A

HISTORY OF EGYPT

During the XVIIth and XVIIIth Dynasties

BY

W. M. FLINDERS PETRIE, D.C.L., LL.D.

EDWARDS PROFESSOR OF EGYPTOLOGY IN UNIVERSITY COLLEGE, LONDON
MEMBER OF THE IMPERIAL GERMAN ARCHÆOLOGICAL INSTITUTE
MEMBER OF THE SOCIETY OF NORTHERN ANTIQUARIES

II

WITH NUMEROUS ILLUSTRATIONS

ISBN: 978-1-63923-712-8

All Rights reserved. No part of this book maybe reproduced without written permission from the publishers, except by a reviewer who may quote brief passages in a review to be printed in a newspaper or magazine.

Printed: February 2023

Published and Distributed By:
Lushena Books
607 Country Club Drive, Unit E
Bensenville, IL 60106
www.lushenabks.com

ISBN: 978-1-63923-712-8

A HISTORY OF EGYPT

VOL. II.

THE XVIITH AND XVIIITH DYNASTIES

PREFACE

THE present volume of the history of Egypt comprises only a short period of a few centuries; but a period which is more full of material than any other age of Egypt. The foreign wars, the contact with other nations, the architectural activity, the luxury and brilliance of this cycle, all render it the most attractive in the long history of the country.

The present statement of the material is therefore on a far larger scale than in the previous volume; the standard of leaving no fact or monument referring to the regal history unnoticed, having been maintained throughout.

Such a text-book is of necessity only a work of reference in many parts; but general observations on the condition of the country, and the circumstances of the rule, have given scope for summarising the view suitably for the historical reader. In particular, the decline of Egyptian rule in Syria has been for the first time treated as a consecutive history.

Regarding the references, the various sources have been compared, and the best text selected: where accuracy is equal, the later publications and the English publications have been preferred.

The references by letter or number to the various buildings at Thebes are always based on the plans given in Baedeker's Guide, as these are the most compact and accessible for general use.

Mr. F. Ll. Griffith has again given the most ungrudging help in revising, and often translating, the various documents which are here quoted. And I have also to thank Professor Sayce and Mr. Percy Newberry for many notes and corrections.

LIST OF ILLUSTRATIONS

FIG.
1. Palette of Ta·aa. Scale ½. Louvre
2. Throw-stick of Thuau. Scale 1/12. Ghizeh
3. Coffin of Seqenenra. Ghizeh
4. Gold ring of Aah·hotep. Louvre
5. Dagger of Aah·hotep. Scale ⅜. Ghizeh
6. Axe of Aah·hotep. Scale ¼. Ghizeh
7. Golden boat of Kames. Ghizeh
8. Axe and dagger of Kames. Scale ¼. Ghizeh
9. Spear head of Kames. Scale ¼. Evans
10. Scarab of Aahmes. F.P. Coll.
11. Oxen drawing sledge. Turrah. (L.D.)
12. Coffin of Aahmes Nefertari. Ghizeh
13. Statuette of Nefertari. Turin
14. Plaque of Merytamen. F.P. Coll.
15. Cartouche of Aahmes·hent·ta·meh. F.P. Coll.
16. Figure of Aahmes·sa·pa·ir. F.P. Coll.
17. Cartouches of Amenhotep I. F.P. Coll.
18. Head of Amenhotep I. Turin. (L.D.)
   Coffin of Amenhotep I. Ghizeh
   Tablet of Amenhotep I. B. Mus.
21. Scarab of Aah·hotep. F.P. Coll.
22. Paheri nursing Uazmes. El Kab. (L.D.)
23. Scarab of Amenmes. F.P. Coll.
24. Scarab of Nebta. F.P. Coll.
25. Sensenb. Deir el Bahri
26. Tahutmes I. Deir el Bahri
27. Mummy of Tahutmes I. Ghizeh
28. Obelisk of Tahutmes I. Karnak
29. Scarabs of Tahutmes I. Louvre
30. Head of Queen Aahmes. Deir el Bahri
31. Head of Queen Aahmes. Deir el Bahri
32. Ivory wand of Aahmes. Turin
33. Queen Mut·nefert. Ghizeh
34. Princess Khebt·neferu. Deir el Bahri. (L.D.)

LIST OF ILLUSTRATIONS

FIG.
35. Mummy of Tahutmes II. Profile and front. Ghizeh
36. Portrait of Tahutmes II.
37. Coffin of Tahutmes II.
38. Princess Neferura. Deir el Bahri. (R.S.)
39. Scarabs of Neferura. F.P. Coll.
40. Queen Hatshepsut. Deir el Bahri
41. Sculpture of Deir el Bahri
42. Ships and pile houses of Punt. Deir el Bahri. (D.H.)
43. Egyptian soldiers. Deir el Bahri
44. Statue of Senmut. Berlin
45. Tahutmes II. and sacred cow. Deir el Bahri. (D.H.)
46. Chair of Hatshepsut. B. Mus.
47. Scarab of Hatshepsut and Usertesen III. Louvre
48. Gold ring of Tahutmes III. F.P. Coll.
49. Tahutmes III. B. Mus.
50. Map of approach to Megiddo.
51. Chiefs "smelling the ground." Qurneh
52. Chief of Tunep and artist. Qurneh
53. Syrian chariot. Rekhmara
54. Syrian captives with vases. Rekhmara
55. Syrian dishes
56. Staff with human head. (Pr. A.)
57. Chair. Amen·ken
58. Inlaid table. Amen·ken
59. Golden dish. Syria. (Pr. A.)
60. Jar of wine. Rekhmara
61. Copper vase. Syria. (Pr. A.)
62. Cups from Syria. (Pr. A.)
63. Scarab of Tahutmes III. F.P. Coll.
64. Silver vase. Syria. Rekhmara
65. Silver rings. Syria. Rekhmara
66. Tribute from Punt. Rekhmara
67. Gold vase. Syria. Rekhmara
68. Bows. Syria. Amen·ken.
69. Golden lion's head. Syria. Rekhmara
70. Golden deer's head. Syria. (Pr. A.)
71. Shields. Syria. Amen·ken
72. Quiver. Syria. Amen·ken
73. Bull's head vase. Syria. Rekhmara
74. Falchion. Amen·ken
75. Suit of armour. Amen·ken
76. Silver jug. Syria. Rekhmara
77. Elephant. Syria. Rekhmara
78. Alabaster vase, Tahutmes III. F.P. Coll.
79. Glass bead, Tahutmes III. F.P. Coll.
80. Columns, Tahutmes III. Karnak
81. Lotus pillars, Tahutmes III. Karnak
82. Comparative diagram of obelisks
83. Overseers of works. Puam·ra

LIST OF ILLUSTRATIONS

	PAGE
of Tahutmes III. Karnak	137
ng board in squares. B. Mus.	138
vase of Tahutmes III. (R.C.)	139
ɔ of Tahutmes III. F.P. Coll.	140
ma'ra, from his tomb. Qurneh	141
of Tahutmes III. Deir el Bahri.	143
:ic labels of Nebtau and Takheta	145
ι scarab of Tahutmes III. Long	145
:sen I., old Egyptian type	148
ιew Egypto-Syrian type	149
of servant. Khaemhat. (Pr.A.).	150
of priestess. (Pr. A.).	151
hotep II. and nurse. (L.D.)	154
of Amenhotep II. Karnak.	156
ng statue of Amenhotep II. (L.D.)	160
ɔ of Amenhotep II. as a hawk. F.P. Coll.	162
ɔ of Amenhotep II. with uraei. B. Mus.	162
ɔ of Amenhotep II., born at Memphis. F.P. Coll.	162
and stone vases. Ra. (Pr.A.).	163
ιooting at a target. (D.E.)	166
of Tahutmes IV. (L.D.)	168
of tied lotus, early. (L.D.)	169
of tied lotus, late. (L.D.)	169
ɔ of Tahutmes IV. F.P. Coll.	171
ɔ of Tahutmes IV. F.P. Coll.	171
ɩf Tahutmes IV. F.P. Coll.	171
mes IV. offering to Osiris. (M.A.)	172
Mutemua. (L.D.)	173
of Amenhotep III. (C.M.).	177
ιotep III. and his *ka*. (L.D.)	178
ɩt of Khaemhat. (L.D.)	179
of Tyi. F.P. Coll. (P.A.).	182
of man of Ynuamu. (P.A.)	182
of Nefertiti. Amherst. (P.A.)	182
of Amenhotep III. (L.D.)	184
ιotep III. on his throne. Khaemhat. (L.D)	186
ιotep III. B. Mus.	188
nade at Luqsor	191
ɾom Napata. Berlin	194
y and silver rings, Amenhotep III. F.P. Coll.	195
motto scarabs of Amenhotep III. F.P. Coll.	195
of Khaemhat. Berlin.	199
of Amenhotep III. (L.D.)	202
artist Auta, painting. (L.D.)	204
of Amenhotep IV. (L.D.)	208
of Amenhotep IV. (Pr. M.).	209
ιotep IV. supporting the Aten. F.P. Coll.	210
ιches of Aten. (P.A.).	212
aten and Nefertiti. (L.D.).	213

FIG.		PAGE
133.	Akhenaten, Nefertiti, and daughters. (L.D.)	217
134.	Group of women. (L.D.)	219
135.	Foliage on column. (P.A.)	219
136.	School of music and dancing. (L.D.)	222
137.	Ushabti of Akhenaten. F.P. Coll.	222
138.	Head of Akhenaten. Louvre	224
139.	Scarabs of Amenhotep IV. F.P. Coll.	225
140.	Group of scribes. Florence	228
141.	Death cast of Akhenaten. Ghizeh	230
142.	Nefertiti offering. Amherst. (P.A.)	230
143.	Princesses and Nezem·mut. (L.D.)	232
144.	Rings of Ankh·kheperu·ra. (P.A.)	234
145.	Rings of Ankh·kheperu·ra. (P.A.)	234
146.	Ring of Mert·aten. (P.A.)	234
147.	Head of Tutankhamen. (L.D.)	236
148.	Rings of Tutankhamen. (P.A.)	236
149.	Ring of Ankhsenamen. (P.A.)	237
150.	Pendant of Tutankhamen. (M S.)	237
151.	Alabaster vase of Tutankhamen. F.P. Coll.	237
152.	Ring of Tutankhamen. F.P. Coll.	238
153.	Head of Queen Ty. (L.D.)	239
154.	Ay and Ty, from their tomb. Dr. May	240
155.	Scarab of Ay. F.P. Coll.	242
156.	Head of Horemheb. (L.D.)	245
157.	Negroes and Asiatics adoring. (Pr. A.)	249
158.	Ring of Nezem·mut. F.P. Coll.	250
159.	Scarab of Horemheb. F.P. Coll.	251
160.	Head of Horemheb. (R.A.)	253
161.	Negroes, Silsileh. (L.D.)	254
162.	Map of Syria, under Amenhotep IV.	319
163.	Southern Syria under Tahutmes III.	324
164.	Map of Northern Syria	330

LIST OF ABBREVIATIONS

A.	L'Anthropologie (Journal).
A.B.	Arundale and Bonomi Gallery (Brit. Mus.).
A.E.	L'Archéologie Egyptienne (Maspero).
A.L.	Archæologia, London, Society of Antiquaries.
A.Mus.	Ashmolean Museum.
A.R.	Archæological Report, Egypt Exploration Fund.
A.Z.	Zeitschrift Aeg. Sprache.
B.A.G.	Berlin Anthrop. Gesellsch.
B.C.	,, Catalogue, 1894.
Bd.A.	Breasted, Hymn to Aten.
B.E.	Baedeker, Egypt.
Berl.	Berlin Museum.
B.G.	Brugsch, Geographie.
B.G.I.	,, Geog. Inschrift.
B.H.	,, History.
B.I.E.	Bulletin Inst., Egypt.
B.I.H.D.	Birch, Inscr. Hieratic Demotic.
B.M.C.	Bliss, Mound of many Cities.
B. Mus.	British Museum.
B.O D.	Bezold, Oriental Diplomacy.
B.P.	Birch, Pottery.
B.R.	Brugsch, Recueil.
B.R.P.	Birch, Two Rhind Papyri.
B.Rs.	Brugsch, Reiseberichte.
B.T.	,, Thesaurus.
B.X.	Burton, Excerpta.
C.B.	Champollion, Lettre Duc Blacas.
C.E.	Chabas, Melanges Egypt.
C.F.	Champollion, Figeac Egypt. Anc.
C.L.	,, Lettres, ed. 1868.
C.M.	,, Monuments.
C.N.	,, Notices.
C.O.E.	Congrès Oriental, St. Etienne, 1878.
D.D.	Duemichen, Baugesch. Denderatempels.
D.E.	Description de l'Égypte.

LIST OF ABBREVIATIONS

D.F.	Duemichen, Flotte.
D.H.	,, Histor. Inschr.
D.O.	,, Oasen.
E. Coll.	Edwards Collection.
E.G.	Ebers, Gozen zum Sinai.
E.L.	Études ded. Leemans.
F.H.	Fraser, Graffiti of Hat-nub.
F. Mus.	Florence Museum.
F.P. Coll.	Flinders Petrie Collection.
G.Bh.	Griffith, Beni Hasan.
G. Coll.	Grant Collection.
G.H.	Golenischeff, Hammamat.
G.K.	Griffith, Kahun Papyri.
G. Mus.	Ghizeh Museum.
G.N.	Gardner, Naukratis ii.
G.O.	Gorringe, Egyptian Obelisks.
G.S.	Griffith, Siut.
H.B.	Hawkins, Belmore Tablets (Brit. Mus)
H. Coll.	Hilton Price Collection.
J.A.I.	Jour. Anthrop. Institute.
L.A.	Lepsius, Auswahl.
Lb. D.	Lieblein, Dictionary of Names.
Lb. P.	,, St. Petersburg.
L.C.	Leyden Congress.
L.D.	Lepsius, Denkmäler.
L.K.	,, Königsbuch.
L.L.	,, Letters (English edit.).
L. Mus.	Leyden Museum.
L.T.	Lanzone, Catalogue of Turin.
M.A.	Mariette, Catalogue Abydos.
M.A. ii.	,, Abydos ii.
M.A.B.	,, Album de Boulaq.
M.A.F.	Mission Archeol. Franc., Cairo.
M.B.	Mariette, Catal. Boulaq, 6th edit.
M. Coll.	Murch Collection (Chicago).
M.D.	Monuments Divers.
M.D.B.	Mariette, Deir el Bahri.
M.E.	Musée Egyptien.
M.E.E.	Maspero, Études Egypt.
Mel.	Melanges d'Arch. Egypt (Maspero).
M.F.D.	De Morgan, Fouilles à Dashur.
M.G.	Meyer, Geschichte.
M.I.	De Morgan, Monuments et Inscriptions.
M.K.	Mariette, Karnak.
M.M.	,, Mastabas.
M.S.	,, Serapeum.
M.S. Ms.	,, Serapeum, ed. Maspero.
Ms. A.	Maspero, L'Archéologie Egypt.
Ms. C.	,, Contes Populaires.

LIST OF ABBREVIATIONS

ẑ. . .	Maspero, Enquête Judicaire.	
ʳ. . .	„ Guide Bulaq.	
ƒ. . .	„ Momies de Deir el Bahari.	
ƒ.P.L.	„ Mem. Papyr. Louvre.	
ẑ. . .	Murray, Egypt.	
. . .	Naville, Ahnas.	
?. . .	„ Ahnas, Paheri.	
g. . .	Nicholson, Aegyptiaca.	
. . .	Naville, Bubastis.	
D. . .	„ Deir el Bahri.	
' . . .	Newberry, Beni Hasan.	
ˌll. . .	Owen's College, Manchester.	
. . .	Orcurti, Catalogue Turin.	
. . .	Petrie, Tell el Amarna.	
. . .	„ Hawara.	
. . .	„ Illahun.	
. . .	„ Kahun.	
. . .	Pierret, Louvre Catalogue, Salle historique.	
. . .	Petrie, Medum.	
ıs. . .	Paris (Louvre) Museum.	
. . .	Petrie, Nebesheh.	
ˇ. . .	Prokesch van Osten, Nilfahrt.	
. . .	Petrie, Pyramids of Gizeh.	
. . .	Pierret, Recueil Inscrip. Louvre.	
. . .	Petrie, Season 1887.	
. . .	„ Scarabs.	
ˋ. and ii.	„ Tanis, i. and ii.	
T. . .	Papyri of Turin, Pleyte and Rossi.	
ſus. .	Philadelphia Museum.	
·ˌ . . .	Prisse, Art.	
˪. . .	„ Monuments.	
. . .	De Rougé, Album.	
. . .	Revue Critique.	
. . .	De Rougé, Études Egypt.	
. . .	Rosellini, Mon. Civili.	
L. . .	De Rougé, Monuments Egn. du Louvre.	
i. to xviii.	Records of the Past, series I. i.-xii.; series II. i.-vi.	
. . .	Rosellini, Mon. Religious (del Culto).	
. . .	„ Mon. Storici.	
). . .	De Rougé, Six Dynasties.	
. . .	Recueil de Trauvaux, Egypt.	
A. . .	Revue Archæologique.	
˪. . .	Soc. Biblical Archæol. Proceedings.	
˪.T. .	„ „ „ Transactions.	
˴. F. .	Schiaparelli, Catalogue Florence.	
. . .	Sharpe, Inscriptions.	
. . .	Stuart, Nile Gleanings.	
. ˋ . .	Schuckhardt, Schliemann.	
˪ˌ . . .	Schack-Schackenborg, Unterw. des K. Amenemhat.	

LIST OF ABBREVIATIONS

S.T.	Schiaparelli, Tomba Herchuf.
T. Mus.	Turin Museum.
T.P.	,, Papyrus.
V.G.	Virey, Catalogue Ghizeh.
V.P.	Vyse, Pyramids.
W.G.	Wiedemann, Geschichte.
W.G.S.	,, ,, Supplement.
W.M.C.	Wilkinson, Manners and Customs, ed. Birch.
W.T.	,, Thebes

The above works, and others, can be consulted in the Edwards Library, University College, London.

A HISTORY OF EGYPT

SEVENTEENTH DYNASTY

THE rise of this dynasty is wholly lost to sight under the Hyksos power. It is only with the later kings who began to assert their independence, or perhaps with the intermarriage of an invading and assertive family from the south, that any historical personages appear. The details of the relationships involve so many considerations, and so much acquaintance with the family, that it is better to study them after an outline of the period; they are therefore placed here at the end of this volume, and should be referred to for seeing the reasons for the arrangement adopted.

So far as the details are yet known, it appears that the royal family at the close of the XVIIth dynasty stands thus—

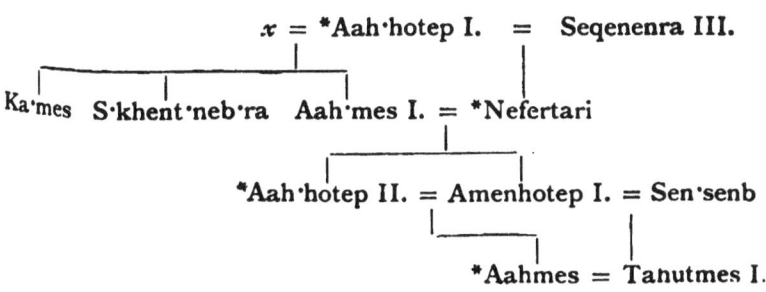

SEVENTEENTH DYNASTY

In order to see how far the ages and other data agree, it is best to tabulate the chronology; not as laying down what is certain, but only as proving that no hidden discordance lies in what is already supposed to be ascertained. The fixed points that we have to deal with are the lengths of the reigns of Aahmes and Amenhotep, — the ages of Seqenenra and Aahmes (about 40 and 55 respectively at death, see Ms. M. 528, 535),—the successive marriages of Aah·hotep,— the eight princes and princesses who were, some, or all, probably her children after the birth of those who came to the throne,—and the general presumption of the ages of marriage. We see in the following table that there will be nothing contradictory among these data; and, with the exception of the very uncertain length of the short reigns of Kames and S·khent·neb·ra (for which an assumption has been made, regulated by the age and family of their mother), there is probably not much uncertainty in these statements.

SEVENTEENTH DYNASTY

B.C. about	Seqenenra	Aah·hotep					B.C. about	
1637	0 born							
1622		0 born						
1621	15 marries x							
1619		16 Kames b.	0 Kames					
1617		18 Skhentneb. b.		0 Skhentnebra			1617	
1615		20 Aahmes b.			0 Aahmes		1615	
1613	22 m. Seqenenra						1613	
	24	22 m. Nefertari b.				0 Nefertari		
								(here follow 8 children in 16 years).
1597	40 dies		24 succeeds				1597	16 m. Aahmes
1595							1595	18 Satamen b.
1593							1593	20 Aahhotep b.
1591			30 dies	28 succeeds			1591	22 Sa·pa·iri b.
1589							1589	24 Amenhotep b.
1587				32 dies	28	20 marries	1587	
1562		50					1562	
1541		75				30 succeeds	1541	
		96 alive				55 dies		

(The only assumptions in this table are the lengths of the short reigns of Kames and Skhentnebra, and the details of the exact ages of Aah·hotep and Nefertari at the births of their children. Only an uncertainty of a few years will rest on these details, which are here approximated, in order to show the general relation of events. The successive order of the facts is fairly certain, as will be noted farther on.)

SEVENTEENTH DYNASTY

We may now approximately arrange the reigns and dates of the XVIIth dynasty—

		B.C. about
XVII. (Beginning of dynasty)		1738
5. ? Se·qenen·ra (I.)	Ta·āa	1660
6. Se·qenen·ra (II.)	Ta·āa·āa	1635
7. Se·qenen·ra (III.)	Ta·āa·ken	1610
8. Uaz·kheper·ra	Ka·mes	1597
9. Se·khent·neb·ra		1591
XVIII. Aahmes		1587
		1562

Of the earlier part of this dynasty we know nothing. The resemblance of Seqenenra III. to the Berber type points to these kings having come down from Ethiopia. A new dynasty beginning with Aahmes seems to have been due to the break in the family, he being descended of an Egyptian and not an Ethiopian father. This dynasty, then, would seem to have been descended from a part of the royal Egyptian line which had taken refuge in the far south to escape from the Hyksos oppression; and was there mingled with southern blood, and became of the dark Berber type. As the Hyksos power decayed, this southern family fought its way northward again, and so laid the foundation of the XVIIIth dynasty. For the date of the beginning of this dynasty we have only the statement of Manetho, which gives 151 years for the duration of it. Of the first eighty years, or so, we have no names remaining; perhaps they should be sought in Nubia rather than in Egypt, as there is no allusion to tombs of the predecessors of the Seqenenras at Thebes.

Rahotep, as we have noticed in vol. i., belongs to

the XVIth rather than to the XVIIth dynasty, as he reigned at Koptos, and therefore quite under the Hyksos power. This points to his being a vassal under the great Hyksos kings, and not one of the fighting family who ejected them, as there is no place for him anywhere in the later part of this dynasty when it was becoming independent.

We will now notice the actual remains of these kings before proceeding to notice their great work of expelling the Hyksos.

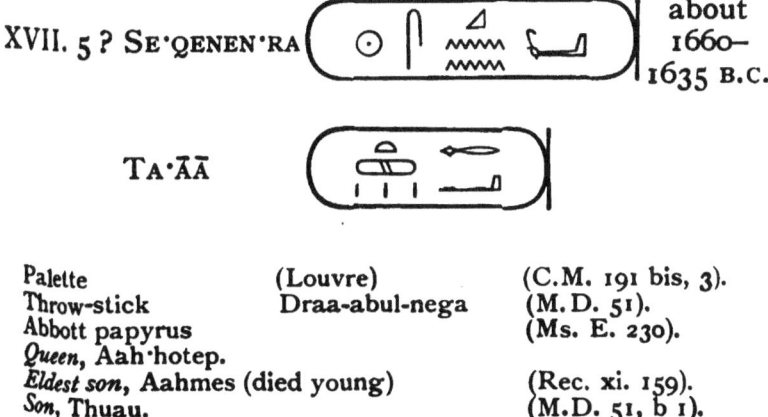

XVII. 5 ? SE·QENEN·RA about 1660–1635 B.C.

TA·ĀĀ

Palette	(Louvre)	(C.M. 191 bis, 3).
Throw-stick	Draa-abul-nega	(M.D. 51).
Abbott papyrus		(Ms. E. 230).
Queen, Aah·hotep.		
Eldest son, Aahmes (died young)		(Rec. xi. 159).
Son, Thuau.		(M.D. 51, b 1).
Daughter, Aahmes.		

The existence of this king, as separate from his successors, is shown by the Abbott papyrus containing the Ramesside inspection of the royal tombs. His tomb is there named; and it is followed by that of Sekenenra Ta·āā·āā, or the great Ta·āā, whose name we might otherwise have supposed to be a variant of Ta·āā, remembering the confusion of the Antef names. This king's tomb is named next after that of Sebek·em·sauf, and is described thus: "The tomb of king (Seqenenra), son of the sun (Ta·āā), examined this day by the masons, was found intact." The only contemporary objects bearing the king's name are a palette in the Louvre, on which he is said to be beloved of Amen·ra and of Safekh; a throw-stick found in the tomb of Aqi·hor at Draa-abul-nega, which bears the cartouche Ta·āā, and the name of the king's son Thuau; and an important statue of the king's elder

FIG. 1.—Palette of Ta·aa.
1 : 2. Louvre.

son Aahmes, deceased, made by his father Ta·aa a, his mother the king's daughter and queen Aah·hotep, and his sister Aahmes (Rec. xi. 159). Though at first sight these names Aahmes and Aahhotep would seem to point to this being of Ta·aa·qen,

FIG. 2.—Throw stick of Thuau. 1 : 12. Ghizeh.

yet we have to balance the probability of the Aah names having been earlier in use in the family, against the improbability of Ta·aa·qen being written without his distinctive title *qen*, and being thus confused with his ancestors. This monument seems, then, rather to belong to Ta·aa, whose name is on it, than to either of the following kings.

XVII. 6?
SE·QENEN·RA

TA·ĀĀ·ĀĀ

about 1635–1610 B.C.

Of this king nothing is known except the mention of his tomb in the Abbott papyrus. Following the account of his predecessor's tomb, we read: "The tomb of the king (Se·qenen·ra), son of the sun (Taāā·āā), who is the second king (Ta·āā), examined on this day by the masons, was found intact."

XVII. 7?
SE·QENEN·RA

TA·ĀĀ.QEN

about 1610–1597 B.C.

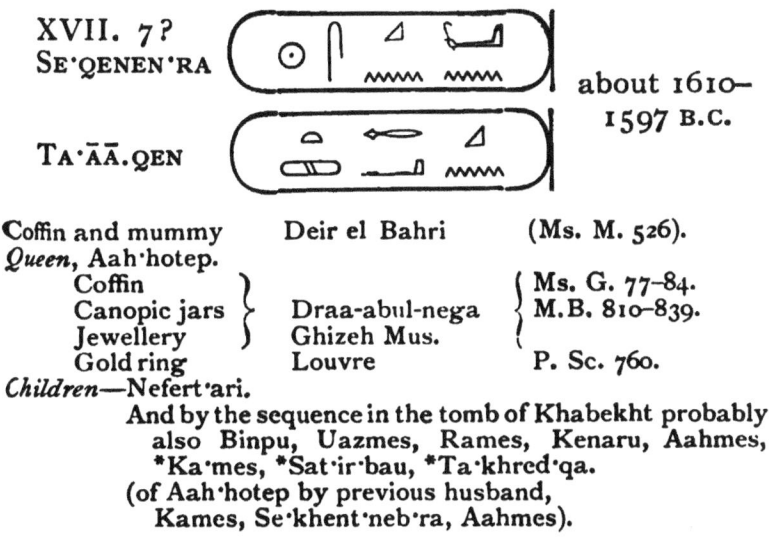

Coffin and mummy Queen, Aah·hotep.	Deir el Bahri	(Ms. M. 526).
Coffin		Ms. G. 77–84.
Canopic jars	Draa-abul-nega	M.B. 810–839.
Jewellery	Ghizeh Mus.	
Gold ring	Louvre	P. Sc. 760.

Children—Nefert·ari.
And by the sequence in the tomb of Khabekht probably also Binpu, Uazmes, Rames, Kenaru, Aahmes, *Ka·mes, *Sat·ir·bau, *Ta·khred·qa.
(of Aah·hotep by previous husband, Kames, Se·khent·neb·ra, Aahmes).

The coffin and mummy of this king were found in the great deposit of royal mummies in the tomb at Deir el Bahri or "the northern convent" at Thebes. The outline of this discovery is given at the close of this volume. The body of Seqenenra had probably been shifted from one hiding-place to another, like the bodies and coffins of the other kings whose removals are inscribed upon them. Lastly, it was laid in the tomb of the priest-kings until removed to the museum at Cairo.

The coffin is heavy in style, like those of the Antefs, with a single line of inscription down the front. The mummy shows that the king died on the field of battle. From the position of the wounds, it appears that he was first struck down by an enemy on his left hand, who attacked him by a violent blow on the side of the head in front of the ear, and the tongue was bitten between the teeth in the agony of the conflict; the next stroke was mortal, an axe crashed through the left side of the head, leaving an opening two inches long; and a dagger-cut above the right eyebrow completed the attack.

FIG. 3.—Coffin of Seqenenra. Ghizeh.

The body was recovered by his subjects, and reverently preserved for embalming and burial. Closely wrapped up, so that the soft parts putrefied instead of drying in the open air, it was carried for many days to Thebes, where it was as fully preserved as the condition of it allowed; but the bones of the body and the left arm were entirely bared of flesh. The king appears to have been of the Berber type, tall, slender, and vigorous, with a small, long head, and fine black hair. The beard was shaved, but not the hair of the head (Ms. M. 527, 771, 776; pl. iii.). A rude stone seal found at Thebes may belong to this, or to a previous king Seqenenra.

His wife Aah·hotep was one of the great queens of Egyptian history, important as the historic link of the dynasties, and revered along with her still more celebrated and honoured daughter Nefertari. We have already noticed how her son Aahmes (so described on Edfu stele, Rec. ix. 93, Ms. M. 626) was of the ordinary Egyptian complexion, while her daughter Nefertari (so placed in the series of Khabekht, L.D. iii. 2a, and called royal daughter) was black. As Seqenenra was Berber, Nefertari might be three-quarters black; while Aahmes, if son of an Egyptian husband, might be three-quarters Egyptian, thus accounting for the difference. The age of Aahmes at his accession, after the insignificant reigns of his brothers, shows that he was the son of a first husband, implying that Aah·hotep first married an Egyptian, and secondly, Seqenenra. The importance of Nefertari as heiress shows that the queen had no daughter by her first husband. The reign of Kames before Aahmes shows that he was the elder brother. And the presence of Se·khent·neb·ra between Aahmes and Kames (tomb of Khabekht, L.D. iii. 2a) shows that he was another brother, who probably reigned briefly between them. Thus we reach the relationships.

FIG. 4.—Gold ring of Aah·hotep. Louvre.

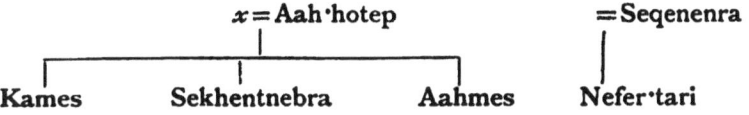

Though the reasons for this arrangement are not very strong, yet there are no objections to it so far known, and the resulting chronology is not discordant.

Two documents serve to show the long life of the queen. A Theban stele of Kames (Rec. ix. 94) states, in the tenth year of Amenhotep I., that Aah·hotep I., the royal mother, was still acting. According to the dates, she would then be eighty-eight years old; and this cannot be abbreviated, as it is made up of fixed amounts, the birth of Aahmes (second or third son) about her twentieth year, his fifty-five years of life (Ms. M. 535), and the ten years of reign of Amenhotep. The other stele, of Iufi (Rec. ix. 92), appears to show that Aah·hotep was still alive under Tahutmes I., when she must have been about a hundred years old. She must certainly have had, therefore, a long life, and have seen the whole revolution of the rise of Egypt,—born under Hyksos rule, and dying with the wealth of Asia around her, won by her son, grandson, and great-grandson.

The name of Aah·hotep is familiar in connection with the beauty of her jewellery, which, till the discoveries at Dahshur, has been an unique treasure. The coffin containing the mummy and jewellery was found slightly buried in the ground at Draa-abul-Nega, the northern and most ancient end of the cemetery of Thebes, where lie the tombs of the XIth dynasty. It is certain that such was not its original site, and that it must have been taken from a royal tomb. By whom? Not by the Arab plunderers of the Deir el Bahri tomb, as has been suggested; nor by any regular tomb thieves, such as plundered the tombs in the Ramesside age. Neither of such parties would encumber themselves with moving a great coffin and a mummy, when all the valuables might be gathered up in a few minutes and put into a bag. Such a reburial of an intact mummy in its heavy case, shows a care and respect for it such as no plunderer would have had. Rather must it have been taken out of the tomb by pious hands, when the disorganisation of government could no longer protect the tombs from thieves or foes, and have been committed unmarked and unseen to the safe keeping of the earth, for fear of the fate which awaited it if left in the well-known tomb. It was a part of that care for the royal dead which led to the kings being moved from tomb to tomb, and lastly hidden at Deir el Bahri. How

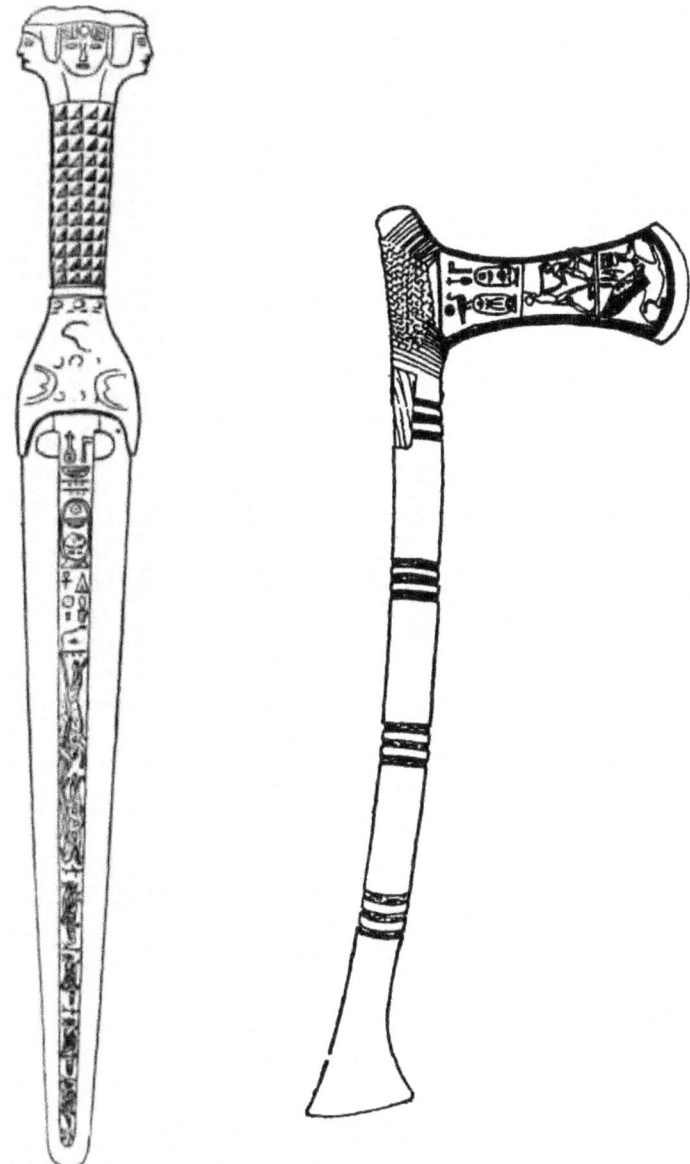

FIG. 5.—Inlaid dagger of Queen Aah-hotep. Scale, 2 : 5.

FIG. 6.—Inlaid axe of Queen Aah-hotep. Scale, 1 : 5.

many more of the royal tombs may have been thus emptied, and their contents safely hidden in the sand, we may never know or suspect. This coffin was only found accidentally by some natives in 1860; was confiscated by the Mudir of Qeneh, and lastly seized by Mariette for the new museum.

The coffin of wood is plain in the body and coloured blue. The lid is massive, entirely gilt, carved with the face and wig, and covered by the wings of Isis over the body, like the Antef coffins. Within the coffin was the mummy, with four canopic jars, and with some jewellery at the side of it, some within the wrappings, and some upon the corpse (M.B. 810). To enter on a full list of

FIG. 7.—Boat of Kames. Ghizeh.

the treasure here would be too lengthy, but we must notice the historical points. On the corpse were a scarab and chain with the name of Aahmes on the fastening, besides three bracelets and a diadem, all with the name of Aahmes; while within the wrappings were the gold axe and the dagger, both with the name of Aahmes. The personal ornaments of this queen were therefore provided by Aahmes, that is to say, when the queen was between fifty and seventy-five years old.

But beside these objects of Aahmes, some with the name of her eldest son Kames were also found. In the coffin were two model barks with rowers: one of gold bore the name of Kames; the other, of silver, was plain. The other objects were a fly-flap and bronze axes, of Kames; and probably other bronze axes and a spear of his, now in England, came from the same source. It has always been assumed that the whole of this outfit belonged solely to the queen. But as no object of Kames was within the bandages, but only loose in the open coffin, there is no such assurance. Rather it would seem that the valuables in the burial of Kames which were outside of his mummy had been hurriedly heaped together into the coffin of Aah·hotep, and so all carried out for safe burial. The two barks would thus belong, one to Kames, the other to Aah·hotep's own burial. And the bronze axes and spear are more likely to have been laid with a warrior king than with the queen. There is a strong suggestion in the arrangement of the lower line of figures in the tomb of Khabekht (L.D. iii. 2a) that Aah·hotep had many other children. After the three brothers, Aahmes, Skhent·neb·ra, and Kames, there follow eight royal sons and daughters who do not belong to any later generation, as they never appear subsequently. These are Binpu (who occurs on a statuette, M.D. 48 b), Uaz·mes, Rames, Ken·aru, Aahmes, and the princesses Kames, Sat·ir·bau, and Ta·khredqa. The uniform order of sons together and daughters together, and the absence of any other important ancestor connected with them, suggests that they are brothers and sisters of Aahmes, and children of Aah·hotep subsequent to Nefertari.

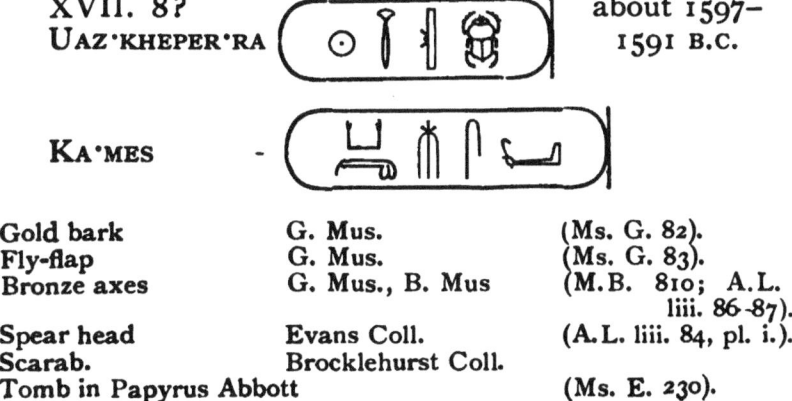

XVII. 8? UAZ·KHEPER·RA			about 1597–1591 B.C.
KA·MES			
Gold bark	G. Mus.		(Ms. G. 82).
Fly-flap	G. Mus.		(Ms. G. 83).
Bronze axes	G. Mus., B. Mus		(M.B. 810; A.L. liii. 86-87).
Spear head	Evans Coll.		(A.L. liii. 84, pl. i.).
Scarab.	Brocklehurst Coll.		
Tomb in Papyrus Abbott			(Ms. E. 230).

The position of this king we have already discusse in the previous pages. His reign has left no trace

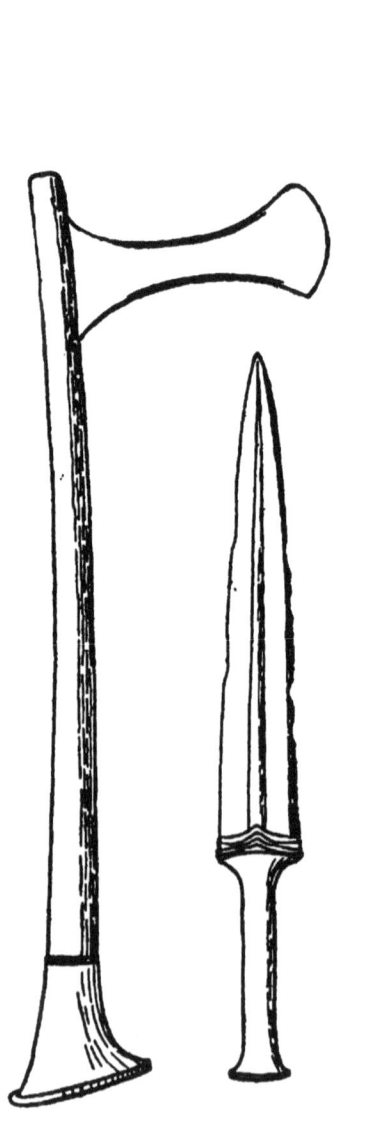

FIG. 8.—Axe and dagger of Kames. 1 : 4. Ghizeh.

FIG. 9.—Spear head of Kam 1 : 5. Evans Coll.

beyond his burial and subsequent adoration of him. That he cannot have come before the Seqenenra kings, is indicated by his jewellery resembling that of Aahmes, and being placed with Aah·hotep, probably owing to his burial being close to hers, or in the same vault. But the absence of any work of his points to a brief reign; and in allowing six years in the history for him we can hardly err much either way. A much longer reign would involve difficulties in the age of his mother.

We have noticed that the objects found loose in the coffin of Aah·hotep probably came from the burial of Kames. Beside these, two bronze axes with his name are known (B. Mus. and Sir John Evans' Coll.), and a bronze spear head with a long inscription (Evans' Coll. See A.L. liii. 84). This reads, "The good god, lord of action, Uaz·kheper·ra. I am a valiant prince, beloved of Ra, begotten of Aaḥ, born of Tehuti, son of the sun Ka·mes eternally strong." Here there is the same fighting tone that we meet in the names Seqenenra, "Ra makes valiant," and "Taāā the valiant." There is also the link to the name of his mother and brother in his being "begotten of Aah." Another interesting link is in his being "born of Tehuti" (a confused idea of a god instead of a goddess bearing him); for it has been already pointed out that the XVIIIth dynasty had strong links to the lunar gods of Eshmunen or Hermopolis, in the names Aahmes and Tahutimes (B.H. 273). Again, in the old Egyptian chronicle of Castor, the XVIIIth dynasty is Hermopolite. And a statuette of black basalt was obtained from Mellawi, and probably came from Eshmunen, bearing the name of a private person, Kames (F.P. Coll.), which shows the observance of the royal names in that town at the time. One scarab of this king was found about 1893, now in Brocklehurst Coll.

The tomb of Kames is mentioned in the Abbott papyrus as having been inspected by the Ramesside officials. "The tomb of King Uaz·kheper·ra, son of the sun Ka·mes, examined in that day, was intact." (MS. E. 230).

XVII. 9?
SE·KHENT·NEB·RA

or SE·NEKHT·EN·RA

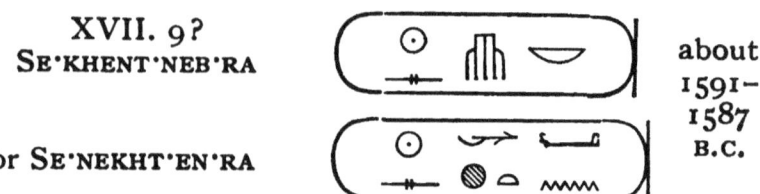

about
1591–
1587
B.C.

This first name is only known in the list of the tomb of Khabakhnet (L.D. iii. 2a), where it occurs between the names of Kames and Aahmes, suggesting that it was that of an intermediate brother-king. It has been suggested that this is a mistake for Se·nekht·en·ra, who is found in the list of Tahutmes III. at Karnak, and on the altar at Marseille (Rec. xiii. 146). From the resemblance of the hieratic writing of the two names, this appears not unlikely. The form Senekhtenra is the more likely to be correct, as being similar to Seqenenra in type and meaning. A king—or perhaps a prince—is named on a bronze dagger, *Sa·ra (Beba· ankh) du ankh*, and is doubtless of this age, though otherwise unknown (Greenwell Coll. A.L. liii. 93).

We now come to consider the great struggle of this age, the expulsion of the Hyksos. As this extended over some generations, it will be best to treat it as a consecutive account, and not to divide the subject amongst the several reigns to which it belongs.

From Manetho we have concluded (in vol. i.) that the Hyksos period consisted of three parts: 100 years of destructive invasion, 2098–1998 B.C.; then 260 years of the reigns of six great kings, who allowed their Egyptian vassals a lifelong rule, as they were thoroughly subdued, 1998–1738 B.C.; lastly, 151 years of weakening of the Hyksos power and continual conflict and rebellion, until Aahmes begins the XVIIIth dynasty. This last period is that of the XVIIth dynasty, 1738–1587 B.C., and is that with which we now have to deal.

From the Berber type of Seqenenra, it seems probable that the dynasty had come from Ethiopia; and the earlier part of it, from about 1738 to perhaps 1660 B.C., of which we have no names, may have dwelt in Nubia, and only harassed the Hyksos from thence. That the Hyksos suzerainty under the great kings extended over the whole land, is shown by the lintel of Apepa I. found as far south as Gebelēn; and by the building in red granite of the same king, showing control of the Aswan quarries. But when we come to the time of Apepa II., Thebes was almost independent. That this is the Apepa of the tale of "Apepy and Seqenenra" is probable; because Apepa I. was much earlier than the Seqenen kings, and Apepa II. has a name, Aa·qenen·ra, closely akin to that of Seqenenra Ta·āā· qen. Apepa II. (see vol. i. p. 242) must therefore be one of the later Hyksos.

The tale of Apepy and Seqenenra was considered to be exact history when first translated; but latterly it has been the rather supposed to be a popular tale founded on the history, probably reflecting very closely the actual events. The papyrus (known as Sallier II., in B. Mus.) containing the tale is unfortunately only fragmentary; and here we give the actual remains, with indication of some restorations (see Ms. C. 278).

"It came to pass that the land of Egypt was a prey to plague (*i.e.* foreigners), and at that time there was no lord and king (*i.e.* no king over all the land). At that time the king Seqenenra was prince (*heq*) of the south; and the plague in the cities were the Amu, and Apepy was prince (*sar*) in Hauar (Avaris), and commanded the whole land with their works, and with all good things of the land of Egypt. Behold king Apepy made Sutekh as lord, and he served not any other god of the whole land except Sutekh. He built him the temple of work good for eternity . . . Apepy. And he went in procession each day to sacrifice the daily offerings to Sutekh, and the chiefs of the king were with garlands, as is done in the temple of Ra Har·em· khuti. And the king Apepy sought words to send a message to the king Seqenenra, the prince (*ur*) of the town of the south (Thebes).

"And many days after this the king Apepy called to him his great [chiefs, his captains, and his prudent generals, but they knew not what to say to the king Seqenenra, prince of the south country. The king Ra-Apepy therefore called unto him his cunning scribes (probably native Egyptians, like the present Copts), and they said to him, 'Oh, lord our master, let this be good before thee,' and they gave to the king Ra-Apepy the words which he desired. 'Let a messenger go to the prince of the town of the south, and say to him, "The king Ra-Apepy sends to say, . . .] the canal of the hippopotami [which are in the canals of the country, that they may let me sleep both by night and by day . . . "] with him in taking, and will not approve to him any god which is in the land of Egypt except Amen Ra, king of the gods.'

"And many days after this king Apepy sent to the prince (*ur*) of the south city the message which his cunning scribes had said to him; and the messenger of king Apepy came unto the prince (*ur*) of the south city; and they brought him before the prince of the south city. Then said he to the messenger of king Apepy, 'What message bringest thou to the south city? Wherefore art thou travelled hither?' The messenger answered him, saying, 'The king Apepy sends to thee, saying, "Let them . . . on the canal of the hippopotami that are in the . . . of the city . . . for sleep by night and by day is not able to come to me."' The prince of the south city was troubled, so that he knew not how to answer the messenger of king Ra-Apepy. The prince of the south then said to him, 'Behold this which thy master sends for . . . the prince of the south land . . . the words which he sent to me . . . his goods . . .' The prince of the south land gave to the messenger all kinds of good things, of meat and of bread, of . . . '. . . all this which thou hast said I intend . . .' The messenger of king Apepy betook himself unto the place where his master was.

Then the prince of the south land called to him his great chiefs, his captains, and his prudent generals, and he told unto them all the words about which king Apepy had sent unto him. And behold they were silent with one accord in great grief, neither knew they to reply either good or evil.

"The king Ra-Apepy sent . . ."

Here unhappily the account ceases in this papyrus; but enough remains to give a clear picture of the bullying by the Hyksos kings, and the terror of their vassals when they chose to pick a quarrel. The meaning of the message is obscure, and makes us the more regret the incompletion of the document. This is the only detailed view of the relations of the Hyksos to the Egyptians in the latter part of their sojourn. The king being named Seqenenra, shows that it must refer to the last century, or so, of the bondage; but there is nothing to show to which king of that name this refers, if, indeed, the writer had any clear idea on the matter.

The only monumental notice of the destructions by the Hyksos is in the inscription of Hatshepsut on the front of the rock-cut temple, known as the Speos Artemidos, just south of Beni Hasan. In this the queen recites her re-establishment of the Egyptian power and worship. She describes the injuries to the country. "The abode of the Mistress of Qes (Kusae on west side) was fallen in ruin, the earth had covered her beautiful sanctuary, and children played over her temple. . . . I cleared it and rebuilt it anew. . . . I restored that which was in ruins, and I completed that which was left unfinished. For there had been Amu in the midst of the Delta and in Hauar, and the foreign hordes of their number had destroyed the ancient works; they reigned ignorant of the god Ra" (Rec. iii. 2).

For the period of the actual expulsion of the Hyksos there are but two documents, Manetho as recorded by Josephus, and the tomb of the warrior Aahmes at El Kab. We see in the tale of Apepa that during the

Seqenenra period, somewhere between 1660 and 1600 B.C., the Theban princedom was completely in the power of the Hyksos, and open war had not yet broken out, or become continuous. But the last Seqenenra died in battle, probably at some distance away, and yet was buried properly at Thebes. This points to the Theban powers having become independent by 1597 B.C., and having a fighting frontier some way to the north, so that ceremonials at Thebes were uninterrupted. During the reign of Kames further advance was probably made by "the valiant prince," as we see that king Aahmes was able to besiege the stronghold of the Hyksos down in the Delta at the beginning of his reign, about 1585 B.C. So probably the Thebans had been gradually pushing their way north, and claiming independence, during perhaps twenty years before the country gathered itself together and made the grand effort of the expulsion under Aahmes; and it was that effort which placed Aahmes on the throne as a victorious conqueror, and founded the XVIIIth dynasty.

Manetho summarised the story, according to Josephus, in this form: "The kings of the Thebaid and of the rest of Egypt made insurrection against the Shepherds, and a long and mighty war was carried on between them, until the Shepherds were overcome by a king whose name was Alisphragmouthosis (var. Mis·phra· gmu·thosis = *Aahmes·pahar·nub·thes·taui*, 'Aahmes, the golden Horus binding together the two lands,' a title of his referring to the united action in the war, and recovery of the Delta), and they were by him driven out of the other parts of Egypt, and hemmed up in a place containing about ten thousand arouras, which was called Auaris. All this tract the Shepherds surrounded with a vast and strong wall, that they might retain all their property and their prey within a hold of their strength.

"And Thummōsis the son of Alisphragmouthosis tried to force them by a siege, and beleaguered the place with a body of four hundred and eighty thousand men; but at the moment when he despaired of reducing them by siege, they agreed to a capitulation, that they would leave Egypt, and should be permitted to go out without molestation wheresoever they pleased. And, according to this stipulation, they departed from Egypt with all their families and effects, in number not less than two hundred and forty thousand, and bent their way through the desert towards Syria. But as they stood in fear of the Assyrians, who then had dominion over Asia, they built a city in that country which is now called Judæa, of sufficient size to contain this multitude of men, and named it Jerusalem."

Here, then, it is represented that Aahmes shut them up in Auaris; and that his son (or rather grandson), Tahutmes I., finally ejected them thence. This is, however, due to a confusion of the capture of Auaris with the subsequent Syrian wars of Tahutmes I., as is shown by the contemporary account of one of the main actors in the struggle, the admiral Aahmes. He would certainly have recited the capture of Auaris under Tahutmes I., if any such conquest had then occurred.

The account of the admiral Aahmes is the best authority that we have for the beginning of the XVIIIth dynasty. We here quote the earlier portion, referring to the Hyksos war:—

"The captain-general of marines, Aahmes son of Abana, *makheru*. He says, I speak to you, all men, in order that I may inform you of the honours which have fallen to my lot. I have been presented with gold seven times in the face of the whole land, and with slaves both male and female; likewise I have acquired much land. The name of one valorous in his acts shall not perish for ever in this land. He saith, I came into existence in the city of Nekheb (El Kab); my father was an officer of king Sekenenra, *makheru*, Baba son of Reant was his name."

"I performed the duties of an officer in his place on board the ship called the 'Sacrificial Ox' in the days of king Neb·pehti·ra, *makheru* (Aahmes). I was too young to have a wife, and I slept in the *semt* cloth and *shennu* garment (age about 20, 1586 B.C.). But as soon as I had a house I was taken to a ship called the 'North' on account of my valour. And I followed the sovereign on foot when he went out on his chariot.

"One sat down before the city of Hat·uart (Avaris), and I was valorous on foot in presence of his majesty. I was promoted to the ship called *Kha·em·men·nefer.* We fought on the water in the Pazedku (canal?) of Hat·uart. Here I captured and carried off a hand, mention of which was made to the royal reporter, and there was given to me the golden collar of valour. There was fighting a second time at this place, and a second time I captured and carried off a hand, and there was given to me a second time the gold of valour. There was fighting at Ta·kemt at the south of this city, and I carried away prisoner a live man. I plunged into the water, behold he was brought as one captured on the road of the town, I crossed over with him through the water (*i.e.* he secured him as certainly as if he had been caught on a high-road). Mention of this was made to the royal reporter, and I was presented with gold once more.

"We took Hat·uart, and I carried off as captives from thence one man and three women, in all four heads; and his majesty gave them to me for slaves.

"We sat down before Sharhana (Sharuhen in the southern border of Palestine) in the year 5 (age about 24, 1582 B.C.), and his majesty took it. I carried off from thence captives two women and one hand; and there was given me the gold of valour. Behold there were given me the captives for slaves.

"But when his majesty had slaughtered the Mentiu of Setet, he went south to Khent·hen·nefer, in order to destroy the Anu Khenti; and his majesty made a great slaughter of them. I carried away captives two live men and three hands; and I was presented once more with the gold, and behold the two slaves were given to me. Then came his majesty down the river, his heart swelled with valour and victory; he had conquered the people of the South and of the North.

"Then came Aata to the South, bringing in his fate, namely, his destruction, for the gods of the South seized upon him. When his majesty found him at Tent·ta·ā, his majesty carried him off as a living captive, and all his men, with swiftness of capture. And I brought off two attendants (?) whom I had seized on the ship of Aata; and there were given to me five heads for my share and five *sta* of land in my own city. It was done to all the company of the marines in like manner.

"Then that enemy named Teta·an came; he had collected rebels. But his majesty slaughtered him and his slaves even to extinction. And there were given to me three heads and five *sta* of land in my own city." He then describes his services in the southern campaigns of Amenhotep I. and Tahutmes I., and the Syrian war of Tahutmes I. He came to old age in that reign, when he would be between sixty-five and ninety years old.

We see here that Aahmes concluded the Hyksos war within five years, and then turned his arms to the South. Two separate attempts were made apparently by the defeated Hyksos subsequently: Aata arose during the absence of Aahmes in his southern campaign, and overran the land as far as the south country; but he was soon crushed. Again, another flicker of the conquered force seems to have arisen under Teta·an, which was likewise soon crushed.

The history of the war of independence then seems to have been, that perhaps for twenty or thirty years before 1600 B.C. the Nubian princes of Thebes had been pushing their way northward against the decaying power of the Hyksos. Active warfare was going on at about 1600 B.C.; and a sudden outburst of energy, under the active young leader Aahmes, concluded the expulsion of the foreigners, and the capture of their stronghold, within a few years, ending in 1582 B.C. A couple of last flickers of the war were crushed during the succeeding years, and the rest of his reign Aahmes was able to devote to the reorganization of the whole country.

One question remains, What effect had the Hyksos occupation upon the people? That there were large numbers of the race is evident; only a considerable mass of people could have thus held down a whole country for some centuries, while yet remaining so distinct that they could be expelled as a separate body. The number reported to have left Egypt—a quarter of a million—from a land which very probably only held then about two millions, as at the beginning of this century, shows how large their numbers were even after they had become intermingled with the natives during some twenty generations. It was not merely the upsetting of a government, as the overthrow of the Turks in Europe would be at present, but it was the thrusting out of a large part of the population, probably the greater part of the inhabitants of the Delta. We cannot doubt, then, that from such a large body of a ruling race there must have been a great amount of mixture with the earlier occupiers of the land. The Semitising of Egypt took place largely then, so far as race was concerned; and bore full effect when the fashions, ideas, and manners of Syria were implanted after the Asiatic conquests of Tahutmes III.

EIGHTEENTH DYNASTY.

ALTHOUGH the succession of the kings of the XVIIIth dynasty is well known from the monuments, yet the chronology of the period, and the connection of the names with those given in the Greek lists, is far from settled as yet. As our only hope of obtaining a scheme of the lengths of the reigns and of the duration of the dynasty depends on an adjustment of the names stated by the monuments to those stated by Manetho, the treatment of the Greek lists is of much historical importance, and deserves full consideration. The following are the actual materials that we have to study :—

MONU-MENTS.	HIGHEST YEAR.	MANETHO.			
		AFRICANUS AND EUSEBIUS.		JOSEPHUS.	
					Y. M.
Aahmes	22	Amōs	25	Alisfragmouthōsis	
Amen·hotep I.	?			Tethmōsis	25·4
Tahut·mes I.	9	Khebron	13	Khebron	13·
Tahut·mes II.	9	Amenōfthis (21)	24	Amenofis	20·7
Hat·shepsut	22?	Amersis	22	Amessēs	21·9
Tahut·mes III.	54	Misafris, Mifris (12)	13	Mefres	12·9
Amen·hotep II.	26	Misfragmouthōsis	26	Mēframouthōsis	25·10
Tahut·mes IV.	7	Touthmōsis	9	Thmōsis	9·8
Amen·hotep III.	36	Amenofis	31	Amenofis	30·10
Akhen·aten	17	Oros (36)	37	Oros	36·5
Ra·smenkh·ka	3	Akherrēs (12)	32	Akenkhrēs	12·1
Tut·ankh·amen	?	Rathōs (Athōris 39)	6	Ratōthis	9·
Ay	4	Khebrēs	12	Akenkherēs	12·5

EIGHTEENTH DYNASTY

MONU-MENTS.	HIGHEST YEAR.	MANETHO.		
		AFRICANUS AND EUSEBIUS.	JOSEPHUS.	
		Akherrēs 12	Akenkherēs	12·3
Hor·em·heb	21	Armais 5	Armais	4·1
XIX Ra·messu I.	2	Ramessēs 1	Ramessēs	1·4
		Amenofath (40) 19		
Sety I.	9	Sethōs (51) 55		
Ra·messu II.	67	Rampsēs (61) 66	Armessēs	66·2
Mer·en·ptah	25	Ammenefthis (8, 20) 40	Amenofis	19·6
			Sethōsis	
			Ramessēs	

In these lists the middle of the dynasty seems well identified at Tahutmes IV. and Amenhotep III., and our consideration of it falls into two divisions, the earlier and the later, which stand quite independent of each other. In the first part the lists have been adjusted thus by Wiedemann:—

MONUMENTS.	AFRICANUS.	JOSEPHUS.
Aahmes	Amōs	Tethmosis
Nefertari and Amenhotep I.	Khebron	Khebron
Amenhotep I.	Amenofthis	Amenofis
Tahutmes I.	Amersis	Amessēs
Tahutmes II. & Hatshepsut	Mifris	Mefres
Tahutmes III.	Misfragmouthosis	Meframouthosis
Amenhotep II.		Omitted.

But there are several objections to such an arrangement. Tethmosis cannot well be Aahmes, but is rather to be assigned to Tahutmes. There is no reason to make a separate king from the earlier years of Amenhotep I.; Tahutmes I. cannot be Amesses, who is stated to be the sister of Khebron; the separate reign of Hatshepsut is omitted; and the reign of Amenhotep II. is also omitted.

In the face of these difficulties, it would seem better to suppose that Amenofthis has been accidentally shifted in Manetho (perhaps owing to the account of

EIGHTEENTH DYNASTY

the Hyksos war passing from Aahmes to Tahutmes I., while the quiet reign of Amenhotep was left till after it), and so it appears two places farther down in the list than originally stated. We must also recognise that Tethmosis in Josephus has been altogether dropped out in the later lists of Africanus and Eusebius. In this view, a more satisfactory adjustment is reached as follows:—

MONUMENTS.	AFRICANUS.	JOSEPHUS.
Aahmes	Amōs	Misfragmouthosis
Amenhotep I.	(placed below)	(placed below)
Tahutmes I.	(omitted)	Tethmosis
Tahutmes II.	Khebron	Khebron
(Transposed from above	Amenofthis	Amenofis)
Hatshepsut	Amersis	Amesses
Tahutmes III.	Misafris	Mefres
Amenhotep II.	Misfragmouthosis	Meframouthosis

Thus the name Khebron is explained by Akheperenra, Tahutmes II.; and Amersis "his sister" is Hatshepsut his sister. There is another point also in the last identification. Amersis is stated to have reigned 21 years 9 months; and though Hatshepsut's length of reign is not declared, yet Tahutmes III. begins his independent action in his 22nd year, and thus his independence coincides with his sister's death. The 54 years' reign of Tahutmes III. cannot be identified with any of the numbers of the lists; so, wherever it is placed, some corruption must be assumed. But the name Mefres is already fixed to Tahutmes III. by Pliny in mentioning his obelisk (Hist. Nat. xxxvi. 15, 69). And the 26 years of Misfragmouthosis agrees with the recent discovery of a wine jar with the date of the 26th year of Amenhotep II. The 36 years of Amenhotep III. on the monuments doubtless covers also the period of some co-regency, while the 30 years 10 months of Josephus will be the length of his sole reign, thus implying a co-regency with his son of 5 years.

We now pass to the second half of the dynasty.

Here Oros is doubtless Akhen·aten, and Armais is Hor·em·heb. We know that Ra·smenkh·ka·ser·kheperu (erroneously called Ra·saa·ka·khepru) was the immediate successor of Akhenaten, as he is named "beloved of Akhenaten"; we know that Tut·ankh·amen next succeeded, as his rings are found at Tell el Amarna, without any later objects; and Ay must come before Horemheb,—who re-used his masonry,—and cannot come between Tutankhamen and Akhenaten, as his name is never found in that group at Tell el Amarna. Now, Josephus says that Akenkhrēs was daughter of Oros, while we know that Ra·smenkh·ka, whose throne name was Ankh·khepru·ra, married the daughter of Akhenaten, and thus succeeded him. The relationship and the name, Akherrēs or Akenkhrēs, agree, therefore, fairly with the monuments. Next, Ratothis is said to be the brother of Akenkhres, while we know that Tut·ankh·amen was the brother-in-law of the previous queen, having married another daughter of Akhenaten; the name Aten·tut·ankh (altered later to Amen·tut·ankh) may have been rendered by the orthodox as Ra·tut·ankh, and so have originated Ratothis. Next, the two Akenkheres' reigns of 12 years and 5 months and 12 years and 3 months are probably a reduplication, as only Ay is known to correspond to them: the names of Ay, Kheperu·ar·maa·ra may have been abbreviated into the Akherres of Africanus. The discrepancy of Horemheb's 21 years with the 4 or 5 years of Armais may be due to his dating from some semi-independent generalship of his, while only the last 4 or 5 years of his life were independent after the death of Ay. And this possibility is suggested by the length stated for the reign of Oros —36 years 5 months: it is certain that Akhenaten only lived 17 or 18 years, but the duration of his Aten worship (veiled under the orthodox name of Horus) appears to have been about 36 years. If Horemheb dated from the restoration of the old worship,—in which he may have taken a large part,—that would imply $36 + 21 = 57$ years from Akhenaten to **Horemheb**

EIGHTEENTH DYNASTY

inclusive, and the reigns in Josephus, with the known reign of Akhenaten, amount to 56 years.

Hence, from these data, the best result, so far as we can at present see, appears to be as follows:—

	MONUMENTS.	LISTS.	YRS. MOS.	B.C. about.
				1587
1	Aahmes	Amōs	25	
				1562
2	Amenhotep I.	Amenōfthis	20·7	
				1541
3	Tahutmes I.	Tethmōsis	25·4	
				1516
4	Tahutmes II.	Khebron	13	
				1503
5	Hatshepsut	Amersis	21·9	
				1481
6	Tahutmes III.	Mefres 53·10 − 21·9 = 32·1		1449
7	Amenhotep II.	Meframouthōsis	25·10	
				1423
8	Tahutmes IV.	Touthmōsis	9·8	
				1414
9	Amenhotep III.	Amenōfis	30·10	
				1383
10	Akhenaten	Oros	18	
				1365
11	Ra·smenkh·ka	Akherrēs	12·1	
				1353
12	Tut·ankh·amen	Ratōthis	9	
				1344
13	Ay	Akherrēs	12·5	
				1332
14	Hor·em·heb	Armais	4·1	
				1328
	(Men·peh·ra	Menophres, 1322?)		

The absolute dates stated here are based on the statement of Mahler (by Sirius and the new moons) of the reign of Tahutmes III., from 1503 to 1449 B.C., adding and subtracting the reigns on either side. This astronomical method was first proposed (though carried out imperfectly) by Basil Cooper (Brit. Quart. Rev. 1860).

Some general checks on this arrangement are given by private biographies, which show through which reigns extended the life and activities of certain officials. The inscription of the commander Aahmes at El Kab gives some indications. He was still young and unmarried when he became commander of a ship, in the reign of Aahmes, and he did many great deeds before the 6th year of that reign. If we put him at 19 to 25 years of age in these six years, we cannot be far out. Thus he would have been born about 1606 B.C. by the dates in the above list. He would then be over 40 when he convoyed Amenhotep I. on his Nubian wars, and was personally fighting. He would be 65 when he convoyed Tahutmes I. to Nubia, but nothing is then said of his own activity; a year or two later he cut off a chariot in the Syrian war. But he next says that he has arrived at old age in that reign, and therefore before the reign of Tahutmes II., when he would have been 90 years old. For a man of special vigour and valour this is not an unlikely life-history. About a generation later there is a biography of Pennekheb at El Kab. His first prisoner was taken under king Aahmes. If he were about 18 at the king's death, this would imply that he was born about 1580 B.C., but certainly not later. He then took prisoners under Amenhotep I. when 18 to 39 years old; other prisoners under Tahutmes I. when between 39 and 64 years old. He brought prisoners, apparently as a captain, for Tahutmes II. when he was over 64; and died under Tahutmes III. at over 77 years old. Here the ages are not at all impossible. Yet in both cases they seem rather beyond what would be likely for such activity; and hence the suggestion given by the datum of Sirius rising on the 9th Epiphi, in the 9th year of Amenhotep I. (which would point to our having seven years too long a reckoning between Amenhotep I. and Tahutmes III.), is rather confirmed; as a reduction of all the above elder ages by seven years would be more likely than not. In any case, we see that the interval from Aahmes to Tahutmes III. could not be longer than we have deduced, nor could it be very much shorter by the age implied.

There is, however, another check, which has been hitherto scarcely used. The mentions of the *Sed* festival, at the close of each of the 28 or 30 year periods, when Sirius rose a week later in the calendar (owing to the month-names shifting earlier), show us equal intervals which are most important to regulate the chronology. And not only can exact statements of the date of celebrating a festival be of value; but even general allusions to the festival give some probability of such a feast having occurred at the time.

Our starting-point is from Mahler's determination of the date of the festival and of the reign of Tahutmes III. from the star-rising combined with the new moons. He deduces that the 53 years of Tahutmes III. range from 20th March 1503 B.C. to 14th February 1449, and that the Sirius festival of rising on the 28th of Epiphi was in 1470 B.C. This is strongly confirmed by a document not yet utilised. A tablet at El Bersheh (now destroyed) was dated in the 33rd year of Tahutmes III.—the year of the feast, according to Mahler; and— more precisely—on the 2nd day of Mesore, which is only three days after the feast day on the 28th of Epiphi. And in this tablet the beginning of a million of Sirius cycles is wished for the king. Such an allusion to the great feast in that year, which took place only three days before this, is a brilliant confirmation of Mahler's astronomical reckoning; for, were that erroneous in any point, it would be entirely wrong, and hopelessly unlikely to agree with such a record. While a very strong reason is thus obtained for crediting the absolute dating already stated, yet in the following relation of the Sirius cycles to the reigns, the internal chronology of the dynasty may be considered and affirmed quite irrespective of the absolute dates in years B.C.

The beginning of the reckoning of the reign of Tahutmes III. has been disputed, as we do not know certainly whether he was a son of Tahutmes I., or of Tahutmes II. As a list in the temple of Semneh is dated in his 2nd year, and a papyrus in his 5th year, there is a strong presumption that his earliest regnal years could not have been contemporary with his father's reign. This is also indicated by his sudden activity in his 22nd year, after the 21 years 9 months' reign of his sister Hatshepsut, according to Josephus. These presumptions are firmly established when we turn to the *Sed* festivals. Tahutmes III held his festival (as we have just seen above) in his 33rd year; so the earlier one would fall in his 3rd year. Now Hatshepsut celebrated her first *Sed* festival in her 16th year (see her obelisk), which is therefore the same as the 3rd year of Tahutmes III. (a difference of 30 years being quite impossible); hence he began to reign in her 13th or 14th year. And this exactly agrees with the intervention of the 13 years' reign of Khebron, Tahutmes II., contemporary with Hatshepsut. Thus we see that Hatshepsut dates her years from her association with her father at the end of his reign, while Tahutmes III. dates his years from the end of his father's reign, 13 years later. In considering these years, we must always remember that, though the 22 years' reign of Hatshepsut is reckoned from her brother's death, yet that her regnal years were at that point 13; and that she reigned in all $13 + 22 = 35$ years. The dates of the heliacal rising of Sirius are as follow :—

B.C.	Shifting Months.		
1546	Epiphi 9th, date of papyrus in 9th year, Amenhotep I.		
1526	Epiphi 14, feast	(undated), Tahutmes I. obelisk.	
1498	,, 21, ,,	16th year, Hatshepsut, obelisk.	
1470	,, 28, ,,	33d year, Tahutmes III., Bersheh.	
1434	Mesore 7, ,,	(undated), Amenhotep II., pillar.	
1406	,, 14, ,,	(undated), Amenhotep II.	
1378	,, 21, ,,	(unrecorded).	
1350	,, 28, ,,	(undated), Tutankhamen, tomb.	
1294	Thoth 7, ,,	(unrecorded).	
1266	,, 14, ,,	(unrecorded).	
1234	,, 22, ,,	41st year, Ramessu II., El Kab.	
1206	,, 29, ,,	2nd year, Merenptah, M. Habu.	

Though the vanity of Ramessu II. led to his transferring the astronomical cycle of 30 years to his personal reign, and starting a series of *Sed* festivals on his 30th year, and even repeating them every 3 years after that, such a perversion does not affect the value of the regular cycle for historical purposes. The years of the recurrence of the festival in the reigns of other kings, the 18th year of Pepy I., the 2nd year of Mentuhotep II., the 16th of Hatshepsut, the 33rd of Tahutmes III., the 2nd of Merenptah, show absolutely that the cycle was not a regnal feast but an astronomical one of regular recurrence. And the occurrence of "the feast of 30 years" in the reign of Tut-ankh-amen, who reigned but 9 years, again shows that this refers to a fixed cycle.

We see, then, in the above list the dates of the festivals of the heliacal rising of Sirius, at intervals of a quarter month, later and later, in the calendar. Out of eleven, four feasts are dated to the year in historical records, three feasts are mentioned in the reigns in which they are required to fall (all which reigns are under 30 years, and need not therefore have included a festival), and of only three feasts have no notice come down to us. One of these, falling in Akhenaten's reign, is likely to have been omitted; but we should certainly hope some day to find a reference to the festivals of the 32nd year of Sety I., or the 9th year of Ramessu II.

The first datum, of the 9th of Epiphi, is the only one which seems divergent from the chronology to which we are led by Manetho, as the 9th year of Amenhotep I. appears to be nine years earlier than this, or Sirius would have risen about two days earlier in his 9th year. If we are to put full weight on this difference, it would imply that the reign of Tahutmes I. must have been shorter than is stated by Manetho. In another point we may see an unexpected agreement. The "era of Menophres," mentioned as the starting-point of the Sirius cycle in 1322 B.C., has often been speculated on; but the best proposal yet made is that the name is Men·peh·ra (Ramessu I.), for no king Men·nefer·ra is known in history. Now, as we see, the date of Ramessu I. here comes to 1328 to 1326 B.C. This difference of four or five years may be due to a little error on either side. But, in any case, the general agreement of these dates deduced from the festivals with those of the lengths of the reigns, gives security to the chronology; it shows that in future we shall probably only deal with rectifications of a few years, and that no great uncertainty of generations or centuries now rests on Egyptian history as far back as the XVIIIth dynasty.

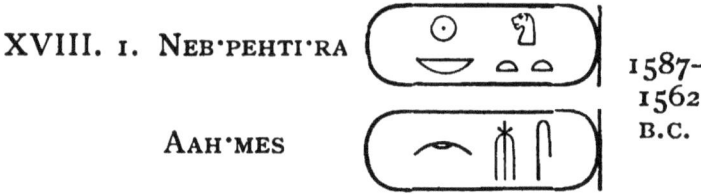

XVIII. 1. NEB·PEHTI·RA

AAH·MES

1587–1562 B.C.

Coffin and mummy, Deir al Bahri, G. Mus. (Ms. M. 533).

Turrah	Inscriptions	(L.D. iii. 3 a b).
Thebes	Brick building	(L.D. iii. 39 e).
Semneh, mentioned by Tahutmes II.		(L.D. iii. 47 c).
(Private monuments)		
Abydos, tomb Sa·ast		(M.A. ii. 53 c).
Thebes, many steles now in Turin, etc.		
El Kab, tomb Aahmes		(L.D. iii. 12 a–d).
,, ,, Pen·nekheb		(L.D. iii. 43 a–b, L.A. xiv. A.B.).
Vase, alabaster	G. Mus.	(M.B. 536).
Hawk, blue glaze	G. Mus.	(M.D. 52 d).
Vase, ring form	G. Mus.	(W.G. 312).
Amulets and scarabs.		
Queen, NEFERTARI.		
Coffin	G. Mus.	(Ms. M. 535).
Mummy	G. Mus. destroyed.	
El Bosra	Inscription	(L.D. iii. 3 c).
Karnak	Statue	(W.G. 316).
Model adze	Turin	(Rec. iii. 124).
Scarabs and cylinders.		
Children (*female)		

By Nefertari {
  *Meryt·amen (Ms. M. 539, 620–2).
  *Sat·amen, infant (Ms. M. 538, 620–2).
  Sa·pa·ir, young (Ms. M. 621).
  *Aah·hotep, queen (Ms. M. 545, 620–2).
  Amen·hotep I. (Ms. M. 536).
  *Sat·kames (Ms. M. 541, 620–2).

By An·hapi, *Hent·ta·meh	Ms. M. 622).
By Tent·hapi, *Hent·tamehu	(Ms. M. 543, 623).
By Kasmut, *Tair	(L.D. iii. 2 a).
By *x*, Sa·amen, 5–6 years	(Ms. M. 538, Ms. G. 344).
By *x*, Turs	(L.D. iii, 2 a, d).
By *x*, Aahmes	(L.D. iii. 2 a, d).

The great event of the reign of Aahmes was the war by which he established his power at the beginning of his reign, that great war of independence which was the most glorious page of Egyptian history. We have already noticed the course of this in the previous chapter. Within four or five years, Aahmes succeeded not only in finally throwing off the suzerainty of the Hyksos kings, but also in driving them out of the Nile valley, in seizing on their great centre of Hauar in the eastern Delta (probably Tanis), and in chasing them across the desert into Palestine, where, in the fifth year, he captured Sharhana, or Sharuhen, upon the southern border, some miles south of Lachish. He also pushed on into Zahi (Phœnicia), where Pen·nekheb states that he took ten hands (L.D. iii. 43 a). Having then slaughtered the Mentiu of Setet, or the Bedawin of the hill country, he turned back, and found the need of his presence on the opposite frontier in the south. The southern races appear to have pushed forward in the rear of the Egyptians on their advance northward, and to have needed repelling, as in the time of Usertesen III. Going, therefore, up the Nile, he made a great slaughter of the Anu Khenti, and is mentioned at Semneh by Tahutmes II. (L.D. iii. 47 c).

His triumphant return, however, was greeted with the news of outbreaks among the remains of the Hyksos people. The expulsion of a race as a whole cannot be effected after several centuries of occupation; and though the foreign army might be driven out, there must have been a large part of the population of mixed race, ready to tolerate the Egyptians if they were the conquerors, but preferring an independent life. From such a source were, doubtless, the two last outbursts of the war. Aata seems to have been of a branch of the

Hyksos party who tried to make headway up the country in the absence of Aahmes; and Teta·an afterwards was the head of a rising of the half-breed race, who refused to accept as yet the new power of the Egyptians. Both were, however, defeated summarily; and after that there seems to have been no further trouble with the Asiatic people. The translation of the biography of Aahmes the admiral, which has supplied the foregoing details, has been given in the previous chapter.

FIG. 10.—Scarab of Aahmes. F.P. Coll.

After this we do not find any great events in this reign. But apparently the organisation of the government, and the repair of the ravages of war, occupied the greater part of the time. After the victory in Syria in the 5th year, and the southern campaign soon after that, there is no mention of any date until the 22nd year, when attention was turned to the rebuilding of the principal temples in the capitals. That the most important religious centres should have remained so long without restoration, shows how much was needful of the more essential material growth of the country, before the objects of luxury and ambition could be developed. It needed a new generation to arise, before the desolation of the oppression and the war could be recovered.

The buildings at Memphis and Thebes have long ago been swallowed up by later alterations and destructions, but the record of them is preserved in the quarries of Turrah, near Cairo, where a royal sealbearer and companion, Nefer·pert, carved two tablets dated in the 22nd year, recording the opening of the quarries for building-stone for the temples of Ptah at Memphis and of Amen at Thebes (L.D. iii. 3 a, b). Special interest attaches to these tablets, as on one of them it is stated that the men employed were of the Fenkhu, a Syrian people who have been generally identified with Phœnicians, though Muller, with his characteristic negation, will not allow this to be so.

Also, below the tablet is a drawing of six oxen attached to a sledge on which is placed a large block of stone; they are attended by three foreigners with short beards. Similar sledges were used in the XIIth dynasty, as pieces of these were found broken up among the filling of the Illahun pyramid.

The coffin and body of Aahmes were found at Deir el Bahri. The coffin is of a new style, different from that which had prevailed from the XIth to the XVIIth dynasty. It is still plain in outline, but is less massive, more shaped to the figure behind, and painted yellow picked out with blue, instead of being gilt all over. The body of the king is fairly preserved, the head long and

FIG. 11.—Oxen drawing sledge. Turrah.

small, the muscles strong and vigorous. He appears to have been somewhat over fifty at his death. The hair is thick and wavy, showing—like Seqenenra—that shaving the head was not then the fashion. May it be that the influence of the dominion of long-haired foreigners had not yet died out? It is not till the XIXth dynasty that a shaven head appears,—that of Sety I. The body has not yet been scientifically examined.

The veneration for Aahmes, and still more for his sister and wife Nefertari, was long continued, and is more frequent than that for any other ruler. Setting aside the examples which cannot at present be dated, the following are the instances of this worship :—

AAH·MES

A. = Aahmes, N. = Nefertari, Am. = Amenhotep I.)

		Abydos	Anāy adoring Osiris and N.	M.A. 1080.
Early XVIII.		Karnak	Nebsu adoring Sitamen, N., Am., Sapair	M.D. 89.
		Thebes	Hymn of praise to N. and Am.	Pap. Tur. 27, 28.
		Thebes	Panekht. Tomb 50	C.N. i. 542.
Tahut. I.		Edfu	Iuf adoring Am. and Aah·hotep	Rec. ix. 93.
Tahut. II.		Thebes	... adoration to Am., N., Tahutmes I. and II., Sapair	Rec. iii. 113.
Tahut. III.		Thebes	Senmen, priest of A., etc.	L.D. iii. 25 bis g.
Tahut. IV.		(P. Mus.)	Pa·āā·aqa mentions the god A.	P.R. ii. 14.
Amenp. III.		(B. Mus.)	Hor: pray *suten·du·hotep* to Hor, Anpu, and N.	T.S.B.A. viii. 144.
Late XVIII.		Thebes	Unnef offering to Am. and N. Tomb 40	C.N. i. 534.
		(B. Mus.)	... adoration to Am., N., and Sat·kames	A.B. 30.
Sety I.		Thebes	... offering to Am. and N. Tomb 32	C.N. i. 520–5.
,,		Qurneh	Sety offering to sacred bark of N.	C.N. ii. 52.
,,		(T. Mus.)	Sety offering to Am. and N.	Rec. iii. 113.
Rams. II.		Karnak	Ramessu adoring N. S. wall, great temple	L.D. iii. 147 a.
,,		Ramesseum	Statues carried of A. and Am. by priests	C.M. 149.
,,		Qurneh	Ramessu offering to N. Room Q.	L.D. iii. 151 c.
,,		,,	Ramessu offering to Amen., N., and Am.	C.M. 150, 3.
,,		,,	Ramessu dancing before Amen and N.	C.M. 150, 2.
,,		,,	Sacred bark of N. borne by 12 priests	C.M. 150 bis.
,,		Deir el Medineh	Kasa adoring Am. and N. Qen adoring Am., N., and sister Merytamen	S.B.A. viii. 226.

Rams. II.	Qurneh	Qen, servant of Am. Huy, priest of Am. Nebra, *kherheb* of Am.	On disc of stone, G. Mus.	Rec. iii. 103.
,, ?	(T. Mus.)	Betehamen offering to	Am., Aah- hotep, N., Satamen, Merytamen Sapair	L.A. xi.
,, ?	Thebes	Amenemapt adoring N. and Am.		C.M. 153.
,, ?	Thebes	Neferhotep offering to Am. and N. Tomb 53.		C.N. 549.
,, ?	Thebes	Penbui offering to Am., N. *x*, Ramessu I., Horemheb		L.D. iii. 173 c.
Rams. III.	(Copenhagen)	Nebnefer adoring N. (older stele usurped)		Rec. ii. 181.
Rams. IV.	Thebes	Anhurkhaui adoring A., N., Am., etc., etc.		L.D. iii. 2 d.
		paintings of N. and Am.		L.D. iii. 1.
Rams. IV.	Thebes	Khabekht adoring A., N., Am., etc., etc.		L.D. iii. 2 a.
Herhor	Karnak	Herhor adoring Amen, Mut, Khonsu, and N.		L.D. iii. 246 a.
XXI dyn.	,,	Graffito on temple of Amenhotep II.		W.G. 315.

There are, besides these, many examples of adoration not dated, such as Unnefer (T. Mus. 1448), Thentnub (T. Mus. 1565), Pa·nefu·em·du·amen (T. Mus. 2430 and Rec. iii. 110), Pa·neshi (T. Mus. 3053); the *sedem asht* officials Uazmes (T. Mus. 1369), Hotepbuaa (T. Mus. 1449), Pen·ta·en·abtu (T. Mus. 3032), Penbua (Rec. ii. 119), and Iairnuf (Rec. ii. 171). Also Tyuti (Rec. iii. 109), Nebmes (Rec. xiii. 119), Mesamen (W.G.S. 35), Ra (M.A. 1097), Zamerkau (Rec. ix. 39), Aa (Rec. iii. 113), ...unba (Pr. M. 25, 1), Nekht (C.M. 162, 2), Ast (C.N. ii. 698), Dudua (Lieb. 553), etc.

From these it is seen that Nefertari was adored as a divinity on the same footing as the great gods of Thebes. She had a priesthood, and a large sacred shrine on a bark borne in processions; and *suten·du·hotep* formulæ were recited to her. Of small remains of this reign there are not many. An alabaster vase (G. Mus.; M.B. 536) bears the name and the *Hor nub* title, *thes taui*. A hawk in blue glazed ware bears the royal names on the crown, and on the under side of the base are three bound captives, negro, Libyan, and Syrian. A ring-shaped vase is said to be in the Ghizeh Museum (W.G. 312). Scarabs and amulets of this king are common; but are of no interest in the types, excepting a plaque of green felspar with names of Aahmes on one side and Amenhotep on the other, probably made in the latter reign for some official who served under both kings. (Abydos, M.A. 1421.)

NEFERTARI or AAHMES·NEFERTARI was the sister and wife of Aahmes; through her descended all the rights of the royal line, and she was adored for many centuries as the great ancestress and foundress. We have already noticed her worship with that of her husband and son. She is styled on contemporary monuments as the "royal daughter, royal sister, great royal wife, royal mother, great ruler (*athy*), mistress of both lands" (L.D. iii. 3 a, b).

Her coffin was found at Deir el Bahri. It is made of layers of linen glued together and covered with stucco. Such a material would not well bear to be formed in long flat masses, and the division of the coffin is therefore around the middle, and not from head to foot. It is 10 feet 4 inches high; painted yellow picked out with blue, like the coffin of Aahmes. The arms are represented as crossed on the breast, holding an *ankh* in either hand. The body is covered with an hexagonal network in relief, and the wig with a chevron net. Within this great coffin were two mummies, one of Ramessu III.; the other was unnamed, and probably of this queen. Unhappily it was left without examination for over four years, amid the damp of the Nile shores;

it was then found to be decomposing, and was "provisionally interred," without any scientific study of its characteristics. The racial details would have been of the highest interest, in comparison with the rest of the family. Thus disappeared the most venerated figure of Egyptian history.

A seated statue of the queen — now headless — lies at Karnak, in the first court, behind the obelisks (W.G. 316); and several smaller statuettes are known, one of stone (T. Mus.) and four of wood (T. Mus. Berl. Stuttgart). A small model adze, *nen*, of wood bears her name (T. Mus.; Rec. iii. 124). Many scarabs of hers are known, but none are of importance. A piece of open work in wood shows Nefertari and Amenhotep seated (T. Mus.).

FIG. 12.—Coffin of Aahmes Nefertari. Ghizeh.

The family of Aahmes was numerous, and needs some notice. His wife and also his children frequently adopted the name Aahmes within their cartouches; and all his children, except Sapair, have their names in cartouches. There was thus an irregularity in the usage which is not found at any other period.

The principal authority that we have for the family is through the subsequent worship of them. The two tombs which we have named before, Anhurkhaui (L.D. iii. 2 d) and Khabekht (L.D. iii. 2 a) agree in naming the following persons, after the ascending line of Amenhotep, his father or mother, and his grandmother; they are, therefore, according to all analogy, his brothers and sisters, namely, *Meryt·amen (*Tair, mother *Kasmut), *Sat·amen, Sa·amen, *Sat·kames, *Hent·ta·meh, *Turs, *Aahmes, Sa·pa·ir (females marked *). Those in loops here occur only in the second of these tombs; and from Tair being a royal sister and Kasmut a divine mother, it appears as if Tair was an early child of Aahmes, and therefore important, but by a wife Kasmut who was not in the royal line of descent. The other children were mostly found at Deir el Bahri.

FIG. 13.—Statuette of Nefertari. Turin.

Meryt·amen	A mummy falsely labelled as hers		p. 539
Sat·amen	Coffin and mummy (false)	Died an infant	538
Sa·amen	Coffin and mummy	Died an infant	538
Amen·hotep	Coffin and mummy		537
Aah·hotep	Coffin (no mummy)		545
Sat·kames	Mummy only	Died about 30	541

Also Hent·tamehu, coffin and mummy, dau. of Thenthapi   543
Mes·hent·themhu, coffin and mummy (false)   544

The pages refer to the account of the remains in Ms. M. How many of these were born of Nefertari is not certain. But it seem probable that the order was—

Meryt·amen	Eldest dau. of Nefertari	Died young
Sat·amen	Second dau. of Nefertari	Died infant
Sa·pa·ir	Eldest son of Nefertari	Died young, heir
Sa·amen	Second son of Nefertari	Died infant
Aah·hotep	Third dau. of Nefertari	Queen
Amenhotep	Third son of Nefertari	King
Sat·kames	Fourth dau. of Nefertari	Died about 30

The special worship of these first four chi'dren, although three of them certainly died young, points to their having been elder than the reigning survivors; only such a precedence would be likely to ensure the continued adoration of mere infants. Also, either Amenhotep I. or Tahutmes I. must have been born rather late in the family, in order to fill out the length of the reigns. This mortality of these children would therefore account for the time elapsed.

FIG. 14.—Plaque of Merytamen. F.P. Coll.

Of the other children, Hent·tamehu was born of the royal daughter Thenthapi, as inscribed on her bandages (Ms. M. 544). She lived till the next reign, as she is called royal sister on her coffin, and on a contemporary slab of sculpture (Fig. 15) (F.P. Coll.). Hent·ta·meh was born of the queen Anhapi (C.N. 513; L.D. iii. 8 a).

Tair was born of Kasmut, probably (L.D. iii. 2 a). There has been a question as to the prince Sa·pa·ir, whose name often occurs, and who seems to have died young; from his prominence he was probably the heir, but it was debated whether he can be the same as the king (Ahmes·sa·pa·ir), whose tomb was examined by the Ramesside inspectors and found intact. Noting how

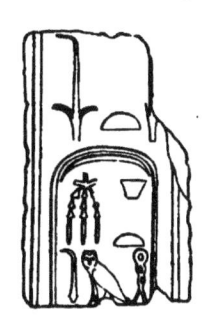

FIG. 15.—Inscription of the Princess Ahmes·hent·ta·mch. Qurneh, F.P. Coll.

loosely cartouches were employed at this time, and how most of the family of Aahmes have his name included with theirs, it seems probable that these two names belonged to one person; and the matter is settled by a part of a stele erected by him, on which he is called "the king's son Aahmes who is named Sa·pa·ir" (F.P. Coll.). The difficulty that he is called king in the Ramesside papyrus is perhaps most likely disposed of by the possibility of the scribe having dropped out *sa* from the title *sa suten*, or king's son. No other king in that document is mentioned without the double cartouche, except Antef IV., who may not have had a second name; and therefore, as this cartouche is single, it is the more likely to belong to a king's son. A limestone stamp for (Sa·ra·sa·amen) found at Thebes is exactly like another for (Seqenenra). But as no earlier Sa·amen is known, it seems not unlikely that these stamps might both have been made at the same time for sealing endowment property of the tombs. The title Sa·ra might be given perhaps to the king's son during his minority, as he was of the divine descent (M.D. 52 b). A scarab (B. Mus.) may belong to this prince (P. Sc. 853).

FIG. 16.—Stele of an official "made by the king's son Aahmes, his name is Sa·pa·ir," with figure of the prince as a boy. Qurneh, F.P. Coll.

A limestone base of a head-rest (?) is inscribed, "Made by the *hon kay* of (Mert·amen) Amenhotep. Hathor over Thebes" (F.P. Coll.); and a bar of wood bears the name of the "royal sister (Aahmes, Amen·mer")" (F. Mus.; S. Cat. F. 1564). Two scarabs are known (B. Mus.; G. Coll.; P. Sc. 854-5). Also a cone of Mahu, chief priest of Meryt·amen (M.A.F. viii. 279, 72).

XVIII. 2. ZESER·KA·RA

AMENHOTEP I.

1562
–1541
B.C.

FIG. 17.—Cartouches from carved wood. F.P. Coll.

Coffin and mummy, Deir el Bahri		(Ms. M. 536).
Inspection of tomb, Abbott Pap.		(Ms. E. 223–4).

Karnak	Granite jamb	(L.D. iii.4 a).
,,	Seated statue, limestone	(M.K. 38 c).
[,,	Named by Taharka	(M.K. 42)].
Thebes	Temple	
,,	Sketch on limestone, G. Mus.	(V.G. 537).
,,	Sketch on limestone, T. Mus.	(Rec. iii. 124).
,,	Statue, Turin Mus.	
Deir el Bahri	Bricks	(L.D. iii. 6 b).
Medinet Habu	Statue, limestone, G. Mus.	(V.G. 698).
Shut er Regal	Inscription	(P.S. 480).
	Inscription of Penaati	(P.S. 476).
Silsileh	Tablet of Paynamen	(L.D. iii. 200 b).
Kom Ombo	Door jamb	(A.Z. xxi. 78).
Ibrim	King under canopy, stele	(R.S. xxviii. 1).
Meroe	Wooden tablets (T. Mus.)	

Statuette	T. Mus.	(L.T. 1372).
Part of stele with head	G. Mus. (V.G. 693)	⎫
Naos fragment	G. Mus.	⎪
Black granite altar	Berlin (2292)	⎬ (W.G. 321).
Vase	Berlin (1637 b)	⎪
Vase	Louvre	⎭
Brick stamp	B. Mus. (5993)	(B.P. 12).
Wooden tablets	Various	
Cylinders, plaques, and scarabs.		

Private monuments, contemporary ?

Aahmes	Tomb, El Kab	(L.D. iii. 12; R.P. vi. 5).
Pen·nekheb	Tomb, El Kab	(L.A. xiv. A.B.; R.P. iv. 5).
Amenemheb	Keeper of palace	(Lb. P. 3).
Amenemhat	Tomb, Qurneh	
Hery	Tomb, Drah Neg.	(C.M. 51 j.).
Tahutmes	Palette	(Sabatier, Rec. xiv. 56).

Sen·em·aah	Stele	(G. Mus.; M.A. 1047).
Ha·nefer	Stele	(P. Mus. C. 47; P.R. ii. 48).
x, Am. I. and Nefertari offering		(L.D. iii. 4 e).
Kars, stele, 10th year Am. I.		(Rec. ix. 94).

Later?

Pen·amen, *kher·heb* of Am. I. P. Mus.		(P.R. ii. 64).
x, adoration of Am. I. F. Mus.		(S. Cat. F. 1563).
Pentaurt statue, with ram's head. Vienna		(Rec. ix. 50).
x, stele, figures of Am. I. and Nefertari. B. Mus.		(H.B. ix. 1).
Pa·amen, part statue. F. Mus.		(S. Cat. F. 1723).
Nekht adoring Am. I. and Sapair		(R.S. xxix. 3).
Coffin, with Am. I. as sphinx. Mealeh		(Rec. ix. 82).
Am. I. and Tahut. I. adoring gods. B. Mus.		(H.B. 1).
Kaha offering to Am. I., time of Rams. II.		(H.B. v. 1).
x adoring Am. I. and Rams. II. Pisa		(Rec. i. 136; iii. 103).
Amenhotep, priest of Am. I.	Book of Dead	(Deveria Cat. 56).
Amen·mes, ,, ,,	Tomb. Thebes	(R.S. iii. 181).
Pa·shed	Altar. B. Mus.	(Lb. D. 566).
Hayt	Stele. B. Mus.	(Rec. ii. 186).
Amennekhtu	Statuette Leyden	(Rec. iii. 104).
Nekhtu	Statuette Berlin	(W.G. 321).
Anhurkhaui	Tomb, Ram. IV. Thebes	(L.D. iii. 2 d).
Khabekht	Tomb Thebes	(L.D. iii. 2 a).
Ta·nezemt adoring Am. I. Papyrus, XX. dyn. Turin		(L.T. 1784).
Ankh·f·en·amen, coffin, Isis, Am. I. and Nebhat Helsingfors		(Lb. P. 71).

(Besides those in list of adorers in previous reign, see p. 38.)

Queens—AAH·HOTEP II. Coffin, Deir el Bahri.
    SEN·SENB   Ostrakon   (A.S. xxix. 117).
                          Temple of Deir el Bahri.

Children (by Aah·hotep)—

Amen·mes	Tomb of Paheri	(N.A.P.X.).
Uaz·mes	Tomb of Paheri	(N.A.P.X.).
Aah·mes, afterwards queen.		
Nebt·ta	Scarab	(F.P. Coll.; L.K. 328).
Mut·nefert	Statue at Karnak	(M.K. 38 b 4).

    (by Sen·senb)—

Tahutmes I.	Ostrakon	(A.Z. xxix. 117).
	Temple of Deir el Bahri.	

For the events of this reign we are dependent on the biography of the admiral Aahmes at El Kab, which we have before quoted in the previous reign of king Aahmes, and the repulsion of the Hyksos. At the beginning of this reign Aahmes was about 44 years old; and he relates: "It was my lot to convey king Zaserkara, *makheru*, on his journey up to Kush for the purpose of extending the frontiers of Egypt. His majesty smote that An Khent in the midst of his troops; brought bound, not one was lost, journeying and leaning over (wearied) as those who exist not.

"Behold I was at the head of our soldiers, and I fought in very truth. His majesty was witness of my valour as I carried off two hands and brought them to his majesty. We pursued his people and his cattle. I took a living prisoner and brought him to his majesty. In two days I brought his majesty back to Egypt from the upper well. And I was presented with the gold, and two female slaves, and . . . beside those which I had brought to his majesty, and I was raised to the dignity of "Warrior of the king." The sub-sequent part refers to the next reign.

FIG. 18.—Head of Amenhotep I.

Another important account is that of Pen·nekheb at El Kab, who also lived through the earlier part of this dynasty. Of this reign he says: "I followed the king Zaserkara, *makheru*. I took for him in Kush one prisoner alive" (L.A. xiv. A. B.). And again he states that on the north of the Amukehak he took three hands (L.D. iii. 43 a).

From these accounts we see that one Nubian campaign was a brief one, a mere raid to sweep the country and crush any opposition; and there is no evidence of any subsequent war there. The capture of the fighting men, and driving of them down into Egypt as slaves, bound and exhausted, almost dead with fatigue in the forced march, is put in a few words. But another important war was that against the Amukehak, who appear to have been a Libyan race, part of the Tahenu or "fair people." There had long been occasional war on this side of the land. Herkhuf had joined in plundering the Temehu of the oases, in the VIth dynasty. The western people had occupied Upper Egypt in the VIIth–IXth dynasties. Usertesen I. had attacked the oases or the Natron lakes in the expedition mentioned by Sanehat. But the rising power of the XVIIIth dynasty was quite able to overcome any opposition in that quarter; and Amenhotep rested secure in his triumph on the south and west, and in his father's triumph on the north.

The tomb of Amenhotep was visited by the Ramesside inspectors, who give a longer account of it than of the others. Its place is at present quite unknown. They state: "The eternal setting (horizon) of the king (Zesarkara), son of the sun (Amenhotep), which has 120 cubits of depth in its great hall, as well as the long passage which is on the north of the temple of Amenhotep of the garden (on which the chief Pa·sar of the town made his report to the monarch Khamuas, to the royal officer Nessu·amen, to the scribes of Pharaoh, to the keeper of the house of the divine adoress of Amenra king of the gods (*i.e.* the queen), to the royal officer Ra·nefer·ka·em·pa·amen, to the herald of Pharaoh, to the supreme magistrates, saying, 'The robbers have robbed it'); examined this day, it was found intact by the masons" (Ms. E. 223–4). We may notice that this tomb was peculiar among those examined for the great depth of the excavation into the rock, over 200 feet long. No other tombs on this outer face of the cliffs approached this extent, the long tombs being all on the other face of the cliff in the valley of the Biban el Meluk. This was, in fact, the first of the class of long sepulchres which prevailed in the XVIIIth–XXth dynasties. The exact position of it is yet unknown, but the temple of Amenhotep has been found (in 1896) on the edge of the desert by Drah abul Negga.

The coffin and mummy of the king were in the great find at Deir el Bahri. The coffin is as simple in form as those of the XIth and XVIIth dynasties; but is much poorer, being only painted and not gilt. It is remarkable that none of the coffins of this or later dynasties approach the magnificence of those which went before; the despised Antefs and the obscure Seqenenra and Aah·hotep lay in far grander state than any of their successors. Apparently the attention and care were directed from the casing of the body to providing the enormous halls and corridors cut in the rock, which then came into fashion. The coffin of Amenhotep shows the rise of the bands of hieroglyphics across it, which were simulated from the bandages of the mummy

FIG. 19.—Coffin of Amenhotep I. Ghizeh

within, and which bore inscriptions adoring the four genii of the internal organs. On the mummy is a mask of wood and cartonnage, like that of the coffin outside. The body is surrounded by wreaths, and has not yet been examined (Ms. M. 536).

This king built at Karnak; probably adding to and adorning the old temple of the XIIth dynasty. A granite jamb remaining shows that he worked in hard stone. He also placed statues there: one of these (M.K. 38 c and text) was later removed and rearranged by Tahutmes III., who added an inscription in his 22nd year; this is of silicious limestone, and the head is somewhat injured; it is placed at the middle of the west wing of the pylon of Tahutmes I. (No. ix. Baedeker). Another statue, perhaps from Karnak, is at the Luxor Hotel, but is much broken (W.G. 320). A very fine statue was found at Medinet Habu (G. Mus. V.G. 698) with a figure of Nefertari on the back-pillar, and the name of Sety I. added. A limestone statuette of delicate work is doubtless from Thebes (T. Mus.; L.T. 1372). Two sketches on flakes of limestone (also from Thebes?) are, one in Turin (Rec. iii. 124) and one at Ghizeh (V.G. 537).

Amenhotep also built on the western side of the river; we have already seen the mention of his temple in the Abbott papyrus, and Lepsius brought a brick of his from Deir el Bahri (L.D. iii. 6 b).

Above Thebes the royal architect Penaati records his office under Amenhotep I., and three following kings, on the rocks at Shut er Regal (P.S. 357, 476). Another graffito, near that, names Amenhotep as "beloved of Horus, lord of Mehit"; that is, the capital of the Oryx nome. And at Silsileh Paynamen carved a figure and inscription of the king. This activity in the sandstone region accords with the adoption of this stone for building material in the XVIIIth dynasty, in place of the limestone which had been mainly in use before.

AMENHOTEP I

At Kom Ombo a door jamb bears the names of this king (A.Z. xxi. 78).

In Nubia a large scene at Ibrim shows the king seated under a canopy, attended by two fly-flappers and a fan-bearer; behind the scene is the goddess Sati, standing as protecting him (R.S. xxviii. 1). And at Meroe were found small wooden tablets engraved with figures (T. Mus.; see below).

Of monuments from unknown sites are,—a good head and cartouches (from part of a private stele of Pa·fu·n·amen) in the Ghizeh Museum (V.G. 693); the fragment of a naos (G. Mus.; W.G. 321); a black granite altar at Berlin (2292); two vases, one in Berlin, with mark of contents of 11 hins, holding 317 cub. ins., or 28·8 for the hin (W.G. 321); the other vase in P. Mus.; and a brick stamp (B. Mus., B.P. 12). The small wooden tablets with carved faces, incised and filled in with blue, are found in several museums; they evidently come from one hand, but may have been discovered in different sites.

FIG. 20.—Wooden tablet, Amenhotep I. Brit. Mus.

The subjects are the king riding in a two-horse chariot (B. Mus., A.B. 30), the king smiting down enemies (five in P. Mus., from Salt Coll., R.S. iii. 1. 107; Tav. ii.), and one in Turin, said to be from Meroe, with two cartouches placed on the *sam* and lotus.

Scarabs are very common in this reign, many of peculiarly rough work; there are also some square plaques, and two cylinders. One cylinder has figures of the king standing (F.P. Coll.); a scarab (P. Mus.) has the king spearing an enemy, accompanied by a hunting leopard. A carnelian stone (G. Mus.) shows an entirely new system of patterning, by altering the texture of it to opaque white; the subject is the same as the last, but around it are circles of small dots, with a larger one in the midst of each circle: as such a pattern is distinctively foreign (Mediterranean), it points to this process belonging to foreign work. The private remains bearing the name of the king are none of particular value historically, and are sufficiently indicated in the list at the head of this reign.

ΛΑΗ·ΗΟΤΕΡ II. The coffin of this queen, who transmitted the line of royal descent, was found at Deir el Bahri. It is like that of her mother Nefertari, already described p. 40 ; and its internal size effectually proves that it belongs to a different queen from that of the coffin in which the jewellery was found (Ms. M. 545). Scarabs of the queen are known (Louvre ; F.P. Coll.), and also a glazed stone *menat* (F.P. Coll.).

FIG. 21.—Scarab of Aah·hotep. F.P. Coll.

We now reach another of the tangled questions of the family history. Amen·mes has been regarded as a son of Tahutmes I., and with him goes also Uazmes, his brother, as stated in the tomb of Paheri. The best ground for this view is the inscription of the 4th year of Tahutmes I. by the "king's great son, commander of the troops of his father." This is *prima facie* ground for ascribing Amenmes as son of Tahutmes I.; but the inscription only states that he commanded his father's troops, and not who his father was. On considering the ages, difficulties at once appear. For, at the first glance, Tahutmes II. was about 30 at his death (Ms. M. 547), reigned 13 years, and therefore succeeded at 17, and was born in the 8th year of the reign of Tahutmes I. Is it likely that Tahutmes I. would have a son old enough to be commander-in-chief in the 4th year of his reign, and yet be succeeded by a son born in the

FIG. 22.—Paheri nursing Uazmes. El. Kab.

8th year of his reign? His successor would then be at least twenty to thirty years younger than his eldest son. When we look in more detail into the ages which are indicated, we find greater difficulties. For Tahutmes I. to have a son commander in the 4th year of his reign would necessitate a series of extreme suppositions,— that Amenhotep I. and Tahutmes I. each had their successors born when only 18 (leaving no room for earlier daughters or children who died), and that Amenmes was commander-in-chief at 18. Nor can these reigns be much lengthened, even if we threw over all Manetho's statements of reigns, as we are tied by the old ages of Aahmes the admiral, over 90 when his tomb was inscribed under Tahutmes II., and Pen·nekheb, over 77 at the carving of his tomb under Tahutmes III. As Hatshepsut was the eldest daughter, it would imply that she was about eighteen or twenty years older than her husband Tahutmes II., and was not married, therefore, till she was about 35 or more. All of this is unlikely. And all the difficulty is avoided if Amenmes was commander of the troops of his father Amenhotep, while dating his monument after his father's death in his brother's reign.

FIG. 23.—Scarab of Amenmes. F.P. Coll.

To render the relative ages clearer, we will here arrange the succession according to the indications that we have, resuming it from the table given before on p. 3, and premising, as before, that the use of this method is to show if any incongruity arises among the data, and not to assert the exactitude of every detail, since many points depend on the more or less vague elements of age.

AMENHOTEP I   [DYN. XVIII. 2.

(See p. 3 for earlier part.)

B.C.								
1589	o Amenhotep I.							
1569	20 m. Aahhotep							
1567	22 Aahmes b.							
1564	25 Tahutmes b.	o Tahutmes I.						
1562	27 succeeds							
1544	. . . . .	20 m. Aahmes.						
1542	. . . . .	22 Neferukhebt b.						
1541	48 dies	23 succeeds						
1540		24 Hatshepsut b.	o Hatshepsut					
1533		31 Tahut. II. b.	o Tahutmes II.					
1516		48 dies	17 succeeds	24 succeeds				
1514			18 Neferura born	25				
1512			20 Merytra brn	27				
1512			20 Tahutmes born	. . . .	o Tahutmes III.			
1503			30 dies . . .	. . . .	9 succeeds			
			Neferura dies					
1495				. . .	17 m. Merytra			
1481				59 dies	31 sole reign			
1469					43	o Amh. b.		
1449					63 dies. .	20 succeeds		
1448						21 marries		
1447						22 Tahut. b.	o Tahutmes IV.	
1430						. . .	17 Amenhotep b.	
1423						46 dies .	24 succeeds	
1414							33 dies	

The data of this arrangement, outside of the chronology and lengths of reigns, as already stated, are as follows:—

Amenhotep I. presumably married Aah·hotep when about 20, and Tahutmes I., son of queen Sen·senb, is not likely to have been much younger than his wife Aahmes, daughter of Aah·hotep.

Tahutmes I. presumably married Aahmes in 1544, at about 20. Nefer·khebt was the elder daughter apparently, and Hatshepsut was probably therefore born about 1540 or later.

Tahutmes II. died at about 30 in 1503, and was therefore born about 1533, or seven years after Hatshepsut, and married, say at 17. Hatshepsut, therefore, would not have married before 24 ; Neferu·ra was her elder daughter, as she is called the "mistress of both lands," or heiress ; and she died at the beginning of the reign of Tahutmes III., as Pen·nekheb in extreme old age in that reign had brought up the deceased Neferu·ra. He was born about 1580 (by his services), and would therefore be 66 at the death of Neferu·ra. Merytra would therefore be born about 1512, after her sister, as Neferu·ra was the elder. Neferu·ra was not married, and therefore died before the adolescence of Tahutmes III. (L.D. iii. 20 c).

Tahutmes III. was probably the son of Tahutmes II., as we shall see farther on. It seems most likely that he was born about the same time as his wife Merytra ; and he is therefore entered here at the same date.

Amenhotep II. was son of Tahutmes III., as recorded on the latter's bandages (Ms. M. 548). He was also son of Merytra, as she was royal mother, and accompanies him on the monuments. From the fact that no wife of his is shown on monuments (which are all of the earlier years of his reign), whereas his mother appears, it seems plain that he came to the throne quite young. He must then have been born when his father and mother were advanced in life. If we place his birth at about 1469, and suppose that he succeeded at 20 years old, we cannot be far out.

We now reach a very tight place in the chronology. That Tahutmes III., Amenhotep II., Tahutmes IV., and Amenhotep III. succeeded as four generations, father and son, cannot be well doubted. The first link is fixed by the mummy bandages (Ms. M. 548); the other three by the tomb of Hor·em·heb, where they are definitely stated to be each sons of the previous one (M.A.F. v. 434, pl. v.). Yet Amenhotep II. was unmarried on his accession; and his marriage, the birth of Tahutmes IV., his growth and marriage, the birth of Amenhotep III., and his growth up to accession, all have to come in the two reigns of 25 years 10 months + 9 years 8 months, or $35\frac{1}{2}$ years in all. That Amenhotep III. was no infant when he succeeded, is proved by his slaying 102 lions between the 1st and 10th year of his reign; hence we cannot place his age at accession below about 15, even supposing that he began lion-hunting so early. This takes 15 off $35\frac{1}{2}$, leaving 19 years; 2 must be deducted to the birth of Tahutmes IV. after the unmarried accession of Amenhotep II.; and thus Amenhotep III. must have been born when Tahutmes IV. was but 17.

It is quite clear, therefore, that it is wholly impossible to shorten these reigns below the figures of Manetho, as has been proposed owing to the absence of monuments; and the principal amount, 26 years, is lately verified by a date on a wine jar. In fact, a few years more would render this history more credible. Still it is not impossible, and unless some new details appear, we must accept this, and observe that it cannot be modified scarcely one year either way. The only points that could give way to release the close fit would be—(1) the non-marriage of Amenhotep II. on his accession; though, even if he had then been married, his mother's prominence, to the exclusion of a supposed wife, would imply his being yet immature; (2) the lengths of reigns in Manetho, which are, however, on the contrary, too long already to seem likely; or (3) the proof that Tahutmes IV. was son of Amenhotep II., for were they brothers, the whole would harmonise well, but yet Horemheb can hardly have made an error in the history of the period of his own lifetime.

What renders these early accessions, of Amenhotep II. at 20, and Tahutmes IV. at 24, the more likely, is that both are represented as children in the tombs of their nurse and tutor respectively. Had they been elderly on their accessions, their childhood would have been hardly so much thought of and commemorated.

To return, then, to the family of Amenhotep I., we may assign to queen Aah·hotep the parentage of the future queen Aah·mes, and probably also of the other queen Mut·nefert and the princes Amen·mes and Uaz·mes. Of the latter, a temple was erected at Thebes, with a stele showing him standing behind his brother Tahutmes I., adored by Tahutmes III.; other mention of him is also found in the same building (M.E. 5, 11), which had been, however, restored by Amenhotep III., a ring of whom was found under the threshold. Nebt·ta was another daughter of Aah· hotep, as stated by Lepsius (L.K. 328). A scarab of hers is known.

FIG. 24.—Scarab of Nebta. F.P. Coll.

From an ostrakon, and from the temple at Deir el Bahri, we know that the mother of Tahutmes I. was named Sen·senb. It has been suggested that the Tahutmes line was of a new family, by both father and mother; but we have seen how the old family reverenced Tahuti along with Aah in the time of Kames, so that the name may well appear in the Aahmes line. And a strong evidence of his descent is given by his wife Aahmes; she was called "lady of both lands," showing her royal heritage, and she was also "royal sister," showing her husband's relation to her and to the family. Above all, he calls himself "king's son of a king's son," claiming descent from Amenhotep and Aahmes (L.D. iii. 18).

FIG. 25.—Sensenb, mother of Tahutmes I. Copy by Mr. Carter. Deir el Bahri.

TAHUTI·MES I

XVIII. 3. AA·KHEPER·KA·RA  1541–1516 B.C.

TAHUTI·MES I.

Mummy	Deir el Bahri	(Ms. M. 581).
Coffin	,, ,,	(Ms. M. 545).

Nubt	Temple	
Deir el Bahri	Temple begun	(C.M. 192, 5).
Deir el Medineh	Bricks	(L.D. iii. 7 f).
Medinet Habu	Offering to Amen	(C.M. 195, 2).
,,	Door	(L.D. iii. 27; 1, 2).
Karnak	Pylons iv. v. viii.	(M.K. ii.).
,,	Scene and inscription	(L.D. iii. 18).
	Osiride figures	(M.K. text 28).
	Pillars	(M.K. 2).
,,	Obelisk	(L.D. iii. 6).
,,	Portions of statues	(W.G. 328).
Aswan	Canal inscription	(Rec. xiii. 202).
Ibrim	Shrine	(C.L. 114).
Semneh	List of gifts	(L.D. iii. 47 c).
Kummeh	Temple	(L.D. iii. 59 a).
Tangur (21° 15′ N.)	Tablet	(S.B.A. vii. 121).
Tombos (19° 40′ N.)	Steles	(L.D. iii. 5).
Arqo (19° 27′)	Stele	(W.T. 472).

Statue seated, diorite, T. Mus. (L.T. 1374).
(portrait in L.D. iii. 292, 25).
Vase, glazed steatite B. Mus. 4762.
,, glazed pottery P. Mus. 502.
Menat blue glaze (Wiedemann Coll.).
Scarabs.

Queens—AAHMES—
    Deir el Bahri   Temple.
    Ivory wand   T. Mus.
    Scarabs   (B. Mus., P. Mus.).
  MUT·NEFERT—
    Statue of Tahutmes II., Karnak (M.K. 38 b, 4).
    Statue, Qurneh   G. Mus. (V.G. 231).

Children of Aahmes—
Khebt·neferu	Deir el Bahri	(L.D. iii. 8 b).
Hatshepsut	,,	,,

of Mut·nefert—
Tahutmes II.	Statue (above).

That Tahutmes was not co-regent with Amenhotep for any length of time, is seen from the dating of a record of a campaign in his second year. Moreover, his coronation edict has been happily preserved, and does not suggest any co-regency. It appears that copies of the royal edicts were officially sent out, and the copy of this despatch for Elephantine was fortunately recovered there lately (A.Z. xxix. 117). It reads thus:—

"A letter of the king to cause thee to know that my majesty is risen as king on the throne of Horus, without equal for ever. My titles are to be made as *Horus Ka nekht, mery·Maat; Samuti Kha·em·nesert·aa·pehti; Hor·nub, Nefer renput, sankh abu; suten biti Aa·kheper·ka·ra; sa ra Tahuti·mes; ankh zet er neheh.* Cause the offerings of the gods of Abu in the south to be made by the will of the prince (l.h.w.) the king of Upper and Lower Egypt, Aa·kheper·ka·ra.

"Cause thou that the oath be administered in the name of my majesty (l.h.w.), born of the royal mother Sen·senb. This is written that thou mayest know it, and that the royal house is safe and strong.

"The first year, Phamenoth, day 21. Day of coronation."

This date, and the coronation of Tahutmes III. on the 4th of Pakhons, give us some data to check the months of the reigns according to Manetho. The lengths of reign he states are Tahutmes I., 25 y. 4 m.; Tahutmes II., 13 y.; Hatshepsut, 21 y. 9 m. Hence, placing in order the months in question thus, we have—

Mekhir, before 21st Hatshepsut dies

Phamenoth 21st, Tahutmes I. begins

Pharmuthi, wars of Tahutmes III. begin

Pakhons 4th, Tahutmes II. dies
        4th, Tahutmes III. begins
  about 4th, Tahutmes II. begins

Pauni,

Epiphi, about 21st Tahutmes I. dies.

Thus we see that Tahutmes II. dated his reign a few weeks before the death of Tahutmes I.; probably on being associated at the occasion of his early marriage with Hatshepsut, who was already named successor to Tahutmes I., between the months of Mekhir and Mesori (see obelisk inscriptions).

The interval between Hatshepsut's death and the beginning of the active wars of Tahutmes III. was very short. It is indicated thus: Tahutmes began his campaign in his 22nd year in Pharmuthi, and passes in the history immediately to Pakhons in his 23rd year; hence he began after 21 years 11 months of regnal inactivity. Now Hatshepsut reigned 21 years 9 months according to Manetho, from Tahutmes IInd's death, leaving only two months for Tahutmes III. to have organised his campaign, so soon as he was master. The coronation of Hatshepsut on Thoth 1st (Rec. xviii. 102) would show that little over a month elapsed between her father's death on Epiphi 21st, and the ceremony of her crowning, probably postponed a little to bring it on the New Year's feast. We now see how these years and months of reigns show no discrepancies with the official dates that are preserved; but, on the contrary, throw additional light upon the facts.

Of the wars of Tahutmes I. we know but little. The invaluable biographies of Aahmes and Pen·nekheb at El Kab are again our best resource. Aahmes relates—

" It was my lot " (at about 65 years old) " to convey

king Aa·kheper·ka·ra (*makheru*) on his journey up to Khent·hen·nefer for the purpose of chastising the disturbance among the tribes, and of exterminating the raiders from the hills. I displayed valour upon his [ships?] on the bad (?) water in the [rescuing?] of the ships at the overturning " (or " at Ta Penayt "), " and I was raised to the dignity of a captain-general of the marines. His majesty " [one line unengraved?] "His majesty became furious at it like a panther, and he shot his first arrow which stuck in the breast of that wretch ; and these [fled ?] fainting before his asp : " (the royal emblem on the cap). "Then was made of them in an instant . . . Their people were carried off as living captives. His majesty returned down the river, all regions being within his grasp. That vile Anu of Khent was kept with his head down in evil plight when his majesty landed at Thebes.

"After this he went to the Ruten for the purpose of taking satisfaction upon the countries. His majesty arrived at Naharina (Upper Mesopotamia); he found that enemy who had plotted conspiracy. His majesty made a great slaughter of them ; an immense number of live captives were carried off by his majesty from his victories.

"Behold, I was at the head of our soldiers, and his majesty saw my valour as I seized upon a chariot, its horses, and those who were on it as living captives ; I took them to his majesty, and I was once more presented with the gold. I have grown up and have reached old age " (over 90 then), "my honours are like . . . and I shall rest in my tomb which I myself have made " (L.D. iii. 12).

Pen·nekheb states : "I followed the king of Upper and Lower Egypt, Aa·kheper·ka·ra (*makheru*): I took for him in Kush two prisoners alive, beside the prisoners brought by me from Kush, I do not reckon them " (L.A. xiv. A.B.). Again he mentions the Kush campaign in another passage (L.D. iii. 43 a). And he also went in the Syrian war: "Again I acted for the king Aa·kheper·ka·ra, *makheru*: I took for him in the land of Naharaina 21 hands, a horse and a chariot" (L.A. xiv.).

Of the Nubian war there are several memorials far up the Nile at Tombos. But the long inscription there, dated in his first year, does not contain any information, beyond a high-flown account of all countries being subject to the king.

FIG. 26.—Head of Tahutmes I. Deir el Bahri.
(From Egypt Exploration Fund.)

Of the Syrian war we learn further in the inscription of Tahutmes III., when he states that "he placed another where was the tablet of his father the king of Upper and Lower Egypt, Aa·kheper·ka·ra"; and further, "His majesty came to the city of Niy on his return. Then his majesty set up his tablet in Naharaina to enlarge the frontiers of Kemi" (L.A. xii.). This points to the limits of the conquests of Tahutmes I.

having been about the district of Niy, which seems to have been on the Euphrates in the region of Aleppo.

It appears, then, that Tahutmes I. must have had the way paved for him by some unrecorded conquests of Amenhotep; as we see that early in his reign he claims general sovereignty, and was soon able to push his frontier as far forward as it was carried by the greatest of his successors, Tahutmes III. He overran the Ruten, or the hill country of Palestine, the land of Naharaina, or northern Syria, and established his frontier boundary on the Euphrates at the place where his son also set up his tablet. Unfortunately we have no detailed record of the cities or tribes subdued by him, such as the later kings engraved, and cannot, therefore, gain a more exact geographical account.

The coffin of this king was found in the great deposit of Deir el Bahri. It was gilded and inlaid, but had been stripped in ancient times. It had been usurped by Painezem I.; but through all the changes the name of the first conqueror of Asia can still be read (Ms. M. 545, 570).

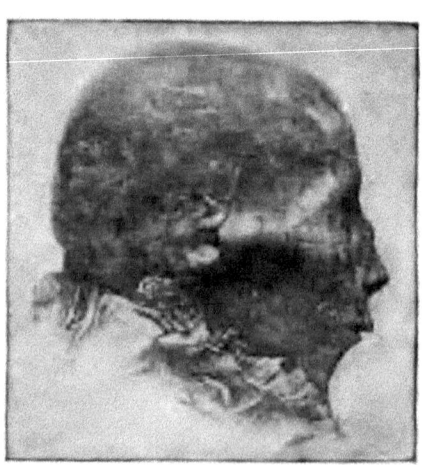

FIG. 27.—Mummy of Tahutmes I. Ghizeh.

The mummy, however, of Painezem was found elsewhere, in the coffin of Aah·hotep II.; and a nameless mummy was found in the coffin of Tahutmes. This body Maspero inclines to believe to be that of Tahutmes, replaced there by pious care when Painezem's usurpation was reversed. The resemblance between this head and that of Tahutmes II.

(Ms. M. vii. viii.) is adduced ; but a stronger likeness of expression and character exists between the portrait of Tahutmes I. at Deir el Bahri temple and the mummy, particularly in front view.

The body shows unusual vigour and a fine form ; it is very well preserved, but unhappily all the wrappings had been destroyed, and so no evidence of the name remained (Ms. M. 581). The locality and the portraiture is all that identifies it.

In the Delta and Middle Egypt no work of Tahutmes I. has yet been found. At Nubt, near Negadeh, he rebuilt the temple of Set, of which doorjambs and a lintel of fine work were found lately.

At Deir el Bahri the temple may have been designed under Tahutmes I., but the sculptures representing him appear to be all due to his great daughter.

At Deir el Medineh bricks of his are found (L.D. iii. 7 f.) ; but at Medinet Habu he founded one of the most important temples of his family ; and the many erasures and alterations of names are a study in family antipathies. His cartouches have been altered from Ra·aa·kheper·ka to Ra·ma·ka by Hatshepsut, and again altered back again by Tahutmes III. (L.D. iii. 27, 1, 2). The decoration appears to have gone on but slowly, and to have reflected the many changes of the time. The lintels of some doors were engraved by Tahutmes I., while their jambs were by the third; other lintels are by the second, and their jambs by Hatshepsut (L.D. iii. 27, 1, 2). The first is seen offering to Amen ; the second offering to Min ; the third on his throne, with his wife Merytra behind him ; or, again, hoeing up a foundation, showing that he founded some parts of this temple (C.M. 195).

In the chapel of Uaz·mes (M.E. v.), a stele erected by a tutor of that prince, figures Tahutmes I. and his little deceased brother Uazmes, adored by Tahutmes III. (M.E. ii.), nearly a year before Hatshepsut's death. There is also a tablet of a tutor of the royal children of Tahutmes I., probably the same person (M.E. vi.).

At Karnak a pylon (IV. Baedeker) fronting the

Amen temple was built by this king, and along the inner face a row of Osiride statues of himself were placed. Another pylon (IX. Baedeker) was also built by him, although the decoration was finished by his sons and Amenhotep II. It is on the north face of this that an important inscription occurs, declaring the co-regency of Hatshepsut. Tahutmes declares that he has led the most distant people, that he has scattered all trouble in Egypt, and put an end to crime and destroyed impiety; that he has brought order in place of the rebellions which appeared in Lower Egypt. Then he prays to Amen to give the lower and upper country to his daughter the king Ma·ka·ra, as it has been given to him (Mel. i. 46). Subsequently Tahutmes III. has altered Ma·ka·ra to Aa·kheper·ka·ra. This document is almost more than an association of Hatshepsut with the king; it prays Amen to give the sovereignty to the daughter as it had been given to the father, making almost an abdication. This suggests that it must have been at the end of the life of the king, when he felt no longer able to rule. The reason of placing the daughter in power rather than the son, is seen in the ages. Hatshepsut was probably 24, and doubtless showed already her vast abilities; while Tahutmes II. was probably not more than 17, and was of no great strength. He was not married to his sister at the time of this inscription. So it appears that on failing health the king placed the power in the hands of his eldest child, who had the sole right to it by the female inheritance; and then, just a few weeks before his death, married Tahutmes II. to her, perhaps to ensure his receiving some respect for his position if not for his character.

Two pillars of Tahutmes I. were re-used later on (between pylons IV. and V. Baed.); but Mariette attributes to this king all the pillars between pylons IV. and V., and those east of pylon V. as well.

This king also placed one of the two obelisks in front of his pylon; but it has been disfigured by Ramesside inscriptions crowded down the blank margins of the inscriptions (L.D. iii. 6). A base for a statue remains in front of this; and fragments of two statues are seen in the place (W.G. 328). The fellow obelisk is due to Tahutmes III. (M.K. ii.).

A very enigmatical block was found here, of which no explanation is yet possible. It has a large cartouche horizontal; within that a small cartouche vertical of Tahutmes I.; on one side of that "year 8," and on a raised oval *Ra·aa·kheper* and an inexplicable curl; on the other side a like oval, with *Ra·aa·kheper·tef·ka·kheper·mery*, and "year 6" (G. Mus.).

FIG. 28.—Part of obelisk of Tahutmes I. Karnak.

At Aswan an interesting memorial remains of the campaign of this king, and his passage up the old canal cut by Usertesen III. for his Nubian wars (see i. p. 179). The viceroy of the south inscribed the rock thus, below the names of Tahutmes I.: "Year 3, Pakhons 20th, his majesty passed this canal in force and power in his campaign to crush Ethiopia the vile. Prince Turo" (Rec. xiii. 202). Another inscription after the titles states: "His majesty came to Kush to crush the vile" (M.I. i. 41, 185). And a third (all dated on the same day), after the titles, states: "His majesty commanded to clear this canal, after he had found it filled with stones, so that no boat could pass up it. He passed up it, his heart rejoicing" (M.I. i. 85, 13).

At Ibrim is a rock shrine with figures of the king seated between Tahuti and Sati (C.L. 114).

The frontier fortresses of Semneh and Kummeh, which were so important under the XIIth dynasty (see pp. 179–181), became again the keys of the south lands under the XVIIIth. Tahutmes I. began the rebuilding here, and a list of gifts to Amen bears his name at Semneh (L.D. iii. 47 c); while at Kummeh his sculptures were usurped by his son Tahutmes II. (L.D. iii. 59 a).

Three records of his conquests remain in Ethiopia: at Tangur (21° 15′ N.), on a rock 60 feet above the Nile, is a record of the return of the king in his 2nd year, with a convoy led by Aahmes, scribe of the troops (S.B.A. vii. 121). And, farther still, at Tombos (19° 40′ N.) is a large stele of the 2nd year, and several smaller ones, referring to his conquests of the Nehasi and of Kush. The historical details of these we have already noticed. Lastly, at Arqo is a stele known as "the golden stone" (W.T. 472).

Beside the royal monuments there are several private inscriptions of interest.

A man named Amenhotep bears the title, "Chief king's son of Aa·kheper·ka·ra"; but as he is shown offering to his father Tehuti·sena, and mother Ta·hured, and to his brother Nefer·hotep, it appears that this king's son must be purely titular, and not related to the king. The "king's son of Kush," as the title of the viceroy of Ethiopia, shows that there were titular "king's sons"; and this Amenhotep would therefore be the chief of such a class (L.D. iii. 9).

Of the officials of this reign there are recorded—

Penaati	Director of works	(P.S. 476).
Pu	Great builder	(A.Z. xix. 67).
Tehuti	Director of hewers	(E.L. 35).
Aa·kheper·ka	Keeper of equipment	(M.A.F. viii. 275, 64).
Userhat	Keeper of the palace	(Rec. iv. 125; L.T. 1456).
Sebekhotep	Guardian of the palace	(S. Cat. F. 1566).
Pet·en·ra	Keeper of the cattle	(M.A.F. viii. 289, 171).
x	Tutor of the princes	(M.E. vi.).

(The keeper of equipment, za·khau, is analogous to the phrase "ship's husband.")

Of priests and adorers there are—

Aa·kheper·ka·ra·senb, canopic jars, P. Mus.	(W.G. 327).
Amenemhat (under Tahut. III.)	(L.D. iii. 29 c).

Neta	Cone	(M.A.F. viii. 297, 261).
Uaz·shemsu	T. Mus.	(Rec. ii. 172; L.T. 1457).
Sebek·nekht	Tomb	(C.N. 512).
Sem·nefer	T. Mus.	(Rec. iii. 113).
x (Silsileh)	Tomb	(L.D. iii. 28, 4 a–d).
Pen·nekheb, *hon ka* (see p. 47)		(L.D. iii. 43 b).
Iufi, praising Aahmes		(Rec. ix. 93).

The king is also mentioned in some tombs at Thebes, Nos. 9 (C.N. 501) and 30 of Amenhotep (C.N. 519); and at Silsileh, in the tomb of Menkh (L.D. iii. 8 c).

Of portable objects there is a seated statue in diorite, about life size, in Turin (L.T. 1374); also two fragments of statues lying still at Karnak, in the hall behind pylon V. A seated colossus remains in front of pylon VIII. at the west end, which was erected by Tahutmes III. in his 42nd year in honour of his father (Mel. i. 46). Two vases and a menat are noted above in the list. Of scarabs there are many, and some peculiar types; one has the ka name down the middle, between the repeated throne name (P. Mus.); another has a sphinx with the name, and on the back instead of a beetle a kneeling figure (F.P. Coll.); another has the joint cartouches of Tahutmes I. and Hatshepsut, she being named *sa ra* (P. Mus.); this was probably made during the brief co-regency at the end of his reign. Of both this king and Hatshepsut there are unusual scarabs

Fig. 29.—Scarabs of Tahutmes I. Louvre.

with the *hor nub* name and the uraeus and vulture names.

Of Queen AAHMES a few objects remain. Her portraits appear at the temple of Deir el Bahri; an ivory wand in the form of an arm bears her cartouche (T. Mus.); and two scarabs of her are known (P. Mus., B. Mus.).

Sat·amen, this king's supposed sister and wife, has been regarded as of far more importance than is warranted, owing to the mistake of attributing a reign in Manetho to her instead of to Hatshepsut (C.B. i. 27).

Fig. 30.—Head of Queen Aahmes, Deir el Bahri. (From Egypt Exploration Fund.)

Fig. 31.—Queen Aahmes. From a photograph by Mr. H. Carter.

In fact, no trace of this supposed queen is to be found, except a green glazed steatite toilet-box in the Louvre

Fig. 32.—Ivory wand of Aahmes. Turin.

(P. Sc. 852); there is no evidence to what reign this belongs, and there seems no reason why it should not have been part of the outfit of the infant heiress of

Aahmes and Nefertari, thus setting aside altogether a later and mythical Sat·amen.

Of queen MUT·NEFERT a fine statue in sandstone was found in the chapel of Uaz·mes (V.G. 231 ; M.E. i.). It bears the inscription on the throne, "The good god, lord of both lands, Aa·kheper·en·ra (Tahutmes II.), made by him his monuments of his mother, royal wife, royal mother, Mut·nefert, *makheru.*" This queen was

FIG. 33. Queen Mut·nefert. Ghizeh.

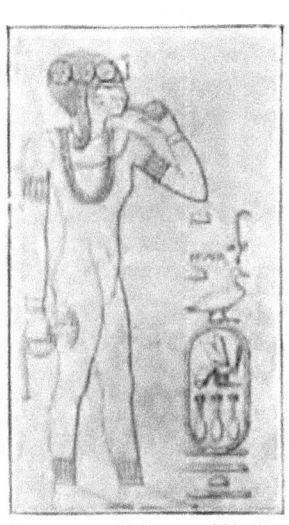
FIG. 34.—Princess Khebt· neferu. Deir el Bahri.

a daughter of Amenhotep, as she appears on the statue of Tahutmes II. as the "royal daughter, royal wife," at Karnak (M.K. 38 b, 4). The royal children were the heiress Khebt·neferu (L.D. iii. 8 b), who died early, as she was not married; and the great queen Hatshepsut, who was married to her half-brother Tahutmes II., the son of Mut·nefert.

XVIII. 4. AA·KHEPER·EN·RA

Tahutimes II.

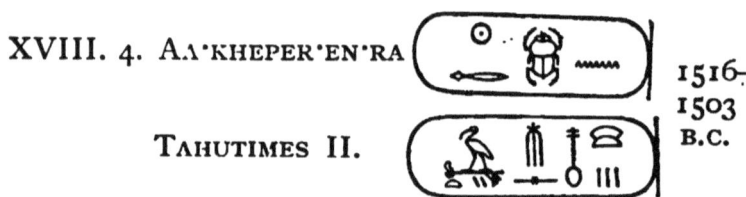

1516–1503 B.C.

Coffin and mummy, Deir el Bahri (Ms. M. 545).

Deir el Bahri, temple, parts	(L.D. iii. 17a, 20a).
	(D.H. ii. 21).
Medinet Habu, temple, parts	(C.M. 195, 4).
Bricks on west side	(Pr. M. 23, 15).
Karnak, pylon IX. begun	(L.D. iii. 14, 15, 16).
2 statues by pylon VIII.	(M.K. 38 b, e).
Chambers X, Y, Z, Z^1	(C.N. ii. 145–6).
Esneh, red granite pillars	(P.R. ii. 3, 43).
Aswan, inscription	(L.D. iii. 16a).
Semneh, inscription	(L.D. iii. 47 c).
Kummeh, alteration of Tahut. I	(L.D. iii. 59 a).
Barkal	(W.T. 472).
El Ayun, Oasis, Stele	(A.Z. 1876, 120).

Pakhen offering to T. II., stele, T. Mus.	(L.T. 1458).
Penaati, director of works, Silsileh.	(P.S. 476).

Isis and Horus. Lee Collection   (Cat. No. 27).
Scarabs and cowroid.
Queens—HATSHEPSUT.
   ASET, wrappings of Tahutmes III. (Ms. M. 548).
Children(by *Hatshepsut*)—Neferu·ra, Assasif (C.M. cxcii. 3 ; cxciv. 1, 3; head best in R.H. ii. 8).
              Meryt·ra Hatshep-
                set
(by *Aset*)   Tahutmes III.   (Ms. M. 548).

That Tahutmes II. was not co-regent for any length of time with his father, is shown by an inscription at Aswan being dated in his first year. This records his expedition to Kush. He states that he was "revered in the lands of the Hanebu (or Mediterranean), and that the Mentiu·setet and Anu·khent (north and south) came with their offerings. His south boundary was to the opening of the level land, and his north bound to the *pehu* of the Setit (the lakes of Syria), all these are serfs of his majesty. His arms were not repulsed from the land of the Fenkhu. . . . Then one came with good news to his majesty, 'that the vile Kush has gone into rebellion . . . to injure the people of Egypt, and to raid their cattle, even beyond the gates which thy father built in his victory to beat back the rebellious foreigners, even the Anu·khent of Khent·hen·nefer, being come to the north of the vile Kush' . . . His majesty raged at it like a panther. 'As I live, as Ra loves me, as my father lord of the gods praises me, I will not leave a male alive.' He sent a great army to the land of Khent in his good and victorious time to overthrow the rebellious; . . . this army of his majesty overthrew these foreigners, they took the life of every male according to all that his majesty commanded; excepting that one of those children of the prince of Kush was brought alive as a live prisoner with their household to his majesty, placed under the feet of the good god. Behold, his majesty was seated upon the throne when were brought the prisoners which the army of his majesty were bringing. This nation being made as bondmen of his majesty, as in old time. The people rejoiced and gave praise to the lord of both lands, exalting the good god." From this it is evident that Tahutmes II. did not go to lead the campaign himself, and this accords with his youth, being only about seventeen at this time. Another war is mentioned by Aahmes Pen·nekheb, who states: "I followed the king Aa·kheper·en·ra, *makheru*, I brought away from the land of the Shasu (Bedawin) very many prisoners, I do not reckon them. . . . the king Aa·kheper·en·ra gave me two gold bracelets, six collars, three bracelets of lazuli, and a silver war axe" (L.A. xiv. ; R.P. iv. 8).

The temple at Deir el Bahri, which is mainly occupied with the scenes of the expedition to Punt, must have been begun to be sculptured toward the end of his reign, as he only appears on some parts of it, and

Tahutmes III. is more usually found there. This
agrees with the expedition having been made late in

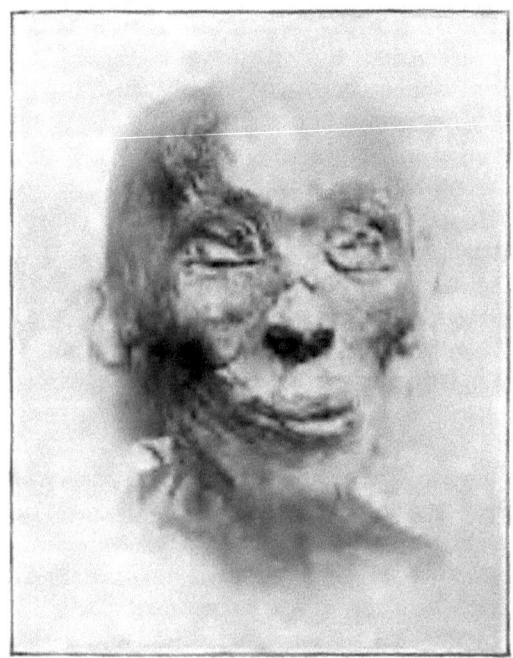

Fig. 35.—Mummy of Tahutmes II. Ghizeh. Profile and front view.

his reign, in the ninth year (Rec. xviii. 103). Thus there were but four years for the expedition and the sculp-

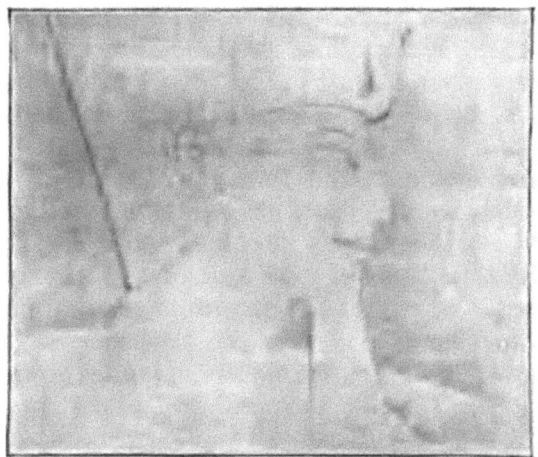

FIG. 36. Portrait of Tahutmes II.

FIG. 37.—Coffin of Tahutmes II.

turing before he died. Even during his life, Hatshepsut appears to have taken the leading part; as she well might, being so much older than he, and having been associated on the throne before him. In short, he appears to be solely the husband of Hatshepsut, and not to have taken any important action in the government. From his mummy it seems that he was not healthy, nor of a strong frame like that of his father or brother. And his early death bears this out.

The great work of the temple at Deir el Bahri we shall consider in the next reign, that of Hatshepsut, who appears to have been the real author of it.

At Medinet Habu there is a scene of this king offering to Min (C.M. 195, 4). But most of the occurrences of his name there are due to the need of filling in some name over the erasures of Hatshepsut's name by Tahutmes III.; some places he filled in with his father's, and some places with his grandfather's, over the loathed cartouche of his great sister (L.D. iii. 7 a, b, c).

At Karnak was the principal work of this reign. The pylon IX. was begun, and half of the doorway inscription completed, the rest being filled in by Tahutmes III. (L.D. iii. 16, d–g). Two statues before this pylon are also of the builder. And several of the chambers were decorated under him; following Champollion's lettering, X shows Tahutmes II. offering to Amen, but usurped by Hatshepsut, while Hatshepsut's original work in this room is unaltered; Y has Tahutmes II. offering to Amen, perfect on the north side, but usurped by Hatshepsut on the south; room Z has bad work of Tahutmes II. in part, and of Tahutmes III. in the rest; and room Z^1 has some fragments of a granite doorway of Tahutmes II. So this decoration must have been running on during the latter part of his reign, and left unfinished at his death.

He also appears to have built at Esneh, as two red granite pillars from there bear his name (both in P. Mus.): one has titles and name, "beloved son of Sati" (P.R. ii. 3); the other has been usurped by Ramessu II., and is a fragment of an obelisk naming the divinities Thenent and Menthu (P.R. ii. 43). These pillars had probably been brought from Taud (opposite Erment), which is named upon them.

At Aswan is the long inscription of the Nubian war in his first year (L.D. iii. 16 a). Others have been attributed to this king (M.I. i.); but reading only Ra·aa·kheper, they might as well be of Tahutmes I. or of Amenhotep II., and are probably of the latter.

At Semneh, Tahutmes II. is named with his father in an inscription recording gifts to Amen on the front wall (L.D. iii. 47 c). And at Kummeh he has converted the name of his father into his own (L.D. iii. 59 a). At Barkal in Ethiopia, remains of his are found (W.T. 472).

In the Oasis of El Ayun (Farafra) is an inscription of this reign seen by Ascherson (A.Z. 1876, 120).

Of private remains there is the stele (T. Mus.) of Pakhen offering to this king (L.T. 1458); and at Shut er Regal the graffito of Penaati, the director of works (P.S. 476). The tomb of Pen·nekheb at El Kab, which is of so much importance for the preceding reigns, was made under this king, as also the grey granite statue of Pen·nekheb (A.Z. xxi. 77).

FIG. 38.—Princess Nefrura. Deir el Bahri.

Of minor remains, a statuette of Isis and Horus has the name of Tahutmes II. on the side of the throne, above groups of bound prisoners (Lee Cat. 27).

Scarabs are not common, and one with the *ka* name is the only type of interest.

The queen Hatshepsut we shall notice by herself in

the next section. The daughter Neferu·ra was the eldest, being the "lady of both lands, princess of the north and south"; and she appears next behind Hatshepsut and Tahutmes III. in scenes. Yet she was never married, which points to her early death before the adolescence of Tahutmes III. As late, however, as the 16th year of Hatshepsut, she was alive, as Senmut was keeper of her palace when he went to quarry the great obelisks (L.D. iii. 25 *bis*, q). This, therefore, points to Tahutmes being then unmarried. Several scarabs of Neferu·ra are known. Meryt·ra

FIG. 39.—Scarabs of Neferura. F.P. Coll.

Hatshepset was the second daughter (*shepset*, singular, distinguishes this from her mother, *shepsut*, plural); she was the wife of Tahutmes III., "great royal wife," but not called heiress; and she was the mother of Amenhotep II. Two or three scarabs of her are known.

The descent of Tahutmes III. has been in much doubt. That his mother was a concubine named Aset is certain, but the evidence varies between Tahutmes I. and Tahutmes II. as his father. The former king has generally been credited, on the strength of a statue of Anebni (B.M., A.B. 51), which names Tahutmes III. as brother of Hatshepsut. But against this there is the statue of Tahutmes II. (so named on the belt), dedicated by Tahutmes III. to "his father" (M.K. 38 b, z); and in the tomb of Anna, Tahutmes II. is said to have "joined the gods, and his son held his place as king, and was prince on the throne of him who begat him" (Rec. xii. 105-7). The last expression, which is much relied on by Maspero (S.B.A. xiv. 178), is not conclusive, as Tahutmes III. occupied the throne equally of Tahutmes I. as of Tahutmes II. So we have the expression "son" (Anna's tomb) and "father" (statue) to set against the "brother" of Hatshepsut (on Anebni's statue). Probably the phrase brother is used for nephew here, or brother's son; and we should see in Tahutmes III. a son of Tahutmes II.

XVIII. 5.
MAAT·KA·RA

HAT·SHEPSUT
(Khnum·Amen)

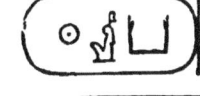

B.C. 1516–1503
with Tahut. II.
1503–1481
with Tahut.
III.

Wady Maghara	Stele, 16th year	(L.D. iii. 28, 2).
Sarbut el Khadem	Glazed bowls	(B.P. 56).
Buto	Seal of temple of Amen	(Ms. G. 91).
Speos Artemidos	Sculpture	(Rec. iii. 1; vi. 20).
Deir el Bahri	Temple	(L.D. iii. 8–27; D.H. passim, N.D.B.).
Qurneh	Bricks	(L.D. iii. 25 bis, 26).
Karnak	Obelisks	(L.D. iii. 22–24; R.P. xii. 127; L.D. iii. 24 a–c).
	Sandstone block	(W.G. 338).
	Chamber sculptures	(C.N. ii. 145).
	Temple of Mut begun	
Medinet Habu	Erased name	(L.D. iii. 7 a, b, c).
	Bricks	(L.D. iii. 26, 4).
El Kab	Inscription	(R.S. iii. i. 130).
Kom Ombo	Gateway	(L.D. iii. 28, 1).
Aswan	Stele of Sen·mut	(L.D. iii. 25 bis, q).

Stele	Dedicated to Tahut. I. by Hatshepsut	(L.A. xi.)
Stele	Vatican	(Rec. ii. 128; C.N. ii. 700).
Stele	G. Coll.	
Statue	Headless, Berl.	(L.D. iii. 25).
,,	Head of, Berl.	(L.D. iii. 25).
Statues, two	Leyden	(A.Z. xii. 45).
,,	Heads of	(L.D. iii. 25).
Ushabti	Hague	(S.B.A. 1885, 183).
Box	Deir el Bahri, G. Mus.	(Ms. M. 584).
Throne	Biban el Meluk, B. Mus.	
Draughtboard	,,	
Set of draughtmen		
Part of cartouche		
Lion's head draughtman		G. Mus. (Ms. G. 123).
Draughtboard		P. Mus. (616).
Plaque		P. Mus. (456).

Alabaster vases	Abydos	G. Mus. (M.A. 1467–8).
,, ,,		P. Mus. (456, 356–7)
,, ,,		Alnwick (Cat. 1380).
Models of tools	P; F; G; Leyden, T. Muss.	
Bead, glass or obsidian		(W.M.C. ii. 141).
Scarabs and plaques.		

Although the reign of this queen is entirely overlapped by those of her co-regents, Tahutmes I., II., and III., yet her importance during the life of her husband, and her independence during the nominal reign of her nephew, until her death, make it most fitting to treat her monuments and acts separately.

Her activity seems to have been entirely given to peaceful enterprises, owing to the vigour and extensive conquests of her father having ensured an age of tranquillity to the realm.

FIG. 40.—Portrait of Hatshepsut. Deir el Bahri. Photograph by Mr. Carter.

In the Sinaitic peninsula she worked the mines. At Wady Maghara, a tablet, dated in her 16th year (= the 3rd year of Tahutmes III.), shows her offering to Sopd, and Tahutmes III. offering to Hathor. It has been suggested that, as he has the crown of Lower Egypt, he was ruler there, while she ruled the upper country; but this cannot hold good, as he has the double crown on her obelisk (L.D. iii. 246), and has the upper crown on the doorway of Kom Ombo, built under her (L.D. iii. 28, 1 b). At Sarbut el Khadem she reopened the mines which had been worked by Amenemhat II. (p. 165); and pieces of glazed vases, bowls, etc., are found there with her name, and the names of later rulers down to the XXth dynasty. This shows that not only the mines were worked, but also potteries of glazed ware, and probably the manufacture of glass and frit coloured with the copper there found. Such work implies the use of a good deal of fuel, and points the more wooded state of the desert in past times, as indicated also by other facts (B.P. 56).

That the Delta began to rise into notice again, is shown by the seal of the temple of Amen at Buto, bearing the name of Hatshepsut (Ms. G. 91).

At Speos Artemidos, near Beni Hasan, an inscription of 42 lines above the façade shows that it was begun by this queen, though the interior was further carved by Sety I. This inscription shows that she had largely refitted the temples, and rebuilt some of them, as we have noticed in the XVIIth dynasty (p. 19). One remarkable phrase is, "my spirits inclined toward foreign people . . . the people Roshau and Iuu did not hide themselves from me"; and, further, the expedition to Punt is mentioned, and the importation of trees and incense. This points to a general taste for geographical enterprise, such as we see illustrated in the great expedition (Rec. iii. 1; vi. 20).

The grand work of this queen was her vast and unique temple at Deir el Bahri, so called because a Coptic convent or Deir was built in its ruins in Christian times, and was called the northern (*Bahri*, often misspelled *Bahari*), in contrast to the southern at Deir el Medineh. Owing to the nearness to this temple of the great tomb cave where the royal mummies were hidden, both have been called by the same name; but that sepulchre has no relation to the temple, and is round a corner of the cliff, in quite another bay. As this temple is now being fully explored, it would be premature to attempt to describe its details.

The general plan is that of a series of three great terraces or platforms, rising one higher than another up the slope of the ground, until the last is backed against the vertical cliffs of the mountain. An axial stairway led from terrace to terrace. Along the front of each terrace the platform was carried on the top of a cloister or colonnade. The upper terrace is headed by a row of chambers, the middle one of which is carried deep into the rock, and lined with sculptured slabs,

Other chambers, and an altar in a courtyard, lie on either side of the upper terrace.

The historical interest is in the representation of the great expedition to Punt. This is shown on the wall which subdivides the upper terrace across. The head of the scene is on the right hand of the spectator. There Amen is seated; before him is a speech of his to the queen in 15 columns. A speech of the queen in six columns is in front of her figure, standing adoring

FIG. 41.—Sculpture of Deir el Bahri.

Amen. Next is the bark of Amen, borne by 24 priests and two high priests, before which Tahutmes III. makes offering of incense. After a speech of the queen in five columns, offering all the products of the land of Punt to Amen, then appear Safekh and Tahuti,—the deities of writing and of numbers,—registering all the offerings. Horus superintends the balance, where rings and bars of electrum are being weighed. Piles of green *ana* incense are being measured out. Following these are the trees, the cattle, the logs of ebony, the tusks of ivory, the boxes of electrum, the leopard skins, the panthers, the giraffe, and the cattle, all of which are offered to Amen.

Following this is a figure of the queen, and of her *ka* behind her, introducing the scenes of the expedition. Eight ships and a boat are embarking the produce of Punt, the trees transplanted in baskets, the sacks and bales and jars, the baboons,—all are being brought in peace to the fleet. Next is the scene of the meeting of the Egyptian troops and commander, with Parohu, the chief of Punt, Aty his wife, their two sons and daughter, the ass on which the queen rode, and three attendants. Behind them is their town; the houses are built on piles and entered by ladders, while palms growing beside them overshadow them. The strange fatness of the queen has been much speculated upon; whether it was a disease such as elephantiasis, or was natural fat, has been debated; but as her daughter shows much the same tendency of curve in the back, it is probably the effect of extreme fat, which was considered a beauty, as in South Africa at present.

Scenes in other parts show the festivities of the return from Punt, the troops eagerly hastening in procession, the sacrifices being cut up and offered, and the dances of the Libyan allies with boomerangs.

Many points of great interest occur in the details. The physiognomy of the Punites is finely rendered; it it is much like that of the early Egyptians (compare the queen and Hesy), and the form of beard is that of the Egyptian gods. The great variety of fishes in the sea beneath the ships is no mere fancy; the species have been identified with the Red Sea fishes, and show close observation. Either the fish were brought back for the artist, or else artists accompanied the expedition—probably the latter, as the queen and her ass, the houses and trees, all seem to have been seen by the designer. Another class of details is the military outfit of the Egyptian troops; the standards which they carry, of figures in sacred barks, lions, heads, and cartouches of

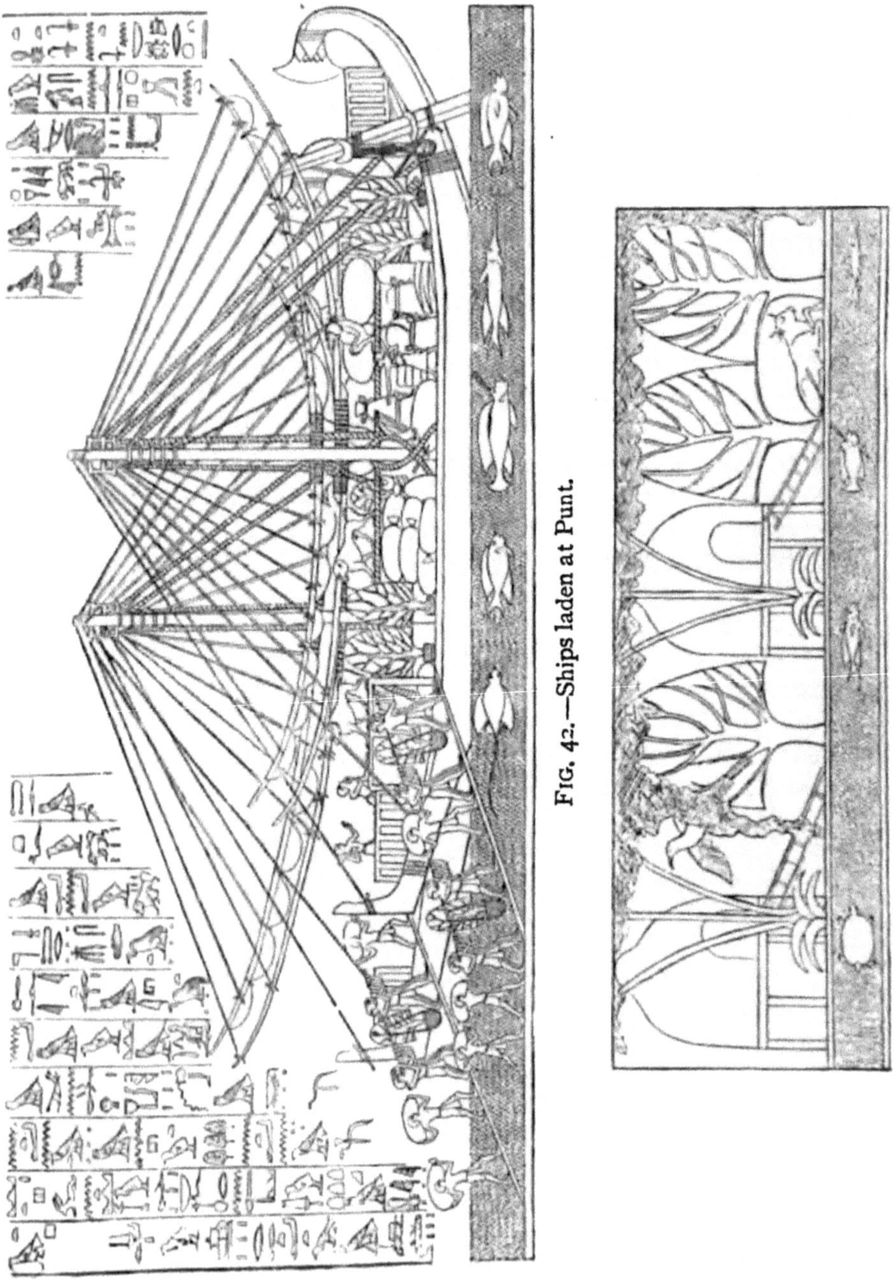

Fig. 42.—Ships laden at Punt.

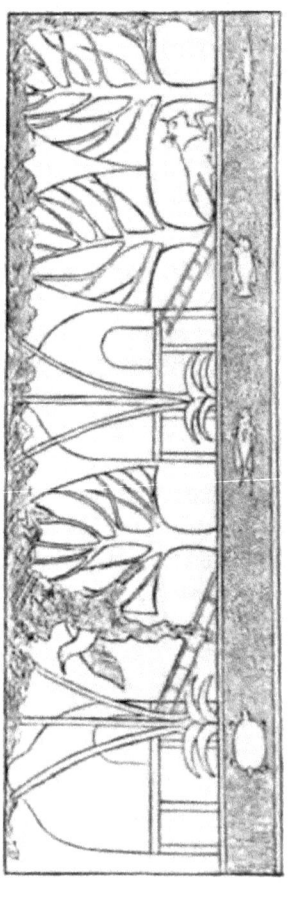

the queen, the axes, bows, spears, and boomerangs, the drum beaten with a hand on either end;—all of these are beautifully represented.

On other parts of the temple, in the colonnade of the middle terrace, are scenes of the royal family. Tahutmes I., queen Aahmes, and the elder daughter, Khebt·neferu, are there posthumously figured. In the chambers cut into the rock at the head of the terraces are also various figures of the family: Aahmes, Hatshepsut, and Tahutmes II. are seated before their tables of offering, with the lists of funeral offerings above. These are true tomb sculptures, and show that these were the funereal chapels of the family. But the places of the tombs are quite unknown. Perhaps they are in the rock behind, entered from some bypassage; but, as we shall see later on, there is evidence that Hatshepsut's tomb is entered from the valley of the kings' tombs, just behind the wall of cliff, and therefore more probably the other tombs of the family adjoin that. It is rather on the other side of the cliff that we must expect the entrance to be found to the tombs, and not on the Deir el Bahri side.

FIG. 43.—Egyptian soldiers. Deir el Bahri.

The next most important works of the great queen are the obelisks at Karnak. The greater one was erected on the *Sed* festival in her sixteenth year. The sides bear the splendidly cut line of hieroglyphics down the middle of each, with the scenes of Hatshepsut and Tahutmes III. offering to Amen in all his various characters, while one scene on each side has been usurped later by Sety I. This great obelisk was recognised as a triumph of work and a marvel of speedy execution; and a long inscription in small lines around the base of it is happily preserved to show with what feelings it was erected. After an adoration to Amen, she states "she hath made this as a monument to her father Amen, lord of the thrones of the two lands, dwelling in Thebes, even hath made for him two great obelisks of hard granite of the south, the point of each is of electrum, the tribute of the best quality of all countries. They are seen on both sides of the valley, the two lands are bathed in their splendours. The sun's disc rises between them, as when it rises from the horizon of heaven. I have done this from a heart full of love for my divine father Amen.

"I have entered upon the way in which he conducted me from the beginning, all my acts were according to his mighty spirit. I have not failed in anything which he hath ordained . . . . I make this known to the generations which are to come, whose hearts will enquire after this monument which I have made for my father, and who will talk enquiringly and gaze upon it in future. I was sitting in the palace, I was thinking of my creator, when my heart urged me to make for him two obelisks of electrum whose points reach unto the sky, in the noble hall of columns which is between the two great pylons of the king Aa·kheper·ka·ra. Behold, my heart led me to consider what men would say. Oh, ye who see my monument in the course of years, and converse of what I have done, beware of saying, 'I know not, I know not, why these things were done' . . . Verily the two great obelisks that my majesty has wrought with electrum, they are for my father Amen, to the end that my name should remain established in this temple for ever and ever. They are of a single stone of hard granite without any joining or division in them. My majesty commanded to work for them in the 15th year, the first day of Mekhir, till the 16th year and the last day of Mesori, making seven months since the ordering of it in the quarry" (R.P. xii. 131).

As Tahutmes I. died about the end of Epiphi (fifteen years before), the sixth of the seven months here named, and as by the change in the regnal year Hatshepsut must have begun to reign in one of those months, and before Tahutmes II. was associated, about early in Pakhons (see p. 61), we see that the association of Hatshepsut on the throne is limited to Mekhir, Phamenoth, or Pharmuthi, that is, between three and six months before her father's death.

The very brief time of seven months for the whole work of this obelisk, of nearly a hundred feet high, in hard red granite, has been a stumbling-block and wonder to all who have considered it. If we exclude the preliminaries, and date from the actual cleaving of it from the bed, we can scarcely write off less than two months for extracting the block and bringing it to Thebes. If it were erected in the rough, and then worked by men on a scaffolding around it, so as to get the greatest number employed at once, we must set off at least a month for erecting it and placing the scaffold. Thus four months is left for men, working by relays, to dress down, polish and engrave, at least three or four square yards of surface for each man. This would be the probable distribution of time; and nothing impresses us more with the magnificent organisation of the Egyptians, than this power of launching hundreds of highly trained and competent workmen on a single scheme in perfect co-ordination. It is no question of a tyranny of brute force and mere numbers; but, on the contrary, a brilliant organisation and foresight dealing with a carefully prepared staff.

The second obelisk has been overthrown, and the upper part of it lies broken off, on a bed of fragments from the neighbouring buildings.

In some of the sculptures of the chambers this queen also appears; sometimes in original work, sometimes in substitutions of her name for that of Tahutmes II. (C.N. ii. 145, rooms X, Y).

At the Tahutmes temple of Medinet Habu she has erased her father's name to make room for her own, *aa·kheper* giving place to *maât* (L.D. iii. 27). In another place her name appears on the jambs, and that of her husband on the lintel. At El Kab an inscription of hers was formerly known (R.S. iii. i. 130).

At Kom Ombo, the great gateway, now washed away, bore her name on it as builder, though Tahutmes III. appears on one jamb, and perhaps Tahutmes II. on the other, now altered to the IIIrd. The absence of feminine terminations makes it unlikely to be a figure of the queen (L.D. iii. 28, 1 ; R.R. xxviii.).

At Aswan the inscription of Senmut on his going to quarry the obelisks is valuable, as showing that Neferu·ra was still living then. The rapid carving of these rock inscriptions on all occasions shows the mastery of tools. As the inscription of Hammamat also shows (i. p. 151), where a long and fine inscription was cut in eight days, as shown by an informal one roughly added below it.

As Senmut was one of the greatest men of his age, we may here notice his remains. His statue is in the Berlin Museum, and bears a long inscription, from which we learn that he was chief tutor to the king's daughter, the heiress of the two lands, Neferu·ra ; that his parentage was not distinguished, as his "ancestors were not found in writing"; that he was created a prince, the companion, greatly beloved, keeper of the temple of Amen, keeper of the granaries of Amen, and director of the directors of works (chief architect). Other official charges were also held by him ; and it is not difficult to see that he was the favoured official of the queen, after the death of her husband and in the minority of her other brother (L.D. iii. 25 h-m). Another statue of his, found in the temple of Mut, shows that he built many temples for the queen. On his funeral stele he perpetuates the memory of his father and mother, though they were not distinguished, as he is shown seated between them ; the father, Rames, embracing him, the mother, Hat·

Fig. 44.—Senmut the architect   Berlin.

nefer, holding a flower before her great son. He appears there to have had special charge of the sacred cattle, of which many are figured and named (L.D. iii. 25 *bis*, a). His stele at Aswan shows him standing before Hatshepsut, and entitled the royal seal-bearer, the companion, greatly beloved, keeper of the palace, keeper of the heart of the queen (see "keeper of the king's conscience," the Lord Chancellor), making content the lady of both lands, making all things come to pass for the spirits of her majesty. It is stated that he there carved the two great obelisks for the queen which we have described above (L.D. iii. 25 *bis*, q). From the stamps on the bricks of his tomb, we see that he was priest of Aahmes, and held offices for the younger daughter, Hatshepset (Meryt·ra), as well as for the elder one, Neferu·ra. His tomb is high up, on the N.E. of the Qurneh hill; it was very magnificent, but the painted facing of the walls is almost entirely destroyed. A staff bearing his name is in the hands of a dealer at Luxor. A clear white glass bead of Senmut was found at Deir el Bahri (1894); and another bead of Hatshepsut appears to bear his name (W.M.C. ii. 141).

A curious point is the religious adoration of Hathor, developed as a familiarity and petting of the sacred kine. On the scenes of Deir el Bahri, Tahutmes II. is being licked by the sacred cow (D.H. ii. 32); and Hatshepsut had favourite cows, as one of them is named on Senmut's stele as "her great favourite, the red." The line of kine down the side of Senmut's stele all have their names, and were probably pet animals of the queen in the sacred cattle farm.

Another keeper of the palace, who took the queen's diadem title as his own name, Uazit·renpitu, is recorded on a rock tablet north of Aswan, below the joint cartouches of Ra·maāt·ka and Ra·men·kheper (M.I. i. 207, 10).

Of minor monuments there are several. A stele in the Louvre is dedicated by Hatshepsut to Tahutmes I., and he is represented seated receiving offerings (L.A.

xi.). Another stele in the Vatican shows Hatshepsut offering to Amen, with Tahutmes III. standing behind her (C.N. ii. 700-1). And a small stele shows the queen suckled by the Hathor cow, as figured at Deir el Bahri (Grant Coll.).

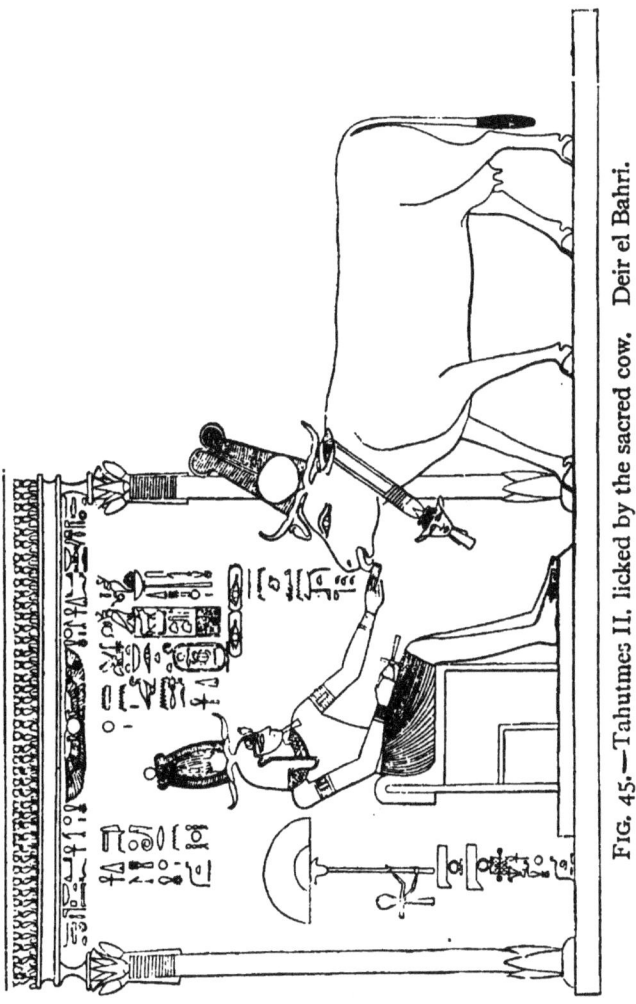

FIG. 45.—Tahutmes II. licked by the sacred cow. Deir el Bahri.

Several statues of the queen are known. The temple at Deir el Bahri had an avenue of sphinxes, all portraits of the queen. Two of these heads are preserved at

Berlin; also the head of a statue, and a headless statue of the queen (all L.D. iii. 25). Two other statues are in Leyden (A.Z. xiii. 45). An ushabti of fine work is at the Hague (S.B.A. vii. 183). A box with the cartouches of the queen was found in the royal deposit of mummies at Deir el Bahri; but as the name of Amen had been erased from it, it must have been accessible during the time of Akhenaten, and was not therefore in the tomb of the queen. The liver which was found in it has been consequently supposed to be that of the later queen

FIG. 46.—Chair of Hatshepsut. Biban el Meluk.

Ra·maat·ka of the XXIst dynasty; though it would be a happy chance if this box had been available some centuries after it was made, so as to be used for a queen of the same name (Ms. M. 584).

An important discovery of objects of Hatshepsut was made a few years ago in the royal tombs (Rec. x. 126). As I believe the circumstances have not been published, I will recount what I have heard from my late friend, Greville Chester, who bought the objects for Mr. Haworth, by whom they were presented to the

British Museum. Mr. Chester was informed by the Arabs that a group of objects, comprising a throne, a draughtboard, many draughtmen, and a piece of a wooden cartouche, were all found hidden away in one of the side chambers of the tomb of Ramessu IX., under the loose stones which encumber the place. This spot was pointed out to Mr. Chester by the Arab dealer who went with him. The place we cannot corroborate, beyond seeing that it is just at the mouth of that side valley which runs up closest to the cliff behind the temple of Hatshepsut, and which is therefore the most likely to contain her tomb. The objects being thus hidden, it would imply that when her tomb had been anciently plundered, the thieves had carried out of it everything portable, in order to be able to remove the objects at leisure, after attention had been called to their attack on the queen's tomb; hence they had buried the articles of lesser value in the already open tomb of Ramessu IX., at the mouth of the valley, until they might find it convenient to remove them. The collocation of the objects shows strongly that they really belonged together. The portion of wooden cartouche was not easily readable, except to anyone who knew the signs by heart; nor did the seller at all profess to read it, hence there was no attempt to connect the find with this queen. But the wooden draughtmen are all in form of lions' heads, of just the type of a fine one of jasper, which bears the name of the queen on the head and the collar (Ms. G. 2965). This latter in the Ghizeh Museum cannot have served as a model to later fabricators, as—to say nothing of the difficulty of copying an object in the museum—they would have certainly copied the cartouche to enhance the value, if they copied at all. Hence the Museum specimen authenticates and dates the similar heads found elsewhere; and it is important to note this, because in the passion of incredulity doubt has been thrown on the authenticity of these lion-head draughtmen. They are then clearly linked with the same queen who is named on the fragment of cartouche found with them. The draughtboard is also probably connected with the pieces for playing. Hence, so far as we can test it, there is good evidence for the truth of the story; and the style of the throne—of rare woods, inlaid elaborately with electrum (the serpent being of the same wood as the cartouche), and its slender and beautiful form—is quite consistent with the taste of the early XVIIIth dynasty. So far, then, as any account can be tested, under the system of secrecy and mystification enforced by an arbitrary and injurious law, there seems no reason to doubt the account which has been given.

A glazed draughtboard and a plaque with the queen's name are in the Louvre. Alabaster vases were found at Abydos, containing black and yellow resin (G. Mus.; M.A. 1467–8). Several rude small alabaster vases with the name were evidently found along with the models of tools, which belong to some extensive foundation deposit, probably from Deir el Bahri; these objects are scattered in the museums of Paris, Florence, Turin, Leyden, and Ghizeh. Another complete series of such models from a foundation deposit have lately been found at Deir el Bahri, in a pit in the rock, by M. Naville. Bricks stamped by Hatshepsut are found at Qurneh; some with the added name of the deceased Tahutmes I., probably made just after his death (L.D. iii. 25 *bis*, 26). Many scarabs and plaques of the queen are known; some have the *ka* name, and the vulture and uraeus name. But the most interesting class are the restored scarabs of earlier kings. Scarabs bear double cartouches of Usertesen III. and Tahutmes III., of Sebekhotep III. and Tahutmes III., and of Amenhotep I. and

FIG. 47.—Scarab of Hatshepsut, with name of Usertesen III. Louvre.

Tahutmes III.; others read doubly Ra $\left\{\begin{array}{c}\text{maat}\\\text{kha}\end{array}\right\}$ ka, Usertesen II. and Hatshepsut; others have these two names both complete; and other scarabs of Men·ka·ra, Nefer·ka·ra, Amenemhat II., Usertesen III., and Amenhotep I. are identical in type and workmanship with the scarabs of Hatshepsut and her brother.

The children of Hatshepsut we have already noticed in her husband's reign.

Some private remains of this reign may be noted. An ostrakon, written on a limestone flake, records Sat·ra, surnamed An, the chief nurse of the queen, who prays a *suten du hotep* to Hatshepsut as a divinity (S.B.A. ix. 183). A statue of Anebi (B. Mus.) praises the queen and Tahutmes III. (L.A. xi.). The tomb of Duaheh, No. 22 at Qurneh, mentions the queen (C.N. 515-6). Tahuti adores Hatshepsut and the gods of Thebes on a statuette of his (E. Coll.).

On noticing the details of the family history, we now see how the position of Hatshepsut, which has caused so much speculation, was a very natural one to occur, and does not imply any particular bad faith on any side. Her father died before he had a son old enough to properly succeed him on the throne; and about five or six months before his death (probably in failing health), he associated his daughter with him, as she was the heiress of the kingdom in the female line, in which royal descent (like that of private families) was specially traced. She was then about 24 years of age, of great capacity and power. Two or three months later, he married to her his eldest son, Tahutmes II., who would otherwise have had no claim to the throne, being the son of Mut·nefert, and not of a royal princess. Ten weeks later he died. Tahutmes II. showed no ability, and seems to have been a weakling: he did not go on the campaign when he was about 18 years old; he never entered on any other war, nor undertook any important work. During his life his sister appears to have ordered and organised public business, and he died about 30. Thus Hatshepsut was

left the sole legitimate ruler at about 37 years of age;
the only person who could challenge her power being
her little nephew, Tahutmes III., then perhaps 9 years
old. He had no claim to the throne, being the son of
a woman, Aset, not of royal blood. But his aunt did
all she reasonably could: she associated him with her
in the kingdom, public dating of documents was
carried on in his name; and though her eldest
daughter, that beautiful and most brilliant girl,
Neferu·ra, had died, she married the second to
him as soon as might be, and so gave him the
position of heir. To throw up the power which she
had more or less wielded for so long, to turn the
affairs of state over from an experienced and large-
minded ruler of mature age at 37 to a boy of 9,
was not to be thought of for a moment. She did
all that was reasonable; and if she held on firmly till
her death to the power which was unquestionably her
right, she only did as any other capable ruler would
have done. No doubt it was galling to a very active
and ambitious young man to be held down to peaceful
pomp and routine; no doubt the etiquette of the court
did not become less precise when, in old age, the queen
held tenaciously to her rights; and no doubt, when
Tahutmes found life passing, and himself entering the
thirties without being allowed free scope, he may well
have chafed and become very sore at everything belonging to the old lady. But all things come to him who
waits. Egypt developed greatly during twenty years of
peace and commerce, and resources were husbanded;
so that, when, at the queen's death at about 59,
Tahutmes — then about 31 — succeeded to the full
power, he found a grand instrument in his hands,
and was able in a few weeks' time to launch out into
that mighty series of campaigns which mark the
highest extent of Egyptian power, and which gloriously
occupied twenty-eight years of overflowing energy.

[B.C. 1503-1449.] TAHUTIMES III

XVIII. 6.
MEN·KHEPER·(KA)·RA

TAHUTI·MES (III.)
HEQ·UAST

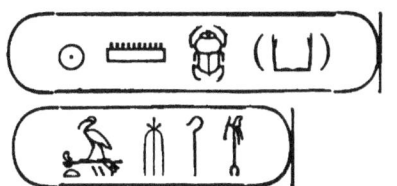

1503–1449 B.C.

Coffin and mummy (Ms. M. 547).

Sarbut el } Khadem	Stele, 23rd year	(L.D. iii. 29 a).
	Stele, 27th year	(photograph).
,,	Jamb of doorway	(,,).
,,	Glazed vase bits	(B.P. 56).
Wady Maghara	Inscription	(My. E. 344).
Kom el Hisn	Foundation deposit	(F.P. Coll.).
Heliopolis	Gate jambs	(B.R. ix. 23 a-b).
,,	,, ,, (Cairo)	(D.E. v. 24, 1).
	Stele, 47th year (Berl.)	(L.D. iii. 29 b).
	Obelisk (Lateran)	(G.O., R.P. iv. 11).
	,, (Constantinople)	(L.D. iii. 60).
,,	,, (New York)	(G.O., R.P. x. 21).
,,	,, (London)	(G.O.).
Abusir	Inscription, Amenemhat	(L.D. iii. 29 e).
Memphis	Temple of Ptah	(Sakhara inscr. B.H. 403).
Gurob	Temple	(P.K. 32, xxii.).
Speos Artemidos	Rock shrine	(L.D. iii. 26, 7).
El Bersheh	Stele	(S.I. ii. 37).
Ekhmim	Stele	(L.D. iii. 29 d).
,,	Inscription	(My. E. 421).
Abydos	Osiris statue	(M.A.; I.).
,,	Two statues of king	(M.A. 348, 9).
Dendera	Founding of temple	(A.Z. iii. 91).
Hammamat	Inscription	(My. E. 326).
Koptos	Temple.	
Nubt	Town and temple, etc.	
Karnak	E. hall of pillars.	
,,	Surrounding courts of temple.	
	Hinder sanctuary.	
	South pylon VII.	
,,	Temple of Ptah.	
,,	Temple of Mut begun?	
Medinet Habu	Temple	(L.D. iii. 7, 17, 27-8, 37-8).
N. of Ramesseum	Temple.	

Deir el Bahri	Completion of Temple.	
,,	Obelisks	(L.D. iii. 60).
Taud	Fragments	(W.G. 362).
Esneh	Stele mentioned	(L.D. iv. 78 a).
El Kab	Temple architecture	(C.N. 266).
,,	Two temples, fragments.	
Edfu	Late inscription on building	(A.Z. ix. 97).
Kom Ombo	Pylon (now lost)	(L.D. iii. 28, 1; R.R. 28).
,,	Lintel	(A.Z. xxi. 78).
Elephantine	Temple (destroyed)	(D.E. i. 34–8).
,,	Block at station	(Rec. ix. 81).
,,	Obelisk (Sion Ho.)	(Birch, Hist. 102).
Aswan	Inscriptions	(Rec. xiii. 203; M.I. i. 101, 207).
Kalabsheh	Granite statue and block	(B.E. 307).
Kuban	Inscription	(My. E. 538).
Dakkeh	Inscription	(S.N. 136).
Korti	Stone and foundation	(L.L. 124).
Amadah	Scene	(L.D. iii. 45).
,,	Gate and lintel	(L.D. iii. 65 b, c).
Ellesiyeh	Scenes	(L.D. iii. 45 d, f, 46 a).
,,	Stele, 42nd year	(L.D. iii. 45 e).
Ibrim	Two rock shrines	(C.N. 79–84).
Wady Halfa	S. brick temple	(B.E. 341).
Semneh	Temple	(L.D. iii. 47–56).
Kummeh	Temple	(L.D. iii. 57–59 a, 64 b).
Sai (20° 42′ N.)	Temple	(L.D. iii. 59 b, c).
Dosheh (20° 30′ N.)	Rock shrine	(L.D. iii. 59 d, e).
Soleb	Temple begun.	
Bahriyeh Oasis	Stele	(B.E. 348).

Statues and portraits—

Seated limestone colossus, base of throne, Karnak	(M.K. 38 d).
Head of colossus, granite, B. Mus.	
Standing, red granite, Karnak	(R.A. 125; V.G. 202).
Seated, black granite, Karnak	(V.G. 214).
Seated, black and white diorite, T. Mus.	(L.T. 1376).
Seated, grey granite, Nubia, F. Mus.	(S. Cat. F. 1503).
Torso Abydos	(M.A. 348).
Throne Abydos	(M.A. ii. 21 e, f).
Seated, black granite, Alexandria.	
Torso, behind temple, Karnak	(W.G. 358).
Torso in small temple of Apet, Karnak	(B.E. 150).
Fragments Luxor	(W.G. 358).
Bust, red granite, Karnak	(V.G. 192).

[B.C. 1503-1449.] TAHUTIMES III 99

Bronze statue, Marseille.		
Statues mentioned by Tahutmes IV.		(M.K. 33).
,, ,, Neb·ua·iu		(M.A. ii. 33).
Sphinxes, red granite, Karnak		(V.G. 221-2, M.K. 32 b).
Figure on wooden canon board,	B. Mus.	(A.B. 33, 148).
Trial piece	T. Mus.	(L.D. iii. 304).

Stele, with Min	T. Mus.	(L.T. 1460).
,, in temple, Uazmes	G. Mus.	(M.E. ii.).
Altar, red granite, high	B. Mus.	(A.B. 34).
,, another still at Karnak		(W.G. 366).
,,	Vatican	(Vat. Cat. p. 215).
,, dedicated to Amen	Salonika	(A.Z. vi. 79).
,, red granite		(M.K. 32 b; V.G. 211).
,, alabaster		(M.B. 98).

Alabaster vase of 9 hins		T. Mus.	(L.T. 3224).
,,	,,	T. Mus.	(Rec. iv. 137).
,,	,, of 21 hins	B. Mus.	(V.G. 446).
,,	,, 2	G. Mus.	(V.G. 702).
,,	,, 3	Berlin	(W.G. 367).
,,	,, P. Mus. Leyden,	B. Mus.	(C.M. 425, R.C. 62, 6).
Glass vases		{ B. Mus.	(Ms. A. fig. 220).
			(C.M. 425).
Ivory tablets		Marseille.	
Wooden labels of princesses			(A.Z. xxi. 123).
Feather of Amen		T. Mus.	(W.G. 368).
Fish-shaped cup glazed green		G. Mus.	(Ms. G. 124).
Scribe's palette		Bologna.	
Papyri,		T. Mus.	(1, 83 B).
,,		Berlin	(L.D. vi. 117 b, c).
,,		Munich	(W.G. 368).
Rings and scarabs, innumerable.			
Gold ring (Ashburnham)			(R. Soc. Lit. 1843, 108).

Queens—MERYT·RA HATSHEPSET—
    Sphinx, Baracco Coll.   (A.Z. xx. 118).
    Temple, Medinet Habu   (L.D. iii. 38 a, b; C.M. 195, 3).
         (L.D. iii. 62 a).
    Tombs {   (L.D. iii. 63 a, 64 a).
         (C.M. 160).
    Scarabs, P. Mus., T. Mus.   (M.A. ii. 40 n).
  ,,   NEBTU   (Rec. ix. 97; B.R.P. xii.).

Son—Amenhotep II.   (L.D. iii. 62, 64).
Daughters (?)—Taui ....
        Ta·kheta
        Pet·ahu·ha
        Pet·pui Ta·khet·aui   (B.R.P. xii.).
        Meryt·ptah   (A.Z. xxi. 124).
        Sat·hora
        Nefer·amen
        Ua·ay
        Henut·anu

In dealing with this reign, which is the fullest in the history of Egypt, it may be best to examine it in the following order—

(1st) Outline of the dated events and monuments.
(2nd) Translation of the annals.
(3rd) The greater monuments.
(4th) The lesser monuments.
(5th) The private monuments.
(6th) The royal family.
(7th) The influence of Syria on Egypt.

The details of the geography of the campaigns appear at the end of the volume.

I. Outline of the Dated Events.

Fig. 48. Gold ring of Tahutmes III., "born at Thebes." Gurob, F.P. Coll.

Born at Thebes (see gold ring, F.P. Coll.).

1st year, Pakhons 4. Coronation, at about 9 years old.

2nd year, Paophi 7. This earliest dating is that of a grand list of gifts to the temple of Semneh, which had been in progress under the father and brother of this king.

5th year, Thoth 1. A papyrus at Turin is dated thus, concerning a scribe User·amen going to offer in the temple of Amen (Pap. T. 1).

15th year, Pakhons 27 is named as the day of a great festival of renewing the offerings in the temple at Karnak (M.K. 15).

22nd year. Renewing the statue of Amenhotep I. (M.K. 38, c. 2).

22nd year, Mekhir 4 (about). Death of Hatshepsut; beginning of independent reign of Tahutmes III.

22nd year, Pharmuthi. The army assembled on the frontier at Zalu, for the first campaign. The chiefs in southern Syria had rebelled some time before.

23rd year, Pakhons 4, on his coronation day, Tahutmes found himself in Gaza; having marched in twelve days about 160 miles, a rapid march for a large army wholly untrained in such movements. On the next day he left. Ten days later he had marched 90 miles farther, to Carmel. There he rested for a few days, and then he insisted on crossing the mountain by a dangerous ravine, in which he acted as guard to secure the passage of the army, which defiled through safely by 1 p.m. Resting that afternoon, he then early next morning gave battle to the assembled chiefs of Syria who were confederated at Megiddo, and utterly routed them in the plain of Esdraelon, or Armageddon. They fled into the town, round which he at once threw a complete circumvallation, only allowing prisoners to surrender at one entrance. The whole of the enemy capitulated, and enormous spoils were taken from them, and from the rest of Syria. A stele was set up this year at Wady Halfa recording the victories over the Fenekhu, Retennu, and Tahennu (B.E. 341).

24th year. The second campaign in Syria brought in great spoils. On Mekhir 30 was a feast of dedication at Karnak (M.K. 12). Mention of the new moon.

25th year. The third campaign in Syria. Large collection of plants brought from land of Retennu, and carved on walls at Karnak (M.K. 31). Stele of Sarbut el Khadem, copper mining (L.D. iii. 29 a).

27th year. Stele at Sarbut el Khadem.

28th year. Tomb of Amenemhat at Qurneh (L.D. iii. 38 e–g).

29th year. Fifth campaign to Retennu (Syrian hill-country), Tunep, Arvad, and Zahi; great spoil from Phœnicia.

30th year. Sixth campaign to Kedesh, Simyra, and Arvad.

31st year. Tribute of Retennu, of Punt, and of Wawat.

33rd year. Set up tablet at boundaries in Naharina. Tribute of Retennu, Sangar, Khita, Punt, and Wawat. Tablet at El Bersheh, 2nd Mesore. *Sed* festival, 28th Epiphi.

FIG. 49.—Tahutmes III., granite head. Brit. Mus.

34th year. Campaign, and tribute of Zahi (Phœnicia), Retennu, Asi (Cyprus).

35th year. Tenth campaign, to Zahi. Spoils of Naharina.

38th year. Thirteenth campaign. Spoils of Anaugasa ; tribute of Asi, Punt, and Wawat.

39th year. Fourteenth campaign in Syria.

40th year (?). Tribute of Asi, Kush, Wawat.

41st year (?). Tribute of Rutennu and Khita.

42nd year. Campaign to Tunep, Qedesh. Erection of long inscription at Karnak. Erection of statue to Tahutmes II. (M.K. 38 b).

47th year. Stele at Heliopolis. Berlin (L.D. iii. 29 b).

50th year. Expedition to Ethiopia. Clearing of canal of the cataract (Rec. xiii. 203).

51st year, Pauni 5. Stele at Ellesiyeh (Br. H. 395).

54th year, Phamenoth 30. Tahutmes died at about 63 years old. Succeeded by his son, Amenhotep II.

II. Translation of the Annals.

The annals of this king are considerable, and they give a most graphic view of the state of Syria, and the wealth and luxury of the inhabitants, at this age. Every allusion in them is of value; and in the first campaign, which had the delight of new-found power about it, the details are very full, and show the character of Egyptian warfare. The geography of these campaigns will be treated afterwards at the end of this volume.

In the following translation the only restorations are such as are necessarily involved by the sense, and they are always marked by square parentheses [ ], while explanatory additions are in curved parentheses. The numbers of the original lines of the text are marked for ease of reference to the inscription.

(L.D. iii. 31 b.)

(^{3}) " His Majesty ordered to be placed [the victories which his father Amen had given to him, upon] (^{4}) a tablet in the temple which His Majesty made for [his father Amen, recording] (^{5}) the expedition by its name, together with the spoil [which His Majesty had obtained by it in] (^{6}) every [country] which his father Amen had given him.

The campaign. The 25th day of the month Pharmuthi in the
XXIInd year of his reign, [His Majesty] proceeded from the city (^{7}) ot Zalu in his first campaign of victory . . .

[to extend] the (⁸) frontiers of Egypt with might ...
(⁹, ¹⁰) [the land had been in confusion] ... (¹¹) the men who were there (¹²) in the city of Sharuhen (in Simeon), beginning from Yeruza (¹³) as far as the ends of the country they rebelled against His Majesty. On the 4th of Pakhons of the
XXIIIrd year, the day of the festival of the royal

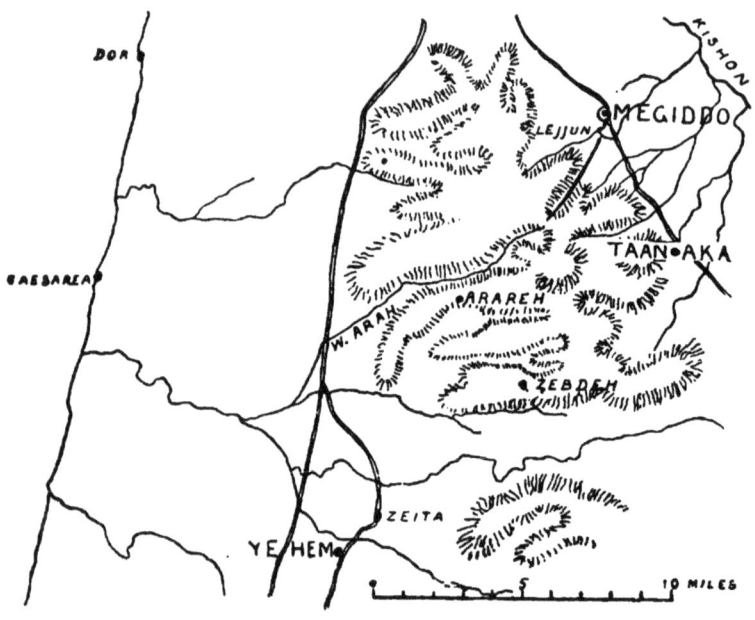

Fig. 50.—Map of approach to Megiddo. Yehem, Megiddo, and Taanaka are certain. Arareh is probably Aaruna, and Wady Arah the line of Tahutmes' approach. Neither Zebdeh nor Zeita appear to agree with Zifta, which was probably west of Megiddo.

coronation (¹⁴) at Gazatu (Gaza), the city occupied by the king. (¹⁵) On the 5th of Pakhons he started from this place in triumph [power], (¹⁶) defence, and justification to overthrow the vile enemy, to extend (¹⁷) the bounds of Egypt according to the command of his father Amen·Ra.

The passage of Carmel. (¹⁸) On the 16th Pakhons of the XXIIIrd year, at the fortress of Yehem (Yemma,

16 m. S.S.W. of Megiddo): commanded His Majesty ([19]) a discourse with his brave troops, saying
"That [vile] enemy ([20]) of Qadesh has come and entered Maketa (Megiddo); he is [there] ([21]) at this moment, and has collected to himself the chiefs of all countries (that were) ([22]) obedient to Egypt, with him as far as Naharaina, consisting of . . . ([23]) the Kharu (Syrians), the Qedshu, their horses and their army ([24]), and he says, 'I shall remain [to fight the king of Egypt] in Maketa.' Tell ye me . . . ." ([26]) They said in reply to His Majesty, "What is it like [that we] should march on this road, ([27]) which becomes a narrow pass? [men have come] saying ([28]) that the enemy are waiting to [attack when there is no] ([29]) passage for a numerous host; does not one (chariot) horse have to follow behind [the fellow, and man behind] ([30]) man likewise? ought our vanguard to be engaged while our rearguard is waiting ([32]) in Aaruna (Ararah? 7 S.W. of Megiddo) without fighting. Now there are two roads, ([33]) one road behold it [will lead] us [to the . . .] ([34]) Taanaka (Tannuk, 5 S. of Megiddo), the other behold it [leads us to] the ([35]) north side of Zefta, and we should come out at the north of Maketa ([36]). Let then our mighty lord march on one of those [two] ways, [which ever] his heart [chooseth], ([37]) but let us not go on that difficult road."

Then [went] ([38]) the messengers [whom the king sent to give his commands] for the disposition of [his army]; ([39]) they said at the beginning of the speeches:—
"The Majesty of the king saith, 'As I live, ([40]) as I am the beloved of Ra, praised by my father Amen, as my nostrils are refreshed with ([41]) life and strength, I will go on this road of ([42]) Aaruna; let him of you who will, go on ([43]) the roads ye name; and let him of you who will, follow my Majesty. ([44]) For they—namely, the enemy, ([45]) abominated of Ra—consider thus, "Has His Majesty gone on ([46]) another road? Then he fears us," thus do they consider.'"

([47]) They said to His Majesty, "As lives thy father Amen·Ra, lord of the thrones of the two lands, who dwells in Thebes, who has made thee, (⁴⁸) behold we follow thy Majesty whithersoever thy Majesty goes, (⁴⁹) even as servants follow [their master]."

(⁵⁰) Command was given to the whole army to . . . [follow] (⁵¹) . . . that road which became [narrow. His Majesty swore] (⁵²) an oath, saying, "Not a man [shall go forth] (⁵³) before my Majesty in . . . [⁵⁴] he shall go forth before his own troops causing to perceive . . . (⁵⁵) by his paces of marching, horse walking after [horse], while [His Majesty protects them] (⁵⁶) of the best of his army." On the 19th of Pakhons of the XXIIIrd year of his reign, watch in . . . (⁵⁷) at the king's pavilion at the fortress of Aaruna. My Majesty proceeded (⁵⁸) northward with my father Amen·Ra, lord of the thrones of the two lands (⁵⁹) . . . before me, Harakhti [strengthening my arms]. (⁶⁰) . . . my father Amen, lord of the thrones of the world, victorious of scimetar, . . . [watching] (⁶¹) over me: went forth [the enemy . . .] (⁶²) with much music . . . (⁶³) the southern wing from Taanaka . . . (⁶⁴) the northern wing from the south corner . . . (⁶⁵) His Majesty cried out at them [and gave battle] (⁶⁶) they fell, behold that vile . . . (two lines lost) [but some of the enemy went toward]

(L.D. iii. 32.)

(¹) Aaruna ; [behold] the rearguard of the valiant troops of His Majesty . . . [were yet in] (²) Aaruna ; while the van was going forth to the valley . . . (³) and occupied the head (or hollow) of that valley, and behold they spake before His Majesty, saying, (⁴) " Behold His Majesty has gone out with his valiant soldiers, and [they] have occupied the [head (or hollow) of] (⁵) the valley, let our powerful lord listen to us this time, (⁶) let our lord keep for us the rear of his army and the people; (⁷) then when the rear of our army comes out to us behind, they will fight (⁸) against these foreigners, and we need not give thought for the rear of (⁹) our army." His Majesty halted beyond them himself (¹⁰) there guarding the rear of his valiant troops; behold, when the van (¹¹) had come forth on this road the shadow turned, (¹²) and when His Majesty came to the south of Maketa on the edge of the water of Qina, it was the seventh hour of the day (?). Then His Majesty's [great] tent was pitched, and command was given before his whole army, saying, "Prepare ye, make ready your weapons, for we move to fight with the vile enemy to-morrow, for the king [will remain] (¹³) quiet in the tent of the king," the baggage of the chiefs was prepared and the provisions of the followers, and the sentinels of the army were spread abroad; they said, "Firm of heart, firm of heart, watchful of head, watchful of head," waking in life at the tent of the king. Came one to report to His Majesty, the country is safe and the army south and north likewise.

The battle of Megiddo. On the 21st day of the month Pakhons, the day of the feast of the new moon, even the same as the royal coronation, early in the morning command was given to the entire army to spread abroad . . . (¹⁴) His Majesty went forth in his chariot of electrum adorned with his weapons of war, like Horus armed with talons, the Lord of might, like Mentu of Thebes, his father Amen·Ra strengthening his arms; the [south] horn of the army of His Majesty was . . . on a hill at the south [of the water of] Qina, the north horn at the north-west of Maketa, His Majesty was in the midst of them, the god Amen being the protection to his body [and strength] (¹⁵) to his limbs. Then His Majesty prevailed over them at the head of his army. When they saw His Majesty prevailing over them, they fled headlong [toward] Maketa, as if terrified by spirits; they left their horses, and their chariots of silver and of gold, and were drawn up by hauling them by their clothes into this city, for the men shut the gates of this city upon them, [and let down] (¹⁶) clothes, to haul them up to this city. Then, had but the troops of His Majesty not given their hearts to spoiling the things of the enemy, [they would have taken] Maketa at that moment; behold the vile enemy of Qadeshu and the vile enemy of this city were drawn up in haste to get them into their city. The fear of His Majesty entered ([17]) [their hearts], their arms failed; . . . his diadem prevailed over them. Their horses and their chariots of gold and of silver were captured, being [taken] suddenly . . . their mighty men lay along like fishes on the ground. The great army of His Majesty drew round to count their spoil. Behold the tent [of the wretch]ed [enemy] was captured, [in] which [was his] son . . . ([18]) The whole army rejoiced, giving praise to Amen [for the victory] that he had given to his son, [and they glorified] His Majesty, exalting his victories. They brought the spoil which they had taken, of hands (of the slain), of living captives, of horses, of chariots of gold and of silver . . .

The siege of Megiddo. ([19]) [And His Majesty gave] commands to his troops, saying, "If ye seize Maketa afterward (?), [I vow great offerings to] Ra this day, inasmuch as every chief of all the countries [who have] rebelled are in it, so that it is as the capture of a thousand cities this capture of Maketa; seize ye utterly entirely at [this mome]nt [on Maketa ([20]) . . . officers of the troops, to each one was appointed his place, they measured the city . . . a rampart formed with the green wood of all their pleasant trees. His Majesty himself was at the eastern tower of this city, [and he commanded ([21]) to surround it] with a thick wall . . . the thick wall [was built], and it was named Men·kheper·ra·aah·setu (Tahutmes III., encloser of the Sati); and men were set to watch over the tent of His Majesty, and they said, "Steady, steady, watch, watch, . . ." His Majesty [then gave orders that ([22]) not one] of them [shall go] outside from behind this wall excepting to come forth to knock at the doors of their gate (none should escape except those who delivered themselves up as prisoners at the entrance). Now, all that His Majesty did against this city, and against the vile enemy and his vile troops, was written from day to day under its date, under the title of "Travels . . . ([23])

[and] placed on a roll of leather in the temple of Amen on this day.

The capitulation of Megiddo. Then the chiefs of this land came, with them that pertained to them, to smell the ground to the spirits of His Majesty, asking breath for their nostrils of the greatness of his power and the mightiness of the spirits of His Majesty ([24]) . . . came to his spirits having their tribute of silver, of gold, of lazuli and malachite; bringing corn, wine, oil, and flocks, for the army of His Majesty; and sent the foreign workmen who were among them

FIG. 51.—Chiefs "smelling the ground."

with the tribute southwards (see chief of Tunep and

FIG. 52.—Chief of Tunep, followed by his artist (*se'ankh*, "he who makes alive") bearing a trophy of gold work. The chief of Kedesh with a vase and a dagger.

his artist). His Majesty appointed chiefs anew (to rule the land).

The spoils. [And this is the account ([25]) of the spoil

taken in the field, even] living captives 340, hands (of slain) 83, mares 2041, fillies 191, *abor*, 6 . . . one chariot worked with gold, with a pole (?) of gold of

FIG. 53.—Syrian chariot.

that enemy, a good chariot plated with gold of the chief of . . . [and 30 chariots of other princes?], (²⁶) 892 chariots of his vile army, total, 924. One excellent suit of bronze armour of that enemy, a bronze suit of armour of the chief of Maketa, 200 suits of armour of his vile army, 502 bows, 7 poles of the pavilion of that enemy of *meru*-wood plated with silver. Behold the army . . . [took](^{27}) . . . 297, bulls 1929, small goats 2000, white flocks (sheep) 20,500.

The plunder and tribute of Syria. The amount of things taken afterwards by the king from the things of the house of that enemy, which was in Yenuamu, in Anaugasa, and in Harnekaru, with all the things of the cities and the fortresses which gave themselves up to his rule and brought . . . (²⁸) . . . *Meruina* belonging to them, 39; sons of that enemy and of the chiefs with him, 87; *meruina* belonging to them, 5; slaves, male and female, with their children, 1796; non-combatants who came all of starvation from that enemy, 103 persons: total 2503. Beside, there was of precious wares, gold, dishes, various vessels, (²⁹) . . . a two-handled vase of the work of the Kharu . . . dishes,

FIG. 54.—Syrian captives with vases.

FIG. 55.—Syrian dishes.

caldrons, and various vases for drinking, great jars, 97 knives : making altogether 1784 *deben* (360 lbs.). Gold in rings, found in the hands of the workmen, and silver in various rings, 966 *deben* 1 *qedt* (200 lbs.). A silver statue made . . . (³⁰) the head of gold, the staff with human heads of ivory, ebony, and kharub wood inlaid

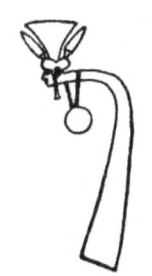

FIG. 56.—Staff with human head.

FIG. 57.—Chair.

FIG. 58.—Inlaid table.

with gold ; chairs of that enemy, 6 ; footstools belonging to them, 6 ; 6 large tables of ivory and kharub wood, inlaid with gold and all precious stones ; a staff used as the sceptre of that chief, inlaid with gold throughout ... statues (³¹) of the fallen chief, of ebony inlaid with gold ; ... vessels of bronze ; various clothing of the enemy. When the land was divided into fields and calculated by the inspector of the king's house, in order to take their harvest, the amount of the harvest brought to His Majesty from the fields of Maketa (the plain of Esdraelon) was 280,500 quadruple *heqt* of corn (150,000 bushels, about 10 square miles of corn land), (³²) beside what was cut as taken by His Majesty's soldiers.

Annual tributes. The tribute of the chiefs of the Ruten in the

XXIVth year, tribute of the chief of Assuru, one great stone of real lazuli weighing 20 *deben* 9 *qedt* (4¼ lbs.), two stones of real lazuli and small stones making 30 *deben*; total, 50 *deben* 9 *qedt* (10½ lbs.) of good lazuli of Bebra. Three *hertet* (agate?) vases of Assuru of [various] colours ... (³³) very many. The tribute of the chiefs of the Retennu, the daughter of a chief, ornaments of silver, gold, lazuli, of the foreigners, ... 30 ; the slaves, male and female, of his tribute, 65 ; 30 [meruina] belonging [to them] ; 4 chariots wrought with gold, the poles of gold ; 5 chariots wrought with electrum, the poles of *aget*, total 10. *Tepau* and *undu* oxen 55, bulls 749, small cattle 5703. Gold dishes ... (³⁴) which could not be measured, silver dishes and pieces, 104 d. 5 q. (21 lbs.) ; a gold *maqersina* inlaid with lazuli ;

FIG. 59.—Golden dish from Syria.

FIG. 60.—Jar of wine or honey.

bronze armour inlaid with gold ... many suits of armour, (³⁵) 823 jars of incense, 1718 jars of wine and honey ... ivory and kharub-wood, meru-wood, pesqu-wood, . . . various of this country . . . (³⁶) to every place which His Majesty visited and where his tent was set up.

(L.A. xii. ; Rev. Arch. 1860, Pl. xvi.)

(¹) **XXIXth** year ; behold His Majesty was in the land [of Rutennu] to chastise the revolted countries in his Vth campaign of victory. The king took the city of Ua . . . the army congratulated the king, and gave thanks (²) to Amen·Ra for the victories which he had given to his son, which the king valued above all else. After this His Majesty proceeded to the storehouse of offerings, he offered a sacrifice to Amen, to Horakhti, of oxen, bullocks, fowls, . . . Men·kheper·ra, giving life for ever. Reckoning of the spoil taken from this city :—

Spoil of Ua . . . From the officers (?) (³) of the fallen of Tunep, the prince of this city, 1, warriors 329, silver 100 *deben* (20 lbs.), gold 100 *deben* ; lazuli, malachite, vases of bronze and of copper; behold they seized a ship . . . laden with all things, male and female slaves, copper, lead, emery, (⁴) and all sorts of good things.

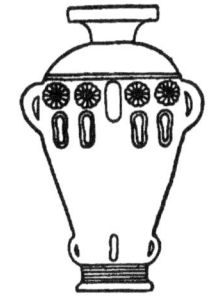

FIG. 61.—Copper vase from Syria.

Then His Majesty proceeded south to Egypt . . . delighted in heart. He smote the city of Aruta (Arvad) with its corn, and cut down all its pleasant trees. Behold [His Majesty] found [the land of] Zahi throughout, its orchards full of their fruit. There were found (⁵) their wines abundant in their wine-presses, as water flows down ; their corn was on the threshing floors . . . more abundant than the sand of the shores. The army was satiated with their shares. The reckoning of the spoil brought to His Majesty in this expedition :—

Spoil of Phœnicia. Male and female slaves 51,

II—8

horses 40, silver cups 10, (⁶) incense of honey *men* vases 470, wine *men* vases 6428; copper, lead, lazuli, green felspar; oxen 618, goats 3636; good bread, and various bread, corn in grain, flour, ... and all good fruits of the land. Then the soldiers of His Majesty were drunk and anointed with *beq* oil every day, (⁷) as in the festivals in Egypt.

FIG. 62.—Cups from Syria.

XXXth year. Then His Majesty was in the land of the Rutennu in his VIth campaign of victory. He drew near to the city of Qedeshu; His Majesty spoiled it, and cut down the trees and reaped its corn. He went to the land of ... tu, he came to the town of Zamara, and came to the town of Arathetu (Arvad), and treated them in like manner. The amount of the tributes brought to the spirits of His Majesty in that year, by the princes of Retennu :—

FIG. 63.—Scarab of Tahutmes III. "Overthrowing Kedesh." F.P. Coll.

Tribute of Retennu. The sons of the princes and their brothers were brought to be placed as hostages in Egypt. If any one of the chiefs died, His Majesty would make his son go to stand in his place. The number of the sons of princes brought this year was ... persons; male and female slaves 181, mares 188, chariots (⁹) adorned with gold and silver and painted, 40.

XXXIst year, Pakhons, 3rd day; assembly of the spoil made by His Majesty in this year, and the spoil brought from the city Anrathu, which is on the bank of the water Neserna :—men taken alive, 490 ... of the sons of the wretched chief of ... 3; chief over the women who were there, 1. Total, 494 persons, mares 26, chariots 13, their equipment ([10]) with all weapons. Behold His Majesty spoiled this town in a short hour, with swiftness of spoiling. The tribute of the princes of Retennu, who came to prostrate themselves before the spirits of His Majesty in this year:—

Tribute of Retennu. Male and female slaves . . . of this country 72, silver 761 *deben* 2 *qedt* (150 lbs.), 19 chariots adorned with silver ([11]) and provided with their weapons. Bulls and . . . 104, bullocks and oxen 172; total, 276. Goats 4622. Native copper, blocks 40; lead . . . gold, copper earrings engraved with horses (?) 42; also all their products ([12]) and all the good woods of this country. Every station which His Majesty came was supplied with good bread and common bread, with oil, incense, wine, honey, fruits, more abundant than anything known to the soldiers of His Majesty, without exaggeration. ([13]) They are placed on the roll of the royal palace; so that their reckoning is not given on this tablet, in order to avoid a multiplication of words. . . .

. . . The harvest of Rutennu was reported, consisting of various corn, ([14]) wheat in grain, barley, incense, fresh oil, wine, fruit, all the good things of a foreign country. They were demanded for the treasury as is reckoned the tribute . . . various, 33, alabaster, all the gems of that country, and various stones in great numbers ([15]) of . . . and all the good things of that land.

His Majesty approached the Delta, and the ambassador of Genbetu (Punt) came, having their tribute of frankincense and gums . . . male negroes for servants 10, bulls and ([16]) bullocks 113, bulls 230; total, 343; beside boats with ivory, ebony, panthers' skins, and the products of [that land. . . . The tribute of Wawat] was . . . of Wawat, 5; bullocks 31, bulls 61; total, 92. ([17]) Beside the boats laden with all the things of that country, the harvest of Wawat also.

XXXIIIrd year, when His Majesty was in the land of

Retennu . . . [he] approached . . . east of that river, he placed another (tablet) where was the tablet of his father, ([18]) the king of Upper and Lower Egypt, Aa·kheper·ka·ra. His Majesty went north, taking the towns and overturning the camps of that enemy of the vile Naharina in . . . [he pursued] after them for the distance of an *atur* without anyone daring to look behind ([19]) him, but they bounded along like a herd of gazelles. The horses . . . by the whole army. Their princes 3, ([20]) their women 30, men taken prisoners 80, male and female slaves and their children 606; those who surrendered women . . . he carried off their grain.

His Majesty then came to the city of ([21]) Niy in going south, when His Majesty was returning and had set up his tablet in Naharina, he enlarging the boundaries of Egypt. . . . The tribute brought by princes of that country :—

Tribute of Naharina. ([22]) Male and female slaves 513, mares 260, gold 45 *deben* 9 *qedt*, silver vases of the work of Zahi . . . chariots with all their equipage, bulls ([23]) calves 28, bulls 564, goats 5323, incense jars 828, sweet *beq* oil . . . all the delicious produce of that country and all its many fruits. Behold ([24]) the forts were provisioned with all sorts of things according to the rate of the yearly tax. The tribute of the land of Remenen was also according to the rate of the yearly tax, and the princes of the land of Remenen . . . birds 2; and one does not reckon the wild fowl ([25]) of that country. Behold they were for the . . .

FIG. 64.—Silver vase from Syria.

The tribute of the prince of Sangar, real lazuli . . . 4 *deben*, artificial lazuli 24 *deben*, lazuli of Bebra . . . of real lazuli, a head of a ram of real lazuli, ([26]) 15 *deben*, and vases.

The tribute of the great Khita in this year was, silver

rings 8, weighing 301 *deben* (60 lbs.), white precious stones 1 great block, *sagu* wood . . . [when returning] toward Egypt, when coming from Naharina in enlarging the frontier of Egypt.

The treasures brought by His Majesty in that year from the land of Punt were dry frankincense, 1685 *heqs* (920 bushels) . . . gold 155 *deben* 2 *qedt* (31 lbs.), male and female slaves 134, bull ([28]) calves 114, bulls 305 ; total oxen, 419 ; beside transports laden with ivory, ebony, panther skins, and all the good

Fig. 65.—Silver rings from Syria.

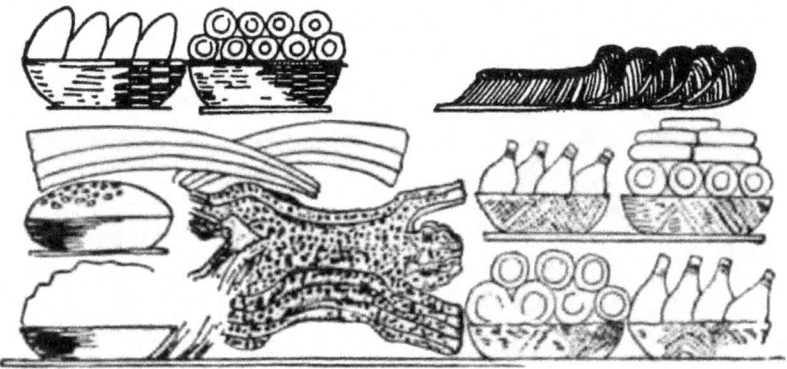

Fig. 66.—Tribute from Punt : ivory, panthers' skins, ostrich eggs and feathers, bags of gold dust, incense, etc.

things of that land. . . . [The tribute of Wawat, male and female slaves 8], male negroes 12 ; total, 20: bull calves 54, ([29]) bulls 60 ; total, 114 : beside boats laden with all the good products of that country, and the harvest likewise.

XXXIVth year, behold His Majesty was in the land of Zahi . . . the whole of that land surrendered. . . . The list ([30]) of the places taken in that year : cities, 3 ; a city surrendered in the territory of Anaugasa ; total, 4. Captives brought by His Majesty . . . taken prisoners, 90 ; surrendered with their wives ([31]) and their children . . . mares, 40 ; 15 chariots adorned with gold and silver, gold vases and gold in rings, 50 *deben* 8 *qedt*; silver vases of that country, and rings, 153 *deben*; bronze . . . bull calves 326, white goats 40, kids 50, asses 70, a great quantity of *sagu* wood, (³²) black wood, kharub wood, chairs with their . . . ; 6 poles for a tent adorned with bronze, as if inlaid with precious stones; and all the good wood of that land.

FIG. 67.—Gold vase from Syria.

The tribute of the princes of the land of Retennu in that year was, horses . . . chariots adorned in gold, silver, and colours, 3[4]; male and female slaves, 70[4]; gold 55 *deben* 8 *qedt*, silver vases various (³³) of the work of that land . . . *men* stone, all kinds of gems, vases, native copper blocks 80; lead, blocks 11; colours, *deben* 100; dry incense, felspar, alabaster . . . ; bull calves 13, bulls 530, asses 84; bronze, much wood, and many copper vases; incense jars 69[5]; (³⁴) sweet *beq* oil and green *beq* oil, 2080 jars; wine, 608 jars; *sagu* wood chariots, and acacia wood, . . . and all the good wood of that land. Each of the stations of His Majesty was provided with all kinds of good things for His Majesty to receive . . . of the land of Zahi, with cedar; the Kefti boats, and the Kapni boats, and the Sektu boats, of their woods and masts, (³⁵) great beams for the [palace] of His Majesty.

Tribute of the chiefs of the land of Asi in that year: blocks of copper 108, *setf*-copper 240 *deben*, lead 5 blocks, ingots of lead 1200, lazuli 110 *deben*, ivory tusks . . . wood chairs 2.

The tribute of the wretched Kush: gold 300 *deben*; daughter of the chief of Arem; slaves, male and female, (³⁶) total, 64; [105] bulls, calves 170; total, 275; beside boats laden with ivory and ebony, and all the products of that land. The harvest of the wretched Kush likewise.

The tribute of Wawat was: gold 274 *deben*; negroes, male and female, 10; bull calves . . . all the good things of the country. The harvest of Wawat likewise.

XXXVth year. His Majesty was in the land of Zahi in his Xth campaign. His Majesty approached the city of Aroana—for behold the miserable chief of Naharina had assembled his cavalry and men . . . ([38]) of the ends of the land, they were many . . . and they made war on His Majesty. His Majesty met with them. The soldiers of His Majesty made a time of attacking them, seizing and spoiling. His Majesty prevailed over these foreigners by the spirits of his father Amen . . . ([39]) of Naharina. They turned and fell down . . . one upon another before His Majesty. The number of things taken by the king himself of these foreigners of Naharina . . . ([40]) Suits of armour 2, bronze . . . *deben*. The number of things taken by the soldiers of His Majesty from these foreigners: live prisoners 10, mares 180, chariots 60, . . . ([41]) . . . bronze armour, bronze . . . for the head 5, bows of Khalu 5. The captures made in . . . ([42]) . . . 226, chariot inlaid with gold 1, chariots inlaid with gold and silver 20 . . . ([43]) *beq* oil jars 953 . . .

FIG. 68.—Bows from Syria.

(L.D. iii. 31 A; L.A. xii. 42–44).

([2]) earrings (?), bracelets (?), abhat stone, stibium, . . . antelopes (?), wood for burning.

The work of the vile Kush, 70 *deben* 1 *qedt* of gold, . . . male and female slaves, . . . oxen, boats laden with ivory and ebony, and all the good things of that land; with the harvest of Kush in that year . . . 34 negro slaves male and female, 94 bulls and steers, beside boats laden with all good things. The harvest of Wawat was likewise.

[([4]) **XXXVIIIth** year.] . . . in his XIIIth campaign of victory. His Majesty destroyed . . . [in the] territory of Anaugasa. The number of the captives brought by the army of His Majesty from the territory of Anaugasa was 50 living captives, horses . . . , 3 chariots . . . with their equipment. (⁵) men surrendered of the territory of Anaugasa. . . . The tribute brought to the spirits of His Majesty in that year was 328 mares, 522 slaves male and female, 9 chariots adorned with gold and silver, 61 chariots painted; total, 70. A collar of real lazuli . . . a goblet, dishes, (⁶) heads of goats, and head of a lion, vessels of all the work of Zahi . . . [copper?] 2821 *deben* 3½ *qedt*; 276 blocks of native copper, 26 blocks of lead, 656 vases of incense, 3 jars of sweet and green *beq* oil, 1752 jars of *seft*, 156 jars of wine, 12 bulls . . . 46 asses, 1 head of a deer, (⁷) 5 tusks of ivory, 3 tables of ivory and locust wood, white

FIG. 69.—Golden lion's head from Syria.

FIG. 70.—Golden deer's head from Syria.

FIG. 71.—Shields from Syria.

FIG. 72.—Quiver from Syria.

menu stone 68 *deben* . . . spears, shields, and bows, . . . all kinds of weapons and fragrant wood of that country, all the best products of that country. Behold every station was supplied with all good things, according to the yearly rate, in going north and going south (forth and back in campaigns), and the work of the Remenen (?) likewise. The harvest of Zahi in corn, green *beq* oil, incense . . .

The tribute brought by the chief of the Asi: the native copper . . . horses . . .

The tribute of the chief of Arurekh in that year: male and female slaves, 2 blocks of native copper, 65 logs of locust wood, with all the fragrant wood of its country.

That which was brought to the spirits of His Majesty from the land of Punt: (⁹) 240 *heq* measures of gums.

The work of the vile Kush: gold 100 [+x] *deben* 6 *qedt*; 36 negro slaves male and female, 111 steers, 185 bulls; total, 296; beside boats laden with ivory and ebony and all the good things of that land, together with the harvest of that land.

The work of Wawat . . . 2844, (¹⁰) 16 negroes male and female, steers 77, beside boats laden with all the good things of that land.

XXXIXth year, His Majesty was in the land of Retennu, in his XIVth campaign of victory after he went [to overthrow] the fallen of the Shasu. The amount [of tribute . . . 197 male and female slaves, (¹¹) 229 mares, gold dishes 2 *deben*, with rings 12 *qedt*, real lazuli 30 *deben*, silver dishes, a goblet, a vase in shape of the head of a bull, 325 various vases, with silver in rings, making 1495 *deben* 1 *qedt*; a chariot . . . (¹²) white precious stone, white *menkh* stone, natron, white *menu* stone, and all the various precious stones of this land. Incense, sweet *beq* oil, fresh *beq* oil, *seft* oil, jars of honey, 1405 jars of wine; 84 bulls, 1183 small cattle, bronze . . . (¹³) . . . of this land with all the produce of this land.

FIG. 73.—Bull's head vase from Syria.

Behold every station was supplied with all good things, according to their rate of the yearly supplies, in going north and south; likewise the harvest of . . . harvest (¹⁴) of the land of Zahi, consisting of corn, incense, dates, wine . . .

(L.D. iii. 30 A.)

XLth year? (¹) [Tribute of the chief] of Asi: 2 tusks of ivory, 40 blocks of bronze, 1 block of lead.

Tribute of [Kush] (²) . . . that year, 144 *deben* 3 *qedt* of gold, 101 negro slaves male and female, . . . bulls (³) . . .

[Tribute of Wawat in that year] (³) . . . 35 steers, 54 bulls; total, 89: beside boats laden with . . .

XLIst year? (⁴) The tribute of the chiefs of Retennu, brought to His Majesty's spirits (⁵) . . . 40 blocks; falchion of . . ., bronze spears, (⁶) . . . that year 26 tusks of ivory, 241 locust trees, 184 bulls . . . goats, (⁷) . . . incense.

FIG. 74.—Falchion.

Also the tribute of the chief of the great Khita in that year was, gold (⁸) 46[+x] *deben* 2 *qedt*, 8 male and female negro slaves, 13 boys for servants; total, 21. Bulls (?) . . . 3144 *deben* 3 *qedt* of gold, 35 steers, 79 oxen · total, 114; beside boats laden with all good things.

(¹⁰) **XLIInd** year? His Majesty was on the road of the shore to destroy the city of Arqantu, and the city of (¹¹) . . . kana. The city and its district was destroyed.

Approaching the land of Tunep, he laid waste the city, took its corn, cutting down its groves, (¹²) and those alive, by the troops; bringing them, they arrived in peace.

Approaching the district of Qedeshu, taking the fortresses in it.

FIG. 75.—Suit of armour.

(¹³) The number of spoil taken in them . . . of vile Naharina who were as defenders among them, with their horses, 691 prisoners, 29 hands [of slain], 48 mares (¹⁴) . . . in that year 295 male and female slaves, 68 horses, 3 gold dishes, 3 silver dishes, 3 craters, a table; together with silver (¹⁵) . . . 47 blocks of lead, 1100 *deben* of lead, colours, emery, all the gems of the land, bronze suits of armour, utensils, . . . (¹⁶) all the excellent wood of the country. Behold every station was provided with all good things, according to the rate of their yearly produce. The harvest of that country ([17]) . . . with dishes, heads in shape of bulls, weighing 341 *deben* 2 *qedt*; true lazuli, one stone weighing 33 *qedt* (11 ozs.); a good *sagu* wood chair, native copper.

([18]) [Tribute of the chief] of Tanai (?): a silver jug of the work of Keftiu, with 3 vases of bronze with silver handles, weighing 56 *deben* 1 *qedt* . . . ([19]) with all the good things of that land.

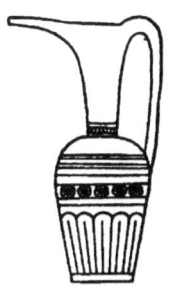

FIG. 76.—Silver jug from Syria.

The harvest of the vile Kush; likewise the work of the Wawat in that year, was, gold 2374 *deben* 1 *qedt* . . . ([20]) Wawat.

Then His Majesty ordered that the victories which he had made, beginning in his XXIIIrd and continuing to his XLIInd year, should be recorded on this tablet on this shrine."

A private inscription of the officer Amen·em·heb is of value, as giving some further details of the northern campaigns. But no distinction is made between different years, and only two distinctive names are found which occur in the Annals; these are Senzaru and Niy, both of which were visited in the XXXIIIrd year. This might well be the date of the active life of Amen·em·heb; for though he appears twenty-one years later under Amenhotep II., he then takes no part in fighting or work, but merely accompanies the king in Egypt. He says (A.Z. xi. 1, 63) :—

I was very true to the prince, pure of heart to the king of Upper Egypt, glorious of heart to the king of Lower Egypt. I followed ([2]) my lord at his goings in the land of the north and south, and he desired that I should be the companion of his feet. He ([3]) performed his victories, and his valour fortified the heart. I made a capture in the land of ([4]) Negeba (the Negeb), I took Amu 3 persons, living captives.

When His Majesty came to Naharina ([5]) I took 3

persons as my spoil thence; I set them before Thy Majesty as living captives.

(6) Again I took spoil in this expedition in the high land of Wan on the west of Khalubu (Aleppo): I brought (7) Amu living prisoners 13 persons, 70 live asses, 13 bronze weapons, and . . . bronze weapons inlaid with gold.

(8) Again I took spoil in this expedition in the land of Karika-masha (Karkhemish). I brought thence . . . persons (9) as living captives. I crossed the water of Naharina with them in my hand . . . (10) [I brought them] before my Lord. Then he rewarded me with a great reward, the amount . . . (11) I saw the power of the king Men·kheper·ra, the giver of life, in the land of Senzaru (Singara); he made . . . (12) I made a capture before the king, I brought a hand thence. He gave me gold of praise, the amount . . . (13) and 2 *deben* silver.

Again I saw his valour, I was among his followers capturing (14) Kedeshu, I did not leave the place where he was; I brought thence 2 *marina* [living prisoners, I placed them] (15) before the king the lord of the two lands, Tahutmes the ever-living: he gave me gold for my valour before all persons (16); the amount was of beaten gold a lion, 2 necklaces, 2 helmets, and 4 rings. I saw my lord in . . . (17) . . . in all his forms in the borders of the land of . . . (18) . . . and again gold was given me for it. I rose to . . .

(19) Again I saw his might in the land of Takhisi . . . (20) I made a captive from it before the king; I brought 3 Amu as living prisoners; gave to me (21) my lord gold of reward, the amount was 2 gold . . . 4 bracelets, 2 helmets, a lion, and a female slave.

(22) Again . . . a second good work done by the lord of the two lands in the land of Niy, he hunted 120 elephants for their tusks . . . (23) the largest one which

FIG. 77.—Elephant from Syria.

was among them began to fight against His Majesty; I cut off his hand while he was alive . . ., (24) I went in the water between two rocks, my lord rewarded me with gold (25). He gave me . . . clothing 3 pieces. The king of Qedshu made a mare come forth (26) in front . . . She ran in the midst of the army, I ran after her (27) on foot, having my weapon. I ripped up her body, I cut off her tail, I gave (28) it to the king, and they praised God for me on account of this. He caused joy to fill my body and pleasure thrilled my limbs.

(29) When His Majesty ordered that every valorous man of his troops should go forth to break through the new walls made for Qedshu, I broke them open, I led all the valiant. No other person went before me, I brought (31) *marina* 2 living prisoners. Again His Majesty rewarded me on account of it with all (32) good things that are pleasing before the king. I made this capture while I was captain . . . (33) I arranged the steering in . . . as the headman of his companions (34) in rowing [the boat of Amen] in his good festival of Thebes, mankind was in joy . . .

(35) Behold the king had ended his time of existence of many good years of victory, power, and (36) justification from the 1st year to the 54th year. In the 30th of Phamenoth of the majesty of the king, (37) Menkheper-ra deceased, he ascended to heaven and joined the sun's disc, the follower of the god met his maker.

When the light dawned and the morrow came, (38) the disc of the sun arose and heaven became bright. The king Aa·kheperu·ra, son of the sun, Amenhotep, the giver of life, (39) was established on the throne of his father, he rested on the *ka* name, he struck down all, he thrust . . . (40) of Deshert, he hewed off the heads of their chiefs, crowned as Horus the son of Isis, he took (41) [possession of] that land.

The remaining lines mention his accompanying the king in Egypt and in the palace.

Greater Monuments.

The most northern monument of Tahutmes III. was the triumphal stele which he erected on his frontier by the Euphrates in the neighbourhood of the city of Niy, by the tablet of his father. This appears to have been as far north as Aleppo; but hitherto it has not been discovered. His other Asiatic remains are the steles in Sinai. At Sarbut el Khadem is a stele of the 23rd year, with the king offering to Hathor, the noble and high officer Roy holding the fan behind him (L.D. iii. 29 a). Another stele dated in the 27th year shows the king again offering to Hathor, the goddess of that region; and a portion of a doorway of his lies near it (from photographs). Pieces of glazed vases are also found there. In the Wady Maghara is an inscription of his (My. E. 344).

The long-neglected Delta began to revive under this reign. At Kom el Hisn, on the north-west, is a town with many Ramesside remains which prove it to be the ancient Amu (G.N. 78). But the rebuilding of the temple here dates as early as Tahutmes III.; as a vase evidently from a foundation deposit (bought in Cairo), names him "beloved of Hathor, lady of Amu" (F.P. Coll.). This is identical in style with the vases of his deposits at Koptos.

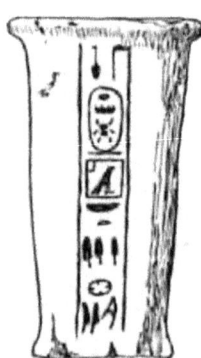

Fig. 78.—Alabaster vase of Tahutmes III., foundation deposit of Amu. F.P. Coll.

At Heliopolis (An) he carried out great works. A large jamb of a gateway was formerly in the citadel at Cairo (D E.Y. 24, 1); it named Tahutmes beloved of Tum of An, and of the spirits of An, and that he made a gate of pure stone of Bekhen. Two other blocks of a gateway were recently still in place (B.R. ix. 23 a, b). A stele of the 47th year (Berlin, L.D. iii. 29 b) informs us that he built a wall with gates around the temple of Ra (L.D. iii. 29 b). Amen·em·ant, whose tomb is at Abusir, was perhaps the architect here, as he was "overseer of works of the temple of Ra." His other titles are prince in Memphis, overseer of all the royal works, and general of the troops (L.D. iii. 29 e). The two obelisks which stood at Heliopolis, erected by Tahutmes III., were dedicated to Tum of Heliopolis. Both were appropriated by Ramessu II., who added lines of inscription on either side of the original line down the middle of each face. Usarkon I. has also added his name. One, and probably both obelisks, were removed from there in the 18th year of Augustus, B.C. 12, as recorded upon the bronze figures of crabs which were placed as ornaments below each corner (A. C. Merriam, Inscrips. on the Obelisk-Crab). They were placed at Alexandria in front of the Cæsareum; and remained there until one (68½ feet high) was removed to London in 1877, and the other (69½ feet high) was removed to New York in 1879. The obelisks of the Lateran and of Constantinople have been reported to belong to Heliopolis; but, as we shall see farther on, they probably come from Thebes.

At Abusir is the tomb of Amen·em·ant, as we have just noticed. At Memphis it appears (according to an inscription at Sakkara, B.H. 403) that a temple was erected to Ptah. At Gurob, at the entrance to the Fayum, a temple was built with a town around it at the end of the great dyke of the Fayum (P.I. xxv.). A lintel (P.I. xxiv. 3), now in Adelaide, and other stones (P.K. xxii. 2), give the king's name; the erasures show that this lasted until the time of Akhenaten; but the temple was soon after ruined and mostly removed, and houses built over its site. This town was ruined in the foreign invasion and expulsion under Merenptah, and was scarcely occupied since.

FIG. 79.—Violet glass bead of Tahutmes III. Gurob, F.P. Coll.

The rock temple of Speos Artemidos, near Beni Hasan, begun by Hatshepsut, was continued by

Tahutmes III. (L.D. iii. 26, 7). At El Bersheh a tablet was carved on the rock, dated in 33rd year, on the 2nd of Mesore, wishing the king millions of the *Sed* festivals, that great feast of 30 years having taken place two or three days before the dating of this stele.

At Ekhmim is a scene carved in a rock chamber, of Tahutmes (written Men·ra·kheper) adoring Amen-Min (L.D. iii. 29 d); and another inscription in the temple site (My. E. 431). At Abydos a colossus of Osiris bears the name of the king on the back (M.A. 1). At Dendera an inscription in a crypt mentions "the restoring of the monument made by the king, lord of both lands, Men·kheper·ra, lord of the crowns, Tahutmes, according to the discovery of ancient writings of the time of Khufu" (D.D. i.); and a block of Tahutmes remains there in the later building (D.D. iii. d). He also dedicated a great sistrum of *mafek* (malachite?), 16 digits (a foot) high, which is figured in the later sculpture (D.D. ii. c). In Wady Hammamat is also an inscription of this king (My. E. 326).

At Koptos he entirely rebuilt the temple. Deep foundations were laid, which lasted through all the successive rebuildings, and through the Ptolemaic clearance, down to Roman times. The front was supported by six large pillars, placed on deep and massive sub-structures. Beneath the walls were several foundation deposits of models of tools, ores, vases in alabaster, and a great quantity of pottery: all of the more valuable objects were inscribed for Tahutmes, "beloved of Min of Koptos." Though the upper building of this temple has been removed, yet fragments show that the walls were all of Silsileh sandstone, in place of the limestone used in the earlier temples. The pillars were of red granite sculptured with scenes of the king offering. They were probably re-used in the later temples, as they remained accessible in Christian times, and were removed from the ruins to build into a Coptic church, of which little remains now but these pillars. Near Ballas, opposite Koptos, is the ruin of the small town of Nubt, built by this king and Amenhotep II., the bricks being stamped with their cartouches. Foundation deposits and a sandstone jamb of Tahutmes III. were lately found there.

Karnak shows the greatest work of this reign. The old temple, which had been renewed and enlarged by this family, had an immense addition made behind it. A great hall was built, over 130 feet long, supported on

FIG. 80.—Columns of Tahutmes III. Karnak.

two rows of pillars and two rows of columns; it lay across the axis of the temple in front of a new sanctuary. Numerous chambers opened around it, forming a complex mass of nearly fifty halls and rooms. In the older part great changes were made. A thin pylon (VI.), or wall, was thrust in between the sanctuary and the pylons of Tahutmes I. It bears some of the most valuable documents, in the long lists of conquered towns and peoples; three lists are of northern, and one is of southern names. Also a casing was built around the lower parts of the obelisks of Hatshepsut, so as to hide all her address to those who should gaze on her work, and desire to know who did it. On the inner side of this pylon of Tahutmes are the two beautiful granite pillars adorned with lotus flowers on each side. The valuable list of ancestors whom the king is represented adoring was in the southern side of the surrounding chambers of the temple; but the whole part was so barbarously destroyed in the surreptitious theft of the sculptures by Prisse, that Mariette could not trace even the position of the chambers.

FIG. 81.—Lotus pillars of Tahutmes III. Karnak.

Leaving the main temple, the southern approach was further decorated by another pylon (VII.), behind the pylon (VIII.) of Tahutmes I. Adjoining that is the eastern wall of the court, and opening from that wall is a small temple of alabaster. The walls bordering the sacred lake here are also of this reign.

To the north the small temple of Ptah was built by Tahutmes; and his name also occurs in the temple of Mut. The brick wall around the whole of the buildings then existing was also the work of Tahutmes III.

At Medinet Habu, this king finished the temple which had been in progress since his grandfather's time, and which was mainly built by his father, and decorated by him and Hatshepsut. It was then but a small building, and was restored by Horemheb, by Sety I., by Ramessu XII., and by Painezem I., according to their successive notices on the front wall. Then Taharqa added a front court and pylon in front, cutting through the temenos of Ramessu III.; the XXXth dynasty added another court in front of that; Ptolemy X. added a great pylon before that; and. lastly, Antoninus added a forecourt in front of all.

At Deir el Bahri, or Assassif, the great design of Hatshepsut was finished by Tahutmes III. after her death; one doorway is entirely inscribed by him (D.H. ii. xxxiv.), showing that the work was not completed by her. The obelisks would be among the later objects, and it is therefore very probable that they were erected or at least inscribed by Tahutmes. The height of the great pair of obelisks is recorded by an inscription in the temple to have been 108 cubits (L.D. iii. 27, 11); and as nothing more than the bases of them have been seen in the temple, we naturally look around to see if they have been carried elsewhere. The length of 185 feet is so much greater than that of any other obelisk, that it is probable that the width was not as large in proportion, as that would have made the weight impossibly heavy to move. The obelisk of Hatshepsut is $97\frac{1}{2}$ feet high, 7 feet 10 inches wide at base, and about 5 feet 8 inches at top (measured from a photograph); the obelisk of Tahutmes III. (Lateran) is $105\frac{1}{2}$ feet high, 9 feet 9 inches wide at base, and about 5 feet 10 inches at top. Taking the lighter obelisk, that of Hatshepsut, which weighs about 300 tons, if the thickness were increased proportionally to the length on 185 feet, it would imply a weight of over 2000 tons. This is so obviously excessive (as the heaviest blocks yet known are the colossi of Ramessu II., 800 tons at the Ramesseum, and 900 tons at Tanis), that we cannot suppose that the thickness was proportionate to the height. Probably, therefore, the missing obelisks should be about the same width at the top as the other great obelisks, and wider at the base.

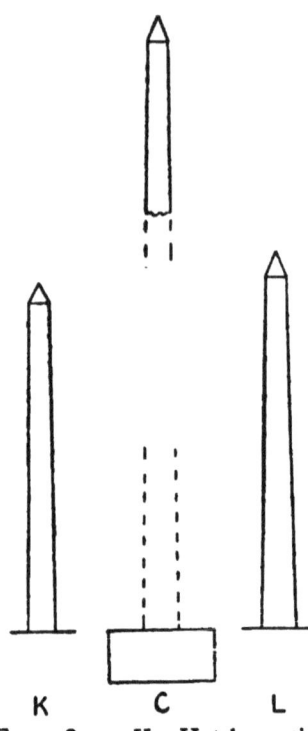

FIG. 82. — K. Hatshepsut's obelisk at Karnak.
L. Tahutmes III. obelisk, Lateran.
C. Broken top of obelisk at Constantinople, continued down to same breadth as Lateran, and making (with the base) a height of 108 cubits as described.

The only obelisk that could fit this requirement is that of Constantinople. It is only the top of a broken obelisk; but the inscription on the south face is exactly parallel to that on the west face of Hatshepsut's obelisk. If it continued like that, its height would come to about 120 feet; but it may, of course, have been a longer inscription. If we suppose that it was 172 feet (or 100 cubits, leaving 13 feet for pedestal), then, as the top is about 5 feet 6 inches wide (by photograph), and the broken end 7 feet wide, the base would have been 10 feet 2 inches wide, there being no perceptible entasis. As the Lateran obelisk is 9 feet 9 inches, this size of base would be very probable for a longer mass. The weight of this Constantinople obelisk would then be about 800 tons, or just of the same class as the two greatest colossi.

The problem, therefore, stands thus. Two obelisks existed at Deir el Bahri 185 feet high, probably including the pedestals. The Constantinople fragment (judging by the inscription) was apparently from an obelisk longer than any other known, and therefore has the best claim to be one of the missing pair. It is so slender that, if protracted to the same base width as the

Lateran, it would be of about the recorded length. If it were of that length, its existing width and slope would imply a weight about the same as that of the heaviest masses known to have been transported. And it was dedicated to Amen, and therefore probably came from Thebes. It is then most likely that we see in this the top of one of the great obelisks of Deir el Bahri. What became of the lower part, and of the other obelisk, we may guess when we see the multitude of obelisks erected by Ramessu II., and remember how ruthlessly he re-worked the stones of his predecessors.

An interesting inscription concerning the obelisks of Tahutmes III. exists in the tomb of Puamra at Qurneh. The king is seated "beholding monuments of great works made by the king, lord of both lands, Men·kheper·ra, to his father Amen in Thebes, great in silver and gold, and all noble things, by the prince, the beloved of the god Puam." Before him stand three of the architects and three of the builders, saying, "Come the overseers of works speaking of these princely things, delighting thy heart by thy creation of all these thy high works." The first three are "overseers of workmen of the temple of Amen"; the other three are "overseers of works of the temple of Amen." Behind them are two great obelisks with inscriptions dedicating them to Amen (L.D. iii. 39 c).

Another tomb shows the king offering two obelisks, with vases, arms, collars, boxes, gold rings (613¼ *deben* weight), etc., to Amen (C.M. 316–7).

The great tomb of Rekh·ma·ra (which we have drawn from in previous pages to illustrate the foreign tribute) shows that he had to do with the monuments of the king, and with the plating of the temple gates with gold from the Rutennu (M.A.F. v. 57). Similarly, Men·kheper·ra·senb states that he had seen Tahutmes make a monolith shrine of red granite entirely plated with ₍electrum, and a colonnade and pair of obelisks likewise covered.

At Taud, above Thebes, are fragments of sculptures

of this reign. At Esneh a great stele of the king is mentioned in an inscription of the time of Claudius (L.D. iv. 8 a). At El Kab an architrave of the temple of Sebek is of this age (C.N. 266); and a small temple surrounded by a colonnade—like the destroyed one of Elephantine—stood here (W.T. 430). At Edfu is a Ptolemaic inscription stating that Tahutmes III. built

FIG. 83.—The overseers of works who made the obelisks. Thebes.

the temple of Hathor at Edfu (A.Z. ix. 97). At Kom Ombo stood a grand pylon to the temenos of the temple, which, though built by Hatshepsut, was carved by Tahutmes III. The lintel of it was a Ptolemaic restoration (L.D. iii. 28, 1; R.R. 28); but all this is now washed away by the Nile. A lintel block of Tahutmes III., perhaps washed out of some later structure, lay on the bank recently (A.Z. xxi. 78).

At Elephantine some temple existed, as is shown by the blocks of Tahutmes III. which remained built into the quay wall. But there is no evidence to which temple they belonged ; and it is more likely that they were part of some ruined temple of Tahutmes rebuilt by the Ptolemies, than that the temple of Amenhotep III. was begun by Tahutmes. A block of this king remains also at the railway station at Aswan (Rec. ix. 81). An obelisk from the temple of Elephantine is stated to be at Sion House (Birch, History, 102). An inscription at Sehel records the clearing again of the canal of the cataract (see i. p. 179): "The year 50, Pakhons 22, under the majesty of king Men·kheper·ra, His Majesty commanded to cut this canal, after he had found it choked with stones so that no vessel crossed on it. His Majesty passed over it, his heart rejoicing that he had slain his enemies. Name of this canal, 'Open the way well by Men·kheper·ra.' The fishers of Elephantine are to dredge this canal every year" (Rec. xiii. 203). Another stele shows the king adoring the gods Khnum Anket and Sati (M.I. i. 101, 218). Probably a temple was built on the island of Bigeh by this king, judging from a statue there (W.T. 470).

In Nubia was one of the greatest fields of architectural activity of Tahutmes III. Almost every site there appears to have been settled by him, and temples built to the local gods. At Kalabsheh is said to be a granite statue in the temple, and a block with his name (Prokesch Nilfahrt 575). At Kuban is an inscription (My. E. 538). At Dakkeh also a mention of the king (S.N. 136). At Korti is a stone of Tahutmes, and the foundations of the temple which was rebuilt later (L.L. 124). At Amadah is a gateway of Tahutmes III. on one jamb, and of Amenhotep II. on the other jamb, while both names occur jointly on the lintel. This points to a co-regency (L.D. iii. 65 b, c). A great stele in the third year of Amenhotep II. shows that the work was done here at the close of the reign of Tahutmes (L.D. iii. 65 a), and that the co-regency was not long. There is also a scene of Tahutmes embraced by Isis-Selk (L.D. iii. 45). At Ellesiyeh are scenes of Tahutmes III. adoring Ra, Dedun, and Usertesen III. (L.D. iii. 45 d), and of Uazet and Mut embracing the king, and his offering to Hathor and Horus of Behen, Maam, and Ta·khens (L.D. iii. 46). A stele here is dated in the 42nd year, Pakhons 14 (L.D. iii. 45 e), showing again that the Nubian works were toward the end of the reign. At Ibrim are two rock chapels; one has a lintel with the king's name, and inside are figures of the king before Horus of Maam; the other chapel shows him before Horus of Maam and Sati (C.N. 79). These shrines were carved by the viceroy Nehi, who is frequently met with in this region.

At Wady Halfa a brick temple was erected by Tahutmes III. to the Horus of Beheni. By the door is a stele of his 23rd year (B.E. 341). Also a grand temple at Semneh (L.D. iii. 47–56), and a fellow one at the other fortress of Kummeh (L.D. iii. 57–59 a, 64 b) were probably both begun by the preceding kings, but completed and adorned by the viceroy Nehi under Tahutmes III. At the island of Sai (lat. 20° 42′ N.) are the remains of a temple of this reign, built by the viceroy Nehi (L.D. iii. 59 b, c). At Dosheh appear Tahutmes III. and Usertesen III. together, and also Tahutmes offering to Horus of Ta·khens (L.D. iii. 59 d, e). And the founding of the temple of Soleb is attributed likewise to this reign.

We see thus the most extraordinary activity in building; and probably dozens of minor temples have passed away which are quite unknown to us, as little suspected as the temples of Kom el Hisn, Gurob, and Nubt were a few years ago. As it is, we can count up over thirty different sites, all of which were built on during this reign. The Nubian buildings seem to be mostly of later date than the others, and the record of clearing the canal in the 50th year shows activity there at that time. It would seem probable that the last ten years of the great conqueror were devoted to affirming his power in the south.

Lesser Monuments.

The statues of Tahutmes III. are numerous, but seldom colossal. At Karnak is the base of a seated colossus in hard white silicious limestone, at the west end of the front of pylon VIII. (M.K. 38 d). The head of a colossus in brown granite is in the British Museum, but the statue of it is unknown.

A standing statue in red granite from Karnak, rather over life size, is in Cairo (G. Mus., V.G. 202); it was found in the axial chamber or sanctuary of the buildings of Tahutmes III. at the east end of the temple (M.K. p. 34). A seated black granite statue was also found at Karnak in many fragments, now rejoined (G. Mus., V.G. 214). Many dozens of statues of this king are also stated to have existed at Karnak (M.K. p. 36). At Turin is a very fine statue in black and white diorite (L.T. 1376; the head, L.D. iii. 292, 30). Another seated statue in dark grey granite, but headless, was brought from Nubia — probably Elephantine, as it names the gods of that place: it is now at Florence (S. Cat. F. 1503). At Abydos remains still a torso, and a throne (M.A. 348–9).

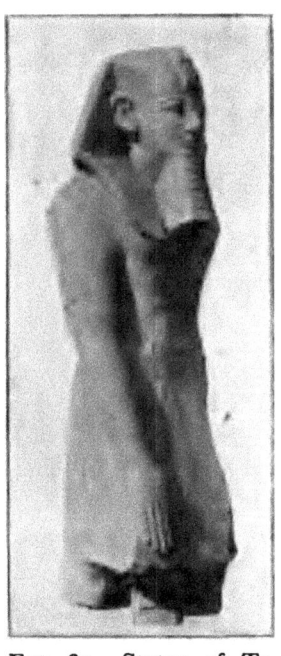

FIG. 84 —Statue of Tahutmes III. Karnak.

At Alexandria stood a statue of the king, "beloved of Anit, lady of Dendera" (B.R. ix. 3, p. 18). A torso lies behind the temple at Karnak, and two fragments of statues before the first pylon of the hypostyle at Luxor (W.G. 358). A bust in red granite was found at Karnak (V.G. 192). A bronze statuette of the king is reputed to be at Marseille, but is not in Maspero's catalogue. Two statues are mentioned in inscriptions by Tahutmes IV. (M.K. 33), and by Neb·ua·iu (M.A. ii. 33).

Two sphinxes in red granite were found in a chamber at the back of the hall of pillars of Tahutmes, along with two tables of offerings probably for offering before them (V.G. 221–2; M.K. 32 b, pp. 34, 55). A drawing of the king on a board divided in squares for the canon

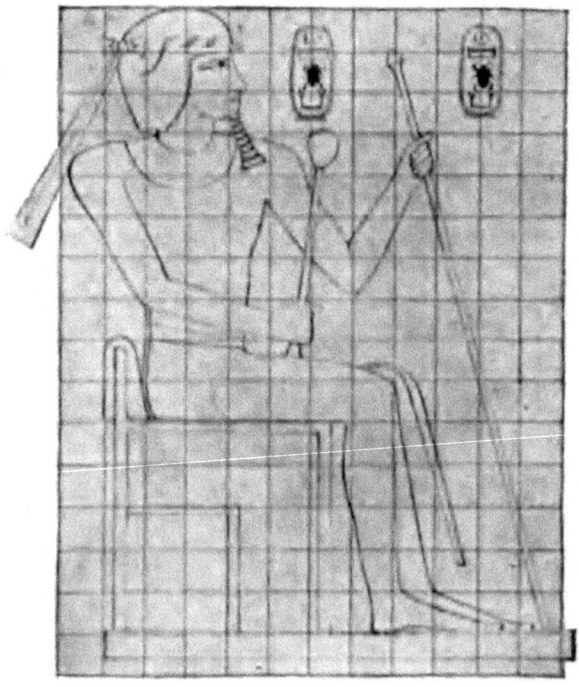

FIG. 85.—Board with figure of Tahutmes III., drawn on squares. Brit. Mus.

of proportion is in the British Museum (A.B. 33); and a trial piece with uncertain heads and this king's name is at Turin (L.D. iii. 304).

A stele, showing Tahutmes adoring Min, is at Turin (L.T. 1460); and one was found in the chapel of Uazmes, showing Tahutmes III. adoring his grandfather and prince Uazmes (M.E. ii.). A large, high block of red granite, with figures half detached in relief, representing Tahutmes held hand in hand by Mentu and Hathor, twice repeated, was found at Karnak. From the size, about 5½ feet high and 3 × 1½ feet at the top, it cannot be an altar; but would be exactly suited as a stand for resting the sacred bark in the temple, when depositing it from the priests' shoulders after a procession (B. Mus., A.B. 34). Another such block is said to be still at Karnak (W.G. 366). A large and very fine altar is in the Vatican (Massi, Guide, 87). An altar of the *kalathos* form was found at Salonika (A.Z. vi. 79). And two fine altars of red granite and of alabaster belonged to the sphinxes of Tahutmes in a back hall of the Karnak temple built by him (Hall Y[1], M.K. 32 b; V.G. 211; M.B. 98).

Many alabaster vases are known, to which references are given at the head of this reign. The important ones are those with the contents marked. One at Turin contained nine hins, but is filled with bitumen (?), so that it cannot be guaged; another at Ghizeh contained 21 hins, and as it measures 581 cubic inches, the hin was 27·7 c. i. in this case. Two glass vases with the name of Men·kheper·ra are the earliest dated glass known, and show much facility in the working and knowledge of the material (B. Mus.; Ms. A. 251; R.C. lxii. 6). Two ivory tablets with the name are reported to exist at Marseille (W.G. 368), but are not apparent in Maspero's catalogue: they are probably those which are now considered false. A very strange series of fourteen labels of wood and one of stone, bearing the names of princesses, three of which have also the name of Tahutmes III., were found in a tomb in Thebes by Rhind. That they were original labels of the mummies of the princesses, seems very unlikely; they may have belonged to slaves or servants of the princesses, as there are so many different names.

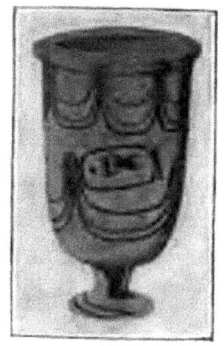

FIG. 86.—Glass vase of Tahutmes III.

From the style of the names they seem to be all of this same period, so they are not likely to be labels which were attached in course of removing a series of miscellaneous royal mummies in later times. The names are stated here in dealing with the family of the king. A feather head-dress of Amen with the king's name (T. Mus.), a fish-shaped dish of green glaze (Ms. G. 124), and a scribe's palette for "Tahutmes III. loved by Amen and Ptah" (Bologna), are of this reign.

A few papyri remain. One in Turin (No. 1) recounts how a scribe User·amen had served royalty for thirty years; as he dates in the fifth year of this reign, he began in the middle of Tahutmes Ist's reign.

Rings are common in all materials, except glazed pottery, which does not appear till Tahutmes IV. One ring in gold found at Gurob (Fig. 48) shows that the king was born at Thebes (*mes uas*). The contemporary scarabs of this reign are commoner than in any other; and the name of Men·kheper·ra continued to be placed on amulets and scarabs in many later times, so that two scarabs out of any three with names are generally of this king. His lasting popularity shows how deeply the glories of his reign had impressed Egyptians with the greatest epoch of their history. Two later kings retook his name, the husband of Isi·em·kheb in the XXIst, and Piankhy in the XXVth dynasty.

FIG. 87.—Scarab of Tahutmes III. F. P. Coll.

PRIVATE MONUMENTS.

We now turn to the remains of private persons, which, from the length and the riches of this reign, are unusually important.

Beginning with those who lived in this reign, there are the following officials and others:—

Aa·ma·thu, vizier, tomb, Silsileh   (L. D. iii. 25 *bis*, o; S. B. A. xii. 103; M. A. F. v. i. 3).

Amen·em·ant, architect and general, Abusir (L.D. iii. 29 e).
Amen·em·hat, keeper of the palace, Heliopolis (L.D. iii. 29 c).
Amen·em·heb, tomb with Rutennu (M.A.F. v.224-285).
Amen·em·hat, tomb, stele, 28th year (L.D. iii. 38 e-g; A.Z. xxi. 132).
Amen·em·ka, cones, second prophet of king (M.A.F. viii. 279, 82).
Amen·em·meruf, *wekil* of the palace, Leyden (Lb. D. 595).
Amen·mes, overseer of north, tomb, Asasssif.

FIG. 88.—Rekh·ma·ra.

Amen·user, tomb 119, vizier (B.E. ii. 191).
Amunzeh, keeper of the palace, tomb (M.A.F. v.337-361).
Antef, chief reporter, tomb, Drah a. Negga.
Bahes·heku, feather-bearer, Turin (Rec. iii. 124).
Humai, governor of Memphis, P. Mus. (S. h. 14).
Kargui, scribe of Nubian treasury, Addeh (W.G. 368).
Kharu, fan-bearer (Lb. D. 591).
Mau·en·hequ, armour-bearer, Turin (L.T. 1459).
Men·kheper·ra·senb, A, keeper of magazines (B.C. 127 cone).
    B, tomb 59 (C.N. i. 557; M.A.F. v. 197-223).

Neb·amen, keeper of granaries, Abbott papyrus.
,, tomb, keeper of audience hall (Rec. ix. 97).
Neby, great builder of the king, Dresden (A.Z. xix. 67).
Nehi, viceroy of Ethiopia (L.D. iii. 59 b, c, etc.; C.N. 79).
Penaati, chief of works (P.S. 357).
,, ,, statue, Turin (S. Cat. F. 1505).
Ptah·mes, high priest, Memphis, naos, Abydos (V.G. 200; M.A. ii. 32).
,, ,, ,, pyramid, Berlin (B.C. 91).
Puam·ra, over the royal monuments, and governor of the small Oasis (D.O. 1, 2 a, p. 22; L.D. iii. 39 c), ushabti-coffin (B.C. 125), stele (V.G. 215).
Rekh·ma·ra, vizier, great tomb, No. 35, Qurneh (M.A.F v.; H.E. xlvi.-xlix.; P.A. 97, 100).
Set, guardian of the palace (Lb. D. 587).
Tahuti, general, gold dish, silver dish, canopic jar (Louvre), gold heart scarab, canopic jar, kohl pot (Leyden), dagger (Darmstadt).
Tahuti, scribes, coffin (M.B. 577), palette (M.A. 1486 and Ms. G. 120).
Tahutmes, *wekil* of the palace (Lb. D. 595, 608).
,, high priest of Memphis (S. Cat. F. 1570).
User, vizier (M.K. 32 g); stele, 24th year, tomb (A.Z. xxi. 132).
User·hat, overseer of serfs of the king (L.P. 26).
Zanuni, scribe of general census, tomb (C.N. 831), stele (Turin; Rec. iv. 13; M.A.F. v. 591).

Priests of Tahutmes III. in later times:—

Bakta, *qemat* of Tahutmes III., stele, P. Mus. (P.R. ii. 77).
Horames, adoring Sopd and Tahutmes III. (E.L. 40).
Hor·em·heb, tomb (C.N. i. 492; L.D. iii. 78 b).
Ima·dua, great tomb under Rams. X. (C.N. i. 563).
Ken·amen, priest, Abydos (M.A. 1108, ii. 49).
Khaemuas, 2nd prophet of T. Tomb of Khonsu (Qurneh)
Khonsu, 1st prophet of T. Rams. II. tomb (Qurneh)
Men·kheper, prayer to royal *ka* (C.N. i. 839).
Ra, priest (L.D. iii. 62 b).
Ran, priest (Berlin, 2067?)
Sakedenu, priest, cones (M.A.F. viii. 299, 294).
Sen·nefer adoring Nefertari, Sa·pair, Tahutmes I. and III., Amenhotep II., seal and palace keeper, tomb, Qurneh (L.T. 1455).

The importance of these private remains is in showing details of the foreign peoples and tributes; these we have already noticed.

Royal Family.

Of the family of Tahutmes III. but little is known. His queen, of whom his heir Amenhotep II. was born, was Meryt·ra Hatshepset, daughter of Hatshepsut; this is shown by Amenhotep being accompanied with his mother in tomb scenes (L.D. iii. 62, 64), and on a scarab (M.A. ii. 40 n). A female sphinx representing her, with the name of her husband on the chest, was found in the temple of Isis at Rome, now in the Baracco collection, and casts of it at Turin and Berlin (A. Z. xx. 118). The queen appears behind her husband at Medinet Habu (L.D. iii. 38 a, b; C.M. 195, 3); and in a tomb (L.D. iii. 63 a).

FIG. 89.—Head of Tahutmes III., Deir el Bahri. Photographed by Mr. Carter.

A strange collection of labels bearing the names of princesses was found by Rhind at Thebes. A tomb sealed under Amenhotep III. had been broken open; in the upper chamber were fragments of coffins and funereal furniture, with these labels lying loose; in the lower chamber were the despoiled mummies. Not having any of the pieces of the coffins dated or preserved, it is possible that they and the mummies all belonged to subsequent interments, but not likely; as, if the place had been cleared out for fresh burials, the entrance would have been regularly opened. And as it is not likely that a whole clearance would have been made within sixty years, the seal of Amenhotep is probably of the same closing of the tomb to which these labels of Tahutmes III. belong.

The question then arises, who were the persons connected with the labels? The little slips of wood, with names written on in rough hieratic with ink, are not at all grand; and Rhind suggested that they might have been for slaves of the various princesses. This is the more likely, as there are three labels of one name, and two of each of two other names: so they must have referred to persons or things belonging to the princesses, and could not be body labels for themselves. But no person is named beside the princesses, except on two labels, the household or funeral officials, namely, an inspector, two guardians, and an embalmer, are inscribed.

Turning next to the names, we read first: "Year 27, Pharmuthi 2. King's daughter Nebtau, daughter of the royal son Sa·tum" (see No. 1). Here the title king's daughter must mean descendant, as Sa·tum was her immediate father. Another inscription bears on this, as Neb·amen was keeper of the house of the royal wife Nebtu (Rec. ix. 97), whose name is probably the same as Nebtau, with a slight blunder in one or other. Neb·amen had served Tahutmes II., then dead, and Nebtu was also dead when he wrote under Tahutmes III. This date of twenty-seven years after Tahutmes II. is not at all impossible to fit his biography. Who, then, was the queen Nebtu? As the date above on the label is forty years after the death of Tahutmes I., it seems more likely that Nebtu was a queen of Tahutmes III., who died young. The tomb appears to have been in use till some time later, by the seal of Amenhotep III.; and hence the various king's daughters named, and stated to be of the house of the royal children of Tahutmes III., were probably his daughters. Their names are recorded—

"Princess Taui . . . of the house of the royal children of Men·kheper·ra; those who follow her, inspector Maa, guardian . . ., guardian Nefer . . ., embalmer . . ."

"Princess Ta·kheta, of the house of the royal children of Men·kheper·ra; those who follow her, the inspector Tugay, guardian Si, guardian Neferu·er·hatf, embalmer Nefer·renpit" (see No. 2).

"Princess Pet·ahuha of Men·kheper·ra" (3).

"Princess Pet·pui, surnamed Ta·khet·aui" (2).

"Princess Meryt·ptah."

"Princess Sat·hora."
"Princess Nefer·amen."
"Princess Uaay."
"Princess Henut·anu" (2).

Bearing on the date, we may notice that the Kheta do not appear named among Egyptian foes till the

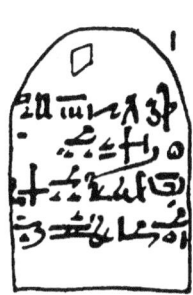 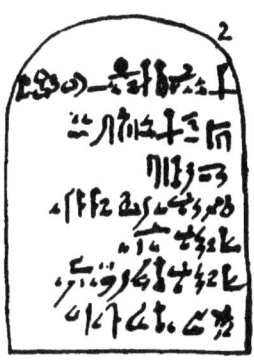

FIG. 90.—1. Label of Nebtau.   2. Label of Ta·kheta.

33rd year of Tahutmes III.; hence Ta·kheta (who was probably the child of some captive of the Kheta) would probably have died late in his reign.

At the close of this reign,—one of the grandest and most eventful in Egyptian history,—we may well pause to look at the new conditions of life which were thus forced on the country.

FIG. 91.—Hæmatite scarab of Tahutmes III., found in Cappadocia, and clearly of Syrian work, both in design and execution. Dr. Long's Coll.

In the previous crises of the land, when it was invaded by the Libyans in the VIIth, by the Amu or Asiatics in the IXth, and again in the XIVth dynasty, but little effect was made upon the national art and character. The invaders were apparently less civilised than the

Egyptians, and had no knowledge to impart to them. The upper classes of the Egyptians doubtless fled southward before the invaders, and only those whose property fixed them to the soil were likely to stay under a hated oppression. Thus very little effect appears on the Egyptian civilisation; the works of the XIth and the XVIIth or of the XIIth and the XVIIIth dynasties, when compared, are barely distinguishable. Clearly no external influence acted on the art or ways of the Egyptians with any obvious result. Not only would the skilled classes flee, but the boundary of the races would be always a fighting frontier where the arts would not be practised.

When we come to the invasion of Syria by the Egyptians, very different causes are at work. This was not a racial invasion by a body of settlers, who hold together and form a rival community to the natives, with a repellent attitude. On the contrary, it was a far-reaching raid of a body of troops passing through many different tribes, and not displacing any of them, but plundering each in turn. Thus the Syrian and the Egyptian were brought into close personal contact.

Then at this period the civilisation of Syria was equal or superior to that of Egypt. No coats of mail appear among the Egyptians in this age, but they took 200 suits of armour at the sack of Megiddo (23rd year Tahutmes III.), and soon after such coats of scale armour commonly appear in groups of valuables sculptured in the tombs. No gilded chariots appear in Egypt, except later than this, and for royalty; but we read of two gold-plated chariots in the sack of Megiddo (yr. XXIII), 10 with gold and silver (yr. XXIV), 19 chariots inlaid with silver (tribute yr. XXXI), chariots adorned with gold, silver, and colours (yr. XXXIV), 20 chariots inlaid with gold and silver (yr. XXXV), and nine more (yr. XXXVIII). Here was luxury far beyond that of the Egyptians, and technical work which could teach them, rather than be taught. In the rich wealth of gold and silver vases, which were greatly prized by the Egyptians, we see also the sign of a people who were their equals, if not their superiors, in taste and skill.

In what way, then, did this civilisation come in contact with Egypt? In the most thorough way possible. No sufficient notice has ever been taken of the great number of captives brought into Egypt. In the biography of Aahmes, of the earlier reigns of this dynasty, we read that he alone had 6 male captives and 7 females, and had 8 others given him from the general booty, making 21 captives taken into the household and estate of one officer alone. In the later biography of Amen·em·heb, under Tahutmes III., we read of his taking as many as 31 or more captives. These were no exceptional instances. Whenever the troops went out, they seem to have usually made many captures: "to every man a damsel or two," like Sisera's custom. We have a general view of the results in the summary of each year's tribute and plunder. In eleven campaigns, of which the details remain, there are 7548 captives and slaves, male and female, mentioned, beside some lost numbers, probably about 8000 in all; and about 400 of these are specified as belonging to the upper classes. And beside this, a tribute of girls appears to have been exacted in the tranquil age of the later reigns.

When we consider whom the Egyptians would select as tribute, it is obvious that they would get the most valuable labourers that they could. In the sack of Megiddo it is specified that the king "sent the foreign workmen with the tribute southwards." The artist of the chief of Tunep is figured as following his captive lord, holding a vase (Fig. 52). And the keenness with which the Egyptians record all the beautiful and luxurious products of the Syrians, shows that the workmen would probably be more in demand than other kinds of slave-tribute. Beside the men who would bring in their arts and skill, large numbers of the captives appear to have been women. We know, in the time of Amenhotep III. and IV., that even the kings married Syrian princesses; and as early as the second campaign of Tahutmes III., the daughter of a chief was yielded to him as tribute. We cannot doubt, then, that the female slaves were taken as wives and concubines by the Egyptians, as also was the Jewish custom. The striking change in the physiognomy and ideal type of the upper classes in the latter part of the XVIIIth dynasty points to a strong foreign infusion. In place of the bold, active faces of earlier times, there is a peculiar sweetness and delicacy; a gentle smile and a small, gracefully-curved nose are characteristic of the upper classes in the time of Amenhotep III. Such features we know to have been found in Syria, as in Thyi, and the Yanuan captive of later time. Being of such a winning type, it is no wonder that they were taken into the Egyptian families.

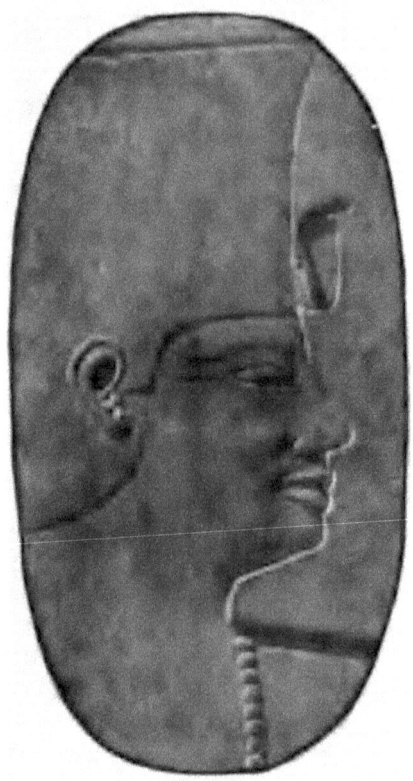

FIG. 92.—Usertesen I., XIIth dynasty. Older Egyptian type.

The condition, then, was that thousands of Syrians, selected probably for their value in either skill or beauty, were brought into Egypt largely as the property of the upper classes, and therefore settled down in their households and domains. Every Syrian workman would be employed on the most valuable work that he could do, as their products were so much appreciated by the Egyptians. Every Syrian mother would teach her children somewhat of her own tongue and her own thoughts. And this was going on among the ruling classes, and imbuing them year by year with the ideas, tastes, and language of a civilisation equal to their own. No wonder that, after a few generations, we find Semitic words, idioms, and thoughts transfused throughout the Egyptian literature. No nation could be proof against such influences.

That large numbers of persons were engaged in unremunerative work in Egypt, and that the economic state of the land had greatly changed, is shown by the requisition for corn. In early days buying corn in Egypt was a matter of course; to the Roman, Egypt was the granary of the empire; in our days the annual millions of the debt are paid for by lines of ships laden with beans and cotton. Egypt has always been an exporting country, except during this XVIIIth dynasty, when it seems to have required imports. From Megiddo the Egyptians carried off 150,000 bushels of corn in one year, beside all that they consumed. And every year large tributes of harvest came in both from Syria and from Nubia. The only possible meaning of this is that a large part of the population was employed on work that did not produce food. For if even half the people were agriculturalists, they would easily sustain the inhabitants without needing imported food.

FIG. 93.—Head of Zey, XVIIIth dynasty. New Egypto-Syrian type.

This intimate connection with Syrian craftsmen and Syrian women altered the nature of Egyptian taste and feelings more profoundly than any influence since the foundation of the monarchy. In language, as is well known, Egypt became Semiticised. In writing, the old thick hieratic, which hardly changed from the earliest examples of the Vth dynasty down to Amenhotep I., suddenly took an entirely different character—thin, flowing, and flourishing. In statuary the ideal type was quite new, and the small-featured and fascinatingly

FIG. 94.—Head of a servant of Khaemhat, XVIIIth dynasty.

graceful faces—such as that of Ptahmes II. in the Florence Museum, and of Zay in the Ghizeh Museum— show that there was an entirely new element in the people. In flat relief a new taste appears, there is far more expression of emotion: the old Egyptian dealt with incident, the new Egyptian with emotions, the flowing postures of the bewitching dance, the girl who has had a drink of wine and is going off on tiptoe, tossing her head back and holding up her hands in delight (G. Mus., V.G. 171), the children following a funeral, and the neglected baby which one has put down clamouring to be taken up again (Neferhotep tomb)—in all these the artist has given himself away in quite a new fashion. And in the small objects and manufac-

Fig. 95.—Head of a priestess, XVIIIth dynasty.

tures as great a change appears; types which were unaltered from the XIIth dynasty until Hatshepsut, vanish entirely, and new designs take their place. In the patterns of beads, in the mode of glazing, in the forms of dress, in the hairdressing, in the designs of furniture, and in the painting of the tombs, the new Egyptian left aside entirely the continuous traditions of his forefathers. Having once broken the old and gradually developing system of ages, dazzled with the taste for incongruous novelties, the Egyptian found it impossible to regain the old life; and thus he passed feverishly from change to change, from worse to worse, until only archaistic revival was possible if an improvement was attempted, and finally all the arts became hopelessly degraded in the Greek period.

XVIII. 7. AA·KHEPERU·RA

AMENHOTEP II.
NETER·HEQ·AN

about 1449–1423 B.C.

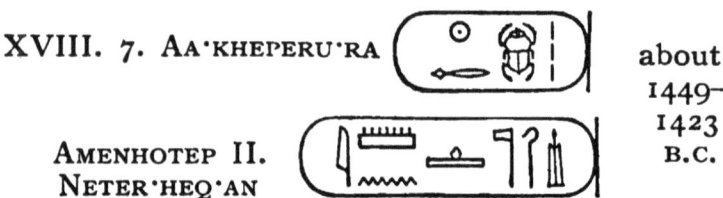

Tell el Hesy	Jar stamp	(B.M.C. 89).
Bubastis	Scenes of offering	(N.B. 31, xxxv.).
Turra	Stele of 4th year	(V.P. iii. 94).
Nubt	Blue glazed uas	(S. Kens. Mus.).
Medamot	Pillar and lintel	(C.N. ii. 291 ; Rec. vii. 129).
Karnak	Wall and halls, between S. pylons, X–XI.	(C.N. ii. 180 ; M.K. 12).
	Scene with king, front pylon IX.	(C.N. ii. 183 ; L.D. iii. 61).
	Red granite stele	(C.N. ii. 185).
	Blocks re-used, before sanctuary	(C.N. ii. 140–4 ; M.K. v.).
,,	Re-erected columns by obelisks	(M.K. 29).
Qurneh	Temple N. of Ramesseum	(L.D. iii. 62).
Erment	Block	(B. Rs. 201).
,,	Stele of conquest, G. Mus.	(A.Z. iv. 33 ; V.G. 158).
Silsileh	Name	(B.E. 258).
Elephantine	Block	(M.I. i. 115).
,,	Obelisk ?	(Rev. A. i. ii. 730).
Aswan	Khaemuas graffito	{ (M.I. i. 90, 87). (M.D. 70, 5).
Sehel	Pa·nehy·amen graffito	(M.I. i. 95, 148).
Bigeh	Statue	(C.N. 160 ; L.D. iii. 63 c).
Kalabsheh	Pronaos	(C.M. 54 bis, 1).

AMENHOTEP II

Ibrim	Painted rock shrine	(C.M. 39). (L.D. iii. 63 d).
Amadeh	Temple finishing	(L.D. iii. 65 a–c).
Halfa, Wady	Brick temple, sandstone columns	(C.M. 2, 7).
Kummeh	Temple scenes	(L.D. iii. 64–67).
Semneh	Name in temple	(My. E. 545)
Sai	Remains of temple	(L.L. 237).
Napata	Temple mentioned	(L.D. iii. 65 a).

Statues—

Before pylon IX.	Karnak	(B.E. 147).
Granite	Bigeh	(C.N. 160).
Kneeling	Beni Naga	(L.D. iii. 70 a–d).
Large kneeling	Turin	(L.T. 1375).
Headless, kneeling	P. Mus.	(S. h. 11).
Body of seated	Karnak	(Ms. G. 426).
Headless, seated	Qurneh temple	(G. Mus.).

Foundation deposits	Qurneh temple.	
Ushabtis	Qurneh (dealers).	
Stele, king adoring Amen	Luxor	(W.G. 376).
Vase, foundation of temple	Qurneh	(Rec. xvi. 30).
Papyrus, 5th year	Paris	(Pap. Rollin, p. 23).
Leather roll, 5th year		(A.Z. xii. 86).
Mummy wrappings of Tahutmes III.		(A.Z. xx. 132).
Toilet box, Rhind Coll., Edinburgh.		
Rings and scarabs : with mother		(M.A. ii. 40 n).
Queen—TA·AA		(A.Z. xxxi. 29).
Sons—Tahutmes IV., and 5 or 7 others		(L.D. iii. 69 a).

As no monuments are dated above the fifth year, it was thought that this reign must have been short, and not have occupied 25 years 10 months, as stated by Manetho. But the Lateran obelisk mentions that it was set up in this reign 35 years after it was abandoned, presumably at the death of Tahutmes III., who ordered it ; and as Tahutmes IV., who finished it, reigned 9 years 8 months, it shows that Amenhotep II. must have reigned over 25 years and 4 months. In short, the obelisk pretty well guarantees all but six months of the two reigns of Amenhotep II. and Tahutmes IV., as stated in Manetho, and must have been set up only just before the death of the latter king. And we see below that the reigns are too short, rather than too long, for the genealogy. Lately the absolute proof of the length of reign has been found on a wine jar dated in the 26th year of Amenhotep II., thus agreeing with Manetho.

It appears that Amenhotep II. cannot have been of mature age at his father's death; he is shown seated on his nurse's knee (L.D. iii. 62 c), and in the tomb of Ra at Qurneh, seated with his mother behind him (L.D. iii. 62 b); again in the great tomb with new year gifts (L.D. iii. 63), though the female figure behind the king is defaced, yet among the statues represented are many of the king, one of his mother, but none of any wife; and also on a scarab found at Abydos his name is side by side with that of the "royal mother Meryt-ra" (M.A. ii. 40 n). Yet he must have been grown up, as in his third year he describes his conquests in Asia on the stele at Amadeh (L.D. iii. 65 a). Hence we may probably assign the age of 18 to him on his accession without erring far on either side. This implies that he was born when his father was about 51; and though it might seem very strange that no older son of the king was preferred, yet there are other cases of such choice. This selection of younger sons as successors is explained once in a way by the record of the succession of Solomon; probably similar influences determined the affairs of the royal harīm in Egypt.

FIG. 96.—Amenhotep II. and his nurse.

Soon after his accession, the young king went forth with his father's veterans to make a customary raid on Asia, and establish his renown. His personal exploits, though of no effect on the war, are chronicled at Thebes. The date of the affair is lost, but it must have been in the first and second years of his reign, because early in the third year a tablet was erected at Amadeh recording the victories. The record at Karnak begins by saying that the king went to some land, as to the city of Shemesh-atuma (in south Galilee): "His Majesty there had success, His Majesty himself there made captives, for behold he was as a terrible lion that puts to flight the country of . . . nen . . . sakhu is his name. Account of that which His Majesty himself took in this day. Living prisoners Satiu 18, oxen 19.

"The 26th day of Pakhons (1st year) passed His Majesty over the arm of water of Arseth (? Harosheth on the Kishon, Arseth LXX.) in this day. His Majesty passed over charging as the valour of Mentu of Thebes. His Majesty turned his head to examine the horizon (shading his eyes with his hand); behold His Majesty saw some Satiu coming on horses, then His Majesty went to attack. Behold His Majesty was armed with his weapons, and His Majesty fought like Set in his hour. They gave way when His Majesty looked at one of them, and they fled. His Majesty took all their goods himself, with his spear . . . and he took the Sati at the frontier, and spoiled him of all his arms. His Majesty returned in joy, his father Amen had given to him his prey. Account of what His Majesty took this day . . . arms of war, 4? bows, a quiver full of arrows with its leather band, and the goods.

"The 10th of Hathor (in 2nd year, nearly six months later) His Majesty went in peace this day to the town of Niy; behold the Satiu of this town, men and women, were on the walls to adore His Majesty . . . " (C.N. ii. 185; A.Z. xvii. 55, xxvii. 39; S.B.A. xi. 422). This expedition was of some importance to establish the power of the new reign; it does not, however, seem to have been a re-conquest, as were so many expeditions, but rather a promenade as far as the Euphratean frontier, to check what disaffection existed, and to assert the Egyptian power over the vassals.

The record of the triumphal return to Egypt remains on a great stele in the temple of Amadeh, where he held a festival of the laying of the foundation stone of the temple on the 15th of Epiphi in the third year, "after he had returned from the land of the Upper Ruten, when he had conquered all the enemies of Egypt in his first campaign.

"His Majesty returned in joy of heart to his father Amen; his hand had struck down the seven chiefs with

FIG. 97.—Head of Amenhotep II. Karnak.

his mace himself, which were of the territory of Takhsi (near Aleppo). They were hung up by the feet on the front of the bark of His Majesty, which was named 'Amenhotep establishes the two lands.' The six of these enemies were hung in front of the walls of Thebes, and the hands (of the slain) in the same manner. Then was brought up the river the other enemy to Nubia, and was hung on the wall of the town of Napata, to show forth for all time the victories of the king among all people of the negro land, inasmuch as he had taken possession of the nations of the south, and had bound the nations of the north and the ends of the whole extent of the earth on which the sun rises and sets, without finding any opposition, according to the command of his father Amen·ra of Thebes."

Though there are no further records of his wars, we see in the great tomb 13 at Qurneh that he claims as captive countries nearly all that his father had held: the south land, the Sekhet Am (Oases), the north land, the Petau, Tahenu (Libyans), Anu (Nubians), Mentiu Satet (Semites), Naharina (around Aleppo), Keftu (Phœnicians), Mennus (Mallus?), and the Upper Ruten (or hill country of Palestine), are all ranged around the base of his throne.

Of the remainder of his reign we know nothing; twenty years of peaceful administration appear to have glided by, intimating that the Egyptian yoke was not too heavily pressed upon Asia.

The public monuments of this reign are of some interest. In Syria, at Tell el Hesy, a jar handle stamped for "the palace of Ra·aa·khepru" was found (B.M.C. 89). In the Delta, work was begun again at Bubastis, where two scenes in a building (which was restored by Sety I.) show Amenhotep offering to Amen (N.B. 31 xxxv.). At the Turra quarries is a large tablet remarkable for the variety of gods to whom the king offers. It is dated in the fourth year, and shows Amenhotep adoring Amen, Horus, Sebek, Up·uat, Hathor of Aphroditopolis, Bast, Ptah, Osiris, Khentikheti, Asthareth, Sekhet, Hathor of Amu, and Uazi. These appear to be in geographical order from Thebes to the western Delta, so that Khentikheti and Asthareth come as Upper Delta deities. The tablet was put up by Min, who was a royal scribe, and "filled the heart of the king in executing his monuments, overseer of the works in all the temples of the north and south"; he also went with the expeditions, and erected the boundary tablets of the empire at Naharina (North Syria) and in Kary (South Ethiopia). The occasion for this tablet appears to have been on reopening the quarries of Turra for some public building (V.P. iii. 94).

In the Delta there is but an uncertain trace of this king in the three much-usurped granite columns found at Alexandria; though probably from the Delta, there is no certainty about them (Rec. vii. 177). In Middle Egypt no remains of the reign have been recorded, except four scarabs at Gurob (P.K. xxiii.; P.I. xxiii.). At Nubt, opposite Koptos, an immense uas of blue glaze was found in the temple (S. Kens. Mus.). At Medamot, near Karnak, a pillar of red granite was seen (C.N. ii. 291), and a lintel also of red granite (Rec. vii. 129).

At Karnak some small works were undertaken. The eastern wall joining the two southernmost pylons (X.–XI.) was built, and the building of unusual type which stands in the middle of this wall. As it is neither temple nor palace, it has been suggested that this was a guard hall, or a resting-place of processions; or it might have been an audience hall. The form is that of a colonnade front facing north-west, and behind it a great court of twenty pillars, flanked on either side by three chambers connected together.

On the front of the pylon of Tahutmes I. (No. IX.) Amenhotep has inserted two scenes of his slaying his foes (L.D. iii. 61; C.N. ii. 183). Several blocks with his name were re-used by Sety II. in reconstructing the buildings before the granite sanctuary; these are seen on the south side of the court with lotus pillars (C.N. ii. 140, 144), and in chamber I. (M.K. v.). He also re-erected the columns in the southern half of the hall containing Hatshepsut's obelisks (M.K. 29). Nothing strikes us as more extraordinary than the condition of injury and confusion in which the most important buildings of Egypt seem to have remained. The most imposing works stood amidst half ruined and unfinished halls for a whole reign; other parts were walled off, to hide offensive memorials; other structures were either incomplete or half ruined. This rage for alteration culminates under Ramessu II., with results fatal for history.

At Qurneh the funeral temple of the king stood next north of the Ramesseum. It was rearranged by Amenhotep III. for his daughter Sitamen. A statue and foundation deposits were found on the site. Until this latter temple was built, there was a regular chronological series of buildings from north to south; Amenhotep's temple was near the end of Drah abul Negga, Tahutmes I. and II. built at Deir el Bahri. Tahutmes III., Amenhotep II., Tahutmes IV., and Amenhotep III. all follow in regular series southwards to the Kom el Hettan.

At Erment a block was noticed by Brugsch (Reisab. 201), and a large stele containing a copy of the inscription of the first half of the Amadeh tablet was found here, and is now at Vienna (A.Z. iv. 33). At Silsileh the king's name occurs by the tomb of Amatu (B.E. 258). A block at Elephantine shows that here again the king had been building or repairing temples (M.I. i. 115). An obelisk described by Prisse (Rev. Arch. 1 ser. ii. 2, 730) perhaps came from there also. Near Aswan are two graffiti of Kha·em·uas (L.D. iii. 63 b; M.I. i. 90, 87), and another adoration of the king with the name lost (M.I. i. 91, 103); while at Sehel is a graffito of Pa·nehy·amen adoring the name of Amenhotep II., set on a stand (M.I. i. 95, 148). On the island of Bigeh, by Philæ, is a granite colossus of a mummified form like Ptah (C.N. 160).

In Nubia, work was continued actively in this reign. At Kalabsheh, on the pronaos, is a scene of the king offering to Min and to the Nubian god Merutru-hor-ra (C.M. 54 *bis*, 1). At Ibrim is a painted rock shrine, showing Amenhotep enthroned in a pavilion, a feather-bearer before him and fan-bearer behind; at the back of the pavilion is Sati; before it comes a procession of men leading captive lions, greyhounds, and wolves. The inscription can still be read, naming 113 live wolves (C.N. i. 84; C.M. 39). Another scene here shows the king offering to Khnum, Sati, Anuke, Sopd, Hathor, and Nekheb (L.D. iii. 63 d).

At Amadeh he appears to have finished the temple sculptures which were in progress at the death of his father; and a short co-regency is indicated by two doorways which have the cartouches of Tahutmes III. and Amenhotep II. arranged evidently at the same time (L.D. iii. 65 b, c); while elsewhere the latter appears alone (d, e). The work was continued here till the 3rd year, at least, when the great historical tablet was engraved.

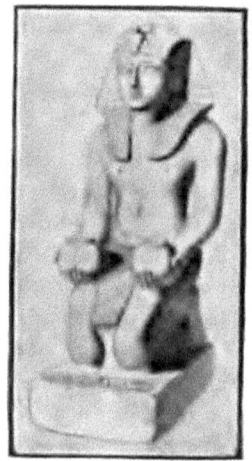 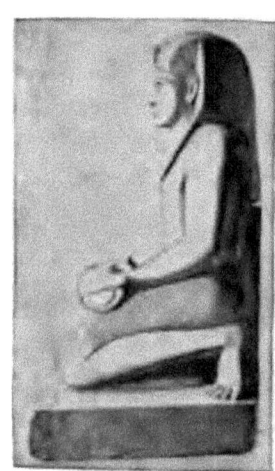

FIG. 98.—Kneeling statue of Amenhotep II. Berlin.

At Wady Halfa the brick temple contained pillars of this king (C.M. 2, 7). At Kummeh the sculptures were also in progress at the death of Tahutmes III., whose name appears on the dividing bands, while the scenes are of Amenhotep II. offering to Khnum and Usertesen III. (L.D. iii. 64 b, 66). Two great doorways are of Amenhotep II. (L.D. iii. 67). At Semneh his name appears in the temple (My. E. 545). At the island of Sai are remains of a temple of this time (L.L. 237). And the temple of Napata in Ethiopia is named on the Amadeh inscription as the place of execution of one of the Syrian princes.

The statues of Amenhotep II. are less common than those of his father. A battered colossus in white limestone stands in front of pylon IX. at Karnak; a very fine torso, with the nose and chin struck off, is also from Karnak (G. Mus.); and the mummiform colossus at Bigeh is in red granite. The seated Osiride statue of grey granite was found in his temple at Qurneh; unfortunately the head is lost (G. Mus.). There are three kneeling statues holding a globular vase of offering in each hand; one at Turin (L.T. 1375), and smaller ones at Paris (Cat. sal. hist., p. 11), and from Beni Naga, at Berlin (L.D. iii. 70). This attitude was apparently introduced for statuary by this king, as two other such images of him are figured in a tomb at Qurneh (L.D. iii. 63, 64).

A stele with the king adoring Amen was in the "French House" at Luxor (W.G. 376). An alabaster vase, from a foundation deposit of the "temple of the west" at Thebes, is in Paris (Rec. xvi. 30). A papyrus, dated in the 5th year, on the 19th of Phamenoth, contains praises of Amenhotep II., saying that he was grown and instructed by the deities Shay and Renent (Pap. Rollin, 15, p. 23). The leather roll at Berlin concerning Usertesen founding the temple of Heliopolis is probably of this reign, and not of Amenhotep IV. (A.Z. xii. 86). On the mummy wrappings of Tahutmes III. is inscribed that "Amenhotep made his monuments of his father, Men·kheper·ra," referring to his embalming. A part of a beautiful toilet box of ebony and ivory bears the cartouches of this king: it was found by Rhind at Thebes (Edinburgh Museum).

The scarabs and amulets of this reign show a new departure. Oval plaques, flat on both sides, and bearing figures, came much into use in this and the next reign, but disappear afterwards; they were specially used for rings, in order to lie flat on the finger. Their disappearance is due to the increase of rings made all in one piece under Amenhotep III. Scroll work on the old pattern reappears at this time (P.Sc. 1097), and the base imitation of it by a row of concentric circles. Another, and characteristic, device was that of two, four, or six uraei, arranged in pairs around the cartouche or an emblem. Sentences also come more into use on scarabs, such as "Amenhotep II., born at Memphis," "setting up obelisks in the house

FIG. 99.—Scarab with Amenhotep as a sphinx, hawk-headed, trampling on a captive. F.P. Coll.

FIG. 100.—Scarab with six uraei. Brit. Mus.

FIG. 101.—Scarab. "Aa·kheperu·ra, born at Men'nefer" (Memphis). F.P. Coll.

of Amen." "The good god, lion over Egypt, lord of might, giving life like the sun;" "lord of glories in the house of Amen," etc. The reference to his birth is of interest, as showing that the court probably resided at Memphis some time in his father's reign.

The private monuments of this age are of great beauty and importance, often preserving records of public affairs in which the various officials were engaged, and particularly of the foreign tributes which they received for the king. The principal private works are as follow:—

Tomb of RA, husband of the king's nurse, high priest of Amen and of Tahutmes III.: contains a fine scene of the king and his mother Merytra, and also of the king on his nurse's lap (L.D. iii. 62). Many fine vases are shown in this tomb (P.A. 102). Qurneh.

Tomb of HOREMHEB, a high official, with scenes of recruiting, receiving tribute, etc.; and recording his devotion to Tahutmes III., to his son Amenhotep II., to his son Tahutmes IV., and to his son Amenhotep III. (M.A.F. v. 432). Qurneh.

Tomb of PA·SAR, a follower of the king in all lands (B.E. 193). Qurneh.

Tomb of AMEN·EM·HEB, with fine painting and important historical inscription of his wars, quoted under the previous reign (M.A.F.). Qurneh.

Tomb of SEN·NEFER and his sister Meryt (B.E.): he was "the noble of the south city," *i.e.* Thebes; and a

FIG. 102.—Glass and stone vases. Tomb of Ra.

statue of him seated was found at Nubt (F. P. Coll.). A stele of a Sen·nefer, perhaps the same, adoring Amenhotep I., Nefertari, Tahutmes I. and III., Sa·paar, and Amenhotep II., is in Turin (L.T. 1455; Champ. Figeac Eg. Anc. pl. 67). Qurneh.

Tomb of AMEN·EM·HAT at Silsileh (S.B.A. xii. 96).

Tomb of Amen·ken (Qurneh), showing the most splendid drawings of a series of new year presents. Amenhotep

II. is seated; with his wife or mother behind him, now destroyed. Before him is a splendid tree of goldwork of conventional forms (which were afterwards developed into the sacred tree of Assyria), and with monkeys climbing about it. A chariot of silver and gold and images of carved work in ebony are mentioned. Then come statues of Amenhotep II. and his *ka*, of Tahutmes I. and his *ka* (which are dark), eight of Amenhotep II., and one of Hatshepset Merytra. Then seven sphinxes of the king, two kneeling statues holding altars, and two kneeling statues with vases, all of the king. Then come rows of collars of jewellery, of shields, quivers, coats of scale armour, daggers, axes, and a gazelle, an oryx, and an ibex, on stands. The materials of the following objects are specified: 330 leather quivers, 680 leather shields, ebony throw-sticks with gold ends and silver handles, 220 whips of chased gold and ebony, 2 pelican heads of bronze, 140 bronze daggers, 360 falchions of bronze, a mirror of carved ebony, variegated glass vases, a throne, feather fans, etc. (L.D. iii. 63 a, 64 a). (See Additional Notes.)

Other private remains are a stele of Nebua at Abydos (M.A. ii. 33 a); a kneeling statue of Anher, a priest of Anher at Abydos (M.A. 372); a group of Kha·em·uas and his wife in the Vatican (W.G. 376); probably the same man whose graffiti occur at Sehel; stele of Nefer·hebt·f, second prophet of Amenhotep II. (B. Mus.), and cones of his (M.A.F. viii. 277, 55); and a piece of a granite statue of a general of Amenhotep (F. Mus., S. Cat. F. 1504).

The queen of Amenhotep II., Ta·āa, is recorded on a double statue of her and her son Tahutmes IV. She is called "royal mother and wife," showing her to be his mother (A.Z. xxxi. 29). She could not have been his wife, as the mother of Amenhotep III. is known to have been Mut·em·ua, so it is impossible that another "royal mother" could have been wife of Tahutmes IV. This is important, as otherwise, from her figure in the tomb of Thenuna (C.N. 481) being only entitled royal wife, along with Tahutmes IV., it was naturally

PRIVATE MONUMENTS

supposed that she was the wife of him, and not of his father, Amenhotep II., as was really the case. Her son Tahutmes IV. is stated to be son of Amenhotep II. in the tomb of Hor·em·heb (M.A.F. v. 434). A princess, Amen·em·apt, is shown on the knee of Horemheb in his tomb; but as he lived through four reigns, we cannot settle her position (M.A.F. v. 434). Probably there were five or seven other sons of Amenhotep II.; for in the tomb of the tutor of Tahutmes IV., Hek·er·neheh (L.D. iii. 69 a), where Tahutmes is a boy on the tutor's knee, there are several other king's sons represented; unhappily all their names have been erased, and from the absence of any other mention of them, it would seem as if their royal brother was unkind to their memory, if not to themselves.

XVIII. 8. MEN·KHEPRU·RA

TAHUTMES IV.
KHA·KHAU

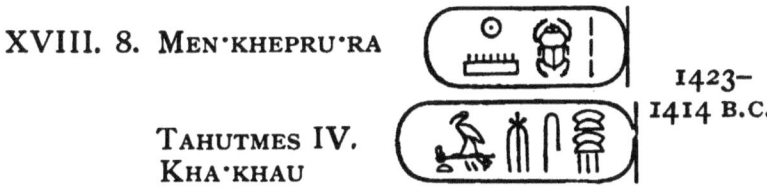

1423–1414 B.C.

Sarbut el Khadem		(My. E. 351).
Alexandria	Columns	(Rec. vii. 178).
Gizeh	Stele of sphinx	(L.D. iii. 68).
Abydos	Statue	(M.A. 350).
Dendera	Fragment	(D.D. iii. b).
Karnak	Scene on pylon IV.	(M.K. 28).
,,	List on wall round obelisk	(M.K. xxxiii.).
,,	Colossus before pylon	(W.G. 378).
Qurneh	Temple S. of Ramesseum.	
Luxor	Scene in birth-hall	(M.A.F. xv. 204).
El Kab	Building of small temple	(L.D. iii. 80 b).
Elephantine	Fragments	(M.I. i. 115).
Konosso	Steles	(L.D. iii. 69 e; M.I. i. 66, 68, 69, 73).
Sehel	Stele	(M.I. i. 90).
Amadeh	In temple	(C.M. 44, 45, 59; L.D. iii. 69 f–i).

Scarabs, rings, uza eyes, etc.

Queens—MUT·EM·UA	Luxor	(M.A.F. xv. 63–7).
	Bark, B. Mus.	(A.B. 34).
Arat?	Konosso	(L.D. iii. 69 e).
Sons—Tahutmes	Scarab	(W.G. 378).
Amenhotep III.	Tomb	(M.A.F. v. 432).

But few public monuments refer to the history of this reign. The first reference to the new king is on a great tablet which he erected between the paws of the Sphinx at Gizeh. He there relates an adventure of his youth. After the usual titles and religious formalities, we read: "He once went afield, pleasing his countenance, on the desert of the Memphite nome, upon its

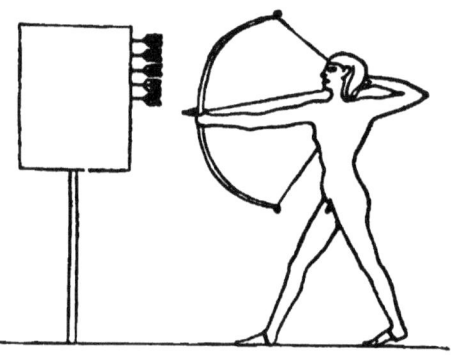

FIG. 103.—Boy shooting at a target.

borders north and south, for shooting at a target with copper (arrows). And he hunted the lions and the gazelles of the desert, riding in his chariot, his horses swifter than the wind, with two of his followers, and no man knew of them.

"Once came an hour of giving rest to his followers, . . . then the sphinx of Khepra, great and exalted, rested in this place, great of spirits, most highly revered, for to him was given the temples of Memphis and of every town upon both sides. Their hands adored his presence with great offerings for his *ka*. One of these times it came to pass a journey was made by the king's son Tahutmes, journeying upon the time of noon. A rest he made in the shadow of this god, sleep fell upon him, dreaming in slumber in the moment when the sun was overhead. Found he the majesty of this noble god, talking to him by his mouth, speaking like the talk of a father to his son, saying, 'Look thou at me! Behold thou me! my son Tahutmes, I am thy father, Hor·em·akht, Khepra, Ra, and Tum, giving to thee the kingdom. On thee shall be placed its white crown and its red crown, on the throne of Seb the heir. There is given to thee the land in its length and its breadth, which is lightened by the bright eye of the universal lord. Provision is before thee in the two lands, and the great gifts of all foreign lands, and the duration of a great space of years. My face is towards thee, my heart is towards thee. . . . The sand of the desert on which I am reaches to me, spoiling me; perform thou that which is in my heart, for I know that thou art my son who reverences me; draw near, and behold I am with thee.'" The rest of the tablet is nearly all destroyed by the scaling of the surface, and only fragments remain, one of which names king Khafra.

Here we see how the young prince spent his youth in hunting and field sports, up in the desert with a couple of followers, lost to the sight of man; this account, and that of the noonday rest in the shadow, are most lifelike phrases to anyone who knows desert wandering.

In the first year of his reign, then, the king ordered this tablet to be set up, in memory of his dream and his clearing of the Sphinx from sand. No great respect was shown for the work of Khafra, as the block taken for the inscription was a granite lintel stolen from the temple of Khafra close by. And although the name of Khafra occurs in this inscription, yet, owing to the unfortunately broken state of it, there is nothing to show whether the Sphinx was attributed to Khafra, whether it was said to be by the side of the temple of Khafra, or in what way the connection with Khafra is involved.

From a stele of Amenhotep, a follower of the king, we learn of his campaigns in the north in Naharina, and in the south to Kari (B. Mus., S.I. 93). And his first campaign was against . . . *a* (probably Naharina), as inscribed on the east face of the wall built around the obelisk of Hatshepsut (M.K. 33). Another fragment mentions a campaign against the Kheta (B.H. 413).

The VIth year is named in the tomb of Duy (C.N. 502).

In the VIIth year, on Phamenoth 8, is dated a rock-

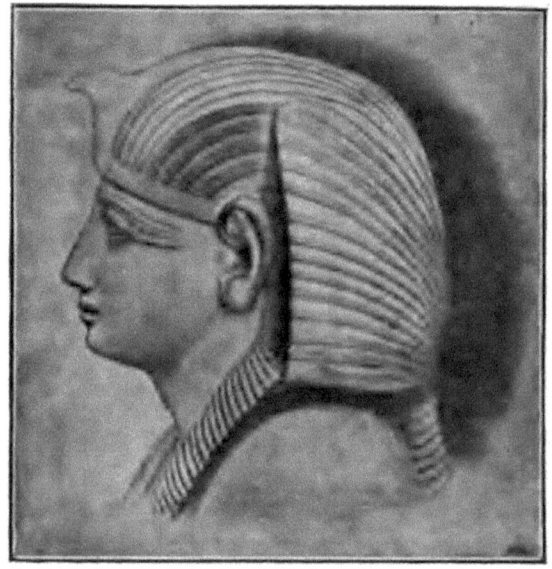

FIG. 104.—Head of Tahutmes IV.

cut stele at Konosso, with a queen standing behind the king, referring to his smiting the Nubians.

In the VIIIth year is dated a long stele at Konosso, on Phamenoth 2, mentioning his smiting Wawat (M.I. i. 66).

It appears, then, that the earlier years of his reign were occupied with asserting his power in Syria, and in the later years Nubia occupied his attention. He died after reigning 9 years and 8 months, according to Manetho.

Turning now to the details of his monuments. He

continued the work at the Sinaitic mines, where his name is found at Sarbut el Khadem (My. E. 351). The columns found at Alexandria (Rec. vii. 178), now at Vienna, may have come from some work in the Delta.

Gizeh was then a deserted group of pyramids and tombs in the desert, as it is now; and the action of the king in clearing the Sphinx must have made a revival of attention to the region. The tablet was, however, merely taken from the neighbouring temple, and no great works were ordered for this business. It is remarkable to see how completely the old tied lotus flowers of the IVth dynasty had dropped out of knowledge by this time; their nature was forgotten, and a senseless imitation of them was made, copied from the old work which was to be seen in this neighbourhood.

FIG. 105.—Original group of tied lotus flowers.

FIG. 106.—Modification of group. Tahutmes IV.

At Abydos a torso of a statue in white silicious limestone was found, with the name on the girdle (M.A. 350). At Dendera a fragment of his work remains (D.D. iii. b).

Karnak was not honoured by any building of this king, but he engraved scenes on a gateway added to the entrance of pylon IV. The south jamb and the lintel has gone; but on the north jamb, on its west and north sides, are his inscriptions. Mariette, however, from the workmanship, regards this part as having been re-engraved by Shabaka (M.K. p. 28; L.D. iii. 69 d). On the east face of the wall which Tahutmes III. had built up around Hatshepsut's obelisk, to hide her inscription, this king added a list of donations to Amen, on his return from his first campaign; and he mentions statues of his grandfather and himself. He also set up a colossus of himself before the pylon of Tahutmes I. (W.G. 378). At Qurneh was the funeral temple, now destroyed, of which fragments of sculpture and part of a colossal head were found.

At Luxor, though Mut·em·ua the queen often appears in connection with the infancy of her great son, yet the king is not shown, as the paternity of Amenhotep III. is ascribed directly to the god Amen (M.A.F. xv. fig. 203–4).

At El Kab the small temple was begun by this king, though finished by his son, who says: "Behold this was made by the majesty the king Maa·neb·ra, beautifying monuments of his father the good god Men·khepru·ra, named everlasting and eternal" (L.D. iii. 80 b).

At Elephantine his name appears on some fragments of the temples (M.I. i. 115). At Konosso are four memorials of this reign; the king appears smiting the negroes before the gods of Nubia, Dedun and He, while behind him stands a queen, who was royal daughter, sister, and wife (L.D. iii. 69 b); her name is written with the uraeus on *neb*, and is read Ar·at; but as this is the only trace of her existence, it may be that this is merely an idiogram for the "goddess queen," and may refer to Mut·em·ua. Beside this, there is a long inscription of forty lines, of which the first twenty-three are published (M.I. i. 66); another inscription, unpublished (*l.c.* 68); a double cartouche (*l.c.* 69); and a scene of Khnum and Min, carved by the divine father Ha·ankh·f·, and the *suten rekh* Neb·ankh (*l.c.* 73). At Sehel is another graffito of the king's son Mes (*l.c.* 84).

At Amadeh, Tahutmes IV. worked considerably (C.N. i. 96–100); the architraves bear his inscriptions (L.D. iii. 69 f): other inscriptions and a scene of his are also published (69 g, h, i), and a figure of the king (C.M. 45, 6).

Of small remains there are many scarabs, rings, etc.

The most important is one with the figure of his son, Prince Tahutmes (Tyszkiewicz Coll., W.G. 378); others bear the usual adulation of this age, "rich in glories,"

FIG. 107.—Scarab of Tahutmes IV., "mighty in glories." F.P. Coll.

FIG. 108.—Scarab of Tahutmes IV., "establishing monuments." F.P. Coll.

FIG. 109. — Green glaze ring, Tahutmes IV. F.P. Coll.

"the glory of all lands," and "establishing monuments." A green glazed pottery ring of his is the earliest such ring known.

The private works of this reign are finer than the public remains. The principal tombs are those of—

Thenuna, fan-bearer, with figures of the king and of his mother Ta·āa (C.N. 480–1, 829). Qurneh.

Amenhotep and his wife Roy, with designs of a sculptor chiselling a royal statue, and the king's name by a second statue; also scribes weighing gold, and many figures of collars, boxes, vases, etc. (C.N. 480; C.M. cliv. 3; cxci.). Qurneh.

Zanuni, with scenes of conscription, and of various soldiers, some bearing square banners with designs of wrestlers, and of the king's name with titles, such as "lord of his might," and "lord of strength" (C.N. 484; C.M. clvii.). He states that he took a "census of the land to its bounds before His Majesty, an inspection of all things, soldiers, priests, royal serfs, artisans of all the country, and of all cattle, all fowls, and all small cattle, by the scribe of troops, loved of His Majesty, Zanuni" (Rec. iv. 130). A stele of this officer is also preserved (T. Mus.; Rec. iv. 129). Qurneh.

Hor·em·heb, a magnificent tomb, with family scenes;

groups of the conscription and registration; lines of foreigners bearing tribute, both Asiatics and negroes; and long processions, with all the varieties of the funeral furniture (M.A.F. v. 413). Qurneh.

x, a fan-bearer: scenes of census-taking, but much destroyed (C.N. 497–8).

Piay, chief prophet and follower of Tahutmes IV., keeper of the boats of Amen in the palace of Tahutmes IV. (C.N. 518–9). Qurneh.

Hek·er·neheh, tutor of prince Amenhotep (= A. III.), and of five or seven other sons of the king whose names are erased (L.D. iii. 69 a; C.N. 569). Qurneh.

FIG. 110.—Tahutmes IV. giving the *hotep* offering to Osiris for Thuna.

Objects are known in this reign of—

Smen sheps, a fan-bearer, and Hesit·na his wife, stele, P. Mus. (P.R. ii. 35).

Pa·aa·aku, a fan-bearer, and adorer of Amenhotep I., stele, P. Mus. (P.R. ii. 14).

Nefer·hat, a follower, stele, with king offering to Nut, Abydos (M.A. 1060; M.A. ii. 47).

Thuna, fan-bearer, seal-bearer, companion, etc., a stele, with the king offering to Osiris *for* the deceased, a real *suten du hotep* scene, Abydos (M.A. 1061 ; M.A. ii. 48). Another stele at Stockholm (Lb.D. 590).

Amenhotep, high priest of Anhur ; and the singer of Anhur, Hent, B. Mus. (Lb.D. 602).

Thenau, "fan-bearer behind the king the noble of princes." Scarab, P. Mus. (P.R. ii. 127).

Ramery, palette, B. Mus.

FIG. 111.—Queen Mutemua.

The king was also adored by—

Horames, under Horemheb (?) (C.N. 517–8).

Nefer·em·hotep. Turin stele.

Rany, priest of his statue, whose south-east tomb boundary is known.

x, under Amenhotep III. offering to Tahutmes IV. (C.N. 499).

The family of this king is obscure. We only have one queen, the celebrated Mut·em·ua, certainly attested. The other queen usually ascribed here, and named Arat, might, as we have noticed, read only "the goddess queen," and refer thus to Mut·em·ua; this is the more likely, as the supposed Arat was "great royal wife," like Mut·em·ua. This name is only found on the Konosso stele of the 7th year, and therefore too far on in the reign to have been an earlier chief wife than Mut·em·ua (L.D. iii. 69 e). Of Mut·em·ua, or "Mut in the sacred bark," there is a fine sacred bark of granite, 7 feet long, with her name and titles around it (B. Mus. A.B. 34). It seems not unlikely that this belonged to the temple of Luxor, where she is specially honoured and worshipped as the mother of Amenhotep III. (M.A.F. xv. 63–67).

Of sons there is Amenhotep the successor and another son, Tahutmes, named on a scarab, as we have mentioned.

XVIII. 9. Neb·maat·ra
(*Nimmuriya*)

Amen·hotep III.
Heq·uast

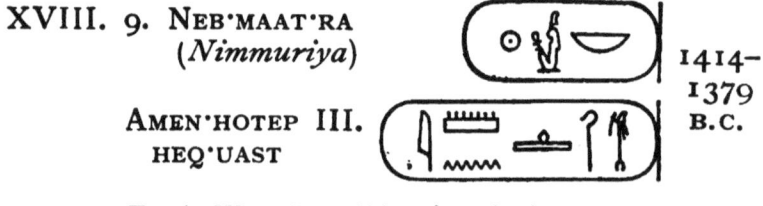

1414–1379 B.C.

Tomb, W. valley of kings' tombs (L.D. iii. 78, 79)
(M.A.F. iii. 174)

Rhodes	Scarab of Amenhotep	(S.S. 316).
Gaza	Two alabaster vases	(Pal. Exp. Fund).
Sarbut el Khadem	Two steles, 36th year	(L.D. iii. 71 c, d).
Bubastis	Four private statues	(N.B. 31–33).
Benha	Agathodaimon slab	(M.D. 63 b).
Turrah	Two steles, 1st & 2nd year	(L.D. iii. 71 a, b).
Memphis	Slab. G. Mus.	(V.G. 230).
,,	Apis tomb	(M.S. Ms. 117).
Gurob	Altar of Tyi	(P.I. xxiv. 7).
,,	Box lid	(P.I. xxiv. 8).
	Kohl tube	(P.I. xvii. 20).

[B.C. 1414-1379.]   AMENHOTEP III   175

Howarte by Minieh	Stone	(My. E. 406).
El Bersheh	Stele 1st year	(S.B.A. ix. 195, 206).
Meshaikh	Temple	(S.B.A. vii. 172).
Rayaneh	Fort	(My. E. 426).
Dendera	Adoration scene, late	(D.D. iv. c).
Karnak	Mentu temple, N.	(C.N. ii. 271-2; M.K. p. 8).
	Small temple E. of it	(M.K. pl. 1).
	Avenue, 122 sphinxes	(M.K. p. 14).
	Pylon III.	(M.K. p. 26).
	Inscription	(M.K. p. 57; pl. 34-5).
	Colossus before pylon XI.	(M.K. pl. 2).
	Pylon VIII., name	(B.Rs. 184).
,,	Building S, name	(C. N. ii. 180).
,,	Temple of Mut, T.	(M.K. p. 15).
Luqsor	Great temple	(L.D. iii. 73-4).
,,	Avenue of sphinxes.	
Kom el Hettan	Temple	(L.D. iii. 72).
,,	Colossi	(D.E. ii. 21-22; My. E. 464).
Qurneh	Stele, black granite.	
,,	Stele, white limestone.	
Deir el Medineh	Temple	(B.I.H.D. xxix.).
El Kab	Small temple E.	(L.D. i. 100; iii. 80).
,,	Fragments	(C.N. i. 266).
Silsileh, E.	Shrine	(S.B.A. xi. 233-4).
,,	Altar, 35th year	(L.D. 81 a-e).
,,	Stele, part	(L.D. 81 f).
Elephantine	Temple destroyed	(D.E. i. 34-8).
,,	Fragment	(M.I. i. 120).
Aswan quarry	Colossus	(M.I. i. 62).
,, ,,	Stele	(M.I. i. 62).
	Stele 5th year	(L.D. iii. 81 g).
,,	,,	(L.D. iii. 81 h).
,,	,,	(C.M. 95, 4).
Konosso	,, 5th year	(L.D. iii. 82 a).
(Other graffiti, see *private monuments*.)		
Semneh	Inscription. B. Mus.	(Arch. Jour. viii. 399).
Soleb	Temple	(L.D. iii. 83-8).
Sedeinga	Temple to Tyi	(L.D. iii. 82 e-i).
Napata, removed from Soleb	Two rams. Berl. Mus.	(L.D. iii. 89, 90 a-c).
	Base of hawk. Berl. Mus.	(L.D. iii. 90 d-f).
	Lions. B. Mus.	(L.A. 13 A.B.).
		(Rec. xi. 212).

Colossi	Kom el Hettan	(D.E. ii. 21-22).
	Before pylon XI.	(M.K. pl. 2).

NEB·MAAT·RA

Colossus	Base, granite. P. Mus.	(R.M.L. 37).
	A. 18	
Statues	White limestone. G. Mus.	(Ms. G. 422).
	Black granite. Thebes	(B. Mus.).
	White limestone. Qurnet Murrai.	
	,, Medinet Habu.	
	Base. Avignon	(W. G. 388).
Portraits	Tomb of king	(C.M. ccxxxii.; C.N. ii. 704; L.D. iii. 70 e).

Ushabtis. Paris. F.P. Coll. (S.B.A. xi. 421).
Group of Amenhotep and Tyi. Saurma Coll. (W.G. 389).
Sphinx, Karnak (C.N. ii. 272).
,, Acad. St. Petersburg (Lb. P. 61).
Sekhet statues, temple of Mut.
Ptah, standing, diorite. T. Mus. (L.T. No. 86).
Ptah, seated, limestone. T. Mus. (L.T. No. 87).
Anpu, seated, basalt. Sabatier (Rec. xiv. 54).
Wooden tablet, with Haremakhti. B. Mus. (P.L. No. 344).
Wooden label, with titles. T. Mus. (Rec. iii. 127).
Wooden stamp (?), not yet engraved. T. Mus. (Phot. 292).
Ostrakon, letter of palace-keeper. B. Mus. (B.I.H.D. xiii.).
Ostraka on coronation-day. B. Mus. (B.I.H.D. xv.).
Papyrus, copied from a roll. B. Mus. (A.Z. ix. 104, 117).
Papyrus, medical. B. Mus. (A.Z. ix. 61).
Stick. Leyden (I. 82).
Ivory inlaying, box handle. B. Mus. } (Arch. Jour. viii. 396).
,, inscribed strip. B. Mus. }
Inlaying from boxes, tomb. G. Mus. (M.D. 36 a).
Kohl tubes, wood. P. Mus.
,, ,, with Tyi. P. Mus. G. Mus. (Ms. G. 95).
,, ,, T. Mus. (Rec. iii. 127; phot. 161).
,, glazed, with Hent·ta·neb (P.I. xvii. 20).
Glazed tubes. Temple of Amenhotep II
Glazed jar, polychrome, with Tyi. G. Mus. (V.G. 747).
Vase, blue, double cylinder. B. Mus.
,, alabaster. Leyden.
,, pottery. P. Mus. (P.L. 361).
,, glazed, with Tyi. P. Mus. (P.L. 362).
Dish. G. Mus.
Scarabs—Marriage with Tyi. E. Coll. (R.P. xii. 39).
    Arrival of Kirgipa (A.Z. xviii. 82; Rec. xv. 200).
    Slaying 102 lions. E. Coll. (R.P. xii. 40).
    Making great tank (A.Z. xv. 87).
Scarabs, with titles, etc.
Rings, beads, etc.
Queens—TYI, daughter of Yuaa and Thuaa (A.Z. xviii. 82).
    Cartouche in quarry. Tell el Amarna (P.A. 4, xlii.).

AMENHOTEP III

Ushabti, alabaster	(D.E.V. 60, 7).
Toilet case. Turin	(Rec. iii. 127).
Figure with son. Tell el Amarna	(L.D. iii. 100 c).
Trial piece. Tell el Amarna. F.P. Coll.	(P.A. i. 6).
Adored as Osirian	(Pap. T. xii. 7).
(Frequently with Amenhotep III. on statues, scenes, scarabs, etc.).	
Scarabs, rings, etc	
KIRGIPA or Gilukhipa	(A.Z. xviii. 82).
Sons—Tahutmes	(L.K. 385).
Amenhotep IV.	(L.D. iii. 100 c).
Daughters—Ast. Soleb	(L.D. iii. 86 b).
Hent·mer·heb. Soleb	(L.D. iii. 86 b).
Hent·ta·neb. Gurob	(P.I. xvii. 20).
Sat·amen, box. B. Mus.	(Arch. Jour. viii. 397).
stele. G. Mus.	(M.A. ii. 49).
dish. A. Mus.	(P.A. xiii. 16).
Bakt·aten, daughter of Tyi	(L.D. iii. 100 a, c, 101).

We have seen from the presumptive dates that Amenhotep III. was probably only 16 at his father's death. There would be much difficulty in supposing him to have been born earlier in the family history; and yet, as his lion-hunting began in the 1st year of his reign, we can scarcely place his age at anything less. Again, his birth is the great subject of the temple he built at Luqsor, and his mother Mut·em·ua is the prominent figure in those scenes, pointing to her being important as queen-mother in the early part of his reign, and his infancy being then still a well-remembered subject. No mention appears of his celebrated, brilliant, and

FIG. 112.—Youthful head of Amenhotep III.

much-loved queen Tyi, until the 10th year of his reign; and he married another Mesopotamian princess, Kirgipa, or Gilukhipa, in the same year, which would well agree to his being about 25 then. Another

FIG. 113.—Amenhotep and his *ka*.

sign of his youth is that he is represented as king with the boy's side-lock of hair, and there is no expedition of his until the 5th year, when he would have been about 20. The various indications thus agree to the presumptive age which I have stated.

OUTLINE OF THE DATED RECORDS.

Born at Thebes, scarab (F.P. Coll.).
Ist year, Epiphi 13, Amenhotep was crowned (Ostrakon 5637 B.M.; see B.I.H.D. xv. 2): age about 16.
Ist year, Epiphi 20 + x, quarry opened at El Bersheh (S.B.A. ix. 195, 206).
Ist year, quarry opened at Turrah (L.D. iii. 71 a).
IInd year, quarrying at Turrah (L.D. iii. 71 b).
IIIrd year, black granite stele (G. Mus.).
Vth year, expedition to Ethiopia (stele, Konosso, L.D. iii. 82 a, and stele erected Athyr 2, at Aswan, L.D. iii. 81 g): age about 21.

Xth year, lion-hunt record (R.P. xii. 40): 102 slain between ages about 16 to 26.
Xth year, marriage with Kirgipa, and already married to Tyi (A.Z. xviii. 82): age about 26.
XIth year, Athyr 16, festival, tank inscription (A.Z. xv. 87).
XIth year, Khoiak 6, decree of building temple, Deir el Medineh (late copy in B.M., see B.I.H.D. 29).
XIVth year, Papyrus Turin (Pap. T. p. 7).
XXXVth year, Pakhons 1, altar at Silsileh (L.D. iii. 81 c).
XXXVIth year, Mekhir 9, steles at Sarbut el Khadem (L.D. iii. 71).

It does not appear that this king undertook any great wars after the Ethiopian campaign in his 5th year. The condition of the kingdom seems to have been one of acknowledged supremacy abroad, and peaceful development at home. Tahutmes I. had

FIG. 114.—Chariot of Khaemhat.

broken the power of Syria; Tahutmes III. had thoroughly grasped that country. He had taken the sons of the chiefs to be educated in Egypt; and as the Egyptian kings married Syrian princesses, it is most probable that the sons of the Syrian chiefs were married to Egyptians at the close of their education. It was only stipulated that they should be restored to their homes to succeed their fathers; and thus they may have lived until middle life in Egypt. In this way, the rulers of Syria were assimilated in thoughts and ways to the suzerain power, and were very unlikely to attempt to be independent. The correspondence of the cuneiform tablets shows that the northern kingdom of Mitanni and Karduniyas were in close diplomatic and family connection with Egypt; and no troubles appear to have disturbed the empire until late in the reign of Akhenaten. The reign of Amenhotep III. was thus free for commercial extension and the cultivation of the arts; and we find in it the greatest activity in this direction.

The reign began with the execution of some large buildings during the minority of the young king; and the quarries of Turrah (L.D. iii. 71; A.Z. v. 91) and El Bersheh (S.B.A. ix. 195) were opened for the fine limestone, of which so much was used, but which has almost all disappeared in the limeburners' kilns. The amusement of the young ruler was lion-hunting, and this he kept up most actively until his marriage in the 10th year of his reign, slaying 102 lions in ten years (R.P. xii. 40). His first and only recorded war was in the middle of this, his athletic age. He went out to the limits of the Egyptian power, and smote many tribes whose names never appear before or after. The tablets about the cataracts mention his victories; and in the land of Abeha alone he took 740 prisoners, and slew 312 more of the negroes (Semneh tablet, B. Mus.). We must not, however, assume that every tribe figured on the monument as a captive had been recently subjugated; in this reign we find at Soleb figures of the Syrian peoples, of Naharina, Kedesh, and other parts, where the Egyptians appear to have been in peaceful political occupation as a suzerain power. The figure of a captive town or people only implies the submission of that region to the Egyptian power. At Soleb the Syrian figures are named Kefa, Khit . . . , Sengar, Tares, Qarqamish, Asur, Apthethna, Makautuash, and Mehpeni; all these are with a fillet on the head and long hair. The other Syrian type is with close-cut hair and no fillet, found in Naharina, Kedshi, Pah . . . , Tita, Arerpaq, and Kedina. Names which have lost the figures are Tanepu and Aka..rita; and perhaps western districts in Sekhet Am, Menaunu Setet, Matnun, Tahennu, Asha . . . , Sekhet Am. Of the southern and negro peoples appear Matur, . . . nutaa, Azenunian, Samanurika, Kary, Maitariaa, Katha . . . , May, Fuersh . . . , Narkihab, Tarobenika, Tarosina, Aken . . . , Manuāreb, Mataka . . . , Abhat, Akina, Serenyk, Aururek, Atermaiu, Maiu, Gureses, the Sunuga, Ayhatab, Akhenuthek, Tartar, and Tursu. Of the Red Sea region are Shasu and Punt, and probably allied to this Aar . . . . This list shows the power of the king, ruling from Karo to Naharina, from Abyssinia to northern Mesopotamia.

His marriage in or before the 10th year of his reign was a great turning-point in his history. These Syrian marriages were so influential in the royal family of Egypt, that it is well to notice them carefully. From the Tell el Amarna tablets we can glean the following table of relationships:—

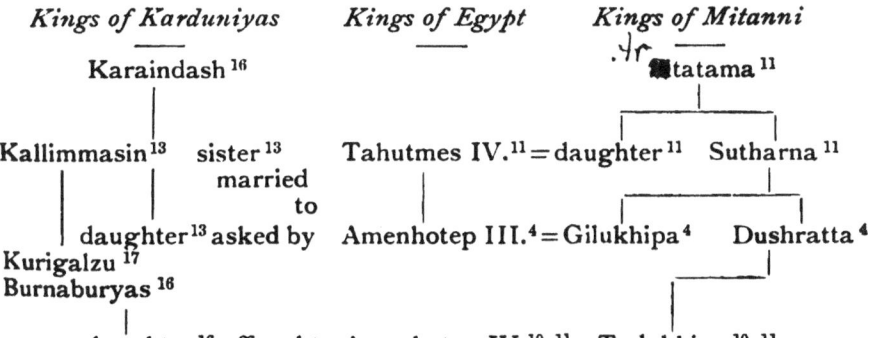

The numbers refer to the summaries of the letters in the chapter on the Decline of Egypt in Syria.

AMENHOTEP III

The marriage to Gilukhipa, daughter of Su . . . in letter 11, is evidently that described on the large scarab, when "the daughter of the chief of Naharina, Satharna, even Kirgipa and the principal of her women, females 317," came into Egypt (A.Z. xviii. 82). As on

FIG. 115.—Head of Tyi.

FIG. 116.—Head of man of Ynuamu.

the same scarab Tyi, daughter of Yuaa and Thuaa, is named as the great queen of Amenhotep, it is evident that Kirgipa cannot be an earlier name of Tyi. Who then was Tyi? Her face (P.A. i. 6) bears a strong likeness to that of her son Akhenaten (P.A. i. 5, 10), and differs from any type seen before in Egypt. There is, however, a close resemblance between this type and that of a man of Ynuā or Ynuamu among the captives on the north wall of the Great Hall at Karnak (misnamed Mitanni, P.A. i. 2). This city appears to have been in the region of Tyre, and so this type may belong to northern Galilee. Another clue, however, may be in the type of Nefertiti, the wife of Amenhotep IV. Her face (P.A. i. 15) has much the same features as that of

FIG. 117.—Head of Nefertiti.

Tyi, insomuch that both are probably of the same race. And it is most probable that Nefertiti is the other name of Tadukhipa, the daughter of Dushratta, as no other queen ever appears with Amenhotep IV. This would connect Tyi with the race of Dushratta in Mitanni. In either case, we must conclude that Tyi belonged to northern Syria. The nationality of her parents has been much disputed; their names, however, may as easily be Egyptian as foreign. But her titles are noticeable; she is called *hent-taui*, "princess of both lands," and "chief heiress, princess of all lands" (L.D. iii. 82 g), just as Nefertiti is called *hent res meh, nebt taui*, "princess of south and north, lady of both lands." These titles seem to imply hereditary right; indeed, it is very doubtful if a king could reign except as the husband of the heiress of the kingdom, the right to which descended in the female line like other property. Now we can see that the daughter of Dushratta, Tadukhipa = Nefertiti, would very probably be in the Egyptian royal line; Dushratta's application for a princess rather later is recorded (letter 28), and it is most likely that the Mitannian kings had Egyptian princesses, as the Egyptian kings had Mitannian princesses. Hence Nefertiti would be a rightful heiress of the Egyptian throne; and, similarly, Tyi may easily have been the grand-daughter of an Egyptian king and queen, her mother Thuaa having been married to some north Syrian prince Yuaa. Thus she would have the right to be a "princess of both lands"; her name might be Egyptian; and she would rightfully fill the prominent place she did in Egypt; while her physiognomy would be Syrian. This view cannot be yet proved, but it certainly fulfils all the conditions closely.

There can be little doubt of the powerful influence of queen Tyi; she appears closely associated with the king on his monuments, her figure is seen side by side with his on scarabs, her name appears along with the king's on innumerable objects, a temple was built in her honour at Sedeinga, and she acted as regent for her son during his minority, when letters were addressed to her by Dushratta (letter 9). Her evident influence on her young son shows in what direction she had been turning affairs during her husband's reign; and the peculiar taste and style, the rich decoration, and the new ideas which blossomed out under Amenhotep IV., guided by his mother, can be seen rising and budding under the reign of the great king Amenhotep III., inspired by his wife's influence.

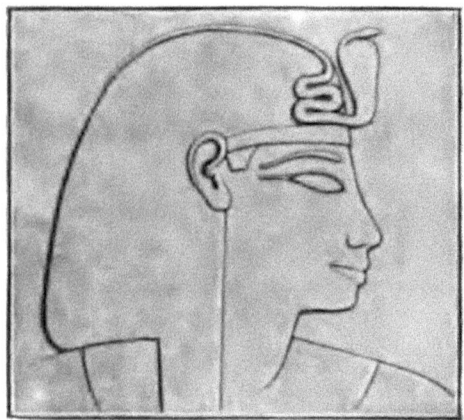

FIG. 118.—Young head of Amenhotep III.

Immediately after his marriage, we find the king engaged in public works; in the 11th year, on Athyr 1st, he "ordered to make a tank of the great royal wife Tyi in the city of Zaru (or Zal, the eastern frontier fort of Egypt). Its length 3600 cubits, its breadth 600 cubits, made by His Majesty in the first festival in Athyr 16, sailed His Majesty in the bark Aten-neferu in his saloon" (A.Z. xv. 87). This tank or lake was nearly a quarter of a mile wide, and over a mile long: that implies an amount to be moved which would be all but impossible in fifteen days (from 1st to 16th Athyr), even if the greatest number of workers were crowded in. But as Zaru—sometimes identified with Sele—was in any case in the region of the isthmus of Suez, with its various lakes and depressions, it rather seems that this tank or lake was made by flooding some natural hollow: the date would be on the 25th October, and therefore just before the fall of the inundation, a time when flooding would be taking place down the canals. The name of the king's barge, "the beauties of Aten," shows that already the worship of the Aten, or the sun's disc, was coming forward, in advance of its nationalisation under the son of Tyi. The founding of the temple of Deir el Medinet also belongs to this year, three weeks later than Amenhotep's *fantasiyeh* on the new lake ; it is unlikely, therefore, that he was at Thebes at the time, and as the record only names private persons, we shall notice it further on.

After this there are no landmarks in this reign until the close ; not a single war is recorded, and the Syrian letters show no trouble there, beyond a well-repelled attack by the Khatti on the king of Mitanni, the ally and brother of the Egyptian king (letter 4). What went on during this long peace is pictured in a little biographical letter, which we may quote complete as a picture of the life of a Syrian prince:—" To the king, my master, my god, my sun, this is said ;—Yatibiri thy servant, the dust of thy feet, at the feet of the king, my master, my god, my sun, seven times, and seven times more, I fall down. Behold, I am thy servant, true to the king my master. I look on one side, and I look on the other side, and there is no light ; but I look on the king my master, and there is light. A brick may be taken out of its place, but I shall move not from under the feet of my master. And now the king my master enquires about me of Yankhama, his agent. When I was young, Yankhama took me into Egypt, and placed me with the king my master, and I dwelt at the door of the king my master. Now the king my master asks his agent how I have guarded the gate of Gaza and the gate of Joppa. As for me, I am with the auxiliaries of the king my master ; wherever they go, I go with them, and whenever they go, I am with them. The yoke of my master is on my neck, and I bear it" (letter 117, S.B.A. xv. 504). Yatibiri seems to have had even his name changed in Egypt, as this is probably the Syrian writing of Hotep-ra.

The temple of Soleb in Nubia is a monument of these silent years of tranquil government. There is shown a great festival, which began on the 26th of Mesore, and ended in Thoth. The king was accompanied by Tyi and two daughters, and probably two sons also; hence this sculpture can hardly be earlier than the 18th or 20th year of his reign.

Toward the close of the reign it seems that Amenhotep IV. must have been associated with him. There are dates of his 35th and 36th year, and yet Manetho

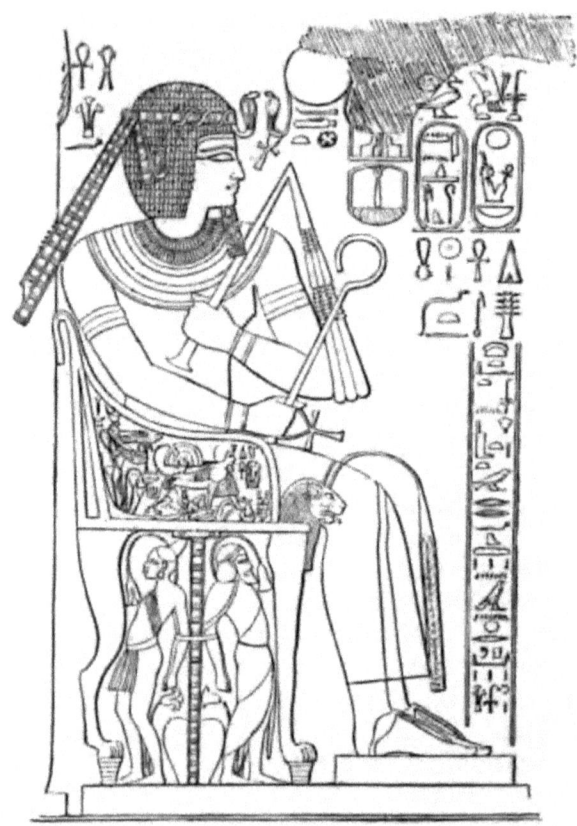

Fig. 119.—Amenhotep III. enthroned. Tomb of Khaemhat.

only gives 30 years and 10 months for his reign. That this difference cannot be due to co-regency with Tahutmes IV. is pretty certain, as there are quarry inscriptions of the 1st and 2nd year of Amenhotep III. But a little point shows that Amenhotep IV. was probably married near the time of his father's death. In a letter Dushratta refers to Amenhotep III. sending to him to fetch a wife from D. to be the mistress of Egypt (letter 6). This cannot refer to either queen of Amenhotep III.; Gilukhipa was given by the father of Dushratta (letter 11), and Tyi was married yet earlier (Rec. xv. 200). Nor can it refer to another queen for Amenhotep III., as the great Tyi could hardly be superseded as mistress of Egypt. It must rather refer to seeking an alliance with Mitanni for the young Amenhotep IV. And we see that Dushratta, writing to Tyi, before Amenhotep IV. took up affairs, greets Tadukhipa his daughter, Tyi's daughter-in-law (letter 9).

Now there is no dating of Amenhotep IV. before his 5th regnal year, and in the 6th year his second child was born, pointing to his marriage in his 4th year. If, then, he were associated in the 31st year of his father's reign, the date of the 36th year of the old king would just follow the marriage of his son, and agree with the earliest date being of the 5th year. This also agrees with letter 8, in which Dushratta greets Tadukhipa his daughter, writing therefore after her marriage, while the letter reached Egypt in the 36th year, by the docket.

MONUMENTS.

We now turn to the great works of this age. This king was the first we know of who placed his tomb out of sight of the Nile. Instead of occupying some part of the wide cemetery overlooking the plain, he retreated an hour's journey up a wild and desolate gorge of the desert, and there hewed out grand galleries for his sepulchre, extending some hundreds of feet into the mountain. This was a magnificent new departure, and served as a type followed century after century by later kings. A long corridor leads to a chamber with two pillars at right angles to it; thence two more galleries lead to the sepulchral chamber, containing six pillars, out of which branch seven other chambers (D.E. ii. 79, 5). The entrance was skilfully concealed by lying behind a spur of rock; but the great banks of chips outside it point to the tomb. The greater part of the tomb was stuccoed and painted, but most of this covering has now disappeared. The execution of what remains is far finer than that of any of the later royal tombs. Three excellent heads of the king are published (C.M. ccxxxii.; L.D. iii. 70 e). The tomb in modern times contained only the lid of a sarcophagus in red granite, and fragments of ushabtis and funeral vases, etc. (D.E. ii. 80, 81; E. and F.P. Colls.).

The earliest dated Egyptian objects found in Europe are the scarabs of Amenhotep and of Tyi, of which several have been discovered in connection with Aegean pottery.

In Syria, two alabaster vases of this king were found at Gaza (Palestine Exploration Fund). At Sarbut el Khadem, in Sinai, two steles show him offering to Amen and to Hathor of Mafket; it appears that work was done at the mines in the last year of the reign.

In Egypt, work was carried on in the Delta. Four statues of officials of this age were found at Bubastis; two of a governor Amenhotep, one of a royal scribe Kherfu, and one unnamed (N.B. 31-33). And at Benha a large slab of black granite was found, with the figure of the guardian serpent of the temple of Har·khenti·khety (M.D. 63 b).

Fig. 120.—Amenhotep III. in middle age.

The steles at Turrah mention that "the king gave orders to open fresh chambers to quarry white excellent stone of An, in order to build his chambers for a million of years,

When His Majesty found the chambers which were in Rufuy going to great decay since the time of those who were at the beginning, by my Majesty they were made anew" (L.D. iii. 71 c, d). This was in the 1st and 2nd years; and a block at his temple of Kom Hettan at Thebes dates the quarrying in the 1st day of the 1st year.

At Memphis, the earliest of the Apis tombs belongs to this time; it was a rock chamber reached by a sloping passage, and with a chapel built over it (M.S. Ms. 117). A slab of this reign was found at Memphis, and is now in the Ghizeh Museum (V.G. 230).

At Gurob, an interesting altar was dedicated by Tyi to her husband's funereal service: "She made her monuments of her beloved brother Neb·ma·ra." A box lid and a kohl tube also name the king, his wife, and daughter Hent·ta·neb (P.I. xvii. xxiv). A block of Amenhotep was found in a town at Howarteh, near Minieh (My.E. 406). At El Bersheh is a stele of the 1st year in a quarry (S.B.A. ix. 195). At Mesheikh, nearly opposite Girgeh, stood a temple of this king (S.B.A. vii. 172). At Rayaneh is a fort the bricks of which are stamped by Amenhotep III. (My. E. 426). In Upper Egypt, at Dendera, is a Ptolemaic sculpture of the king in the guise of Hapi, with the cartouche *Ra·maa·neb* on his head.

At Karnak is the great mass of work of this reign. At the north end was built a temple of Mentu (N in Baedeker), with a pylon, and obelisks of red granite (C.N. ii. 271). The columns were polygonal, and the temple contained many fragments of black granite statues of the king and of Sekhet, and an exquisite small sphinx of Amenhotep. It was restored and altered by Merenptah, Ramessu V., and the Ptolemies II., III., IV., and VI. (C.N. ii. 272; B.E. 161). On the east of this was another lesser temple of this reign (M.K. pl. i., marked C, but referred to as B in text, p. 9).

A long avenue of 122 sphinxes, carved in sandstone,

extends before the temple of Khonsu; these bear the name of Amenhotep, and point to a temple of this reign having stood on the site where Ramessu III. afterwards built the existing temple.

A vast pylon was built by the king, as a new front to the great temple of Amen. This was afterwards used by Sety I. as the back of his great hall of columns, and partly refaced on that side by fresh masonry. On the north half of the west face are shown two great ships. One, over forty feet long, is the royal vessel, with the king standing on the poop, and cabins in the middle with cornices. It is propelled by thirty or forty rowers, and tows the barge of Amen, which bears the small processional bark of Amen in a shrine, and on the prow a sphinx and altar. The ends have great sacred collars below the rams' heads of Amen, the so-called *aegis*. On the east face are scenes of offering to Amen by the king, and a long list of the offerings in 71 lines (M.K. xxxiv.–v.). The colossus before pylon XI. (of Horemheb) is not in its original place. Only the pedestal and a foot now remain; and the little toe of that has been barbarously cut away in late years at a tourist's whim. The work is in quartzite sandstone; and on the base are figures of the king as a youth with the side-lock, showing that it belongs to the beginning of his reign. The statue must have been of the same magnitude as the colossi on the western shore.

Inscriptions of Neb·maa·ra have been added to the pylon of Tahutmes III. (pylon VIII.) and to the building of Amenhotep II. in the great southern court (S).

At the south end of Karnak stood a large and important temple of Mut (T), crowded with hundreds of lion-headed statues of Sekhet, which have been dispersed among the collections of the world. The lake round the sides and back of this temple still remains. The building was re-worked by Sheshenk I.

At Luqsor, a mile and a half farther south, a great temple was built by Amenhotep to his father Amen, with special reference to the divine conception of the king. This was probably not connected at this time with the temples of Karnak, as the axis of this temple and the Karnak avenue of sphinxes have no alignment, intersection, or relation to each other. The connection of Luqsor and Karnak is rather due to the alterations of Ramessu II. This Luqsor temple consists of five portions, which have three slightly different axes. The shrine—which is a processional resting-place, open

FIG. 121.—Colonnade at Luqsor.

in both front and back—has a hall before it, a columnar gallery at the back, and chambers at the sides. In front of this is an open court. Then a hypostyle hall, of four rows of eight columns, the axis of which is rather more to the north, instead of northeast like the shrine. Then a court with colonnades around it, which recovers the same direction as the shrine. Lastly, before this, and the massive pylon which formed its face, an avenue of fourteen columns was added as an approach, with a lesser pylon in front of it.

On the western side of the Nile a great temple was built in this reign; to which the well-known colossi belonged, standing in front of the now-vanished pylon. These colossi have obtained a celebrity through Greek and Roman authors, which has little to do with their importance in history. They were noble pieces of work, but are now so fearfully injured that the group of the Niles on the sides is the only part of artistic value. The height of the figures is recorded by their architect (in the inscription on his statue) as being 40 cubits; with the pedestal and crown they appear to have been exactly this size. At the sides of the legs, against the throne, are statues of Mutemua the mother, and of Tyi the wife, of the king. The Greek inscriptions of visitors who came to hear the sunrise crackling of the stone are published in D.E. ii. 22; v. 55. Other colossi lie a little way behind these, and a vast stele of sandstone about 14 feet wide and 30 feet high, which decorated the forecourts of the temple. Remains of the buildings of the temple chambers, at the back of all, form the Kom Hettan, or "mound of chips." On the edge of the desert to the north of this are the remains of the temple of Merenptah, which was entirely formed from the plundering of Amenhotep's temple. The avenue of jackals with statues of the king between the paws, the inscribed bases on which they stood, the colossi, the sphinxes, the steles, the sculptured blocks, and even the bricks, were all plundered and destroyed for the sake of materials. Thence come the black granite stele (usurped by Merenptah), and the white limestone stele of Amenhotep's triumph, now in the Ghizeh Museum. The chapel of Uazmes was restored by Amenhotep III., whose ring was found under the door sill. The small temple of Deir el Medineh was founded by the great architect of this reign, Amenhotep, son of Hepu; but none of the original building remains, the whole being now Ptolemaic. The inscription about it is noticed below under the architect's name.

At El Kab, a beautiful little temple, formed of a single square chamber with four pillars and a court, stands back in the desert valley. It was begun by Tahutmes IV. and finished by Amenhotep III. (L.D. iii. 80). The name of the king also occurs in the ruins of the great temple (C.N. i. 266).

At Silsileh stood a shrine in the quarry, surmounted by a hawk which now lies by it (S.B.A. xi. 233–4); and also an altar which was dedicated in the 35th year of Amenhotep (L.D. iii. 81 a–e). Probably of the same time is a rock tablet of his in the same place (L.D. iii. 81 f).

At Elephantine stood one of the most perfect and beautiful examples of a temple of this age. It had the usual processional form (with the sanctuary open front and back), and a colonnade of seven pillars at the side and four in the front around the outside. An unusual feature was that it stood on a raised hollow platform reached by a flight of steps. Happily it was passably published in the *Description* (i. 34–8), for soon after that, in 1822, it was swept away by the local governor for stone (a fragment is quoted in M.I. i. 120).

By the quarry at Aswan lies a granite colossus, which was in course of being removed; though partly buried, its proportion indicates a height of about 25 feet. A rock tablet in the quarry shows the sculptor adoring the king's names, and saying that he had "made the great image of his majesty the lion of princes" (M.I. i. 62–3). The other steles at Aswan refer to the war in the Sudan, and are dated in the 5th year, as we have noticed (L.D. iii. 81 g, h; C.M. 95, 4; L.D. iii. 82 a). A stele from Semneh gives some other details of this Nubian campaign (Arch. Jour. viii. 399).

At Sedeinga (20° 32' N.) are the remains of a beautiful temple built in honour of queen Tyi. An inscription says that Amenhotep "made his monuments for the great and mighty heiress, the mistress of all lands, Tyi" (L.D. iii. 82).

The great temple at Soleb (20° 24' N.) was built in

this reign to commemorate the conquest of the Sudan. The king is shown in the dedication festival, with all his officials, entering in at the great gates, which each have a name; it is stated that "all her gates were made of best white sandstone," and the names "Neb·maa·ra . . . nekht" and "Amenhotep Neb·maa·ra s . . r . . ." remain for the great pylons.

At Napata (Mount Barkal), the Ethiopian capital

Fig. 122.—Colossal ram from Napata. Berlin.

(18° 30′ N.), were monuments which had been taken from Soleb. Many of these are now in Europe; two rams and the base of a hawk at Berlin (L.D. iii. 89, 90), and two lions (partly usurped by Tut·ankh·amen) in London (L.A. 13 A.B.; Rec. xi. 212).

Turning now to the portraiture of the king, there are several colossi; two standing at Thebes, the upper part of one entirely built up in Roman times; another of the same size buried behind these; another farther back; and a group of four figures in one block, the heads lost (My. E. 464). Great colossi of Amenhotep in white limestone were removed from his temple and broken up; the remains having been found in the buildings of temple of Merenptah and Medinet Habu. Of statues there are two, one in white limestone (G. Mus.; Ms. G. 422), and one in black granite (B. Mus.), beside a base at Avignon. A group of the king and Tyi is in the Saurma collection. Three excellent drawings of different ages are published from the tomb (C.M. 232; L.D. iii. 70).

FIG. 123.—Pottery and silver rings of Amenhotep III. F.P. Coll.

A beautiful small sphinx was seen by Champollion at Karnak (C.N. ii. 272), and may

FIG. 124.—Scarabs of Amenhotep III. Scale 1 : 2. F.P. Coll.
1. "Born at Thebes."
2. "Beloved of all the gods in the palace."
3. "Prince, making decrees."
4. "Seizing Sangar."

be one of the sphinxes now in front of the Academy at St. Petersburg (Lb. P. 61).

Of divine figures of this age there are the innumerable

statues of Sekhet in black granite, which were mainly placed in the temple of Mut; the standing Ptah in diorite (in Turin), and a seated Ptah in limestone (Turin); Anpu, seated, in basalt (Sabatier Coll.).

The various minor objects of this reign are sufficiently catalogued at the head of this section. The scarabs are peculiar from their large size and long inscriptions. The text of the more important passages has been already quoted; and beside the long texts, there are many scarabs of unusual size with phrases of honour, such as "beloved of all the gods in the palace," "seizing Singar," "the lion of princes," etc.

Private Monuments.

The tombs and tablets of the great officials of this reign are of much importance. The wealth and leisure of all classes led to the construction of magnificent works, which far exceed in extent and beauty the royal remains of most other ages.

We begin with the most celebrated official of Egypt in any age, *Amenhotep*, the son of Hepu, the great architect and administrator. On his statue found at Karnak he states: " Mustering (of troops) was done under me, as royal scribe over the recruits. I trained the troops of my lord, my pen counted millions. I appointed recruits in place of the veterans. I assessed estates according to their just number, and when workmen left their estates for me, I filled the number of the serfs from the spoil smitten by his majesty in battle. I examined all their gangs, I disciplined the decayed. I appointed men over the road to repel foreigners from their place, enclosing the two lands in watching the Bedawin on the way. I did likewise on the water way, the river mouths were joined by my parties, beside the crews of the royal ships. Behold, I guided their ways, they obeyed my orders. I acted as chief at head of my mighty men to smite the Nubians. . . . I counted the spoil of the victories (as chief recorder). I was appointed overseer of all works.

". . . I did not imitate what had been done before. . . . I acted with the love of my heart in undertaking his likeness in this his great temple, in every hard stone firm as heaven. I undertook the works of his statues, great in width, and higher than his pylon; their beauties eclipsed the pylon, their length was 40 cubits in the noble rock of quartzite. I built a great barge, I sailed it up the river (*i.e.* from Jebel Ahmar), and I fixed the statues in his great temple firm like heaven."

The statue bearing this inscription is of the quartzite breccia of Gebel Ahmar (Fraas), and is now at Ghizeh (V.G. 212; M.K. 36-7). The family was of importance, as an Amenhotep surnamed Hepu (who was already dead early in Tahutmes III.) is named in the tomb of Aahmes Pen·nekheb (L.D. iii. 43 b). The high position of this architect is shown by his acting in the absence of the king (then visiting the Delta) at the founding of the temple of Deir el Medineh. The stele which records this is apparently a later hieratic copy; it states that "XIth year, Khoiak 6, under Amenhotep, etc. This day there was in the temple of Kak, the heir, the royal scribe Amenhotep. There came to him the governor Amenhotep; the treasurer Meriptah; and the royal scribe of the troops. He said to them before His Majesty, 'Listen to the orders which are made for the management of the temple of Kak by the heir, the royal scribe Amenhotep, named Hui son of Hap.'" He recites them the gift of male and female servants, and curses any who should remove the endowment (B.I.H.D. xxix.; C.E. ii. 324; A.Z. xiii. 123). Beside this high position, the reputation of this great man lasted till late ages. The copy of the above stele is Ptolemaic. And in a Ptolemaic sculpture in the rock chapel at Deir el Bahri he is represented standing with an "adoration by the scribe of recruits, Amenhotep son of Hepu" (D.H. ii. 7). He was correlated with Imhotep both at Medinet Habu and at Deir el Bahri (A.Z. xxv. 117). Papyri were attributed to him, as one in Paris, entitled "Book of the mysteries of the form found by the royal chief reciter Amenhotep son of Hapi, and which he made for himself as an amulet to preserve his members." This is a litany of magic names (Ms. M.P.L. 58). Lastly, Josephus names him, saying that king Amenophis desired to see one of the gods, "he also communicated his desire to his namesake Amenophis, who was the son of Paapis, and one who seemed to partake of a divine nature, both as to wisdom and the knowledge of futurities"; and, further, he "called to mind what Amenophis son of Paapis had foretold him" (Cont. Ap. i. 26; see also A.Z. xv. 147). The other officials known are:—

Amenhotep, vizier, law-maker, overseer of all works of the king, who may be the same as the above son of Hepu. Two statues found at Bubastis (N.B. 32).

Amenhotep, royal scribe, general, adoring cartouches at Bigeh (C.N. i. 161).

Amenhotep, royal scribe, Soleb (L.D. iii. 83).

Amenhotep, royal scribe, tablet (B. Mus. 151).

Amenhotep, the *am·khent*. Tomb, Thebes. Bears a sphinx with the *ka* name of Amenhotep III. Also two bearers of sceptres with titles and names of Am. III., making monuments to his father Ptah (M.A.F. i. 28).

Aahmes, governor of the town, adoring cartouches, Konosso (L.D. iii. 82 d).

Aa·nen, seal-bearer, second prophet of Amen. Statue, Turin (Rec. iii. 126).

Amen·em·hat, called Surer, chief *semer*, fan-bearer, royal scribe, keeper of palace, born of royal favourite Mut·tuy. Statue kneeling holding stele, Louvre (P.R. i. 1); statuette, Louvre (P.R. ii. 38); tablet, Aix (P.R. ii. 38); torso, B. Mus. (Lb. D. 604).

Amen·nekht, princess, prays with her mother, Mut·nefert, before Amenhotep III., because "he praises her beautiful face and honours her beauty." Ushabti box, Berlin (B.C. 90).

Amu·n·zeh, tomb finished under Am. III. ; royal follower (M.A.F. v. 352 ; Rec. vii. 45). Qurneh.
Anhur·mes, scribe of works of temple of Am. III. Cone (P.S. xxiii. 84).
Baken·khonsu, high priest of Amen, overseer of prophets of all the gods. Naos, red sandstone, Karnak (R.E. ix. 28).
Heby·khetf, prince of Memphis, adoring cartouches, Aswan (M.I. 28, 8).

FIG. 125.—Head of Khaemhat. Thebes, Berlin.

Hor, architect, stele, B. Mus. (T.S.B.A. viii. 143).
Hor·em·heb, royal scribe. Tomb, Thebes (M.A.F. v. 432).
Hotep, fan-bearer before Am. III. and Thyi, Aswan (M.I. i. 41, 181).
Kahu, stele, B. Mus. (Lb. D. 674).
Kha·em·hat, royal scribe of the granaries of south

and north, etc. Tomb, Thebes (M.A.F. i. 116; C.N. i. 498; C.M. 160; Pr. A.; L.D. iii. 76–7); slab at Berlin (B.C. 103).

Kherfu, treasurer, royal scribe, keeper of the palace, adoring cartouches, Aswan (M.I. i. 44, 4); statue, Berlin (B.C. 83); base of statue, Bubastis (N.B. 33).

Men, son of Hor·ammu, sculptor. Stele in style of Tell el Amarna, at Aswan; adoration of Am. III. as a great statue, and his *ka*; by the chief of works in the red mountain, over the artists of great monuments of the king. (Tablet of his son Bak, see next reign) (M.I. i. 40, 174).

Mermes, royal son of Kush, adoration before cartouches, Aswan (P.S. 274); adoring, with Kherfu, Aswan (M.I. i. 39, 177); Konosso (L.D. iii. 82 b); Sehel (M.I. i. 91, 96); alabaster canopic jar (B. Mus.); cones.

Mery, *sam* priest. Soleb (L.D. iii. 84).

Nebt·ka·bani, nurse of princess Satamen. Stele, Abydos, G. Mus. (M.A. ii. 49).

Nefer·sekheru, royal scribe, keeper of palace (C.N. i. 524). Tomb, Qurneh.

Pa·nehesi, prophet of king, Turin, statue (Lb. D. 607).

Pa·sar, in tomb of Horemheb (B.R. ii. 66 c; not in M.A.F.).

Ptah·mer, noble, eyes and ears of the king, keeper of the palace of Maa·neb·ra. Stele, Leyden (Lb. D. 608).

Ptah·mes, A, father, Menkheperra; son, Paneterhon; noble heir, high priest of Memphis, *chancellor*, *sole companion*. Statue, breccia, Florence (S. Cat. F. 1505); naos, Abydos, G. Mus. (M.A. ii. 32; S. Cat. F. p. 203). Living under Tahutmes III. and Amenhotep III.

Ptah·mes, B, father, Tahutimes; brother (?) Ptah·mer; son, Khay; noble heir, high priest of Memphis, *overseer of all the prophets of the south and north*. Statue, grey granite, Thebes, Florence (S. Cat. F. 1506); stele, Memphis (S. Cat. F. 1570);

stele, Leyden (S. Cat. F. p. 205); cubit, Leyden (S. Cat. F. p. 205); palette, basalt (P.R. i. 93). A or B is adored on stele of Ptah·ankh (S. Cat. F. 1571). B living under Amenhotep III.

(The above persons have been confused, but their parentage and titles serve to distinguish them. Paneterhon of Florence, 1679, cannot be the son of Ptah·mes A, as his father is Mahuy. The very different styles of the Florence statues, 1505 and 1506, would well agree to the beginning and the end of the long reign of Amenhotep III.)

Ptah·mes, C, high priest of Amen, governor of south Thebes. Stele, Avignon (W.G. 395).

Ra·men·kheper, son of king Amenhotep II.? Stele, Bigeh (C.N. i. 161).

Ra·mes, A, vizier, at Soleb dedication (L.D. iii. 83); rock stele, Bigeh, adoring cartouches (P.S. 334); another stele, Bigeh (C.N. i. 614); rock stele, Sehel, adoring cartouches and Anket (M.D. 70, 21).

Ra·mes, B, general, overseer of palace. Tomb, Tell el Amarna (M.A.F. i. 10).

Sa·ast, called Pa·nekhu. Stele, Turin (Rec. iii. 125).

Sa·mut, *kher heb*, at Soleb dedication (L.D. iii. 84); = (?) treasurer, translator of the messengers in the palace, second prophet of Amen. Tomb, Thebes (C.N. i. 539).

Sebek·mes, treasurer. Rock stele, Aswan, by river (M.I. i. 44, 2).

Sebek·nekht, noble heir, keeper of palace. Stele, Munich (Lb. D. 611).

Tahutimes, father of Ptahmes B (? son of Ptahmes A). Stele, Leyden (S. Cat. F. p. 205); stele, Florence (S. Cat. F. 1570).

Tahutimes, overseer of serfs. Stele, B. Mus. (Lb. D. 605).

Userhat, keeper of palace of Tyi in Thebes; in tomb of Khonsu, Qurneh (Rams. II.).

Amenhotep was adored as a god after his death, but not as much as might be expected. At Soleb his son Akhenaten (so written) appears in regular royal dress, and not in his peculiar style, adoring the king. At Aswan, Men, the sculptor, adores the great statue. At Memphis the king was also adored (Pap. Sall. iv., pl. 2, verso). A stele of a priest of Amenhotep III. bears an adoration to Osiris, Isis, Amenhotep, and Tyi (C.N. ii. 703). And a statue at Karnak bears a *du hotep suten* prayer to Sokar, Nefertum, Sekhet, and Amenhotep III. (S.B.A. xi. 423).

FIG. 126.—Aged head of Amenhotep III., from his tomb.

ROYAL FAMILY.

We have already noticed the relation of the king to the Mesopotamian rulers of Mitanni and Kardunyas; and the uncertainty about the parentage of his great queen Tyi, who appears to have had hereditary rights to the Egyptian kingdom — probably through her mother. The monuments of Tyi are numerous. She appears at the sides of the colossi of her husband, and with him in official scenes, as at Soleb. Her parentage is recorded on the large scarabs, which name her father Yuaa, and her mother Thuaa (A.Z. xviii. 82).

Her figure was sculptured in the tomb of Huy (No. 2), at Tell el Amarna (L.D. iii. 100 c; Pr. A.). Two trial pieces left in sculptors' shops at Tell el Amarna show her face (P.A. i. 6). Her ushabtis of alabaster were found in the tomb of her husband (D.E. v. 60, 7). She dedicated altars to the *ka* of Amenhotep after his death, of which one has remained in the remote country town of Gurob (P.I. xxiv.). Toilet boxes bear her name, from Gurob (P.I. xxiv.) and at Turin (Rec. iii. 127), while numerous scarabs and cowroids show her name, sometimes conjoined with that of her husband; in two cases their figures appear together (B. Mus., Brocklehurst Coll., P. Sc. 1305–9), and on one scarab she is shown seated (B. Mus.; P. Sc. 1308). Her name appears alone in the quarry at Tell el Amarna, probably after her husband's death (P.A. 4, xlii.).

Of queen Kirgipa only one mention appears in Egypt, on a scarab recording her entry into the land with 317 women attendants, who, doubtless, spread the Syrian tastes in the Egyptian court (A.Z. xviii. 82). Her father is said to be Satharna; and this leaves no question but that she is Gilukipa, daughter of Su . . . king of Mitanni, named by Dushratta in his cuneiform correspondence (letters 4 and 11).

Of the children of Amenhotep III. but little is known. Beside his son, afterwards Akhenaten, there is one son, Tahutimes, who may be only a titular prince and not a relation (L.K. 385). Two daughters are known from the scenes on the temple of Soleb, named Ast and Hent·mer·heb (L.D. iii. 86 b); Satamen is named on an ebony slip from a toilet box (B. Mus.; Arch. Jour. viii. 397), and on a dish from Tell el Amarna (P.A. xiii. 16), and is shown seated as a child on the knees of her nurse, Nebt·ka·bani, on a stele from Abydos (G. Mus.; M.A. ii. 49); while Hent·ta·neb is only known by a piece of a glazed pottery kohl tube of hers found at Gurob (P.I. xvii. 20).

The princess Bakt·aten has been usually placed as a seventh and youngest daughter of Akhenaten. She occurs, however, in a tomb of his 12th year, or only six years after the second daughter was born; and she never appears among the daughters where four (L.D. iii. 93) or six (L.D. iii. 99) are shown, hence there is a difficulty as to her position, unless she died very young. Her real origin is, however, intimated in the tomb of Huya, the only place where she is represented. She is there always associated with Tyi; she sits by the side of Tyi (L.D. iii. 100 c), while the daughters of Akhenaten side by their mother; she alone follows

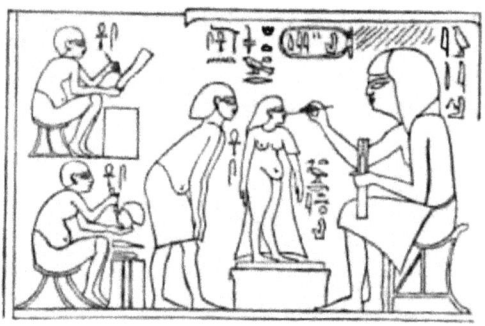

FIG. 127.—Court artist Auta painting a statue of Bektaten.

Tyi (L.D. iii. 101) in a procession where no other children appear; and her figure is painted by Auta, court artist to Tyi (L.D. iii. 100 a). Moreover, she is never called other than a king's daughter, whereas all the other princesses in every inscription are entitled daughters of Nefertiti. Thus, by the difficulty about her position in the family, by her constant association with Tyi, and by her being differently entitled to all the others, it seems clear that she was the youngest and favourite child of Tyi.

AKHENATEN

XVIII. 10.
NEFER·KHEPRU·RA
(*Nap·khura·riya*)

AMEN·HOTEP IV.
NETER·HEK·UAST

Or later
AKHEN·ATEN

1383–
1365
B.C.

Tomb	Valley at Tell el Amarna	(P.A. xxxiv.)
Heliopolis	Fragments of granite	(A.Z. xix. 116; Rec. vi. 53).
Memphis	Fragments in Cairo	(A.Z. xix. 116; S.I. ii. 48).
	Tablet with cartouches	(M.D. 34 e).
	Re-used blocks, Sydney Mus.	(N. Aeg. 117–134).
,,	Stele of Huy	(M.D. 56, 2).
Gurob	Fragments of scene	(P.I. xxiv. 10).
Kahun	Papyrus, 5th year	(P.I. 50).
Eshmunen	Granite pedestal	(Rev. Arch. I. i. 730).
Tell el Amarna	Palace	(P.A. 7, pls. ii.–x.).
,,	Temple of Aten	(P.A. 18).
	Three rock steles, W. bank	(P.A. 5; Pr. M. xiv.; L.D. iii. 91 a–f).
	Eleven rock steles, E. bank	(P.A. 5–6; Rec. xv. 36; L.D. iii. 110 b, 110 a; Pr. M. xii.).
	(Private tombs, see list below).	
	Death mask, G. Mus.	(P.A. front).
	Statues, B. Mus., Amherst	(P.A. 18).
	Colossi	(P.A. 9).
	Ushabtis, G. Mus., F.P. Coll.	(P.A. 17).
	Triad, F.P. Coll.	(P.A. i. 1).
	Sculpture and trial piece	(P.A. i. 5, 9).
	Steles, E. Coll., G. Mus., A. Mus., Amherst, in pavement house	(P.A. xii.; V.G. 150, 207).
	Fragments of steles, sculptures, vases, etc.; A. Mus., F.P. Coll., Ph. Mus., etc.	(P.A.).

Tell el Amarna	Jar sealings, A. Mus	(P.A. xxi.).
,,	Rings	(P.A. xiv. xv.).
Hammamat	Rock cuttings	(L.D. iii. 91 g; G.H. i. 6; G.H. i. 8, iii. 5).
Qus	Blocks	(W.M.C. iii. 52).
Thebes	Fragments used by Horemheb	(Pr. M. x.-xi.; L.D. iii. 110c-g; 100c= Berl., B.C. 2072, p. 101; Rec. vi. 51.)
,,	Stone on quay, Luxor	(W.G. 399).
,,	Three stones, Karnak	(W.G. 399).
Erment	Block	(W.G. 400).
Silsileh	Stele about building	(L.D. iii. 110 i).
E. Silsileh	Stele of Amen Ra	(S.B.A. xi. 233).
Aswan	Stele of Bak	(M.D. 26 u).
Soleb	King worshipping father	(L.D. iii. 110 k).

Statuette	P. Mus.	(L.D. iii. 294, 44).
Shoulder of statue, limestone	G. Mus.	(W.G. 402).
Fragments of statues	Amherst Coll.	(P.A. 18).
Body of quartzite	F.P. Coll.	
Head of statuette, limestone	T. Mus.	
Portraits, best	Young, Karnak	(L.D. iii. 294, 42).
,,	Older, P. Mus.	(L.D. iii. 294, 43).
,,	Death mask	(P.A. front).
Steles	Quartzite (G. Mus.)	(V.G. p. 72).
,,	(Paris Cab. Med.)	(Rev. Arch. I. v. 63).
,,	Alabaster (E. Coll., Berl.)	(B.C. 2045, p. 97).
,,	Stone (Berl.)	(B.C. 10187, p. 101).
Door jamb fragment	(Berl.)	(B.C. 2069, p. 101).
Cartouche blocks, limestone (Turin)		(L.T. 1378).
,, red granite (Sabatier Coll.)		(Rec. xiv. 55).
,, limestone and blue glaze, (Amherst)		(P.A. 18, 19).
Part of altar, granite (G. Mus.)		(V.G. 708).
Part of mortar, red granite (F. Mus.)		(S. Cat. F. p. 53).
,, ,, (F.P. Coll.)		

Vase, alabaster, Leyden.
Rings, gold and copper, scarabs, plaques, etc.
Gold plated heart scarab. Maudsley.

Queen—TADUKHIPA (?) NEFERTITI.
Fragments of   Amherst Coll.   (P.A. 18, i. 13, 15).
5 statues
Portraits   Best   (L.D. iii. 111; P.A.
                                  14, xii.).
Building   Tell el Amarna   (P.A. 8, x.).
Vases   Fragments   (P.A. xiii. 23-34).
Rings, etc.   (P.A. xv.).
Daughters— Mert·aten, mar. Ra·smenkh·ka (L.D. iii. 99 a).
Makt·aten, died before the king.
Ankh·s·en·pa·aten = Ankhsenamen, mar. Tut·ankh·
amen.
Nefer·nefru·aten (L.D. iii. 93).
Married son of Burnaburyas, see letter 16.
Nefer·nefru·ra (L.D. iii. 99).
Sotep·en·ra (L.D. iii. 99).

The dated documents of this reign are not many
Only one bears the name of Amenhotep, in
Vth year, Phamenoth 19, papyrus letter, Kahun
(P.I. 50). Of Akhenaten there are the numerous dated
rock steles, all of the VIth and VIIIth years (the
doubtful reading IVth year in L.D. 110 b should
certainly be VIth year, as shown by one daughter being
figured).
XIIth year, Mekhir 8, visit of Tyi, recorded in tomb
of Huya (L.D. iii. 100 c).
XVIIth year, series of wine jar inscriptions ceases;
end of reign.

The beginning of the reign of Amenhotep IV. is
obscure. That Tyi for a brief time held the power at
Tell el Amarna, is indicated by her name appearing
alone in a quarry at that place (P.A. 4, xlii.); but this
may have only been for a few weeks.
We have already noticed that from Dushratta's
letter (6) it appears that Amenhotep III. was negotiat-
ing for his son's marriage before his death; and from
another letter of Dushratta (9) we learn that Tadukhipa
was the daughter thus married to Akhenaten, and who
was known in Egypt as Nefertiti. Moreover, Dush-

ratta alludes to the marriage in a letter addressed to Amenhotep III. This all points to Akenhaten's marriage having occurred just about the time of his father's death, and certainly before he took over affairs from his mother Tyi (see Dushratta's letter 9).

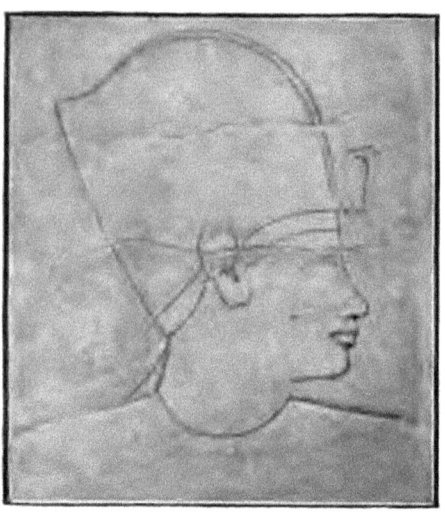

FIG. 128.—Young head of Amenhotep IV.

Now, from the monuments showing sometimes only one daughter (with a record inserted later) and sometimes two daughters in his 6th year, it is clear that his second daughter was born in the close of the 6th year of his reign. This would point to his marriage having taken place early in the 4th year. And hence he may very probably have been co-regent with his father in the years before his marriage.

Now Manetho in Josephus states that Amenhotep III. reigned 30 years 10 months, and yet his latest monument is in his 36th year, Mekhir 9. But this is just capable of a complete explanation by the co-regency of his son. For, as Amenhotep III. was crowned on the 13th Epiphi, his reign of 30 years and 10 months would lead us to date the beginning of Amenhotep IV. about the middle of Pakhons in his father's 31st year. Hence the date of the Sarbut el Khadem stele on Mekhir 9 in the 36th year would be just 40 days before the earliest date of Amenhotep IV. on Phamenoth 19, year 5, which implies the decease of his father. The old king appears then to have died within the few weeks between these dates.

As there are many works of the 6th year of Amenhotep IV., his father was certainly then dead; and this limits us to fix his father's death in any case within a few months after the stele of his 36th year. (See further the endorsement on Tell el Amarna, letter No. 8).

The parentage of Nefertiti has been assigned (Rec. vi. 52) to Tyi; a view which is contradicted by the express reference of Dushratta (letter 9) to Tadukhipa his daughter, Tyi's daughter-in-law. This view has been based on a misreading of the title of Tyi, *seten·mut·seten· hemt·urt*, as if it

FIG. 129.—Head of Amenhotep IV.

were *seten·mut·en·seten·hemt·urt* (L.D. iii. 100 c). That the first is the true reading, is plain from a repetition of the title twice in the same tomb (pl. 101), where there is no *n* after *seten*, and where the titles are inserted as *seten·hemt·urt·seten·mut*, so that the meaning is evidently that Tyi was not "royal mother of the king's wife," but "royal wife and royal mother." This is also shown by Nezem·mut being distinguished as "the sister of Nefertiti" (L.D. iii. 109), and not as "daughter of Tyi," which would have been the more important relationship had it existed.

That Nefertiti had an hereditary claim to the Egyptian throne, is shown by her titles: she was the *erpat urt, hent hemtu neb*, the "great heiress, princess of all women," and "the princess of south and north, the lady of both lands." These titles, like the titles of Tyi, imply an hereditary right to rule Egypt; and such a right would exist had Dushratta married an Egyptian princess who became mother of Tadukhipa Nefertiti. Such a marriage is very probable, looking at the letters that passed, the equality of terms between Dushratta and his brother-in-law Amenhotep III., and his asking as a matter of course for an Egyptian wife for himself.

It seems, then, that we may approximately reckon that the accession of Amenhotep IV. was in Pakhons in his father's 31st year; that about Epiphi, or early in his 4th year, he married Nefertiti (= Tadukhipa, daughter of Dushratta), who did not at first take the name Aten·nefer·neferu (P.A. xiii. 23); that in his 4th year he still worshipped Ra Har·akhti (Ostrakon, P.A. 33); that in his 5th year, Mekhir 9, his father was yet alive, but probably died before Phamenoth 19. That in the end of the 5th year the tomb of Rames at Thebes was begun before the artists had given up the boyish face of Amenhotep, and adopted the new style of art; also a great building of Silsileh stone was begun at Thebes (L.D. iii. 110 i) under the old style of art. Then, early in his 6th year, he shook off the worship of Amen, and even of the hawk-headed Horus, adopted the Aten worship, took the name Akhenaten, established a new capital at Tell el Amarna, and erected the rock tablets defining the new city, before the birth of his second daughter in the 6th year. After the second daughter was born came the change of his name at Thebes (Pr. M. xi. 3), and still later the change of his facial type at Thebes (Pr. M. x. 1, 2).

FIG. 130.—Amenhotep IV. supporting the cartouches of the Aten: from a scarab. F.P. Coll.

Having now traced the detail of his earlier years, we

turn to the great phenomenon of this reign, the conversion of the king and the court. This change took place, as we have seen, early in the 6th year of the reign. The age of Akhenaten is an all-important factor in the question; and this is indicated in two ways. His marriage was only just before his conversion, perhaps two years at most. The conversion cannot then be put before his 18th year, or probably rather later. But, on the other hand, all his portraits before the change show a distinctly boyish type, and are like his father Amenhotep III., while after the change they are like his mother Tyi. Such a transition from the type of one parent to that of the other on reaching adolescence is not unlikely, but it certainly could not be put later than the fixation of the features at about 15 or 16 years of age. The artistic recognition of the change lagged, no doubt, and more at Thebes than at Tell el Amarna; but the change being shown not earlier than his 18th year of age, points to his not being much beyond that age in any case. Now this consideration of his age points plainly to his not being a principal in the revolution, but being acted on by some older and more responsible party. A lad of 18 cannot be supposed to have thought out a new system of religion, ethics, and art for himself, and to have defied the whole feelings of his country. The steady rise of the Aten into notice in the later years of his father (even before the son was born, as in the boat-name Aten·neferu in the 11th year), shows that an older influence was working. And yet it was an external influence, as the whole system utterly vanished without any party remaining in Egypt to support it, when it once collapsed. Tyi was undoubtedly the main mover in this change, as it was carried out completely just when she had the greatest power, as regent after her husband's death, and controlled the boy-king. Nefertiti—of the same race as Tyi—was also a great supporter of the movement, and probably her marriage precipitated it.

But here we are met by the reminder that the Aten was the old worship of Heliopolis, that the high priest had the title of that of Heliopolis, and that there was nothing new to Egypt but a few externals. This may no doubt be technically true so far as mere words go, but a glance at the feeling and character of the whole age marks it out as due to some completely un-Egyptian influence, which no Heliopolitan source could ever have originated. That the sun was worshipped as the Aten in what appears to have been the old centre of the invading Mesopotamian race and religion at Heliopolis, does not disprove that the Syrian Ádon had anything to do with it; but only points to the worship of the sun as lord, Adon, having come in ages before, and being used as an Egyptian stem on which to graft a re-importation of the foreign ideas in the later age. The old Aten worship does not exclude the influence of the Adon, but is rather the very thing itself, ready to revert to its foreign and un-Egyptian type when a fresh wave of Asiatic ideas came in. That the name Adon, for lord, was an old Syrian word, apart altogether from the Semitic influence of the Jewish conquest, is shown by the names of Adonizedek, king of Jerusalem, Adonibezek, king of Bezek, and the general use of the name Adonis in northern Syria, there applied not to the sungod, but to the vegetation god.

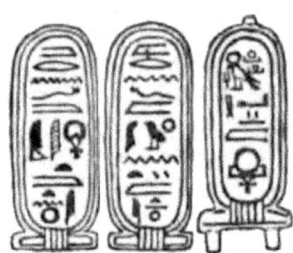

FIG. 131.—Cartouches of the Aten.

The religious changes were profound. In place of the devotion to Amen, which had completely enthralled the previous kings, the very name of Amen was proscribed and erased throughout the country. One only of the old deities, Maat, appears on the sculptures of Akhenaten; once as a full-sized protecting deity before his conversion (tomb of Ra·mes, Thebes), and after that only as an emblem of truth, a small figure held in the hand. Maat is also constantly named by the king, but only as the abstract idea of truth, and not as a deity. Before each of his cartouches he adopted the title

Ankh·em·maat, " Living in Truth"; and in face of his overwhelming devotion to the Aten-sun, it is clear that this refers to the abstract quality and not to a concrete deity.

FIG. 132.—Akhenaten and Nefertiti. The rays holding a uraeus, an *ankh*, four supporting the king, another holding an *ankh*, and three supporting the queen.

The same tendency to the abstract is shown in the sun-worship. Other ages had worshipped the human-figured sun-god Ra, or a hawk as his emblem; and when the sun itself was represented, it was as a concrete solid ball. But a more refined and really philosophical worship was substituted for this by Akhenaten, that of the radiant energy of the sun, of the sun as sustaining all life by his beams. No one — sun-worshipper or philosopher—seems to have realised until within this century the truth which was the basis of Akhenaten's worship, that the rays of the sun are the means of the sun's action, the source of all life, power, and force in the universe. This abstraction of regarding the radiant energy as all-important was quite disregarded, until recent views of the conservation of force, of heat as a mode of motion, and the identity of heat, light, and electricity, have made us familiar with the scientific conception which was the characteristic feature of Akhenaten's new worship. In every sculpture he is shown adoring the Aten, which radiates above him; an utterly new type in Egypt, distinct from all previous sculptures. Each ray ends in a hand, and these hands lay hold of the king and queen, and support their bodies and limbs, sustain their crowns, give the power symbolised by the royal uraeus, and the life symbolised by the *ankh* pressed to their lips. If this were a new religion, invented to satisfy our modern scientific conceptions, we could not find a flaw in the correctness of this view of the energy of the solar system. How much Akhenaten understood we cannot say, but he had certainly bounded forward in his views and symbolism to a position which we cannot logically improve upon at the present day. Not a rag of superstition or of falsity can be found clinging to this new worship evolved out of the old Aten of Heliopolis, the sole lord or Adon of the universe.

The great hymn to the Aten is evidently an original composition of this reign, and in view of the large share in the new worship taken personally by the king, it is probable that this hymn is partly or wholly his own composition. It has been fully edited by Professor Breasted, and is here translated by Mr. Griffith. After an introduction stating that the king and queen adore the Aten, the hymn begins :—

(*Aten ruling the course of the day.*)   [*Morning*
Thy appearing is beautiful in the horizon of heaven,
The Living Aten, the beginning of life ;
Thou risest in the horizon of the east,
Thou fillest every land with thy beauty.
                                            [*Noon*
Thou art very beautiful, brilliant and exalted above earth,
Thy beams encompass all lands which thou hast made.
Thou art the sun, thou settest their bounds,
Thou bindest them with thy love.
Thou art afar off, but thy beams are upon the land ;
Thou art on high, but the day passes with thy going.
                                            [*Night*
Thou restest in the western horizon of heaven,
And the land is in darkness like the dead.
                                            [*Men*
They lie in their houses, their heads are covered,
Their breath is shut up, and eye sees not to eye ;
Their things are taken, even from under their heads, and they
    know it not.
                                            [*Beasts*
Every lion cometh forth from his den,
And all the serpents then bite ;
The night shines with its lights,
The land lies in silence ;
For he who made them is in his horizon.

(*Aten ruling all living beings.*)
The land brightens, for thou risest in the horizon,
    Shining as the Aten in the day ;
The darkness flees, for thou givest thy beams,
    Both lands are rejoicing every day.
                                            [*Men*
Men awake and stand upon their feet,
    For thou liftest them up ;
They bathe their limbs, they clothe themselves,
    They lift their hands in adoration of thy rising,
Throughout the land they do their labours.
                                            [*Animals*
The cattle all rest in their pastures,
    Where grow the trees and herbs ;
The birds fly in their haunts,
    Their wings adoring thy *ka*.
All the flocks leap upon their feet,
The small birds live when thou risest upon them.

[*Waters*
The ships go forth both north and south,
For every way opens at thy rising.
The fishes in the river swim up to greet thee,
Thy beams are within the depth of the great sea.
          (*Aten the source of life.*)   [*Man*
Thou createst conception in women, making the issue of mankind;
Thou makest the son to live in the body of his mother,
Thou quietest him that he should not mourn,
Nursing him in the body, giving the spirit that all his growth may live.
When he cometh forth on the day of his birth,
Thou openest his mouth to speak, thou doest what he needs.

[*Animals*
The small bird in the egg, sounding within the shell,
Thou givest to it breath within the egg,
To give life to that which thou makest.
It gathers itself to break forth from the egg,
It cometh from the egg, and chirps with all its might,
It runneth on its feet, when it has come forth.
          (*Aten omnipresent.*)
How many are the things which thou hast made!
Thou createst the land by thy will, thou alone,
With peoples, herds, and flocks,
Everything on the face of the earth that walketh on its feet,
Everything in the air that flieth with its wings.

In the hills from Syria to Kush, and the plain of Egypt,
Thou givest to every one his place, thou framest their lives,
To every one his belongings, reckoning his length of days;
Their tongues are diverse in their speech,
     Their natures in the colour of their skin.
As a divider thou dividest the strange peoples.
          (*Aten watering the earth.*)
When thou hast made the Nile beneath the earth,
Thou bringest it according to thy will to make the people to live:
Even as thou hast formed them unto thyself,
Thou art throughout their lord, even in their weakness.
     Oh, lord of the land that risest for them.

Aten of the day, revered by every distant land, thou makest their life,
Thou placest a Nile in heaven that it may rain upon them,
That it may make waters upon the hills like the great sea,
Watering their fields amongst their cities.
     How excellent are thy ways!

Oh, lord of eternity, the Nile in heaven is for the strange people,
   And all wild beasts that go upon their feet.
The Nile that cometh from below the earth is for the land of Egypt,
   That it may nourish every field.
   Thou shinest and they live by thee.
         (*Aten causing the seasons.*)
Thou makest the seasons of the year to create all thy works ;
The winter making them cool, the summer giving warmth.
Thou makest the far-off heaven, that thou mayest rise in it,
That thou mayest see all that thou madest when thou wast alone.

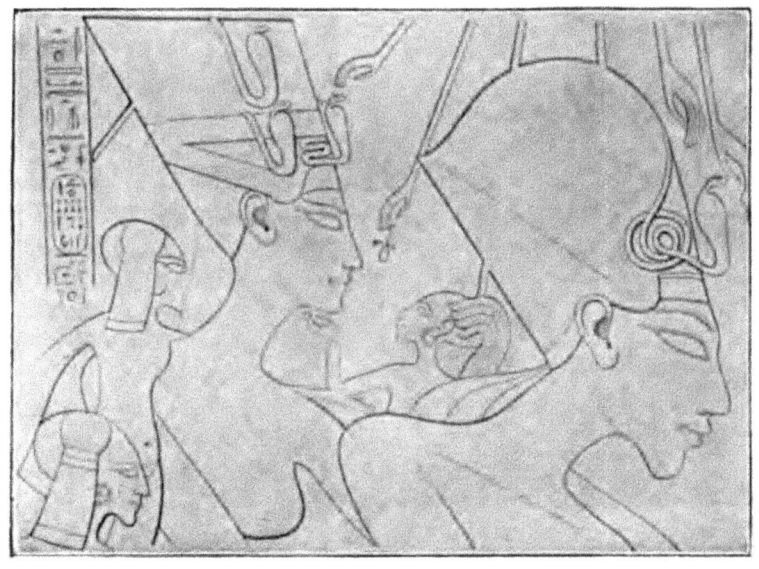

FIG. 133.—Akhenaten, Nefertiti, and daughters.

Rising in thy forms as the living Aten,
Shining afar off and returning,
The villages, the cities, and the tribes, on the road and the river,
All eyes see thee before them,
Thou art the Aten of the day over all the land.
         (*Aten revealed to the king.*)
Thou art in my heart, there is none who knoweth thee, excepting thy son Nefer·kheperu·ra·ua·en·ra ;
Thou causest that he should have understanding, in thy ways and in thy might.

The land is in thy hand, even as thou hast made them :
Thou shinest and they live, and when thou settest they die ;
For by thee the people live, they look on thy excellencies until
    thy setting.
They lay down all their labours when thou settest in the west,
And when thou risest they grow . . . .
Since the day that thou laidest the foundations of the earth,
Thou raisest them up for thy son who came forth from thy sub-
    stance,
The king of Egypt, living in Truth, lord of both lands, Nefer·
    kheperu·ra·ua·en·ra,
Son of the sun, living in Truth, Akhenaten, great in his duration ;
And the great royal wife, his beloved, lady of both lands,
    Nefer·neferu·Aten,
Nefert·iti, living and flourishing for ever eternally."

In this hymn all trace of polytheism, and of anthropomorphism, or theriomorphism, has entirely disappeared. The power of the sun to cause and regulate all existence is the great subject of praise ; and careful reflection is shown in enumerating the mysteries of the power of the Aten exemplified in the animation of nature, reproduction, the variety of races, and the source of the Nile, and watering by rain. It would tax any one in our days to recount better than this the power and action of the rays of the sun. And no conception that can be compared with this for scientific accuracy was reached for at least three thousand years after it. The impress of the new Aten worship on the old formula is curiously given by a stele found at Sakkara. It reads, "a royal offering to the Aten" (or, on the other side, "to Aten, prince of the two horizons, the sole god"), "living in truth, made by the overseer of the merchants of the temple of Aten, Huy." Here not only is the god's name changed, but the *ka* has disappeared, and the offering is "made by" (*an*) such an one (M.D. 56, 2).

In ethics a great change also marks this age. The customary glorying in war has almost disappeared ; only once, and that in a private tomb, is there any indication of war during the reign. The motto " Living in Truth " is constantly put forward as the keynote to the king's character, and to his changes in various lines. And domestic affection is held up as his ideal of life, the queen and children being shown with him on every occasion.

Fig. 134.—Group of women. Tell el Amarna.

In art the aim was the direct study of nature, with as little influence as possible from convention; animals in rapid motion, and natural grouping of plants, were specially studied, and treated in a manner more natural than in any other Oriental art. This may be best seen in the pavement frescoes, and the columns covered with creepers, found at Tell el Amarna (P.A. ii.–viii.).

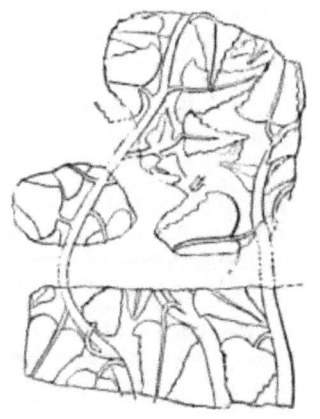

Fig. 135.—Foliage on column. Tell el Amarna.

The length of the reign is indicated by the dating on the series of wine jar fragments found at Tell el Amarna. These extend to year 17, and point therefore to a reign of 17 or 18 years. From these same jar datings we glean that the succeeding king, Ra·smenkh·ka, was co-regent with Akhenaten for a time; there are no dates of the first year, and no wine dates of the third year, but plenty of the second. This points to Ra·smenkh·ka having been associated in his first year, independent in his second, and having left the place in the third year. Such a co-regency is also pointed out by the frequency of the rings of his naming him "beloved of Ra·nefer·kheperu," or "beloved of Ua·n·Ra"; thus indicating his being dependent on Akhenaten. Of such rings there are 25 known, against only 18 with the name *Ra·ankh·kheperu* alone. So by the proportion he would seem to have lived at Tell el Amarna mainly as a co-regent.

Monuments.

The tomb of Akhenaten was excavated in a branch of one of the great valleys which open on the plain of Tell el Amarna. The situation resembles that of the tomb of Amenhotep III. at Thebes, but is more remote, being seven miles from the river (P.A. xxxiv.). The entrance is at the floor of a small side valley; the passage, after descending a short way, has a chamber on the right hand, which is covered with scenes of the mourning for the second daughter, Makt·aten, showing that she died before her father. A passage also on the right side leads round to what seems to have been the beginning of a parallel tomb to the main one, but it was left unfinished. The main tomb passage descends onward until it reaches a level chamber supported formerly by four pillars; on the right side of this is a smaller chamber. The main chamber has been all carved and painted on a stucco coat; this has now dropped off, or been destroyed, leaving only traces of the work where it had been cut through to the limestone rock. In this chamber were fragments of a red granite sarcophagus covered with sculpture, and many pieces of granite ushabtis. The tomb was discovered by the natives many years ago, and a heart scarab with gold plate was then sold at Thebes. In 1891, M. Grébaut obtained knowledge of the tomb, and it was cleared irregularly and without continuous supervision, the men employed selling the objects that were found. I describe it here from memory; and the only plan yet published is a sketch in A.R., E.E. Fund, 1892, p. 12.

Near it are two other tombs in an adjacent branch of
the valley; but these are equally unpublished, and, so
far as I know, not yet cleared.

In considering the positions of the works of Akhenaten, it must always be remembered that (unlike those of any other reign) they were very extensive at Tell el Amarna, and were all completely swept away from there in a short time. Hence they would not be used up—like other buildings—simply for local purposes; but they had to be quickly got rid of, at any cost, somewhere. They are, therefore, likely to have been taken to far greater distances than the remains of other kings; and it is only when fragments are found in position, or state the locality of their erection, that we can infer that a building of this reign existed outside of Tell el Amarna.

At Heliopolis there certainly was a temple built, as a piece of red granite found there gives the name of Mert'aten, and mentions the "building of Ra in An."

At Memphis slabs have been found re-used (N. Aeg. 117–134), bearing portions of the Aten rays and name of Akhenaten; and many other pieces about Cairo, by the mosque of Hakem and the Bab en Nasr, may have come from here or from Heliopolis. A stele at Sakhara of an "overseer of the merchants of the temple of Aten" named Huy, has been taken to prove the existence of a temple at Memphis; but the official might have been of Heliopolis. The remains at Gurob, Eshmunen, and Qus, may have come from Tell el Amarna.

At the capital of the new faith an enormous amount of work was done. The palace—a group of unconnected buildings—occupied a space of about 1500 × 500 feet or more (P.A. xxxvi.). The great temple of the Aten was about 250 feet square; it stood in an enclosure nearly half a mile long, within which were scattered various other buildings. Another temple, and many large buildings, taxed the royal resources; while a town of private mansions and houses was the work of the bureaucracy. The palace appears to have been deserted early in Ra·smenkh·ka's reign, and the town was abandoned in the next reign of Tut·ankh·amen; but even apparently as late as Hor·em·heb a cartouche was cut on the temple (P.A. xi. 5), although that king destroyed the buildings of the new faith. Of the great

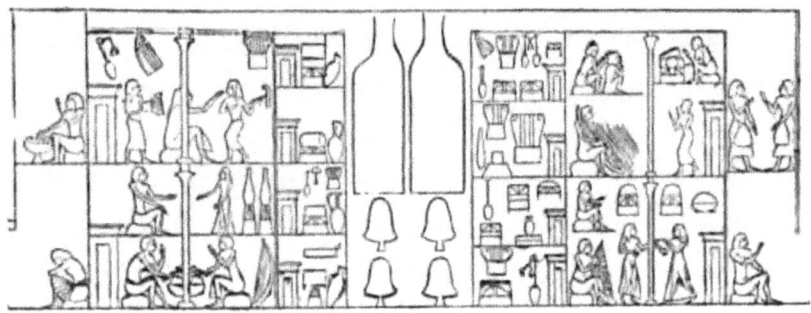

FIG. 136.—School of music and dancing.

temple most interesting views are given in the tombs; the most intelligible in connection with the plan (P.A. xxxvii.) is that in L.D. iii. 94; in side view it is less clear (L.D. 96); and another view abbreviates the long enclosure (L.D. 102), but shows the position of the numerous statues of the king, queen, and Tyi, the fragments of which have been found (P.A. 18). Around the town many rock tablets were engraved, stating its boundaries. Of these, three are known on the west bank, and eleven on the east bank. They are fully stated in P.A. 5–6; but only some of the most striking have been published, and those not exhaustively or correctly (L.D. iii. 91 a–f, 110 a, b; Pr. M. xii.–xiv.; Rec. xv. 36).

FIG. 137.—Part of ushabti of Akhenaten.

The plaster cast taken from the head of Akhenaten after his death (P.A. front) was found along with the granite fragments of the working of his funeral furniture, and the broken and spoiled granite ushabtis (P.A. 17).

In many collections are examples or portions of the stone steles with which the palace was profusely decorated. These steles are always curved and slightly slanting at the top, and bear the scene of the king, queen, and daughter, offering, without any inscription beyond the names and titles. They are cut in all materials, limestone, alabaster, quartzite, black granite, red granite, etc.; and their purpose is unknown. Such slabs are now in the Ghizeh Museum; in the room built over the pavement at Tell el Amarna; in the Ashmolean Museum; Berlin Museum; Cabinet des Medailles, Paris; Lord Amherst's Collection; and the Edwards Collection.

Many minor pieces of sculpture, artists' trial pieces, fragments of sculptures and of vases, etc., are scattered in the various collections. A large quantity of jar sealings are to be found in the storehouses at Tell el Amarna (see Ashmolean Mus.); they bear names of Amenhotep as well as of Akhenaten. A great variety of glazed pottery finger rings, as well as the moulds for making them, were also found in the town and rubbish heaps of the capital (P.A.).

South of the capital there are some rock tablets in the Hammamat valley; one by an official Amen·hotep (G.H. i. 6), and another by an Amen·mes (G.H. i. 8), both probably early in the reign: a tablet with a scene has been altered by Sety I., but shows the remains of the Aten rays (G.H. iii. 5).

At Thebes there certainly was building going on in the earlier years of the reign, the blocks there having the youthful figure of Amenhotep IV., and even showing the hawk-headed human figure of the god Har·akhti (L.D. iii. 110 c; see also Pr. M. 10-11). This building was all broken up, and re-used by Tut·ankh·amen and Hor·em·heb for other constructions at Karnak; and that it was at Thebes is proved by an inscription at Silsileh recording the making of "great sandstone obelisks of Hor·akhti in Apt·asut" (L.D. 110 i).

Another monument of importance at Silsileh (E. bank) is a large rock tablet showing the king adoring Amen Ra; it is, therefore, one of the earliest objects in his reign (S.B.A. xi. 233).

At Soleb, Akhenaten appears in the usual Egyptian style, adoring his father Amenhotep III.; unhappily the faces are destroyed (L.D. iii. 110 k). This concludes the public monuments of the king; and we now turn to minor remains.

The most important small work of the reign is the beautiful and perfect statuette of the seated king in the Louvre (well figured in L.D. iii. 295, 44). Beside the head (B. Mus.), and the mass of fragments (Amherst Coll.), from the temple statues, there is also a shoulder in limestone (G. Mus.; W.G. 402), a torso with cartouches in red quartzite (F.P. Coll.), and other fragments from the prolific ground of Tell el Amarna.

FIG. 138.—Head of statuette in Louvre.

The best portraits are, in youth, the Karnak head (L.D. iii. 294, 42) and the head on the tomb of Ra·mes at Thebes; in older life, the head in a group (L.D. iii. 111), and the head of the statuette (L.D. iii. 294, 43); and, at the end, the very facsimile of the man in his death mask (P.A. front). The poorer quality of portraits are found in uncounted instances on tombs and fragments carved in this reign.

A special class of objects of this king are the tablets bearing cartouches of the Aten on the face, and those of the king on the sides. These tablets were sometimes borne by kneeling statues of the king in adoration

(P.A. 18, 19); and larger ones stood separately as acts of devotion in the temple (L.T. 1378; Rec. xiv. 55). The tablets are sometimes of limestone, all in one with the statue; others are of red granite and of blue glaze.

Of minor objects of this reign there is a great amount (P.A. xiii.-xx.). Rings of pottery are the commonest; and rings of gold or of copper are frequent, as much so as scarabs. Some points indicate that the scarabs belong to the beginning of the reign; a large one with the king supporting the Aten cartouches gives his name as Amenhotep, showing it to be before his 6th year; other scarabs name him as "beloved of Amen," "beloved of Atmu," "beloved of Tahuti," "beloved of Hor·akhti," "lord of the sweet wind," etc. The rings, on the contrary, are severely Atenistic. For the letters found at Tell el Amarna, see the chapter on the Decline of Egypt in Syria.

FIG. 139.—Scarabs of Amenhotep IV.

PRIVATE MONUMENTS.

The private tombs of this age are numerous, and afford nearly all the information that we possess for the period. The names of the principal persons are as follow, with the numbers of their tombs at Tell el Amarna as officially re-numbered in 1891, and published in the plan (P.A. xxxv.) The descriptions are from my own notes.

    Aahmes, tomb 3. "True royal scribe, fan-bearer on right of the king, keeper of the storehouses, keeper of the palace." Not much sculpture, some unfinished painting; statue at end. Figure of Aahmes and prayer to the Aten (L.D. iii. 98 a; B.H. 449).

    Aniy, tomb 23. Son of Pa·kha. A peculiar tomb in every way: the inscriptions are of black inlaid in white plaster, and the face of Aniy is curious. He was keeper of the palace to Amenhotep II., and scribe of the royal table. Two princesses are shown (Rec. xv. 43).

Anui, stele from Tell el Amarna. G. Mus. (V.G. 691).

Apiy, tomb 10. Keeper of the palace. Figures of royal family, three princesses: fine work, no exaggeration, and heads perfect.

Apuy, tomb at Thebes. Overseer of the offerings of Amen in Apt. Scenes of Amenhotep IV.; architecture in the other scenes of same age. (Name of Ramessu II. painted on a boat probably later; like name of Alexander added on an amulet in XVIIIth dynasty, tomb of Sen·nefer.) (M.A.F. v. 604.)

Auta, court artist of Tyi (L.D. 100 a). Father Nauy and brother Kharu were scribes of sculptors; wife, Nezem·men·nefer, sister of Huy (?) (Lb. D. 1168).

Ay, tomb 25. Fan-bearer at right of king, keeper of the mares, true royal scribe, divine father, afterwards king Ay; wife Ty, nurse of the queen. Largest tomb, of splendid work, but quite unfinished, no tomb chamber. Five princesses. Scenes of the royal family and the populace (L.D. iii. 103–106 a; Rec. xv. 45–9; Br. A.). Three discs of ivory with the above titles and " *sem* in the divine feasts" are in Turin (Rec. iii. 127).

Ay, tomb 7. Same titles, and probably earlier tomb of same man; scenes of tribute: royal family, three princesses and queen's sister Nezem·mut (L.D. iii. 107 d–109; Rec. xv. 37).

Bek, " overseer of works in the red mountain for the pylons, chief of the artists for the very great monuments of the king in the temple of Aten in Akhet·aten, son of the chief of the artists Men, born of Roy in An," adoring the king and Aten on a rock tablet, Aswan (M.I. i. 40).

Her·sekheper, tomb 13; or Nefer·kheperu·her·se·kheper: prince of Akhet·aten. Interior unfinished, inscription on door (Rec. xv. 38).

Huy, overseer of merchants, stele Sakkara, wife Nezem·nefer (M.D. 56, 2).

Huya, tomb 1. Scribe of treasuries of Tyi, overseer of works in the palace. Scenes of visit of Tyi in 12th year; Aken·aten borne on a throne; views of temple; prisoners of Kharu; two princesses and Bekt·aten (L.D. iii. 100-102).

Kedet, ushabti with *suten du hotep* to the Aten for his sister Ket. Zurich Mus. (S.B.A. vii. 200).

Kha·em·uas, tomb, Memphis (Ms. G. 427).

Mahu, tomb 9. Chief of the Mazau (police). Much fine sculpture; scenes of king and queen in a chariot; of runners capturing a man; sentry-houses joined by a rope. One princess. Short hymn to Aten (M.A.F. i. 16).

May, scribe, offering to Any in tomb 23 (Rec. xv. 45).

Mery·neit, keeper of temple, tomb Sakkara, fragments. G. Mus. (M.M. 449). Berlin (B.C. 2070, p. 199); and see worship of Neit at this time (P.A. 33).

Nanay, statue, Thebes (B.G.I. i. p. 274).

Nekt·pa·aten, tomb 12. Hereditary prince, seal-bearer, vizier (?); tomb only begun (Rec. xv. 38).

Pa·ari, tomb at Thebes; priest of Amen; father, Shery; sons, Ptah·mes, User·hat, Amen·hotep. A hieratic inscription by a priest Atefsenb is dated in the third year of a king "Ra·nefer·kheperu, son of the sun Aten·nefer·neferu . . ." Probably this is an early variant of Akhenaten's name, which he afterwards transferred to his queen on his marriage (M.A.F. v. 588).

Pa·aten·em·heb, tomb 24. Royal scribe, overseer of works in Akhet·aten. Chamber only begun (Rec. xv. 45).

Pa·nehesi, tomb 6. Scenes of royal family adoring: four princesses; horses and chariots; palace front; etc. Sister, Abneba (L.D. iii. 91 h-p).

Penthu, tomb 5. Scene with fine gateway; royal family with three princesses: long wide passage to chamber (L.D. iii. 91 q).

Ptah·mery, tomb at Gizeh. Chief of goldsmiths of temple of Aten (Ms. G. 304).

Ra·mery, tomb 2. Scenes of king in garden canopy, queen straining wine into his cup, six princesses; dancers and wrestlers; Lybians, Amorites, and Syrians kneeling to the king. Mert·aten married to Ra·smenkh·ka, whose cartouches appear as the king in whose reign the tomb was finished (L.D. 98 b, 99 a, b).

FIG. 140.—Group of scribes. Flor. Mus.

Ra·mery, tomb 4. High priest of Aten. Large tomb, scenes with views of temple with altars of burnt-offering; palace and gardens; royal family with four princesses; guard carrying lantern; blind harper with blind singers (see W.M.C. Fig. 218) (L.D. 92–97 d; Pr. A.; C.N. ii. 319): name on shard (P.A. 33).

Ra·mes, tomb, Thebes, with portraits of the young Amenhotep IV. and older Akhenaten.

Ra·mes, tomb 11. Royal scribe, general, keeper of palace to Amenhotep III. Scenes of king, queen, and one princess (M.A.F. i. 9). Ushabti and carnelian serpent head inscribed: with a dealer at Thebes, 1895.

Rud·ua, tomb o (before tomb 1); name over north corner of door.

Suta, tomb 19. Keeper of the treasury. Long passage unfinished, nothing on façade.

Suti, tomb 15. Fan-bearer behind the king; hall of columns begun, lintel and jambs inscribed (Rec. xv. 42).

Tutu, tomb 8. Am·khent; grand tomb, hall of 12 columns, long texts and scenes, but badly wrecked recently. Scenes of king, queen, and three princesses. The columns are decorated with groups of ducks, as in the palace (L.D. 106 b–107 c; Rec. xv. 37).

. . . amu, tomb 18; born of Pa·aten·ankh; wide passage, well cut, end unfinished.

. . . . . tomb 14. Fan-bearer at the right of the king, general, keeper of the temple of Ra in Heliopolis, high priest of Aten, keeper of the temple of Aten, keeper of all the works of the king. Scenes of the king, queen, and three princesses; five boats, etc., all painted in black outline. The owner was degraded, and his name and his figure everywhere erased and covered with plaster (Rec. xv. 42).

For names of inspectors on ostraka, see P.A. 33.

ROYAL FAMILY.

The marriage of Tadukhipa, daughter of Dushratta, we have already noticed; and there can scarcely be a doubt but that she is the same person as the evidently foreign queen Nefertiti, who is the only wife ever represented with Akhenaten, and was mother of all his children that are known. Her hereditary claim to the throne, and probably Egyptian descent, has already been noted. She was married early in the 4th year of his reign, shortly before his father's death; at first she took only the name of Nefertiti (P.A. xiii. 23), while her husband was known as Amenhotep (IV.). Before adopting the name Akhenaten, he seems to have occasionally (in his 3rd year) used the name Aten·nefer·neferu, or "the beautiful excellency of Aten" (M.A.F. v. 588), which name he transferred later to the queen, who on all the Aten monuments is known as Aten·nefer·neferu·nefertiti. She appears to have had six daughters, and to have survived Akhenaten, as she is shown actively waiting on him in his last days. From her age it is likely that she lived on till Horemheb, or even Sety I.

FIG. 141.—Death cast of Akhenaten.

The best portraits of the queen that are published

FIG. 142.—Nefertiti making an offering.

are in the large group (L.D. iii. 111), see Fig. 133, and the stele fragment (P.A. xii. 1), see Fig. 142; while for detail of physiognomy and perfect vitality, nothing can exceed the fragment of a statue (Amherst Coll.; P.A. i. 15), see Fig. 117. Other portions of five statues of hers (or possibly some of Tyi, L.D. iii. 102) have been found by the Aten temple at Tell el Amarna (Amherst Coll. P.A. 18).

A building specially belonging to the queen, in the palace at Tell el Amarna, was probably her court or *harim* (P.A. xxxvi). The columns were of glazed tile-work (P.A. 9), the walls painted with scenes (P.A. v.), and the floors frescoed over with paintings of pools, birds, cattle, wild plants, and bouquets (P.A. ii. iii. iv.). In the courtyard of this building was a well, covered with a canopy on beautifully carved columns, and round the coping of the wall ran a band of inscription with the queen's titles (P.A. x.). Many fragments of sculpture and of vases bear the queen's name; and there are rings of hers, one of gold in the Louvre, others of pottery; but no scarabs are known, that form having been early renounced by the king, probably before his marriage.

Mert·aten, the eldest daughter, is shown on nearly all her father's monuments, standing behind her parents. She was born in probably the 4th year of his reign, as the second daughter was born in the 6th year; and she was married to Ra·smenkh·ka, probably just before Akhenaten's death, as her husband was co-regent with Akhenaten at the last, and his and her names are found together in a tomb of which the decoration was in progress under Akhenaten (L.D. iii. 99 a).

As Akhenaten reigned certainly 17, and probably 18 years, this would make her about 13 when she was married. Her husband appears to have reigned for 12 years, so that she was only 25 at his death. Rings with her name are known, but none show the transition to Amen worship; from this and the total absence of scarabs of hers, it seems that she passed into obscurity before the fall of Atenism.

Makt·aten, the second daughter, died very shortly before her father; she appears in a group of six daughters (L.D. iii. 99 b), so she probably died between her 9th and 11th year. Her tomb was a side chamber in the passage of her father's sepulchre; and the royal family are there shown mourning for her.

Ankh·s·en·pa·aten, born about the 8th year of her father's reign, must have been but 10 years old at his death. After that, therefore in her sister's reign, she was married to Tut·ankh·aten. After his accession he revived the Amen worship, and rings of his bear the double reading A $\left\{ \begin{array}{c} m \\ t \end{array} \right\}$ en·kheperu·neb; while later he was solely named Tut·ankh·amen. Her name was changed to Ankh·s·en·amen, "Her life is from Amen." She was probably only 31 at her husband's death, and nothing further is known of her. A few pottery rings with her name are found at Tell el Amarna, all apparently made at one time, perhaps for presents on her birthday.

Of the other daughters, Nefer·neferu·aten, Nefer·neferu·ra, and Sotep·en·ra, nothing is known beyond their figures and names on general monuments (L.D.

FIG. 143.—Three princesses, their two nurses, and Nezem·mut.

iii. 99). One of them married the son of Burnaburyas (see letter 16). The queen's sister, Nezem·mut, who is shown in one tomb (L.D. iii. 109), may be the same Nezem·mut who was the queen of Hor·em·heb. If she were about 10 at the queen's marriage, she would have been about 24 at Akhenaten's death, and 62 at the death of Hor·em·heb. The difficulty is that his inscription implies that he did not marry her till his accession, when she would be 58. The marriage to a royal high priestess of Amen was, of course, purely a political necessity to legitimize the king's position; but it would be strange if no younger priestess of the royal line could be then found. The parentage of Bakt·aten has been discussed at the end of the last reign.

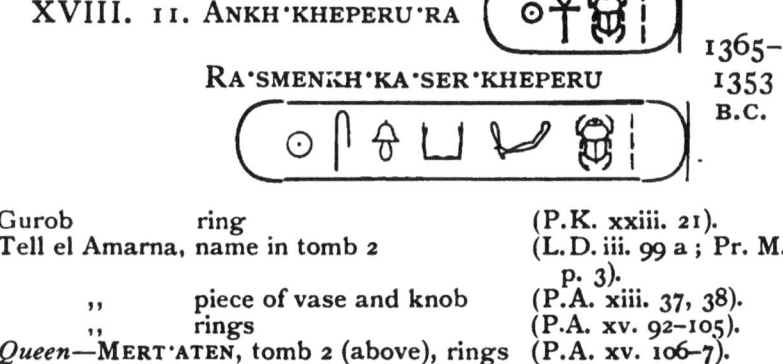

XVIII. 11. ANKH·KHEPERU·RA

RA·SMENKH·KA·SER·KHEPERU

1365–1353 B.C.

Gurob	ring	(P.K. xxiii. 21).
Tell el Amarna,	name in tomb 2	(L.D. iii. 99 a; Pr. M. p. 3).
,,	piece of vase and knob	(P.A. xiii. 37, 38).
,,	rings	(P.A. xv. 92–105).
Queen—MERT·ATEN, tomb 2 (above), rings		(P.A. xv. 106–7).

Excepting a ring found at Gurob, this king is solely known from his remains at Tell el Amarna; yet he does not seem to have lived there for more than two or three years after the death of Akhenaten, for in the great hall of pillars in the palace a heap of wine jars had accumulated, which bear dates of the 2nd year. This cannot be Akhenaten's 2nd year; nor is it likely to be Tut·ankh·amen's date, as there is but one mention of Ra·smenkh·ka in all the tombs here, showing that he did not spend much of his twelve years' reign in the place. It seems, therefore, that he abandoned the palace in his 3rd year, and may have moved from there before that. This will account for the rarity of his monuments, as any at Thebes would be worked up by Horemheb.

In the latest tomb at Tell el Amarna (No. 2), where Akhenaten has all six daughters figured, the decoration went on after his death, with the names of Ra·smenkh·ka and Mert·amen. This is the only sculpture giving the names of this king, and the reading of the personal name has been uncertain: Lepsius read it Ra·se·aa·ka·nekht·kheperu (L.D. iii. 99 a); Prisse as Ra·se·hek·ka·ser·kheperu, but he shows that it was injured in his time (Pr.M. p. 3); unhappily it has all been destroyed in the horrible mutilation which has recently befallen the tombs here. The rings which bear this name are now our best authority for it (P.A. xv. 103–105); they show that Prisse was certainly right as to *ser*; but they

FIG. 144.—Rings of Ankh·kheperu·ra.

FIG. 145.—Rings of Ankh·kheperu·ra.
1. "Beloved of *Nefer·kheperu·ra*."
2. "Beloved of *Ua·n·ra*."
3. *Ankh·kheperu·ra* (alone).

give a different reading to the *aa* of Lepsius, or the *hek* of Prisse, for they indicate *menkh* as the sign.

During his residence at Tell el Amarna this king always claimed his authority from his predecessor. His rings that belong to his residence here, being found in the palace rubbish, all read "beloved of Nefer·kheperu·ra," or "beloved of Ua·n·ra," the names of Akhenaten. Other rings found in the town bear only his simple names, belonging probably to the later part of his reign. A piece of an alabaster vase, and a green and violet glazed box handle, also bear his name (P.A. xiii. 37, 38).

FIG. 146.—Ring of Mert·aten.

His queen we have already fully noticed under her father's reign.

XVIII. 12. RA·KHEPERU·NEB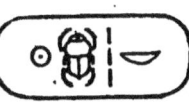

1353–1344 B.C.

AMEN·TUT·ANKH·HAQ·AN·RES

Memphis	Serapeum, burial of Apis II.	(M.S. iii. 2; M.S. Ms. 125).
,,	Pottery rings	F.P. Coll.
Gurob	Alabaster vase	F.P. Coll. (P.K. xviii.).
,,	Wooden cubit	F.P. Coll. (P.I. xxiv. 12).
,,	Rings and pendants	(P.K. xxiii.; P.I. xxiii.).
Tell el Amarna	Rings and pendants	(P.A. xv.).
Ekhmim	Tomb	(B.I.E. ii. ser. 6, 87).
Abydos	Stele of Khonsu G. Mus.	(M.A. 1109).
Karnak	6 blocks in pylon	(A.Z. xxii. 41; Pr. M. xi. 1).
	Block usurped by Horemheb	(L.D. 119 b).
,,	Block and statue (?) (Temple of Mut).	
Thebes	Restored temple of Tahutmes IV.	} (S.B.A. x. 130).
	Inscription on wood H. P. Coll.	
,,	Tomb of Hui	(L.D. 115–8).
Scribe's palette with cartouche		(C.M. 191, 2).
Knob handles	Leyd. M.; G. Coll.; F.P. Coll.	
Kohl tubes	Leyd. M.; B. Mus.	(Rev. A. i. iii. 715).
Portrait		(L.D. iii. 296).

Queen—ANKH·S·EN·ATEN or AMEN.

Alabaster vase	F.P. Coll. (P.K. xviii.).
Wooden cubit	F.P. Coll. (P.I. xxiv. 12).
Kohl tube	(Rev. A. i. iii. 715).
Scarabs and rings.	

Of this reign we know scarcely anything, except from the fine tomb of Hui. The paintings on that show that the princes of the Rutennu in Syria, and of

Kush in the Sudan, were both subject to Egypt, and brought offerings and tribute. This points to a continuity of Egyptian power, and shows that what-

FIG. 147.—Head of Tut·ankh·amen.

ever changes had gone on in the fall of Akhenaten's ideals, the vitality of Egypt abroad was not entirely destroyed.

The main feature of this reign was the reversion to the worship of Amen. This is indicated by the double reading of a ring as Amen or Aten (P.A. xv. 118); and also by the king's name, Tut·ankh·amen. In the long period assigned to Horos, 36 years in Manetho, which cannot

FIG. 148.—Rings of Tut·ankh·amen.
1. *Aten-Amen, Ra·kheperu·neb.*
2, 3. *Ra·kheperu·neb, Setep·amen·ra.*

be applied to the 17 or 18 years reign of Akhenaten, we may see perhaps the duration of the Aten worship under the orthodox name of Horos. This would point to the occurrence of the change in this reign.

The claim of Tut·ankh·amen to the throne was through his wife, Ankhsenpaaten, altered to Ankhsenamen, the daughter of Nefertiti and Akhenaten; he may also have been descended of the royal family, though the fact that he calls Amenhotep III. his father (on the Barkal lions, B. Mus.; Rec. xi. 212) cannot be taken as proving a natural relationship.

FIG. 149.—Ring of Ankhsenamen.

FIG. 150.—Pendant of Tutankhamen. Serapeum.

The monuments of this reign are not wide spread, for they only appear in the heart of Egypt, from Memphis to Thebes. At the Serapeum one Apis was buried in this reign. The tomb contained four canopic jars, and some glazed pendants with the name of the king, "beloved son of Hepu" (M.S. III, pl. 2, p. 8; M.S. Ms. 125).

At Gurob some objects of this reign were found; pieces of an alabaster vase, and a wooden cubit, inscribed for the king and queen, and rings and pendants also (P.K. xviii. xxiii.; P.I. xxiii. xxiv.).

FIG. 151.—Alabaster vase inscription of Tutankhamen and queen. F.P. Coll.

At Tell el Amarna there are no buildings or tombs of this reign, but the town was not yet deserted, as rings of his are found scattered about. Private remains of a tomb at Ekhmim, and a stele from Abydos, are known (B.I.E. ii. ser. 6, 87 ; M.A. 1109).

At Karnak the only remains of buildings are in blocks re-used by Horemheb in his pylon X. (Pr. M. xi. 1 ; W.G. 404 ; and apparently in the same pylon, A.Z. xxii. 41) ; and a block in the temple of Mut. A large grey granite statue there is probably of this king also. On the western bank Tut·ankh·amen restored a temple of Tahutmes IV., as we learn from a fragment of the furniture (H.P. Coll., S.B.A. x. 130). The fine paintings of the tomb of Hui we have already noticed ; unhappily they have been largely injured since the copying by Lepsius (L.D. 115–8).

A few small objects and scarabs, and many rings and ring moulds, are known. The best portrait of the king is that copied by Lepsius (L.D. iii. 296, 49). See Fig. 147.

Fig. 152.—Bronze ring of Tutankhamen. F.P. Coll.

The queen, Ankh·s·en·amen, was very important, and her name is almost as often found as that of her husband. Such prominence points to her descent being more important than that of her husband, owing to her being the daughter of Nefertiti and Akhenaten. No children are known.

XVIII. 13. RA·KHEPER·KHEPERU·AR·MAAT

DIVINE FATHER AY,
NETER·HEQ·UAS

1344–1332 B.C.

Tomb   Valley of kings' tombs   (L.D. 113 a–g).

Memphis	Rings	F.P. Coll.	
Gurob	Rings	F.P. Coll.	(P.K. xxiii.; P.I. xxiii.).
Ekhmim	Shrine		(L.D. iii. 114 a–d).
Karnak	Blocks re-used		(C.N. ii. 45).
Shatawi (22° 17′ N.)	Shrine of Pasar		(L.D. iii. 114 e–h).
Portrait	From tomb		(R.S. xv. 63).
Stele of Min·nekht, 4th year		Berlin Mus.	(L.D. 114 i).
,, ,,		Louvre Mus.	(P.R. ii. 90; S.B.A.T. viii. 306).
,, Tutu		B. Mus. 130.	

Rings, gold, Leyd. Mus.; pottery, various. Scarabs.

Queen—TY.
    Head at Ekhmim shrine   (L.D iii. 114 d).
    Figure in king's tomb   (B.E. 226).

The descent of this king and his queen is unknown;

FIG. 153.—Head of Queen Ty.

and we can only presume that one or other were of royal blood, from their being allowed to take possession of the throne. The queen is called the "great heiress," which would indicate her royal descent (L.D. 113 c). Ay was not a king's son, but only calls himself "divine father," a priestly title. There can be no doubt but that he is the same divine father Ay, whom we have seen to have the grandest tomb at Tell el Amarna; for that tomb being un-

FIG. 154.—Ay and Ty, from the great tomb, Tell el Amarna.

finished (as also a yet earlier one of the same man), there is no evidence against his having made a fresh tomb in the royal valley at Thebes when he there attained to power. The Ay of Tell el Amarna had a wife, Ty, and the same name appears for the queen of Ay. Ay had been fan-bearer at the king's right hand, keeper of the mares, true royal scribe, and divine father; and Ty, his wife, was "great nurse, nourisher of the goddess queen, adorner of the king" (L.D. 105 f). The likeness of this nurse to queen Ty is evident in the above figures. And Ay the official is also like King Ay.

Ay shows a complete reversion to the older worship. His first tomb (7 at Tell el Amarna) has three princesses, and was therefore decorated about the 9th year of Akhenaten (about 1374 B.C.), so that he can hardly have been born later than 1400 B.C. His second tomb (25 at Tell el Amarna) has five princesses, so it belongs to about the 13th year, and was sumptuously worked during the last six or eight years of Akhenaten. These dates would place the working of his third tomb (Thebes) to as late or later than the 56th to 68th year of his age. There was thus plenty of time for him to forget the new faith, for which he had taken so strong a part in his early days. And in place of the suppression of the *ka* formula, as under Akhenaten (M.D. 56, 2), the figure of the king's *ka* is put forward in his tomb (L.D. 113 a). For a portrait from the tomb see R.S. xv. 63.

The principal monument of this reign is a shrine cut high up on the face of the cliffs behind Ekhmim. A grand rock-cut façade with figures and inscriptions, some twenty feet high, rises above a rock cell or chapel (L.D. iii. 114 a–d). The tomb of the king in the western valley at Thebes (L.D. 113 a–c) contains a red granite sarcophagus, with figures of Isis, Nebhat, Selk, and Neit at the corners, embracing the block with their wings (L.D. 113 d, g ; Pr. A.). A re-used block at Karnak, on the south side of the pylon II., shows that Ramessu II. destroyed some building of Ay (C.N. ii. 45).

At Shatawi, a few miles south of Abusimbel, on the east side, is a rock-cut shrine made by Pa·sar, the prince of Kush. He there adores Anpu, Sebek, Usertesen III., and Anuke; while the king offers to Amen, Ra, Ptah, Mentu, Hor, and Sati (L.D. iii. 114 e–h).

Of private remains there are two steles of Min·nekht,

RA·KHEPER·KHEPERU·AR·MAAT [DYN. XVIII. 13.]

who was overseer of works in the temple of Ay, prince, first prophet of Min and Isis in Apu (Ekhmim), overseer of storehouses of all the gods in Takahti, and of Min in Khenti. These steles probably come from Ekhmim. One stele is in Berlin, dated in 4th year (L.D. iii. 114 i; S.B.A.T. viii. 312); the other in the Louvre (P.R. ii. 90; S.B.A.T. viii. 306). A stele of this reign, for Thuthu, royal scribe, keeper of the palace, is in the British Museum (Lb. D. 615).

FIG. 155.—Scarab of Ay. F.P. Coll.

Of small objects the finest is a gold ring at Leyden (P.Sc. 1355). Pottery rings are found at Memphis; but such are not common, and the scarabs are even scarcer.

Queen Ty is only shown in the tomb (defaced), and on the Ekhmim stele (L.D. iii. 114 d). Her earlier figure (before accession) is at Tell el Amarna (L.D. iii. 105 f). No children are known.

XVIII. 14.
RA·SER·KHEPERU
(SOTEP·EN·RA)

HOR·EM·HEB
(MER·EN·AMEN)

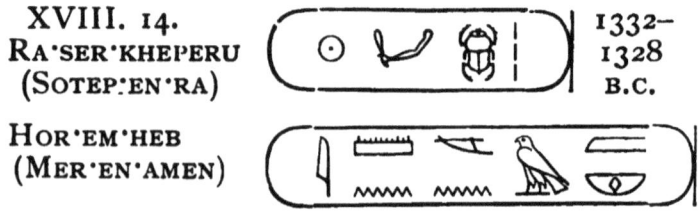

1332–
1328
B.C.

Royal tomb unknown.

Memphis		Tomb before accession	(M.D. 74, 75; S.I. ii. 92; A.Z. xv. 149; R.E. ii. 104–6).
		Apis burials, Serapeum	(M.S. iii. 4, 1–6; M.S. Ms. 66).
		Piece of stele	(F.P. Coll.).
	,,	Capital in Cairo	(W.G. 409).
	,,	Rings	(F.P. Coll.).
Gurob		Rings	(P.K. xxiii.; P.I. xxiii.).

[B.C. 1332–1328.]   HOR·EM·HEB   243

Tell el Amarna	Fragment in Aten temple	(P.A. xi. 5).
Abydos	Frog with queen's name	(M.A. ii. 40 m).
Karnak	Pylon X.	(C.N. ii. 180).
,,	Pylon XI.	(L.D. iii. 119 e; R.A. 64).
	Connecting walls of pylons	(C.N. ii. 180; M.D. 88; B.E. 165–6).
	Avenue of 128 sphinxes	(C.N. ii. 174; M.K. plan).
	Wall between pylon V. and sanctuary	(C.N. ii. 139).
	Stele	(A.Z. xxvi. 70).
	Inscription in temple of Ptah	(M.K. 47 d).
	Block in pylon of Khonsu temple	(C.N. ii. 217, 221).
Luxor	Usurped colonnade	(B.E. 129).
Deir el Bahri	Restoration inscription	(C.N. i. 574; L.D. iii. 119 c).
Medinet Habu	,, ,,	(L.D. iii. 202 d).
Silsileh	Rock temple, scenes of gods	(L.D. iii. 119 f, g, h).
,,	,, ,, Sudan war	(L.D. iii. 120–1).
Kom Ombo	Block re-used by Ptolemies	(P.O.N. 479).
Kuban	Lion-headed statue	(My. E. 538).
Gebel Addeh	Rock shrine	(L.D. 122 a–f; plan in C.M. ii. 5).

Steles (3) as general	P. Mus.	(P.R. ii. 57).
Stele ,,	L. Mus.	(A.Z. xxiii. 80).
Fragment (from tomb?)	Zizinia Coll.	(S.B.A. xi. 424).
,, ,,	Vienna	(S.B.A. xi. 425).

Statues, colossal, M. Habu	Berl. M.	(L.D. iii. 112 c).
,, ,, seated,	Luqsor Hotel	(W.G. 411).
,, with queen	T. Mus.	(L.T. 1379; R.S. xliv. 5,A.; T.S.B.A. iii. 486).
,, with Amen	T. Mus.	(C.F.E. pl. 85).
,, with Horus (Castel Cattajo)		(W.G. 411).
Bust from kneeling statue	F. Mus.	(S. Cat. F. 1507).
Hathor cow suckling king	F. Mus.	(S. Cat. F. 1225).
Portraits, best, from statue		(L.D. iii. 112 c).
,, ,, from pylon		(L.D. iii. 112 a; R.A. 64).
Ostrakon, 21st year	B. Mus.	(B.I.H.D. 14; B.H. 473).
Papyrus, 6 lines broken	G. Mus.	(W.G. 411).
Wooden vase		(W.G. 412).

Bronze plaque	P. Mus.	(P.L. p. 108).	
Rings, amulets, and scarabs		(W.M.C. ii. 342, etc. etc.).	

Queen—NEZEM·MUT.

Statue with king	T. Mus.	(L.T. 1379; xliv. 5, A.).	R.S.

Rings (F.P. Coll.); scarab (Berl. M.).

The first question that arises in this reign is whether the king is the same person as the general Horemheb, the portions of whose tomb from Sakkara are so well known. This tomb belonged to an official whose dignities closely correspond to those which king Horemheb states that he exercised before his accession. Not only is there a wide claim to having been only second to the king in all respects, by both the general and the hereafter king, but the precise positions occupied by each are practically exclusive of any other such official. We read on the statue at Turin about the king, and on other monuments about the general as follows:—

KING.	GENERAL.
King Horemheb before accession had been	the general Horemheb was
(6) Appointed to fix laws;	chosen to regulate both lands, hearer of trials alone (M.D. 74);
(6) Alone without a second;	sole companion, chief above the chiefs, great above the great (M.D. 74);
(7) He satisfied the king about quarrels in the palace;	keeper of the palace (M.D. 74); judge in the palace, chief of secrets of the palace, fan-bearer of the king (R.E. ii. 104-6);
(9) Governed Egypt for many years;	prince in the land to its limits (S.I. ii. 92);
(11) As chief and heir of the whole land.	chief general, great chief of the people, heir (M.D. 74).

When we further see that the "many years" of king Horemheb must extend through the reign of Ay, and perhaps back into that of Tut·ankh·amen; while the general's monuments begin at the end of the Aten period, which was under Tutankhamen, and go on into the full polytheism which succeeded that, it is evident that these two great viceroys were contemporary. Is it possible, then, to suppose that two different persons of the same name wielded the same unique powers over the whole country, at the same period? I think not. Horemheb the general must, in face of such statements, be the same as Horemheb the hereafter king, and as such we treat him here.

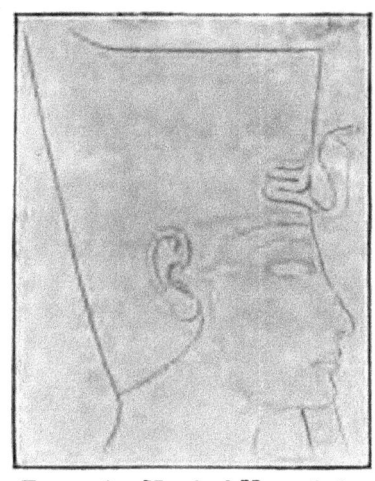

FIG. 156.—Head of Horemheb.

A discrepancy exists between Manetho and the monuments in the chronology of the reign. We have seen how in previous reigns the years, and even the months, stated by Manetho fit together with the monumental record, showing scarcely any signs of error; and we should therefore try all hypotheses before resorting to the rejection of the historian's statements. In Manetho, summarised by Africanus, we find 5 years, in the more detailed copy by Josephus, 4 years 1 month, a slight difference, due, perhaps, to the treatment of odd months in other reigns. But, beside monumental dates of the 1st and 3rd years on important work, we find on one ostrakon the 7th and 21st years are named. In judging between the short reign of 5 years and the long one of 21 years there are a few external points. It is true that two Apis burials probably belong to this reign; but one of these was added by cutting a side chamber in the tomb of the other, and finishing it before the plastering and decoration of the outer tomb. The junction of the tombs points to one burial closely following on the other; and the decorating of the first tomb appears not to have been done till the second was used. The name of Horemheb is only found in the ruins of the chapel over the first tomb. Certainly the conditions do not impose a long reign on the history: for the second Apis seems to have been buried in an emergency, soon after the first, yet not necessarily in the same reign. Looking to the future, the reign of Ramessu II. is tied by the Sirius festival of Merenptah; but we might shorten the reign of Sety to make room for 21 years for Horemheb; yet if we did so, the relation of the era of Menophres to Men·peh·ra would be certainly thrown out.

There is one solution of the discrepancy which seems quite possible. If Horemheb dated his monuments from his accession for the first few years; and then, on his finally destroying the Aten worship, if he dated back his reign from the time of Amen being re-established under Tut·ankh·amen, we should have a solution. That Horemheb had helped to re-establish Amen appears very likely; but that he did not abolish the Aten until some way on in his reign, is shown by his name being carved in the Aten temple when not yet destroyed at Tell el Amarna. We conclude, then, that the 1st and 3rd years are dated from the accession to sole power, but that, on final abolition of the Aten worship, Horemheb glorified himself by dating back throughout his viceregal period to the time when he had come into favour as the restorer of Amen. The ostrakon dated in the 21st year, and referring to the 7th year, would then be of the 5th year of his sole reign, and refer back to the 3rd year of Ay, reckoned as the 7th of Horemheb. This is the best result yet attainable.

The earliest monument of Horemheb is a stele at Leyden (A.Z. xxiii. 80), where he is figured in the style of Akhenaten, adoring the god Hor·akhti. He was already "great general." This may well be towards the middle of the reign of Tut·ankh·amen, say 1350 B.C.; and if the "great general" was then 40, he would have been born about 1390. Next come three steles in Paris, where he adores the gods of Abydos, Up·uat, Anpu, and Hathor; he is called royal scribe and general (P.R. ii. 57). Next he began the decoration of his tomb at Memphis, and a stele (B.M. 551) bears a hymn to Tum Hor·akhti, born of Hathor, son of Ptah, and names Tahuti, Maat, Osiris, and Horus (A.Z. xv. 149).

The door jambs show him bearing the royal uraeus (a sign of the supreme judge), and name him as "Heir, chancellor, sole companion, chief over the chiefs, great over the great ones, hearer of trials alone, keeper of the palace, great general, overseer of the prophets of Horus, follower of the king, royal scribe, great prince of the *rekhitu*, sent by the king at the head of his soldiers against the lands of the south and north, he whom the king has chosen to regulate both lands, general of the generals of the king, he who makes joy in the whole land, chief of the secrets of the palace, acting alone, treasurer of the royal guard, companion of his master on the field of battle that day he overthrew the Sati" (M.D. 74-5).

Somewhat later may be the other parts of the tomb, in which he is further entitled "Judge of the palace, and fan-bearer at the king's right hand" (R.E. ii. 104-6). While later still the door jambs (B. Mus.) add that he was "prince in the entire land, scribe of the recruits, overseer of works in the mountains of quarrying abundantly for the king in both lands" (S.I. ii. 92). Thus all military, judicial, courtly, religious, and business power had gradually come into the hands of this great noble during the feeble reign of Ay. The general cannot have been very strong at the beginning of Ay's reign, or the "divine father" would never have reached the throne. It seems as if there had been a great outburst of Amen worship at the close of Tut·

ankh·amen's reign, and a religious representative stood firmest in the kingdom; while real power steadily accumulated in the strong hands of the general who became viceroy.

A most valuable picture of his rise is given in his autobiography after his accession. On the granite group of him and Nezem·mut at Turin we read that "Amen king of the gods dandled him, and Horus was his protection like amulets on his body; when he came forth from the womb he was enveloped in reverence, the aspect of a god was upon him; the arm was bowed to him as a child, and great and small did obeisance before him. When he was a youth and unlearned, the form of a god was in his aspect, in beholding his figure one was strengthened. His father Horus stood behind him, forming and protecting him . . . knowing the day of his peace to give to him his kingdom. Behold this god advanced his son in the face of all people, he made wide his way until the day came when he should receive his office, until in his time the heart of the king was satisfied with his matters, rejoicing in his choice. He placed him at the head of the land to secure the laws of the two lands, as Heir of the whole land. He was alone without a rival, and the ways of the people were according to his command. He was called before the king, for if there were a quarrel in the palace he opened his mouth and answered and satisfied the king with his speech. All his ways were regulated even as the pace of an ibis, his wisdom was that of the lord (Tahuti) of Hesart (Eshmunen), rejoicing in truth like Khenty, pleased of heart therewith like Ptah.

"Behold he was governing both lands for many years, the controllers reported to him in obeisance at the gates of the palace, the chiefs of the foreigners (nine bows) both south and north came before him with their arms stretched out, they adored his face like a god. What was done, was done by his command; his reverence was great before the people, and they prayed for him wealth and health (part of the royal ascription). He was truly the father of both lands, with the perfect wisdom of the

divine gift to secure the laws. Years passed over these
things while the heir of Horus was as chief and heir of
the entire land.

"Behold this noble god Horus, lord of Hat-suten,
desired in his heart to establish his son upon his throne
of eternity. Horus proceeded in rejoicing to Thebes,
the city of the eternal lord, with his son in his embrace,
even to Karnak, until he came into the presence of

FIG. 157.—Negroes and Asiatics adoring the king.

Amen in order to give to him his office as king, to make
his length of days. Behold Amen appeared in his noble
feast in southern Thebes; and when he saw the majesty
of this god, even Horus of Hat-suten and his son with
him, in the royal entry, to give him his office and his
throne, then behold Amen·ra met him in rejoicing. In
the day of giving his satisfaction then he conveyed himself to this chief heir and prince of both lands Horemheb; he went to the house of the king, going before

him to the palace of his great and noble daughter. She made obeisance, she embraced his beauties, she placed herself before him, and all the gods rejoiced at his appearing."

From this account it would seem that Horemheb was not married to Nezem·mut until his accession, when he legalised his position by becoming husband of the high priestess of Amen, as in the arrangement under the later dynasties (M.A.F. i. 748–764). This marriage was an affair of politics solely, considering the age of the parties; Horemheb was probably between fifty and sixty at the time, and if the queen Nezem·mut was the same as Nefertiti's sister Nezem·mut, she must have been of about the same age as Horemheb. No children are known of this marriage to contradict such a supposition.

FIG. 158.—Ring of Nezem·mut. F.P. Coll.

Much confusion has arisen in modern works from a false identification of Horemheb with Horus of Manetho; even to the present time Horemheb is often called Horus, whereas it is clear from the lists that Horus is Akhenaten, or the duration of Atenism, while Horemheb is named as Armais. The confused account of classical authors about Sesostris leaving Armais in charge of the kingdom cannot refer to the king Horemheb, but probably to some other prince of this name. It is possible that the eldest son of Sety I. was called Horemheb (S.B.A. xii. 258; L.D. iii. 128 a); but the general Horemheb of the Memphite tomb cannot be as late as Sety by the style of his work.

Of the reign of Horemheb we know very little. By an inscription of the first year, Khoiak 22, we learn of his attention to the worship of Ptah (M. K. 47 d, in temple M.K. plan G). And in his third year the tomb of Neferhotep is dated (D.H. xl. e). But there is no evidence that his wars in the south and conquest in the Sudan, or his war with the Ha·nebu in the north, was during his brief reign. Such activities would be more in place during his earlier life, and he may well have executed these monuments to record the triumphs of his generalship. The only later dates are on an ostrakon, on which a man petitions about the tomb of Hai his father, saying that it was granted in the 7th year of Horemheb, and now in the 21st year— no king named—he received title-deeds of it. There is no proof that the 21st year might not refer to Sety's reign; but, as we have noticed, it is quite possible that, after Horemheb abolished Aten worship, he dated his reign from his generalship. That the Aten worship, though displaced from its pre-eminence under Tut·ankh·amen, was not abolished, appears from Horemheb's name being carved on the Aten temple at Tell el Amarna (P.A. xi. 5), and the expression "Ra, his body is Aten" remaining in the 3rd year of this king (M.A.F. v. 499); but soon Horemheb swept away all trace of it, carrying away even the foundations of Akhenaten's work, and also re-using the buildings of Tut·ankh·amen and of Ay in his pylons at Thebes.

FIG. 159.—Scarab of Horemheb. "Founding the temple of Amen." F.P. Coll.

The great work of his reign appears to have been to regulate the country. Having come to the throne through the power of the soldiery, he found it needful to check that power and prevent the abuses of it which were only too certain in a military rule. A long inscription at Karnak might be entitled "The Justice of the King," being occupied with tales of his decisions against the plundering by the soldiers; set up much like a list of convictions by a railway company. We can only give an outline of the lengthy story: the first tale is of a poor man who made a boat and sail to follow the king, probably a sutler of the court-camp; he was robbed of his goods because he could not pay the duties. The king decided that anyone who oppressed a poor man "who pays taxes to the breweries and kitchens of the king by the two agents of the soldiers," should be punished by cutting off his nose and sending him to Zaru. This banishment to the eastern frontier is like the later mutilation of the nose and exiling to Rhinocolura, mentioned by Pliny and Diodorus. Also if a wood-seller had his boat plundered, the penalty should be the same on the thieves. The servants of the palace, when making requisition for the king, shall not take more for themselves. The two divisions of the soldiers, south and north, were incessantly plundering, and even took the skins or hides which were already stamped by the State for payment in kind. The collectors of the skins had this complaint made to them. Each soldier who after that date should go about plundering the skins, shall receive 100 blows so that five wounds are opened, and have the skins taken from him. These abuses had been inquired into under Tahutmes III., who went up and down the river examining them. But fraud had come even into the inspection, "and the officers put in charge also went to the officials, saying, Give us the profit of the fraudulent inspection." So now Horemheb himself goes on inspection on the feast of Apt (Rec. vi. 49; A.Z. xxvi. 70).

This account shows how bitterly the country was paying the price of its foreign conquests, in its oppression by a standing army. No form of tyranny in the East is so bad as that of an undisciplined army, as soldiers ravage over a whole country, and have not even the discretion which a local oppressor or robber has, to avoid destroying his future supplies.

Of the end of Horemheb we know nothing; but, considering his age, he may well have died a natural death.

At Memphis were the remains of his private tomb, and the burials of two Apis bulls in the Serapeum already noticed. A capital in the Derb el Gamamiz in Cairo probably came from here (W.G. 409), as also a piece of an inscription dated in year $5+x$ (F.P. Coll.), and many green glazed finger rings.

At Gurob many rings of his were found (P.K. xxiii.; P.I. xxiii.) : there were none, however, at Tell el Amarna, showing that the town was deserted, although the Aten temple was inscribed under this reign. From Abydos comes a frog with the queen's name (M.A. ii. 40 m).

At Karnak two great pylons belong to this king, as also the connecting walls at the sides of them. The pylons (X. and XI. of Baedeker) were built out of the blocks of a temple of Akhenaten (B.E. 165) and Tut-

FIG. 160.—Head of Horemheb.

ankhamen which stood here (Rec. vi. 53); pylon XI. has a magnificent doorway of red granite, sculptured with four scenes on each side of the door, and on both faces of the pylon, but the S.E. corner is now destroyed (L.D. 119 e; R.A. 64); pylon X. has had the doorway renewed by Ramessu II. (M.K. plan), and was reinscribed by that king (C.N. ii. 180). On the E. wall joining the pylons are the figures of the chiefs of Punt (figures M.D. 88, inscription B. Rec. 57), and the captives of the Ha·nebu and Khita conquered by

Horemheb (S.B.A. xi. 423). On the W. wall of the court is figured the sacred bark of Amen (B.E. 165–6).

Before the pylons there stretched an avenue of 128 sphinxes, to the temple of Mut. These sphinxes are described as being the finest at Thebes; the form is a lion's body with a ram's head (C.N. ii. 174). A wall was built also between pylon V. and the granite sanctuary (C.N. ii. 139). The great stele of the king's justice at Karnak, about 16 feet high and 10 feet wide, we have already described.

At Luqsor, Horemheb placed his name on the grand columns of Amenhotep III. in the colonnade before his temple (B.E. 129). At Deir el Bahri he claimed to have restored the monuments of Tahutmes III., "father of his fathers"; and it really seems not unlikely that the recarving and painting of the scenes erased by Tahutmes III. might have been due to this king; his fervour for Amen would account for such care: also Punt had come forward into notice again in this reign, and the re-working is too good for anything of the XIXth dynasty (C.N. i. 574). At Medinet Habu he also claims restorations, in a line of inscription on either side of the main entrance at the N. end of court M (L.D. iii. 202 d).

At Silsileh the large rock temple cut in the western cliff is specially devoted to scenes of the negro war. The soft sandstone is not adapted for fine work, and the execution is but poor compared with earlier carving. There is some good natural posing, however, in the figures and expressions of the negroes (L.D. iii.

FIG. 161.—Negroes, Silsileh temple.

119–121). At Kom Ombo a block of this king was re-used by the Ptolemies (P.O.N. 479). And at Kuban in Nubia a lion-headed statue of this reign is said to have been seen (My. E. 538). A rock shrine at Gebel Addeh is an important work, but appears to be purely religious, and not to contain any reference to the Nubian war. This makes it the more likely that the war was past and over before Horemheb came to the throne, and that it was only brought forward as the great event of his life on the Silsileh temple, and not as an action of the time of the sculpture.

Of statues there are admirable examples. The upper part of a colossal figure from Medinet Habu (Berlin M.) is very fine (L.D. iii. 112 c); as also the group in white limestone of Amen and the king (T. Mus.). The group with the queen in syenite is valuable for the long inscription which we have quoted (T. Mus.). A colossal figure at the Luxor Hotel, and a group with Horus at Battaglia (in Castel Cattajo), are only mentioned by Wiedemann (W.G. 411). The bust in red basalt (?) at Florence evidently came from a kneeling statue leaning forward making an offering; but the face is not much like Horemheb, and there is nothing to show the name (S. Cat. F. 1507). The hinder half of a Hathor cow suckling the king, in red granite, is of rude work (Flor. Mus.; S. Cat. F. 1225). The best portrait published in the round is from the Berlin statue (L.D. iii. 112 c), and on the flat from the pylon (L.D. iii. 112 a, and another photographed in R.A. 64). The small objects of this reign do not need any particular notice. A fine gold ring in Leyden bears the Hor·nub and vulture and uraeus names of the king. Scarabs, plaques, and rings are all usual.

PRIVATE MONUMENTS.

There are not many private remains of this time, and this accords with the shortness of the reign.

Amen·em·apt, overseer of the palace and of the granaries of south and north, has left a wooden cubit, bearing long inscriptions (Lepsius, Elle. No. 1).

Hor·em·heb·pa·hor·ur, priest of Amen, is on a stele at Leyden (Lb. D. 619).

Khonsu·hotep, priest of the *nub·kau* of the palace. Coffins and mummy at Leyden (Lb. D. 616).

Nefer-hotep, divine father of Amen. Tomb at Qurneh, N.E. of the tomb of Sen·em·aah. Dated in 3rd year of Horemheb; Aten not yet proscribed, the formula "Ra his body is Aten" being used. Published in M.A.F. v. 489, also in D.H. 40–40 e, portions in B.R. 37, and song of the harper in A.Z. xi. 58, 73; M.E.E. i. 130, 162; R.P. vi. 129. Patterns of the coloured ceiling in Pr. A.

Penbui offers to several kings down to Sety I., including Horemheb; T. Mus. (Rec. ii. 178).

Roy, royal scribe, overseer of the palace of Horemheb and of the temple of Amen. Tomb, Thebes, C.N. 544, 853. Whole scene, W.M.C. iii. pl. 68; portions, C.M. 177–8; R.C. 128–9; Pr. A.

The queen Nezem·mut we have already noticed. There are not many remains of her of any kind. The sister of Nefertiti is figured in the tomb of Ay (No. 7) at Tell el Amarna (L.D. iii. 109), and is probably the same as the future queen. A statue of hers with the king is at Turin, but not published in drawing. The figure of the queen as a female sphinx, on the side of this group, is given by Rosellini (R.S. xliv., quin. A). One scarab is known (Berl. Mus.), and one ring (F.P. Coll.); and a frog with her name was found at Abydos (G. Mus.; M.A. ii. 40 m).

We may here notice some kings who have been attributed to the close of this dynasty.

TETA appears as Teta·mer·en·ptah, adored by Amen·uah·su, on a naos at Marseille. The figure of the king is placed in a triangle, which is suggestive of a pyramid (as *men·nefer* is written with the same triangle on this naos), and of the king being considered to be in a pyramid. Rather than suppose a new king at this period, we should see in this the worship of a pyramid king, Teta of the VIth dynasty (A.Z. xvi. 69). The same king appears to be indicated on a stele from the Serapeum (M.S. iii. 6), which has given rise to discussion. The cartouche is so rudely carved that it was read as "Akhenaten" at first, but afterwards as "Se·ra·Teta." If this be the correct reading, which is not certain, it need only imply that May, who set up the stele (in XVIII.-XIX. dyn.), was devoted to Teta (of VI. dyn.), and figured the king as making an offering from him to the gods. Such figures of kings making the *hotep·suten* for private persons are often seen on steles (see M.A. ii. 41, 47, 48, 51, 52). What points to this is that *Se·ra·Teta* is all in one cartouche, and this writing of the title along with the name does occur on the VIth dynasty monuments of Teta, but is rare otherwise; hence it seems that the old usage was copied from an early sculpture of this king. The scarabs that have been attributed to Teta are certainly not of this king.

NEFER·AY was read on an hieratic ostrakon in the Louvre, but it is much effaced and not certain in the reading (Dev. Cat. MSS. p. 202). Possibly it may be some variant of the divine father Ay.

Other names have been brought forward, but none stand on certain ground. Ra·en·tuy or Khutany may possibly be a name, or some connective between the names of Ramessu I. and Sety I. on either side of it (M.A. ii. 17). Ra·user·kheper is a mistake for Ra·kheper·kheperu, Ay. Mer·kheper·ptah is an error for Mer·neb·ptah (tale of Setna), and this is perhaps a Ptolemaic bungle for Maat·neb·ra·mer·ptah, Amenhotep III. Rahotep is already placed about the XVIth dynasty; see vol. i. p. 246. Ra·pe·am is an error for

Horemheb. Ra·user·maat·ra·neb·maat is probably a combination of Ramessu V. and VI. Ses or Sesu appears to be a variant name of Ramessu II. Thus the various reputed kings which are not in the regular lists are not of historical substance, but are only linguistic questions.

THE DECLINE OF EGYPT IN SYRIA

For the age of the decline, when the great conquests of Tahutmes I. were all gradually lost, we possess a store of information in the cuneiform correspondence found at Tell el Amarna. The tablets were all deposited in "The place of the records of the palace of the king," as it is called; and thence, a few years ago, they were dug out by natives, contemptuously neglected by the authorities to whom they were shown, and only a part of them at last saved, in a much injured condition, when their value became recognised. They were scattered among various public and private collections, and copies and translations have been issued in many different forms and places. No attempt has yet been made to combine them into a consecutive history; but, after making abstracts of them all, and comparing them, tabulating all the proper names (over 250), and arranging the sequence of them, it appears that we may construct some provisional narrative from them.

They fall into three main classes:—(1) Those of the age of full Egyptian power, when troubles were only casual, principally the correspondence of the northern kings in alliance with Egypt. (2) Those recording the loss of northern Syria, the main correspondent being Ribaddu. (3) Those referring to Palestine, the backbone of which is the set of Ebed-tob's letters. In the present account an abstract is given of each letter, containing all the proper names, relationships, presents, and political details. The letters are arranged as nearly in order of time as may be; but where earlier letters only throw light on the individual, and not on previous events, they are grouped with regard to the person. The later translations have generally been preferred to the earlier; but even now some uncertainty may rest on many of the versions here given. The variable spelling of names is here purposely left as translated; in some cases it is due to variation in the cuneiform, and where due to translators it may show uncertainty in the reading. When we see such variable spellings of the well-known name of Amenhotep III.—Nimutriya, Nipmuaria, Nimmuriya, Mimmuriya—in cuneiform, it is obvious that less important names of obscure persons and places may easily vary, and have no very precise authority.

The sources are indicated thus:—R.P. xiii.–xviii., "Records of the Past," series ii. vols. i.–vi. S.B.A., "Proceedings of the Society of Biblical Archæology." M.A.F., "Mission Archéologique Française." B.O.D., Bezold, "Oriental Diplomacy," and "The Tell el Amarna Tablets," same numbers. P.A., Petrie, "Tell el Amarna." In some cases there are discrepancies between these sources and the following abstracts, owing to my taking advantage of a revision which Professor Sayce has been kind enough to make.

POSITIONS OF THE PRINCIPAL PERSONAGES NAMED.

Abdisullim, gov. of Hazor
Abisharri or Abimelekh } gov. of Tyre
Aitugama, gov. of Qedesh
Akizzi, gov. of Qatna
Ammunira, gov. of Beyrut
Arzawiya, gov. of Giscala
Aziru, gov. of Amorites
Beya, gov. of Rabbah
Bikhura or Pakhura } gov. of Kumidi
Biridiyi, gov. of Megiddo
Buaddu, gov. of Urza (Yerza?)
Burnaburyas, king of Babylonia
Dushratta, king of Mitani
Ebed-asherah, father of Aziru, Abdimilki, Abdirama, Iddin-adda, and Salmasalla

Ebed-tob, gov. of Jerusalem
Kallimmasin, king of Babylonia
Khaip (after Ribaddu), gov. of Simyra
Khayapa, commissioner
Labai, gov. (?) inland of Joppa
Ribaddu, gov. of Simyra and Gubla
Tiuyatti, gov. of Lapana
Yankhamu, gov. of Yarimuta
Yapakhi, gov. of Gezer
Yidya, gov. of Askelon
Zimrida, gov. of Zidon and (?) Lachish
Zitatna or Sutatna } gov. of Akko

SYNOPSIS OF CORRESPONDENCE.

	LETTERS		LETTERS
First Section.		Ribaddu in Gubla	91–93
Dushratta on alliances	4–12	Ribaddu appeals .	95–96
Kallimmasin and Burna-buryas	13–18	Ribaddu in extremity .	97–102
Alasiya, commercial	20–26	Ribaddu flees to Beyrut	103–105
Details of governors	28–39	Abdashirta's excuses	106
Second Section.		Beyrut fallen	108
Troubles with Khatti	40–41	Ribaddu's last letter	109
Troubles near Akko	42–49	*Third Section.*	
Aziru acting for Egypt	50–54	Ebed tob and Labai in trouble	110–114
Ribaddu in peace	55–58	Towns by Tiberias fallen	116
Ribaddu in trouble at Simyra	59–72	Troubles in Judea	119–123
Abisharri attacked	75–79	Labai against Egypt	124–126
Aziru protesting fidelity	80–84	Akizzi to Amenhotep IV.	127–128
Simyra fallen	85	Loss of Megiddo .	129–132
Tunip in extremity	86	Raid E. of Tyre	133
Tyre in extremity	87	Troubles in Judea	134
Ribaddu attacked at Gubla	88, 89	Loss of Gezer	135–137
Aziru's and Abdashirta's excuses	90, 94	Labai's excuses	138–139
		Milkili and Suyardata .	140–147
		Ebed-tob's last letter	148
		Unplaced	149–173

One of the earliest letters is from a king, who appears by his name to be a Hittite.

I.

TARKHUNDARAUS to NIMUTRIYA. T. sends Irsappa for a daughter of N.; and sends a *shuka* of gold, and will send a chariot, etc. Prince of Khatti on mountains of Igaid (Igaidai of the Mohar) sends a *shuka* weighing 20 manahs, 3 *kak* of ivory, 3 *kak* of *pirkar*, 3 *kak* of *khussi*, 8 *kak* of *kusittiu*, 100 *kak* of lead . . . 5 *kukupu* stones . . . 10 thrones of *usu* wood . . . 2 *usu* trees. (S.B.A. xi. 336.)

The language of this tablet is unknown. It relates to one of the many marriages between the royal families, which were always accompanied with a considerable equivalent of valuables.

Two other glimpses of the friendly relations of the Khatti or Hittites during the age of Egyptian supremacy also remain in the following letters:—

II.

ZI ... AU to king of Egypt. When messengers went to the Khatti, Z. alone sent presents; and now he sends 8 slaves, and asks for gold in return. (S.B.A. xiii. 132.)

III.

King of KHATTI? to KHURI (short for Nipkhuriya, Amenhotep IV.). Asks for an alliance, as between their fathers. Sends a *bibru* of silver 5 minas, another 3 minas, 2 *gaggaru* of silver 10 minas, and 2 great . . .

(S.B.A. xiii. 549.)

From this we see that the treaty of Ramessu II. with the Khita was only the last of a long series of compacts, which began at least as early as Amenhotep III.

The most important letters showing the family relationships are those of Dushratta, king of Mitanni.

IV.

DUSHRATTA to NIP'MUARIA. D. greets Gilukhipa his sister. Soon after his accession, Pirkhi attacked his land and people; but D. repulsed him, and slew D.'s brother Artash·shumara, whom P. supported. D. notifies N. of this, as N. was friends with D.'s father, who gave him D.'s sister. Artash·shumara raised the Khatti, and brought them into D.'s land, but

D.'s god Raman gave them into his hand.
D. sends a chariot, 2 horses, a lad, and a girl,
of the booty of the Khatti. Also 5 cars and
trappings. Also to D.'s sister Gilukhipa a
tutinatum of gold, an *anzabatum* of gold, a
mash-hu of gold, and a jar of oil. Sends Gilia
a messenger and Tunip·ipri. Let N. return
them soon. (S.B.A. xv. 120.)

Here there is the usual oriental tale of a rivalry between two brothers for the throne; one supported by a foreign prince, as an excuse for invasion.

V.

DUSHRATTA to NIMMURIYA. N. sent Mani to
ask for daughter of D. to be mistress of
Egypt. Giliya, D.'s messenger, reported
words of N. which rejoiced D. And D. asks
much gold, as N. sent to his father Sutarna a
dish, cup, and brick of solid gold. D. sends
Giliya, and a present of a gold goblet set with
crystals; a necklace of 20 crystal beads and
19 of gold, in middle a crystal cased in gold;
a necklace of 42 *khulalu* stones, and 40 gold
beads; and an amulet of *khulalu* stone in
gold, 10 pairs of horses, 10 chariots of wood,
and 30 eunuchs. (R.P. xv. 84.)

Here Dushratta is sending grand presents, besides being willing to give up a daughter to Egypt. This points to his being a tributary, and not entirely independent. Amenhotep III. sends an envoy to negotiate for a princess to be the "mistress of Egypt," and this was not for himself, but for his son, as the later letters show. To Dushratta's letter above, Amenhotep replied by accepting the present, and sending again to fetch the princess. His request is acknowledged in the next letter, while the princess was preparing for the journey.

VI.

DUSHRATTA to MIMMURIYA. Mani, A.'s messenger, has come to fetch a wife from D. to be the mistress of Egypt. Land of Khani-rabbat, and land of Egypt . . . [Giliya, D.'s messenger, will be sent in 6th month with Mani, A.'s messenger. Dowry will be sent. Much gold asked for. (S.B.A. xiii. 552.) Or [After 6 months Giliya and Mani were now sent with the queen. Nakharamassi sent by D. with letter. D. asks for much gold; has sent a spear of wood, an *isissu* of Aleppo stone, and a *khulal* stone set in gold. (R.P. xv. 74.)

In the next letter Dushratta calls himself father-in-law to Amenhotep III., referring to some previous marriage, and not to the one just negotiated, as the last was of Amenhotep IV., as shown by letters IX. X. and XI. The position of the letter is indicated by Nakhramassi being sent.

VII.

DUSHRATTA to NIMMURIYA. D. is father-in-law to N. May Istar bless N. Mani the messenger and Khani, dragoman of N., have brought presents. Nakhramassi is now sent by D. with a necklace of crystal and alabaster and some gold. (R.P. xv. 73.)

VIII.

DUSHRATTA to NIMMURIYA. D. greets Tadukhipa his daughter, and Nimmuriya his son-in-law. Sends statue of Istar of Nina, to be honoured by N. and returned.

(S.B.A. xv. 124.)

On the back of this is an hieratic docket, apparently in the 36th year of Amenhotep III., month of Pharmuthi. This is the very last date in the reign, and would be two or three weeks later than the papyrus of Kahun dated under Amenhotep IV. (see p. 208). It is possible that the docket is misread, or that the dating was put in terms of Nim·muriya's reign after his death, as the letter was addressed to him.

(S.B.A. xv. 124; B.O.D. 10.)

After Nim·muriya's death, Dushratta hesitated to address the son, who was so young, and wrote to Teie, whom he already knew.

IX.

DUSHRATTA to TEIE. D. greets Teie and Napkhurariya her son, Tadukhipa D.'s daughter, T.'s daughter-in-law. Appeals to old friendship of D. with Mimmuriya; T. alone knows their negotiations. T. had sent Giliya the messenger to propose to maintain relations as before. D. asks that Napkhurariya will send the *gargar* of gold. Names Yuni D.'s wife.

(S.B.A. xv. 127.)

Giliya, the messenger of Dushratta, had probably brought the previous letter VIII., arriving just at the death of Amenhotep III. He was sent back with the news by Tyi, as here stated; and the above is Dushratta's reply. We see here plainly that Tadukhipa is Tyi's daughter-in-law, and was therefore married to the IVth and not to the IIIrd Amenhotep. Nap·khura·riya is Nefer·kheperu·ra, Amenhotep IV.

X.

DUSHRATTA to NAPKHURRURIYA. D. salutes Teie thy mother, Tadukhipa my daughter thy wife. Pirizzi and Bubri D.'s messengers sent. Manē N.'s messenger and Umeatu D.'s messenger sent before. D. asks for return

of his messenger. D. has projects with N.'s father, which Teie, N.'s mother, alone knows.
(M.A.F. vi. 304 ; R.P. xv. 89.)

The importance of Tyi here in diplomacy is explained by her relationship to Dushratta which appears in the next letter. It has been said that these terms of brother and sister only refer to an official brotherhood of fellow kings, and not to natural relationship. But this is directly contradicted by the precision with which son-in-law, father, and father-in-law is named, and daughter-in-law, mother, and mother-in-law.

XI.

DUSHRATTA to NAPKHURRIYA. N. is D.'s son-in-law. D. salutes Teie "my sister and thy mother," and Tadukhipa "my daughter and thy wife." D. has done all that Nimmuriya desired, as "Teie thy mother knows." Let N. enquire of Teie. The father of Nimmuriya (Tahutmes IV.) sent a messenger to Artatama, father of D.'s father, asking for a daughter ; only granted on 7th application. Nimmuriya sent Khamasi (Kha·em·uas) to Sut(arna) asking for a daughter from D.'s father, namely, D.'s sister, granted the 7th time. (S.B.A. xiii. 559.) Giliya brought back gold, etc., to Nimmuriya, and Nimmuriya sent his envoy Nisag with slaves and gold. Nimmuriya lately died and Dushratta is much grieved. The envoy Artatama is sent by D.
(R.P. xv. 79.)

This is the most important letter of the series, for the relationships which it states. It shows that Tahutmes IV. married a Mitannian princess, likewise Amenhotep III., and lastly, Amenhotep IV.; and it shows that Tadukhipa was the queen, "mistress of Egypt" (letter VI.), Nefert·iti, wife of Akhenaten.

XII.

DUSHRATTA to NAPKHURURIYA. Khani N.'s envoy has come. N. desired that as D. had been friends with his father Mimmuriya, so he should be with N. Asks for a wife from N., and promises to send ten times as much presents. D. had asked for two *gargar* of gold, one for himself and one for Tadukhipa his daughter. M. promised him also rock crystal, more also, *patala* and *gargar*. But N. did not send them, but other things. Khamassi is the messenger of N.

(S.B.A. xiii. 556.)

Here Khani is the dragoman named before in letter VII.; and he played an important part as resident in Syria during the period of decline. Khamasi or Kha·em·uas was envoy in the previous reign, as the last letter shows. Dushratta here seeks to strengthen further the ties between the kingdoms, by having a sister of Amenhotep IV. This is the last letter from him that remains, and soon after the intercourse was broken by the insurrection of the intervening peoples of Syria.

The next most important alliance of Egypt was with the kings of Karduniyas, or Babylonia, with whom they intermarried.

XIII.

NIPMUARIA to KALLIMMASIN, king of Karduniyas. N. (Amenhotep III.) had asked for a princess from K.; but K. complains that his sister, who was given to N. by K.'s father, has not been seen again. N. replies, send a high official who knew her to verify her state. The present messenger Zakara is only a shepherd, and none of the others knew her.

K. complained that his messengers did not know his sister to be such, and N. believes that K. says that if a girl of Gagaya or Khanigalbi (or Khani·rabbat) or Ugarit is produced she may impose as his sister on the messenger. [N. promises by Amen that he will not impose on the messengers by another woman?]

If K. doubts in this way, does he demand to see his daughters who are married to other great kings? And why was K.'s sister sent but that presents should be returned, as was done?

N. is cold to K.'s messengers because they bring nothing; they received much silver, gold, oils, purple, and all things, and only brought this bad message, and spoke evil in private. K. has said that his chariots presented were mixed up with those of the governors, etc.; but N. has them duly. Scribe Kistu·nizaz·anni. (S.B.A. xv. 26.)

From this we see Amenhotep III. had married a Karduniyan (Babylonian) princess; but that her brother Kallimmasin was not satisfied about her safety. Amenhotep appears, however, to have reassured him, so that he was induced to send another princess—his own daughter—to Egypt.

XIV.

KALLIMMASIN to the king of Egypt. K.'s daughter Sukharti ("the younger") will be sent as asked for. K.'s father sent a messenger who was returned; but K.'s messenger was detained five years, and then only 30 manahs of gold were sent by him. (S.B.A. xiii. 130.)

The following letter, from the tone of it, appears to be also from Kallimmasin; but the names are all lost.

XV.

x to *y*. *x* refers to a former request and refusal of a daughter of Egn. king for a foreign prince.

A foreign princess having been promised to the Egyptian king before; but the Egyptian ambassador did not bring enough gold. More gold asked for in months Duzu or Abu; if even 3000 talents are sent to x, it will not be accepted, nor will x send y his daughter.
(S.B.A. xiii. 128.)

Next we find that Kallimmasin had died; and after three other reigns (as we learn from the Babylonian records) he was succeeded by Burnaburiyas, who begins by appealing to the past friendship between the royal families, and opening negotiations to get an Egyptian princess betrothed to his son.

XVI.

BURNABURIYAS to NAP·KHURA·RIYA. Kings of Karduniyas and of Egypt have been friends since king Kara·īndash. Messengers have come thrice without valuables, and B. has nothing to send. Ten minas of gold sent were not full weight. B. has some girls, N. may ask who he likes, and B. will send her; also an ——? of ancient work. When Sindisugab, B.'s messenger, leaves, N. is to send chariots at once, for B. to make 9 others on the pattern. B. sends 2 minas of *uknu* stone (crystal or lazuli); and for N.'s daughter, wife of B.'s son, (he?) sends a collar (?) of stone, . . . 10 of *uknu* stone weighing 1048 (end lost). (S.B.A. xv. 117.)

The marriage of Napkhurariya's daughter here stated cannot have been effected at the time, as this letter was written certainly long before the daughters were grown, and Burnaburyas sends a present to Egypt for her. This must then refer to a betrothal, and not to an actual marriage. Of the three elder daughters one died, and two married successive kings of Egypt, so that the daughter here named must have been the fourth or later, and born, therefore, as late as the 10th year of Akhenaten's reign. The sample chariot was evidently sent, as the next letter shows the others to have been made from it.

XVII.

BURNABURIYAS to NIPKHURRIRIYA. B. and N.'s fathers were allied. B. received two minas of gold, but expects more. B.'s father was Kurigalzu ; in his time the Kunakhâu (Canaanites) sent to him to revolt and invade Kannishat (?), and he refused. B. sends three minas of rock crystal (or lazuli), 10 sets of harness (or 5 pairs of horses), and 5 chariots. (S.B.A. xiii. 540 ; see R.P. xv. 63.)

Next we see that the marriage was actually carried out, by letter

XVIII.

BURNABURIYAS to NAPKHURARIYA. A list of the gold and ivory thrones, etc., sent by Shuti, which formed a part, or the whole, of the dowry of the Egyptian princess who was to marry his son. (B.O.D. 4.)

A portion of a similar list—perhaps on the same occasion—also remains.

XIX.

No names. Fragment of inventory of carvings, thrones, sceptres, etc. (S.B.A. x. 519.)

This marriage, even if a child-marriage, must have been far on in the reign, as the fourth daughter was not born till the 10th year; and so this ceremony might be in the 14th or 15th at the earliest. As Syria appears to be clear then for messengers, the decline and loss of the empire must have come very quickly in just the last year or two of the 18 years' reign of Akhenaten. This agrees with a successful campaign in Syria being represented on one of the tombs carved under Akhenaten.

Another kingdom with which there were commercial relations was that of Alashiya, or Alosa in Egyptian, as endorsed on the tablets in hieratic. This was probably the northern end of the Syrian coast. No personal name of the king is stated.

XX.

King of Alasiya to king of Egypt. Sends a tank of bronze, three talents of hard bronze, one tusk of ivory, one chair, and a ship.
(S.B.A. xi. 340.)

XXI.

King of Alashiya to king of Egypt. Despatch of 100 talents of bronze, a couch, a chariot, horses, etc., appears to have been lost on the road ; on account of this the king of Alashiya fears the displeasure of Amenhotep. Although the king of Alashiya has sent gifts regularly to the king of Egypt, from the time of his ascending the throne, Amenhotep has sent him nothing.
(B.O.D. 6.)

XXII.

King of Alasiya to king of Egypt. Sent his messenger with the Egyptian. Sent five talents bronze, much in A., and wrought there. Asks for gold, and oxen, and oils, 2 jars of *kukubu*, and 60 men. Will send wood. Man of A.

has died in Egypt and left goods; widow and son claim them, asks that A.'s messenger may bring them. Asks for gold, and will send double of what is sent to A. by kings of Khatti and Sankhar. (S.B.A. xiii. 544.)

The next appears to relate to a specified tribute, as the amounts are much the same as in letter XXL; while the rest of the business differs from that.

XXIII.

King of Alashiya to king of Egypt. Sends 100 talents of bronze, and asks for a couch of *ushu* wood inlaid with gold, a chariot inlaid with gold, two horses, etc. Names a quarrel between A. and E. merchants. Desires equal treatment and reception of A. and E. envoys. Asks for oils, and has sent a *khabanat* of excellent oil to E. (S.B.A. xv. 133.)

The commercial relations of Egypt and Alashiya seem to have been important. The remaining letters are but short.

XXIV.

King of Alasiya to king of Egypt. Asks for messengers back quickly, as the traders go. Mentions ships of Alasiya. (S.B.A. xiii. 547.)

XXV.

King of Alasiya to king of Egypt. Introduction of a messenger bearing a costly gift. Docket in hieratic "Letter from Alosha."
(S.B.A. xi. 334.)

The next letter seems to show the troubles beginning.

XXVI.

King of Alasiya to king of Egypt. Protests that the king of Egypt is mistaken about people of Lukki who come into Alasiya. The Alasiyans are not allied to the Lukkians. If proved to be so they shall be punished.

(S.B.A. xv. 130.)

These Lukki, whom the Alasiyans repudiate, are doubtless the Luka or Lykian pirates and sea-rovers, who were the mainstay of the Mediterranean confederacies in the following dynasties. They here appear for the first time in connection with another maritime people, the Alasiyans.

Another alliance, that with the king of Assyria, also appears.

XXVII.

ASSUR·YUBALLIDH to NAPKHURIYA. A. received the ambassadors, and sent a chariot with two white horses, another chariot, and a seal of white crystal. Asks for gold, and arrears due. A.'s father, Assur·nadin·akhi, received 20 talents of gold from Eg. King of Khani·rabbatu (E. Kappadokia) received 20 talents. Asks for as much. The Suti (Satiu) had waylaid Eg. ambassadors.
(King of Assyria)

(R.P. xv. 61.)

The system of setting up nominees of Egypt in the conquered provinces has left its mark in the following letter:—

XXVIII.

ADDUNIRAR to king of Egypt. Manakhbiya (Tahutmes IV.), king of Masri (Egypt), raised A.'s father to rule in Nukhasse.
(of Nukhasse)

(S.B.A. xv. 20.)

A fragment of a letter (XXIX.) belongs to Sutarna of Musikhuni. As the place has not been identified safely, it is possible that this is from Sutarna, the father of Dushratta. See XI. (P.A. 36, No. 100 *bis.*)

A view of the duties of the Egyptian governors is given by several short letters.

XXX.

x to *y*. A governor writes to adjacent governors saying that he is going to send Akiya to make his submission to Egypt. He asks if any gifts shall be sent with Akiya. (B.O.D. 58.)

This shows how they united in sending a joint messenger.

XXXI.

YIDYA to king of Egypt. Y. sends food, drink, of As- oxen, etc. as a tribute (B.O.D. 52.)
kelon

XXXII.

YIDYA to king of Egypt. Y. supplied the troops with all necessaries. (B.O.D. 54.)

XXXIII.

YIDYA to king of Egypt. Y. guards Askelon, and sends women. (B.O.D. 53.)

It seems that not only did the Egyptians take thousands of female slaves captive into Egypt, but a regular tribute of girls was rendered from various places. Not only in the above, but also in the two following letters is this shown.

XXXIV.

SHATIYI to king of Egypt. S. guards the spring of Zi ... S. has sent his daughter to the king's household. (B.O.D. 77.)

XXXV.

SUMANDI to king of Egypt. S. asks for Khanya (the dragoman, lett. VII) to be sent; and he sends 300 oxen, and the girls, and votive offerings. (S.B.A. xi. 331.)

The same governor writes briefly in three other letters.

XXXVI.

SHUMANDI to king of Egypt. S. is disabled by illness. (B.O.D. 40.)

In XXXVII. and XXXVIII. he acknowledges the receipt of a despatch, and states that he guards the city. (B.O.D. 38, 39.)

Of another *shekh* or governor far in the East we get a glimpse.

XXXIX.

ARTAMA·SAMAS of Ziri·basani (the plain of Bashan) to the king of Egypt. A. reports his adhesion, with soldiers. (R.P. xvii. 99.)

After this peaceful correspondence of the age of supremacy, we begin the age of troubles; gradually the northern people began fighting with one another; and, not being coerced by the Egyptians, the feuds spread southward through all Syria and Palestine.

Each governor and chief attacked his weaker neighbours, and both parties sent letters to Egypt, each claiming to be acting in the Egyptian interest in fighting the other.

The warlike Khatti, or Hittites, who were never conquered, but only repressed, in their Cappadocian mountains, began to spread into more fertile regions. In letters I. II. III. we have seen them on treaty terms with Egypt; but now they were fighting for their own hand.

XL.

HADADPUYA and BILTI·ILU to king of Egypt. The Khatta have taken Lupakku and the cities of Am from Bin·addu (Benhadad). Zitana and soldiers have gone to Nukhasse. Greeting from Amur·hadad to Bin·ili, Ebed·ip, Bin·Ana, Bin·ziddi, and Anati (hostages in Egypt?).
(R.P. xvii. 99.)

The preparation for this attack is noted elsewhere, in

XLI.

Eda(-gama) to king of Egypt. Eda[gama] (see 94, 130, 135) states that the governor of Kinza is leagued with the Khatti, and attacked the cities of Am. E. defends his city, and will defend it.
(B.O.D. 46.)

When the Egyptians began to withdraw, immediate disorder arose, as shown in

XLII.

x to king of Egypt. The Egyptian troops being gone, the country rebels. (B.O.D. 80.)

XLIII.

YAMA to king of Egypt. Y. defended his cities after the governors fled. (S.B.A. xi. 392.)

The echoes of these difficulties affected even the south, and down at Akku (Acre) difficulties appear, although the land is all nominally Egyptian.

XLIV.

ZITADNA of Akku protests his fidelity. (B.O.D. 32.)

XLV.

NAMYA·ITSA to king of Egypt. Reports his adhesion, with his Bedawin and Sute (Satiu).
(R.P. xvii. 96.)

XLVI.

ZATATNA (Zitadna, XLIV.) of Akku to king of Egypt. Zirdam·yasda revolted. Namya·itsa remains with Suta the Commissioner in Akku. Egn. soldiers are in Megiddo with a female refugee. Suta sent to Zatatna that she has given Zirdam·yasda to Namya·itsa, who does not accept him. (R.P. xvii. 95.)

What Zatatna's course was is seen by the complaints of Burnaburyas, which show that the land was still professedly open to intercourse from Babylonia to Egypt.

XLVII.

BURNABURYAS king of Karduniyas to NAPKHUH-RURIYA. B.'s messengers with Akhi·dhabu (Ahitub) went into land of Kinakhkhi (Canaanites), and on to Egypt. In Khinnatuni of the land of Kinakhkhi, Sum·adda (Shem·Hadad) son of Balumme (Balaam) and Sutatna (or Zitadna, 46) son of Saratum (or Zurata, 132) of Akku, slew them and robbed the presents. B. complains because the Kinakhkhi belong to Egypt, and asks redress; or else B.'s people will slay Egyptian ambassadors, and their agreement be broken; 1 maneh of crystal sent. (R.P. xv. 65.)

Of Sumaddu, who acts as freebooter, we learn that he was governor of Samkhuna (Semekhonitis, Gr. = Merom, 33 m. E. of Akku), whence (XLVIII.) he sent a report of peace to the king. (S.B.A. xii. 328.) But later he excuses his deficiencies by the disturbed state of the land.

XLIX.

SHUMADDU to the king of Egypt. S. is unable to send corn, because the threshers have driven away the overseers. (B.O.D. 66.)

The principal leaders of revolt in Syria were the family of Abdishirta, and particularly one of them, who was a native governor appointed by the Egyptians, named Aziru. The latter appears to have been the most capable and energetic of the rulers, and to have been faithful to Egypt, until it was clear that the Egyptians were hopelessly weak, when he determined to do the best he could for his own hand. His earlier letters are purely in the Egyptian interest.

L.

AZIRU to DUDU (viceroy). A. has done all that the king desired. A. rules in the land of the Amurri (Amorites). (S.B.A. xiii. 217.)

LI.

AZIRU to the king of Egypt. Two men were sent by the messengers to receive the orders for the land of Amurru. (S.B.A. xv. 21.)

LII.

AZIRU to DUDU. Khatib has made report to the king, and is now with D. King of Khatti has invaded Nukhasse.

LIII.

AZIRU to the king of Egypt. A. has carried out all his orders . . . the kings of Nukhasse . . . city of Tsumuri (Simyra). (S.B.A. xi. 410.)

In the next we see Aziru trying to use Dudu as a catspaw to get a subsidy from Egypt.

LIV.

AZIRU to DUDU. The kings of Nukhasse said to A. that his father got all the gold he wanted from the king of Egypt. (S.B.A. xiii. 216.)

We next turn to a most faithful servant of the Egyptians, Ribaddu, governor of Simyra and afterwards of Gabula, who has left the longest correspondence of all; nearly forty letters of his extend from the age of tranquillity to the almost entire loss of Syria.

LV.

RIBADDU to the king. Names the official Amanma or Amanappa). R. marches with 60 chariots . . . Let Yappa·addu be blamed . . . Two ships are sent. (S.B.A. xi. 361.)

Ebed-ashera (or Arad-ashirta) soon appears as the enemy of the Egyptian power. His sons—including Aziru—seem to have been the main rebels, though professing to act in the Egyptian interest.

LVI.

RIBADDU to the king. Sons of Ebed-ashera have taken two horses and chariots, and Yivana (the Ionian) is gone to Tyre. R. sent two messengers to Zemar. Asks for ten men of Melukhkha and ten of Egypt for defence.
(R.P. xviii. 50.)

The following may be about this same period.

LVII.

RIBADDU of Gabla to king. King's guard have stolen goods of R. as well as of the king. Pakhura (Syrian) has sent the Sute and smitten the Serdani (Egyptian). R. rebuts charges.
(R.P. xviii. 66.)

LVIII.

RIBADDU to AMANAPPA (Amenemapt). R. asks A. to deliver him from Arduashirta's soldiers. He was ordered to send ships to Yarimuta. Soldiers patrol the land of Amurri. R. desires that troops be not sent to Akzabu (Achzib).
(M.A.F. vi. 307; R.P. xviii. 62.)

LIX.

RIBADDU to the king. Hostile is Ebedasherah of Barrabarti; he has captured cities, and stirred up Gubla and Tyre, saying, "I am your lord." And Bedawin have done like the city of Ammi . . . the Serdanu. Zemar is still strong for R. (R.P. xviii. 89.)

LX.

RIBADDU to king. R. sent nephews to Tyre for safety. Palace of Tyre is great like that in Ugarita. (R.P. xviii. 63.)

LXI.

RIBADDU to the king. Names the city of Tisa . . . in land of Tsumuri, and the land of Martu (Amurri). (P.A. 35, No. 3.)

The following letter, addressed to the chief of Amurri, was probably sent to Aziru, as he ruled and received orders in the land of Amurra; but no addressee is named. Khanni was formerly dragoman (VII.), but here appears to be administrator.

LXII.

KHANNI to chief of Amurra. The chief of Gubla has complained of an attack by the chief of Amurra, and asked to be protected by Khanni. Chief of Amurra is summoned to a court-martial at Zidon. A woman Mada has gone to chief of Qidsa, driven out by the Amurri to a hostile place. Threats of burning him out. Amurri is in land of Kinakhi. Next year K.'s son must go to Egypt with a settlement of affairs. Asks A. to send in his son to Egypt as a hostage, and allows this year for him to do so. Next year will be too late. Khanni is sent in place of the king, with a black list of enemies. A. is asked to help to bring in Sarru and all his sons, Tuya, Liya and all his sons, Pisiari and his sons, the son-in-law of Mania and his sons and wives . . . Da wife of (or Dasarti) Paluma, and Nimmakhi *hapadu* of Amurri. (S.B.A. xiii. 224.)

A later translation, while agreeing in the names, renders this as a reproach to the chief of Gubla for expelling his brother, who lives in Zituna, etc. But this is not so concordant with the address to the chief of Amurri.

In the next we have an appeal from another city.

LXIII.

IRQATA city, to the king of Egypt. The nobles of Irqata send 30 horses, etc. Men of a town in Shanku, who were before friendly, now are foes. Irqata refuses their offers, and appeals to Egypt. (B.O.D. 42.)

The appeal was in vain, as the next letter shows.

LXIV.

RIBADDU to king of Egypt. R. is distressed by the sons of Ebed·asirta who descend into Amurru. All the land of Tsumura and city of Irqata (Tell 'Arqa) rebel in Tsumura. Governor has left Gubla. Neither Zimrida nor Yapa·addu are with R. Governor sent to them, and they paid 30 manehs. King has sent reinforcements to Tsumura and Irqata, garrison of Tsumura has fled. (R.P. xv. 70.)

LXV.

RIBADDU to king of Egypt. Names Tsumuri and Arad·asirti. (P.A. 35, No. 2.)

The next letter has lost the sender's name, but is doubtless from the faithful Ribaddu.

LXVI.

x to king of Egypt. Owing to Abd·ashirta, Khaya (or Khaip, governor of Zumura) was unable to send ships to land of Amurri. Ships from Arvad, in charge of x, lack men, and x urges that Egyptian ships and men be sent; also that an officer be set over ships of Sidon, Beyrut, and Arvad, to seize Abd·ashirta.

This appeal to secure tne fleet for Egypt failed, as we read in the next letter that the ships were lost.

LXVII.

RIBADDU to the king. May the goddess of Gubla give power to the king. Aziru is his adversary, has taken 12 of R.'s men, and asks 50 of silver ransom; A. has taken in Tambuliya men whom R. had sent to Zumur. Ships of Zumur, Biruta, and Ziduna all are gone over to land of Amuri (*i.e.* to Aziru, see L.). Yapa·addu as well as Aziru attacks R., and have taken his ships. R.'s family will go over to enemy if not succoured. R. holds Zumur, but is surrounded by enemies for two months past. Ask Amanma if R. has not been faithful in Alasiya . . . Yarimuta . . . Yappa·addu.   (S.B.A. xv. 359.)

In the next three letters we see that Ebed-asherah had obtained allies, and was pushing his way still further against Ribaddu.

LXVIII.

RIBADDU to king. Salma·salla son of Ebed-asherah holds Ullazu, Ardata, Yibiliya, Ambi, and Sigata. Kings of Kasse and Mitani have taken land of the king. If help is not sent Zemar will fall also, and R. cannot go to Zemar.   (R.P. xviii. 58.)

LXIX.

RIBADDU to the king. Zemar still faithful. Yappa·addu does not help. Kasites joined Ebed-asherah and Mitani and the Khatti take the land. King has sent troops with Yankhamu, and men of Yarimuta, and commissioner of Kumidi . . .   (R.P. xviii. 59.)

The name of the sender is lost; but the following letter is clearly from Ribaddu, and of this period.

LXX.

x to king of Egypt. *x* held Tsumura. City of Zarak reports that the four sons of Abd·asirti are captured. Yapa·addu and Aziru oppose *x*. Sons of Abd·asirti went against Tarkumiya, and took the land of the king of Egypt, the king of Mitana·nanu, the king of Tarkusi, and the king of Khata (Hittites). Yankhamu the servant of the king of (in ?) Yarimuta, and the Resident Melekh·mi . . .   (S.B.A. xi. 356.)

The report of the capture of the Abd·ashirtites was false, as we find them more active in future.

We next see that even Zemar was in great danger.

LXXI.

RIBADDU to the king. R. in difficulty for Zemar; sends two messengers to king, one of Yarimuta. Asks for help to take Aziru, as sons of Ebed-ashera have smitten cities, Zemar, Ullaza, Sawa. . . . Offers to send to Yankhame and Biri. R. has occupied Amurri in peace, with Yapa·addu and Khatib. Asks for men of Malukh·kha.   (R.P. xviii. 52.)

And next we see that Zemar was lost.

LXXII.

RIBADDU to the king. Ebed-asherah strong against R., and sends to Mitana (Aram Naharaim) and Kasse (Babylonia). E. has collected Bedawin against Sigata and Ambi. Zemar is already lost. (R.P. xviii. 56.)

We turn now to other writers, resuming the later troubles of Ribaddu at No. lxxxviii.

LXXIII.

SU(?)YARZANA to king of Egypt. S. is attacked by
of the city of Tusulti. The Bedawin have taken
KHAZI. Makhzi . . . ti and burnt it, and have gone against Aman·khatbi (Amenhotep), and have taken Gilu, and only Bal·garib survives. They attack Magdali, and Usteru . . ., and Khazi. S. captured 50 Bedawin, and took them to Aman·khatbi . . .
(R.P. xvii. 85.)

Tusulti has been equalled with Tasuret of Thothmes, probably Teiasir 11 N.E. of Shechem, but the rest of these places seem to be lower down in the Esdraelon region, for Khazi is the Khazay of Thothmes, Tell el Kussis, 8 N.W. of Megiddo. The ruler of Migdol was soon in extremities, and wrote as follows:—

LXXIV.

x to king of Egypt. *x* has no authority in Magdalim, and the soldiers of Kukbi have conspired. *x* contradicts Abbikha, who says that his cities have been captured by the enemy.
(B.O.D. 73.)

Abi·sharri, otherwise rendered as Abi·milki, the governor of Tsurri (Tyre), is another important person, whose troubles were like those of Ribaddu.

LXXV.

ABISHARRI to king of Egypt. A. asks for Uzu to strengthen him; for Ilgi ruler of Sidon has defeated him. The ruler of Khazur (Hazor) has come out. (S.B.A. xiii. 323.)

The ruler of Khazur appealed to Egypt.

LXXVI.

ABDI-SULLIM to the king of Egypt. A. will hold his city until the king comes.
of Khazur. (B.O.D. 47.)

Ilgi named above must have soon died or been slain, as a new ruler appears in this next letter.

LXXVII.

ZIMRIDDI to king of Egypt. Z. is governor of Ziduna, which is safe for the king; Z. asks succour. (S.B.A. xiii. 318.)
of Sidon.

This profession of obedience seems to have been only a blind, to draw some supplies; for we read in

LXXVIII.

ABISHARRI to king of Egypt. The king thunders in heaven like the god Addu. The king sent a message and all the land feared. A. is raised to the rank of the great officers. Zimrida governor of Ziduna sends messages to the rebel Aziru, son of Arad·ashratu, for all the Egyptian news. Is that right?
(S.B.A. xv. 518.)

Zimrida soon takes a more active course.

LXXIX.

ABISHARRI to king of Egypt. A. cannot leave his town to come to Egypt, because he cannot get out of the hands of Zimrida of Ziduna, who knows that he wants to leave, and wars against him. Asks for 10 men to guard the town in his absence, and sends a messenger. Asks for wood and water, because placed on the sea they have neither. The messenger, Ilu-milku, bears 5 talents of copper, *subu* and a *ginasu*. Replying to the king's enquiries about Kinaahna, the king of Danuna (Danian, 135 of Tyre) is dead, his brother succeeds, and the land is quiet. The house (?) of the king of Ugarit is half burnt. Of the Khatti nothing. Itamagapapiri of Qidshu, and Aziru, war with Namyapiza. Zimrida collected ships and men of Aziru and came against Abisharri. (S.B.A. xv. 507.)

This phrase of asking for ten men (or officers) is like the modern idiom in Egypt of asking for two piastres, as a modest way of applying for an indefinite amount. The difficulty in Tyre for wood and water has always been common in war.

Aziru, however, gives another version of his relations with Egypt, and asks for supplies from the king, preparatory to his final rebellion.

LXXX

AZIRU to king of Egypt. A. is always faithful to Egypt. The people of Sumuri disturb him. If the king of the Khatti comes against him, he needs men, chariots, etc., to repel him.
(S.B.A. xiii. 219.)

LXXXI.

AZIRU to DUDU (viceroy). Khatib (Hotep) will go to the king; if Aziru also leaves, the king of Khatti will come into Nukhassi, and his revolt will be laid to us.   (S.B.A. xiii. 229.)

LXXXII.

AZIRU to *x*. The king of the Khatti is in Nukhassi and Tunip (Tennib) and Martu.
(S.B.A. xiii. 233.)

LXXXIII.

AZIRU to king of Egypt. A. and Khatib are now leaving; but the king of the Khatti is in Nukhassi and in Tunip.   (S.B.A. xiii. 232.)

LXXXIV.

AZIRU to KHAI (viceroy). A. and Khatib will soon leave. The king of the Khatti is in Nukhassi, and went into the land of Martu (=Amurri), and ravaged the city of Dunip (Tennib).
(S.B.A. xiii. 231.)

A very different version of these affairs is given by the other side.

LXXXV.

ABI·SHARRI to king of Egypt. The king is like the sun-god, like the god Addu in heaven. The king set A. in Tyre, and A. asks for 20 soldiers. . . . Aziru . . . Arad·ashratu . . . revolted Khabi. If a messenger had been sent there Zumur would not have been given

to Aziru. Zimrida has taken Uzu (Hosah) from A., and A. has no wood or water, or burial-ground. Zimrida of Ziduna and Aziru, and men of Arvada, have sworn together, and assemble ships, chariots, and soldiers, to take Tyre. They took Zumur on the word of Zimrida, who brought a false message (see LXXVIII.) to Aziru. No wood nor water.
(S.B.A. xv. 511.)

This mentions the fall of Zumura, which Ribaddu reported in LXXII. And Zimrida, who was beleaguering Tyre in LXXIX., here is joined with Aziru and the Arvadites.

Tunip also besought the king against Aziru.

LXXXVI.

TUNIP people, to king of Egypt. Manakhbiria (Men·kheper·ra, Tahutmes III.) received their allegiance. His statues are in the town. They have sent messages twenty times. By the god Addu they demand a reply. Aziru has maligned them as enemies to Egypt and to the Khatti. Aziru will treat them like the people of Ni, who have broken allegiance to Egypt. Aziru took Zumur. The writers desire a reply. (S.B.A. xv. 18.)

This is the last appeal of Tunip; and below is the last appeal of Tyre.

LXXXVII.

ABISHARRI to king of Egypt. The king gave orders to supply wood and water, but nothing is done. A. is the servant of Salmayati, and Tyre is the city of Salmayati. (S.B.A. xv. 515.)

LXXXVIII.

RIBADDA to king of Egypt. Reports conspiracy of Aziru, fall of Zumura, and death of governor Khaib. Therefore Bikhura will not be able to hold Kumidi. (B.O.D. 18.)

Here we learn the name of the unlucky governor of Zumura, whom we have met before in letter LXVI. Bikhura saved himself by joining the victors, as Ribaddu laments in the next.

LXXXIX.

RIBADDA to king of Egypt. R. attacked by Bikhura, governor of Kumidi, who incited the Sute (Bedawin), with Abdirama, Iddin-adda, and Abdi-milki (or Abdisharri), sons of Abdashirta, to attack him. (B.O.D. 20.)

Next Aziru sends a polite series of excuses for his falseness.

XC.

AZIRU to king of Egypt. When envoy Khani came, A. was at Tunip, and knew it not. Followed him in vain. A.'s brother and Bitil received K. well, and supplied him. Another time Khani came, and received A. as a father. King orders A. to rebuild Zumur. Kings of Nukhassi have fought A. and taken town, urged by Khatib, and A. has not rebuilt. Khatib has taken half of what king gave him, and all the gold and silver. King has asked why A. refused his envoy and welcomed that of the Khatti; but he has received the envoy well.
(S.B.A. xv. 372.)

Here the king has heard of the fall of Zumura, and ordered its restoration, but Aziru tries to throw the blame of its destruction on the kings of Nukhassi and Khatib the Egyptian, who were apparently leagued with Aziru. He also tries to abuse Khatib as false to the king.

Another lament from Ribaddu follows; the sender's name is rendered Rabimur or Ilu·rabi·khur, but this is apparently from Ribaddu.

XCI.

RIBADDU (?) to king of Egypt. A. ruled in Gubla. Aziru has smitten Aduna king of Irqata, the land of Ammiya and the king of Ardata, and taken Tsumura and other towns. Only Gubla is left to the king. The city of Ullaza and Palasa are captured by Aziru. Sarnu . . . Itakama smote the land of Am. The king of the Khatta, and king of Nariba . . .
(S.B.A. xiii. 220; R.P. xvii. 90.)

XCII.

ILU-RABI·KHUR of Gubla to king of Egypt. Aziru has leagued with the kings of Ammiya and Ni against the king. He asks for 30 to 50 men to guard the city and Zumur, and warns the king against Aziru.   (B.O.D. 45.)

Ribaddu again reports his afflictions in the next.

XCIII.

RIBADDU to king of Egypt. Zumuru captured. Biri an Eg. officer slain and men scattered. R. applied to Pakhamnata, who would not help, and was present when Zumuru was destroyed. Troops of Gubla slain at Zumuru. No corn in Gubla, serious state.
(B.O.D. 24.)

Pakhamnata, evidently an Egyptian envoy, seems to have played false ; and we see old Arad·ashirta claiming to be faithful and submissive to the envoy.

XCIV.

ARAD·ASHRATU to king of Egypt. A. guards the whole land of Amuri. A. tells Pakhanati his inspector (or Resident) to take the auxiliaries . . . A. guards Zumur and Ullaza (taken by Aziru, see XCI.). When the inspector brings word from the king, A. will give up Zumur.
(S.B.A. xv. 502.)

A new governor was sent to try to improve the affairs, and Ribaddu at once seeks to take action.

XCV.

RIBADDU to KHAYAPA. R. prostrates before K. sent as commissioner. R. asks for troops against Zemar. Ebed-asherah is strong among the Bedawin, and sent 50 convoys of horses and 200 soldiers into Sigata, which he holds, and also Ambi.
(R.P. xviii. 56.)

He also appeals to another governor, but in vain.

XCVI.

RIBADDU to AMANAPPA. R. prostrates himself before A. May the goddess of Gubla protect him. Asks why he does not speak for him, that A. may come with troops and take land of Amuri. Amuri have a stronghold and no longer belong to Arad·asirta ; they drill day and night, and we must do the same. All the governors desire action since Arad·asirta has ordered people of Ammiya to slay their master. R. asks A. to tell all this to the king. A. knows R. and his acts at Zumur.

(S.B.A. xv. 355.)

Ribaddu appears to have discovered some defection in the enemy's party, and wished to encourage the new envoys to take active steps. For a time it seems as if the Egyptian interest was succeeding, as in the next letter, after they had been short of corn for two years, and Ribaddu was limited to Gubla, the governor ejected Ebed-asherah from Amurri.

XCVII.

RIBADDU to king. For two years no corn; all families of garrison have gone to Yarimuta. King has sent 400 men and 30 convoys of horses to Shuta, who will defend city. Yankhamu says "king gave corn to Ribaddu, therefore give to Tyre." And likewise Yapa-addu. King did not give corn in Zemar, but gives it in Gubla. The king of Tarizi marched to Zemar and Gubla; the governor has destroyed Ebed-asherah out of Amurri. E. had occupied Tyre. (R.P. xviii. 67.)

But we next find that for three years there had been no corn, and Ribaddu cannot move out.

XCVIII.

RIBADDU to the king. R. protests his family fidelity. But brigands oppress the land, and R's people have fled to Yarimuta. For three years no cultivation; only Gubla and two other places are left to R. Arad-asirta has taken Sigata, and said to men of Ammiya, "Slay your master," and they submitted. R. fears much, he is shut up as a bird in a cage in Gubla. Asks that Aman-appa (Amen·em·apt, letter CII.) shall state case. (S.B.A. xv. 351.)

XCIX.

RIBADDU to AMANAPPA. Reports attacks on city, corn scarce for three years. Names Amurri, Mitani, Zumuru, and official Yankhamu who supplied corn. (B.O.D. 21.)

C.

RIBADDU to king. R. asks for troops to protect Gubla, etc. (B.O.D. 25.)

Then even Gubla became insecure for Ribaddu.

CI.

RIBADDU to AMANAPPA. Gubla is surrounded with foes; people of Ambi stirred by Abd-ashirta have rebelled; and R. is surprised that Amanappa should have ordered him to Zumuru. (B.O.D. 23.)

Treachery began within the city.

CII.

RIBADDU to the king. R. went to Khamuniri (=Ammunira, CIII.). R.'s brother tries to drive him from Gubla, and has guard and Yanazni with him. R. has never seen the king, but now sends his son. R.'s brother wishes to give Gubla to sons of Ebed-asherah, who are hostile in Puruzilim. R. begs for help. (R.P. xviii. 70.)

Then Ribaddu flees to Beyrut.

CIII.

RIBADDU to king of Egypt. The men of Gubla and R.'s family demanded that he should submit to Arad·asirta. R. sent an account to the king, but no reply came. Corn ran short: so R. fled to Ammunira, governor of Biruta (Beyrut), who shut him out. Meanwhile R.'s family fled. (S.B.A. xv. 362.)

Of Ammunira we learn a little before this, in the following :—

CIV.

AMMUNIRA to king of Egypt. A chief of Biruta has obeyed the king's orders, and gone forth at the head of his soldiers with horses and chariots. (S.B.A. xv. 366.)

of Biruta.

But his account of Ribaddu's flight seems to show that he gave him shelter.

CV.

AMMUNIRA to king of Egypt. A. will guard Biruta until auxiliaries come. Ribaddu of Gubla has taken refuge with A. R.'s brother is in Gubla, and has given the sons of R. to the rebels of Amuri. (S.B.A. xv. 368.)

The other side of the story comes from the rebel Abd·ashirta.

CVI.

ABD·ASHIRTA to the king of Egypt. A. protests his fidelity in Gubla, and asks for assistance. Acknowledges receipt of letter, and sends in answer ten women. (B.O.D. 33.)

After Ribaddu fled, the garrison followed his example.

CVII.

RIBADDU to king of Egypt. Owing to corn not coming from Yarimuta, the garrison rebelled and left Gubla. R. is no longer governor, and the cities are ruled by Aziru, leagued with Abd·ashirta. (B.O.D. 19.)

Lastly, Beyrut fell, as Ribaddu reports.

CVIII.

RIBADDU to AMANAPPA. R. asks for an explanation of the censures on him. Though Biruna (Beirut) has fallen, R. supplied soldiers and chariots to protect it. (B.O.D. 25.)

The last letter from Ribaddu is a final appeal to the king to act strongly.

CIX.

RIBADDA to king of Egypt. Reports Abd·ashirta coming, and the fall of Biruta. Unless the king sends chariots and soldiers at once, all the coast from Biruta to Egypt will fall to enemy. A little help from Egypt will enable R. to hold out. (B.O.D. 17.)

We now turn to the letters concerning Southern Syria, the principal personages in which are not found in the preceding series. Two or three times a link occurs between the Northern and Southern series, and no doubt the earlier letters that here follow were written before the later letters which we have already summarised. The main clue to the order in the following letters is the alliance of Labai with Ebed·tob in the Egyptian interest at first, and his later union with the Syrian party. Many of the letters are so short and unallusive that they can only be fitly grouped by the personages.

The first letter here has lost the sender's name; from the tenor of it, we can hardly be wrong in attributing it to Ebed·tob, especially as he defends Urushalim (Jerusalem), which was that governor's place.

CX.

x to king of Egypt. . . . as to Urushalim, if the land remains to the king why is not Khazati the capital? Gimti-Kirmil (Gimza) is fallen to Tagi and men of Guti (Gath). He is in Bit-Sani (Beit Shenna, 4½ S.E. Gimzu?), and E. arranged that Lab'ai should give . . . to the Khabiri. Milkilim sent to Tagi; and granted requests of Kelti (Keilah) We have delivered Urushalim. The guard left in it Khapi son of Miyariya (Hapi son of Mery·ra). Addalim (Hadad-el) remains in Khazati.

(R.P. xvii. 73.)

Zimrida, the letter naming whom was found at Lachish by Dr. Bliss, appears as governor of that city here. In the letter CXI. he is named as in the Syrian interest; so we must only look on the present letter as a polite blind, like Aziru's letters LXXX. to LXXXIV. Whether this Zimrida is the same as Zimrida of Zidon, whom we last saw in letter LXXXV. as taking Tyre, is uncertain; if there be but one Zimrida, this letter must come after No. LXXXV. Anyhow, No. CXII. records his end.

CXI.

ZIMRIDI to king of Egypt. Z. the chief of Lakisha has received orders and will execute them.

(S.B.A. xiii. 319.)

CXII.

EBED·TOB to king of Egypt. E. protests fidelity. Suta (Suti) the commissioner has come, and E. has given him 21 women and 20 men slaves. There is war against Egypt as far as mountains of Seri (Surah, on hills 6 S.E. of Gath) and Guti-Kirmil (Gath). The Khabiri are capturing forts. Turbazu (Egyptian) was killed in Zilu (Zelah). Zimrida (Syrian) of Lachish is slain. Yaptikh-addu (Egyptian) was killed in Zilu. E. begs for reinforcements, the land being in extremity.
(R.P. xvii. 68.)

CXIII.

EBED·TOB to king of Egypt. E. is accused of revolt. E. asks the governor why he favours the Khabiri, and often has reported to the king the attacks on the land. Asks for Yikhbil-Khama. Ili-milki (Elimelech) is destroying king's land. Khabiri are wasting all.
(R.P. xvii. 66.)

CXIV.

SUYARDATA to king of Egypt. S. ordered to attack Kelte. Ebed·tob sent 14 pieces of silver to men of Kelte to attack S. Ebed·tob took Kelte, Bel·nathan (?), and Hamor (?). Lab·api (Labai) and Ebed·tob occupy . . . ninu. *Docket*, repeated refusal.
(S.B.A. xi. 348; R.P. xvii. 77.)

This letter is the last naming Labai as being on the Egyptian side; and the first to bring in Suyardata, whom we frequently find later. We turn now to a short connected series which belong to about this time.

CXV. (in full, see p. 185).

YATIBIRI to king of Egypt. Yankhama took Yatibiri (Hotep·ra) into Egypt when young, and Yatibiri lived in the palace. Later Yatibiri was guarding Azzati (Gaza) and Yapu (Joppa), and always went with the auxiliaries.
(S.B.A. xv. 504.)

Yankhama appears as viceroy in the next, which is from the region of Tiberias.

CXVI.

MUT·ADDA to YANKHAMU. Ayab and king of Bitilim fled, and the enemy are in the city. Refers Y. to Bininima and Isuya. Names city of Ashtarti. The cities of Udumu, Aduri, Araru, Mestu, Magdalim, Khinianabi, Zarqizabtat, Khayini and Ibilimma are hostile.
(R.P. xviii. xvii.)

CXVII.

SHIBTI·ADDA to king of Egypt. Acknowledges letter. Yankhamu is faithful.
(B.O.D. 65.)

CXVIII.

BAYAWI to king of Egypt. Owing to Yankhamu, rebels have seized the country.
(B.O.D. 60.)

This was the usual device of a man who was rebelling, to accuse the Egyptian party falsely, in order to hide his defection of attacking them. Beyawi, or Beya, next appears as an adversary.

CXIX.

ADAD·DAYAN to king of Egypt. There is war in Tumur (Tumra? 7 N.E. Gaza). Mankhate (Wady el Menakh, 7 S. Gezer) was taken by Beya. Rianap retook it, and Ghezer and Rubute. Ransoms are 30 of silver for some men, and 100 for Beya's men.
(M.A.F. vi. 299.)

Another translation varies thus:—The city of Tumur and city of Mankhate revolt. Addu·kinumma (the writer) took . . . from Beya, and gave it to Rianap. Beya of Rubute has not reported lately. For provisions for men 30 pieces of silver; for city of Beya 100 pieces.
(S.B.A. xi. 394.)

Rianap (*Ra·em·apt*) was an Egyptian governor, as we see in the next.

CXX.

BUADDA to king of Egypt. B. guards his land. B. was rebuked for his conduct to Rianappa, and promises now to look on R. as on the king.
(B.O.D. 56.)

CXXI.

BUADDA of Urza to king of Egypt. B. advised Shakhshikhashi (?) not to help the enemies.
(B.O.D. 55.)

CXXII.

BUADDA of Pitazzi to king of Egypt. Report of peace. (S.B.A. xi. 329.)

Another glimpse of Beya appears.

CXXIII.

x to king of Egypt. The troops sent to Tyre were taken prisoners by Biya son of Gulati; now Biya is expelled from the city, and the city is in right hands. (B.O.D. 71.)

Returning now to Labai's party.

CXXIV.

ADDU·ITLU to king of Egypt. Two sons of Lab'ai have joined A.'s enemy; they complain that the king gave to Su·ila·giti a city that Labai took. They have stirred up men of Gina (Janiah, 7 W. Bethel), besides smiting Avanu (Beth Aven, near Bethel); and they addressed an Egyptian prince Namya·itsa. Sons of Lab'ai say they war like their father when he was set over Sunama (Selmeh? 3 E. Joppa) and Burqa (Bene-beraq, 5 E. Joppa) and Kharabu (El Khurab, 11 E. Joppa?), and took Giti-Rimuna (Gath-rimmon, near Joppa, Jos. xix. 45) Messengers of Milkilim.
(R.P. xvii. 83.)

CXXV.

TAGI to king of Egypt. T. is father-in-law of Milkili, and asks that main roads be still guarded by Milkili. (B.O.D. 70.)

This relationship explains the next letter.

CXXVI.

EBED·TOB to king of Egypt. Milkilim joins sons of Labai and sons of Arzai to take the country.

Milkilim joined with Tagi and took Rubute (Rabbah). Puru (or Pauru = Paari) is in Khazati (Gaza). Requests that Yikhbil-Khamu be sent. (R.P. xvii. 71.)

We now turn to another group of letters concerning Labai and Arzai, or Arzawiya; prefixing two which are of an earlier date before the great troubles, and which belong to the North, but which throw light on the same people.

CXXVII.

AKIZZI to NAP·KHUR·RIYA. A. is governor of Qatna; he names services in victualling the army; asks for troops to be sent to occupy country around, which would welcome them. Men of Qatna seized by Aziru; asks for rescue or ransom. Statue of Shamash taken from Qatna by king of Khatti, asks N. to send ransom. (B.O.D. 36.)

CXXVIII.

AKIZZI to NAP·KHUR·RIYA. King of Khatti has obstructed him. Aitugama of Qedesh, Tiuyatti governor of Lapana, and Arzauya governor of Gizzi, are leagued; but kings of Nukhashshi, Ni, Zinzar, and Kinanat are faithful. A. asks for troops soon, as kings with Aitugama and Dasha in the land of Am are going to take Aup. Timasgi is in the land of Aup. (B.O.D. 37.)

CXXIX.

YASHDATA to king of Egypt. Men of Takh . . . have raided Y. Y. is allied with Biridiyi governor of Megiddo. (B.O.D. 59.)

CXXX.

BIRIDI to king of Egypt. Labai wars against B. City of Aveti (or Abitu, CXXXIII. Abdeh, 15 S. of Tyre) received the Egyptians. Labai attacks Megiddo. B. desires forces.

(R.P. xvii. 81.)

CXXXI.

BIRIDI to king of Egypt. Megiddo is besieged, and there are rebels in the low country.

(R.P. xvii. 82.)

Labai failed, it seems, but succeeded in escaping.

CXXXII.

x to king of Egypt. x chased Labaya, who was with Yashdata, but could not claim him, as Labaya had been taken at Megiddo by Zurata, who would have sent him to Egypt by ship; so x gave money to Zurata to get hold of Labaya, but Zurata took L. to his house in Khinatuna, and then Labaya and Addamikhir escaped. How is x to get back his money spent for the king? (B.O.D. 72.)

This looks as if Labai had been ransomed by his friend out of the Egyptian hands; and then they were scheming to make the Egyptians repay the money.

The next gives the last notice about Namyayiza, named in CXXIV. and many earlier letters.

CXXXIII.

x to king of Egypt. Names rebels. Biridashyi stirred up city of Inu-amma (Yanuh, 7 E. Tyre); they took chariots in city of Ashtarti (Ashteroth,

21 E. Gennesaret); kings of Buzruna (Bozrah) and Khalunni (Golan, 'Allan) league with Biridashyi to slay Namyayiza, who refuged in Timasgi, and, being attacked by Arzauya, declared himself Egyptian. Arzauya went to Gizza (Gish, 22 S.E. Tyre) and took Shaddu; Itakkama of Qedesh ravaged Gizza, and Arzauya and Biridashyi wasted Abitu (Abdeh, 15 S. Tyre); *x* will guard the city of Kumidi.
(B.O.D. 43.)

We now continue the history of the attacks by Labai and Milkili on the region nearest to Egypt.

CXXXIV.

EBED·TOB to king of Egypt. Gezer, Asqaluna, and La(chish) have given supplies. Urgent need of troops. E. occupies Urushalim. Milkilim and Labai have given country to the Khabiri. As to the Kasi (Babylonians?), let the king ask the commissioner how strong the temple is. Pauru (Pa-ari) will come to Urushalim to deliver Adai. E. has made roads in the plain and hills. Consider Ayaluna (Ajalon) E. not able to make road. (R.P. xvii. 74.)

Gezer, however, was in difficulties before the end, as we read from the unlucky governor.

CXXXV.

YAPAKHI of GAZRI to the king of Egypt. Acknowledges letter, and asks for support in Gezer.
(B.O.D. 49.)

CXXXVI.

YAPAKHI to king of Egypt. Acknowledges letter; a raid of the Sute. (B.O.D. 51.)

CXXXVII.

YAPAKHI to king of Egypt. Y.'s younger brother has joined the rebels in Mu(ru?)khazi. Y. asks for instructions. (B.O.D. 50.)

Labai sends in his version of affairs.

CXXXVIII.

LABAI to king of Egypt. The king's soldiers behaved as enemies. (B.O.D. 61.)

CXXXIX.

LAB'AI to king of Egypt. Excuses attack on Gazri (Gezer) because the people had taken property of L. and Milkilim. The king sent to Bin·sumya. (R.P. xvii. 78.)

Milkili we see to have been in the service of Egypt by the following :—

CXL.

MILKILI to king of Egypt. Acknowledges letter, asks for troops. (B.O.D. 63.)

CXLI.

MILKILI to king of Egypt. M. announces bringing a despatch. (S.B.A. xi. 371.)

CXLII.

MILKILIM to king of Egypt. M. and Suyardata have enemies; asks for forces to protect them; desires that Yankhama be questioned.
(R.P. xvii. 80.)

Suyardata was another of the Egyptian allies originally.

CXLIII.

SHUARDATA to king of Egypt. S. is carrying out orders. (B.O.D. 69.)

CXLIV.

SHUARDATA to king of Egypt. S. has sent all his soldiers to the Egyptian army, and also girls and a dragoman to the king. (B.O.D. 67.)

CXLV.

MILKILI to king of Egypt. M. receives orders, and has obeyed them. (S.B.A. xiii. 325.)

CXLVI.

MILKILI to king of Egypt. The enemy has come against him and Suyardata.
(S.B.A. xiii. 326.)

CXLVII.

MILKILI to king of Egypt. Yankhamu has carried off M.'s wives and children. Desires chariots and soldiers to protect them. (B.O.D. 62.)

The last letter of Ebed·tob shows that even the South was lost.

CXLVIII.

EBED·TOB to king of Egypt. Milkilim and Suardatum join forces of Gazri (Gezer), Gimti (Gimzo), and Qilti (Keilah), and occupied Rubute (Rabbah). Land gone over (?) to

Khabiri. King still has Urushalim, city of the temple of Uras, whose name is Shalim.
(R.P. xvii. 72.)

One letter remains from a hopeless queen, who evidently belonged to the South.

CXLIX.

URASMU ... or NIN·UR·ZIKARI to king of Egypt. The country is exposed to the *khabbati* (plunderers or Bedawin), who have sent to Ayaluna (Ajalon) and Zarkha (Zorah) ... two sons of Milkilim. The sender is queen of Zapuna.

This completes the letters containing allusions which enable them to be connected with others. Other letters may here be mentioned in order to complete the catalogue. All with names are addressed to the king of Egypt.

CL. Abdi·ashtati. Acknowledges letter. (B.O.D. 34.)
CLI. Amakizi names the king's house before city of As(or Dil)nate ..... In 3rd year A.'s father did .... (S.B.A. xi. 385.)
CLII. Dagantakala. Father and grandfather obeyed the king. (S.B.A. xiii. 327.)
CLIII. Dagantakala, asks for help. (B.O.D. 74.)
CLIV. Dasru. Report of peace. (S.B.A. xi. 327.)
CLV. Dashru. Acknowledges letter. (B.O.D. 75.)
CLVI. Gesdinna. Report. (S.B.A. x. 496.)
CLVII. Khumyapiza (? Namyapiza, letters 50, 82, 125, 134). Reports his arrival with his troops. (S.B.A. xi. 333.)
CLVIII. Nampipi or Khuzam. Report. (S.B.A. x. 493.)
CLIX. Pidas of Dilbarlugil? Report. (S.B.A. x. 491.)
CLX. Zidri'ara. Acknowledges letter, and performs orders. (B.O.D. 76.)
CLXI. Zinarpi. Report. (S.B.A. x. 499.)
CLXII. From *x*. Names city of Biduna. (S.B.A. x. 498.)
CLXIII. From *x* of Gubbu, who sent soldiers to the king's army. (B.O.D. 78.)
CLXIV. Fragment naming Sid(?)nina a king. (S.B.A. x. 517.)

CLXV. x to Nabkhurriya. x conferred with Mimmuriya .... 14 pieces of crystal of the mountain .... 4 papyri. (S.B.A. xi. 383.)
CLXVI. From x. refers to Napkhurriya and Mimmuriya. (M.A.F. vi. 311.)
CLXVII. From x. Acknowledges orders, and sends tribute. (B.O.D. 81.)
CLXVIII. From x. Received 200 pieces of silver (obscure). (S.B.A. xi. 375.)
CLXIX. From x. Complaint of army exactions. (S.B.A. xi. 369.)
CLXX. From x to y. x is accused, and asks y to refer his case to the king for trial. (B.O.D. 79.)
CLXXI. From x. A fragment. (S.B.A. xi. 372.)
CLXXII. From x. Broken; the burden of each sentence is "The king my Lord my sun god," like Ps. cxxxvi. (S.B.A. xi. 364.)
CLXXIII. Mythological text about a plague demon. (S.B.A. xi. 386.)

Fragments of dictionaries and letters. (P.A. 36.)

Forms of Egyptian Names.

Amanappa	Amen·em·apt	55, 58, 96, 98, 99, 101, 108	Nap·khura·riya Nap·khuru·riya	Nefer·kheperu·ra 9, etc. ,, 12, 47
Amankhatbi	Amen·hotep	73	Nip·khurri·riya	17
Amanma	Amen·mery	55, 67	Mim·mur·iya	Neb·maat·ra 9, 12, 165, 166
Ammunira	Amen·ra ?	103–105		
Dudu	Tutu (tomb 8 T.A.)	50, 52, 54, 81	Nim·mur·iya Nimut·riya	,, 5, etc. ,, 1
Khamasi	Kha·em·uas (tomb Memphis)	11, 12	Nip·mua·riya Pakhanati	,, 4, 13 Pa·kha·en·ta (?) 94
Khapi	Hapi	110	Pakhamnata	,, 93
Khaip	,,	88	Puru	Pa·ari 126, 134
Khayapa	,,	95		(tomb Thebes)
Khaya	,,	66	Rianappa	(Amen)·ra·en·apt 119, 120
Khatib	Hotep 52, 71, 81, 83, 84, 90		Suta	{ Suta (tomb 19 T.A.) 18, 46, 112 or Suti (tomb 15 T.A.)
Khuri=Nap·khu·riya		3		
Manakhbiria	Men·kheper·ra	86	Shuta Shuti	} 97 18
Manakhbiya	Men·kheperu·ra	28		
Miya·riya	Mery·ra (tomb 4 T.A.)	110	Teie Yankhamu	Tyi 9, 10, 11 (?) 69–71, 97, 99, 115–118, 142, 147
Nab·khur·riya	Nefer·kheperu·ra	127, 128, 165	Yatibiri	Hotep·ra 115
Nap·khu·riya	..	166		

(The references given to tombs at Tell el Amarna, etc., are to illustrate the names at this period, but are not necessarily of the identical persons.)

INDEX OF PERSONS.

(For Egyptian kings see previous list.)

Abanappa	Assur·yu·ballidh 27	Iddin·adda 89
(v. Amanappa)	Ayab 116	Ilgi 75
Abbikha 74	Aziru 50–54, 67, 70,	Ilumilku 79, 113
Abdashirta 56, 58,	71, 78–86, 88, 90–92,	Ilurabikhur 92
59, 64–66, 69–72,	107, 127	Irsappa 1
78, 85, 89, 94, 96–98,	Balgarib 73	Irtaba 14
101–103, 106, 107,	Balumme 47	Isuya or Yishuya 116
109, 150 (?)	Bayawi ⎱ 118	Itagama (v. Aitu-
Abdi·milki 89	Beya ⎰ 119, 123	gama)
Abdirama 89	Bikhura 88, 89	Itamagapapiri 79
Abdisullim 76	Bilti·ilu 40	Kallimmasin 13,
Abi·milki, or	Binaddu 40	14, 15
Abisharri 75, 78,	Binana 40	Karaindash 16
79, 85, 87, 89	Binili 40	Khabi 85
Adad·dayan 119	Bininima 116	Khaip 88
Adad·puya 40	Binsumya 139	Khamasi 11, 12
Adai 134	Binziddi 40	Khamu·niri 102
Addalim ... 110	Biri 71, 93	Khanni ⎱ 7, 12, 35,
Addamikhir 132	Biridi or Biridashyi	Khanya ⎰ 62, 90
Addu·itlu 124	129–131, 133	Khapi 110
Addu·kinumma 119	Bitil 90	Khatib 52, 71, 81, 83
Addu·nirar 28	Buadda 120–122	84, 90
Aduna 91	Bubri 10	Khaya (v. Khaip) 66
Aitugama 41,	Burnaburyash 16,	Khayapa 95
91, 128, 133	17, 18, 47	Khumyapiza 157
Akhidhabu 47	Da ⎱ 62	Khuzam ? 158
Akiya 30	Dasarti ⎰	Kistunizizanni 13
Akizzi 137, 138	Dagantakala	Kurigalzu 17
Amakizi 151	152, 153	Labai ⎫ 110, 114,
Amanappa 55, 58,	Dasha 128	⎪ 124, 126,
96, 98, 99, 101,	Dashru 154, 155	Labapi ⎬ 130, 132,
108	Dudu 50, 52, 54, 81	⎪ 134, 138,
Amankhatibi 73	Dushratta 4–12	Labaya ⎭ 139
Amanma 55, 67	Ebed·asherah	Liya 62
Ammunira 103–105	(v. Abdashirta)	Mada 62
Amurhadad 40	Ebed·ip 40	Mani 5, 6, 7, 10
Anati 40	Ebed·tob 110, 112–	Mania 62
Arad·ashirta	114, 126, 134, 148	Melekh·mi ... 70
(v. Abdashirta)	Edugama (v. Aitu-	Milkilim 110,
Artama·shamas 39	gama) 41	124–126, 134, 139–
Artash·shumra 4	Gesdinna 156	142, 145–149
Artatama 11	Gilukhipa 4	Miyariya 110
Arzai 126	Gilya 5, 6, 9, 11	Mutadda 116
Arzauya 128, 133	Gulati 123	Nakharamassi 6, 7
Assur·nadin·akhi 27	H. see A.	Nampipi ? 158

Namyapiza	45, 46,	Shatiyi	34	Yama	43
or	79, 124,	Shibtiadda	117	Yanazni	102
Namyaitza	133	Shumandi	35-38	Yankhama	69-71,
Nimmakhi	62	Shuta	97	97, 99, 115-118, 142,	
Nin·ur·zikari	149	Sidnina ?	164	147	
Nisag	11	Sindisugab	16	Yapa·addu	55, 64,
Pakhamnata	93, 94	Sitatama	11	67, 69-71, 97	
Pakhura	57	Suilagiti	124	Yapakhi	135
Palasa	91	Sukharti	14	Yaptikh-addu	112
Paluma	62	Sumadda	47-49	Yashdata	129, 132
Pauru (*v.* Puru)	134	Suta	18, 46, 112	Yatibiri	115
Pidas	159	Sutarna	5, 11, 29	Yidya	31-33
Pirizzi	10	Sutatna (*v.* Zatadna)		Yikhbil·khama	
Pirkhi	4	Suyardata	114,		113, 126
Pisiari	62	142-144, 146, 148		Yishuya or Isuya	116
Puru	126	Suyarzana	73	Yivana	56
Rabimur		Tadukhipa	8, 9, 10,	Yuni	9
(*v.* Rib·addu)	91		11, 12	Zakara	13
Rianappa	119, 120	Tagi	110, 125, 126	Zatadna	44, 46, 47
Ribaddu	55-61,	Tarkhundaras	1	Zi ... an	2
64-72, 88, 89, 95-		Tarkumiya	70	Zidriara	160
103, 105, 107-109		Teie	9, 10, 11	Zimrida in Zidon 64,	
Salmasalla	68	Tiuyati	128	77-79, 85; in La-	
Saratum (*v.* Zurata)		Tunipipri	4	chish 111, 112	
	47	Turbazu	112	Zinarpi	161
Sarru (Saratum ?)	62	Tuya	62	Zirdamyasda	46
Shakhshikhashi (?)		Umeatu	10	Zitana(*v.*Zatadna)40	
	121	Urasmu ...	149	Zurata	47, 132

INDEX OF PLACES AND TRIBES.

Abitu	Abdeh (15 S. Tyre) 130, 133	Avanu	Aven, Haiyan (2 S.E.		
Aduri	Toran? (10 W. Tiberias) 116		Bethel)		124
Akku	Akka	44, 46, 47	Aveti	(*v.* Abitu)	130
Akzabu	Achzib (8 N. Akka)	58	Ayaluna	Ayalon	134, 149
Alasiya	N. Syrian coast	20-26, 67	Azzati	Gaza? Azotus?	115
Am	Imm (21 E. Antioch)	40,	Barrabarti		59
		91, 128	Belnathan (?)		114
Ambi	101, 95, 72, 68		Biduna		162
Ammi or Ammiya (E. of Simyra)			Biruta	Beyrut	66, 67, 103-105,
	59, 91, 92, 96, 98				108, 109
Amurra	Upper Orontes 50, 51, 58,		Bitilim	Bethel ?	116
	62, 64, 66, 67, 71, 94, 96,		Bitsani	Beit Shenna (4 S.E. Gimzo)	
	97, 99, 105				110
Araru		116	Burqa	Bene baraq (5 E. Joppa) 124	
Ardata	Artusi (9 N.E. Tripoli)		Buzruna	Bozrah	133
		68, 91	Danuna	Danian (13 S. Tyre)	79
Arvada	Arvad, Ruad	66, 85	Dilbarlugil ?		159
Arzawa		1	Gagaya		13
Ashtarti	Ashteroth (29 E. Tiberias)		Gaturri	Gezer { 119, 134, 135, 139,	
		116, 133	Gazri	„ { 148	
Asnate		151	Ghezer	„	
Asqaluna	Askelon	33, 134	Gilu		73
Aup		128	Gimti	Gimzu (14 S.E. Joppa) 110, 148	

INDEX OF PLACES

Gina	Janiah (7 W. Bethel) 124		Murukhazi ?		137
Gitirimuna	Gathrimmon 124		Musikhuni		29
Gizza	Giscala, Gish (22 S.E. Tyre) 128, 133		Nariba	Nerab (2 E. Aleppo)	91
Gubbu	Gapa?(12 S.W. Hamah)163		Ni, Nina	(E. of Aleppo) 8, 86, 92, 128	
Gubla	Gibla (14 S. Laodicea) 57, 59, 62, 67, 91–93, 96–98, 100–103, 105–107		Nukhassi	(around Aleppo) 28, 40, 52–54, 81–84, 90, 128	
			Pitazzi		122
			Puruzilim		102
Guti-kirmil	Gath 110, 112		Qatna	Katma ? (23 W.N.W. Aleppo)	127
Hamor (?)	114				
Ibilimma	Ibleam 116		Qideshu	Qedesh (22 S.E. Tyre) 79, 128, 133	
Igaid	1				
Inuamma	Yanuh (7 E. Tyre) 133		Qidsa	Qadisha (Tripoli)	62
Irqata	Arkas (14 E.N.E. Tripoli) 63–64, 91		Qelte	Keilah 110, 114, 148	
			Rubute	Rabbath (6 N.E. Beit Gibrin) 119, 126, 148	
Kannishat	17				
Karduniyas	(Babylonia) 13–18		Rukhizi		
Kasi	(Babylonians) 68, 69, 72, 134		Samkhuna	Semekhonitis (Merom) 48	
Kelte	(v. Qelte)		Sankhar		22
Khabiri	Hebronites 110, 112, 113, 134, 148		Sawa . . .		71
			Serdani	Shardana 57, 59	
Khalebu	Aleppo 6		Seri	Surah (6 S.E. Gath) 112	
Khalunni	Golan 133		Shaddu		133
Khani gabbi or	(E. Cappadocia) 6, 13,		Shanku	Shakku (10 S.W. Tripoli)63	
Khani rabbatu	27		Sigata	Tell Saukat(16 S. Laodicea) 68. 72, 95, 98	
Kharabu	El Khurab ? (11 E. Joppa) 124		Sunama	Selmeh ? (3 E. Joppa) 124	
Khatti	Hittites 1, 2, 3, 4, 40, 41, 69, 70, 79–84, 86, 90, 91, 127, 128		Suti = Satiu	Bedawin 27, 45, 57, 89, 136	
			Takh . . .		129
			Tambuliya	Zambul (22 E. Tripoli) 67	
Khayini	116		Tarkusi		70
Khazati	Gaza, Azotus ? 110, 126		Timasgi	Damascus 128, 133	
Khazi	Tell Kussis (8 N.W. Megiddo) 73		Tisa . . .		61
			Tsumura	(v. Zumuri)	
Khazur	Hazor(13 S.E. Tyre) 75, 76		Tsurri	Tyre 56, 59, 60, 85, 87, 97, 123	
Khinatuna	Kanatha 47, 132		Tumur	Tumrah?(7 N.E. Gaza)119	
Khinianabi	116		Tunip	Tennib (18 N. Aleppo) 82–84, 86, 90	
Kideshu	(v. Qideshu)				
Kinanat	128		Tusulti	Teiasir?(11 N.E. Shechem) 73	
Kinanna	Canaanite 79				
Kinakhkhi	,, 47, 62		Uduma	Adamah (5 W.S.W. Tiberias) 116	
Kunakhau	,, 17				
Kinza	Hanezi (43 W. Aintab) 41		Ugaritu	13, 60, 79	
Kukbi	74		Ullaza	68, 71, 91, 94	
Kumidi	69, 88, 89, 133		Urushalim	Jerusalem 110, 134, 148	
Lakisha	Lachish 111, 112, 134		Urza	Yerza ? (11 N.E. Shechem) 121	
Lapana	Elbin(20 W.S.W. Aleppo)? 128		Usteru . . .		73
Lukki	Lykians 26		Uzu	Hosah (6 S. Tyre) 75, 85	
Lupakku	40		Yapu	Joppa	115
Magdali	Magdalim 73		Yarimuta	50, 67, 69–71, 97, 98, 107	
Magdalim	Magdala (3 N. Tiberias) 74, 116		Yibliya		68
			Zapuna		149
Makhzi . . ti	73		Zarak		70
Mankhate	Wady Menakh (7 S. Gezer) 119		Zarkha	Zorah (11 W. Jerusalem)149	
			Zarqizabtat	Kaphar Sabti (7 W. Tiberias) 149	
Martu	(v. Amurra) 61, 82, 84				
Megiddi	Megiddo 46, 129–132		Ziduna	Zidon 62, 66, 67, 75, 77–79, 85	
Melukhkha	56, 71		Zilu	Zelah (N. Jerusalem) 112	
Mestu	Mushtah (14 W. Tiberias) 116		Zinzar	Shinshar (11 S. Homs) 128	
			Ziribasani	Bashan	39
Mitanni	(E. of Karkemish) 4–12, 68, 69, 72, 99		Zumuri or Zemar	Simyra 53, 56, 59, 61, 64, 65, 67–72, 80 (falls), 85, 86, 88, 90–97, 99, 101	
Mitana·nanu = Mitanni	70				

NOTES ON THE IDENTIFICATIONS OF PLACES.

Heb. Hebrew; *Gr.* Greek; *Italics, modern names.*

Most of the proposed identifications of names with sites in the foregoing index are based strictly on geographical indications. The sense of each narrative letter was followed as closely as possible; and, after the positions were marked, all the letters were read over, using the map as a scheme of positions, and tracing the relations indicated, to make certain that no difficulties were involved in the proposed arrangement. Far more reliance is placed on position than on any exact details of transliteration, though none of the forms here suggested are unlikely modifications. That the transliterations were not strictly philological, is proved by the variable forms of the same name. I here make notes on such names as need observation; many are commonly agreed on, and many others cannot be identified at present.

ABITU was apparently near Tyre, being named with Gizza. *Abdeh* is in a likely region for this.

ADURI was in the Tiberias region, in which *Toran* lies; this is not satisfactory, but is the nearest modern name.

ALASIYA is entirely a coast region, the Egyptian Alosa, for all the references are to commerce and shipping, and nothing is said about the surrounding peoples, who were cut off by the Pierian mountains. The north end of the Syrian coast agrees with all the indications, but Cyprus has lately been suggested.

AM is a district in the north. It was taken by the Khatti, and lay north of Tyre and Damascus. *Imm*, Gr. Imma, is the main city of a populous region, 21 m. E. of Antioch and within reach of the Khatti. Kinza also, in the far north, attacked Am.

AMMIYA is a district which is not the same as Am, as both occur separately in one letter. It is placed between Irqata and Ardata, and was not very far from Sigata. There is no indication of the name in later sources.

AMURRA were a people whom Aziru and Abd·ashirta ruled over, before beginning to conquer Syria. In some tablets this region is named as Martu, a variant form of the name. Reports on Amurri are sent from Zumuri. The Amurri attack Gubla early in the war; they drove a refugee to Qidsa (Tripoli), and took Gubla. All this limits them to the hinterland of Gubla and Zumuri. If, as seems likely, these people are the same as the Amar, conquered by the Egyptians in the XIXth and XXth dynasty, it would seem that they were pushed down Syria by the advancing Khita.

ARDATA is apparently not the same as Arvada; and from its linking between Irqata and Zumuri (94) it is probably the neighbouring port of Orthosia (Gr.), *Artusi*.

ASHTARTI was over the Jordan, by its link with Bozrah and Damascus. Probably it is Ashteroth (Heb.), *Ashtarah*; or else the neighbouring city of Ashteroth-Karnaim.

AVANU, Heb. Beth-aven. This is not Bethel, for Ai was beside Beth-aven on the east of Bethel (Jos. vii. 2). Aven, Avanu, can hardly be other than *Haiyan*, 2 m. E.S.E. of Bethel.

AZZATI is usually considered = Khazati, and both the same as *Ghuzzeh*, Gaza. It would be tempting to suppose some confusion between Gaza or Azzah (Heb.) and Ashdod or Azotus. Khazati being stated as west of Gimti, and being taken by the Gimtites, would point rather to Azotus than to Gaza.

BITSANI is linked with Guti and Gimti, apparently close to the latter. This points to its being *Beit Shenna*, 4½ S.E. of *Gimzu*.

BURQA is doubtless Benebarak, being linked with Giti-rimuna.

BUZRUNA is Bozrah, as the king joins a party at Ashtarti to chase a fugitive to Damascus.

DANUNA is near Tyre, as Abisharri sends news of it

while he was besieged. It is clearly *Danian*, Heb. Danyaan, the natural stronghold on the top of *Ras Nakura* (the Hor-Nakura of the Egyptians), which is the southern boundary of view from Tyre, 16 m. distant.

GIMTI is usually rendered as Gath; but as in one letter the men of Guti, Gath, are said to have taken Gimti, the two names must refer to two places. Immediately after taking Gimti they were in Bitsani; and the close relation of Gimzo and Beit Shenna (4½ m. apart) points to these being the places in question.

GINA is near Avanu, and therefore is *Janiah*, 7 m. W. of Bethel.

GITIRIMUNA is Gathrimmon (Heb.) which was close to Joppa (Jos. xix. 45).

GIZZA was near Tyre, and was raided along with Abitu, apparently by the party returning from Bashan. This points to its being *Gish*, Gr. Giscala, 22 S.E. of Tyre.

GUBBU may be *Tell Gapa*, 12 S.W. of *Hamah*, but is probably a misreading for Gubla.

GUBLA. This most important place has always been supposed to be Gebal, *Gebail*, Gr. Byblos. There is, however, another coast city, with a name slightly closer to Gubla, namely, Gabula (Gr.), *Gibleh*, 14 S. of Laodicea. The question between these two sites is fixed in letter xcviii., where Ribaddu has lost Sigata and was then shut up "like a bird in a cage," showing that Sigata was close to Gubla. Within two miles of Gabula is the outlying fort *Tell Saukat*, which is manifestly Sigata, and thus fixes Gubla to the northern site.

GUTI has always been assigned to Gath, to which all indications agree.

INU·AMMA is the Egyptian Ynuāmu (or Yanu of the Amu, Syrians), which is almost certainly *Yanuh*, Heb. Yanoah, 7 m. E. of Tyre.

IBILIMMA, named at the end of the Galilean towns, must be Ibleam (Heb.).

GEOGRAPHICAL POSITIONS

IRQATA near Zumuri is plainly *Arkas*, Gr. Arke, 14 E.N.E. of Tripolis.

KHABIRI means only "the confederates." They were in Judea and pressed from the hills down into the plain; the name points therefore to Hebron, though, of course, the confederates may not have already settled at Kiriath-arba so early. Hebron was so named between the time of Abraham's visit and the Exodus.

KHALUNNI was near Ashtarti and Buzruna. This brings it to Golan; and though Khalunni would normally form Holan ('Alem), yet as there is some variation in what seems to be the forms of this name, Golan for the city and region, and '*Allân* for the river traversing it, Khalunni may well represent the original name, which has been modified to Golan and '*Allân* by later peoples.

KHATTI are doubtless the same as the Khita of the Egyptians, the Hittites. They occupied at this time the mountains, were leagued with Kinza, were above Nukhasse and Tunip, were in Nukhasse and went on to Tunip and Martu, and were allied with Nariba. All this points to their being beyond all the other peoples named, and gradually pushing southward.

KHAZI is Khazay of the Thothmes lists, fixed by that at *Tell el Kussis*, 9 N.W. of Megiddo.

KINZA, which was leagued with the Khatti in attacking the northern district of Am, is probably *Hanesi*, 43 W. of Aintab.

KHINATUNA was on the road from Karduniyas in Babylonia to Egypt. It must be on the east side of Syria, therefore. Messengers were there attacked by chiefs of Samkhuna and Akku, which shows that it was about Bashan. It agrees, therefore, with Kanatha (Gr.), *Kanawat*, which is sufficiently near the cuneiform.

KINANNA, Kinakhi, Kunakhau, are forms of the well-known Canaanite. Amurra was in Kinakhi, and it included Danuna and Kanatha. All this points to a large region, from the upper Orontes down to the Jordan, and from the coast across to Bashan.

LAPANA, near the land of Am, is probably *Elbin*, 20 W.S.W. Aleppo.

LUKKI are a people who professed alliance with the maritime Alasiyans in the extreme north coast, and were repudiated as being objectionable. This leaves no doubt that they are the Luka or Lykians, who appear as sea-rovers during the next two dynasties.

MANKHATE was in the region of Gazri and Rubute; the *Wady Menakh* between these places (7 m. S. of Gezer) preserves the name.

MARTU was the home of Aziru, otherwise called Amurri. It is named next to Nukhasse and Tunip; and after the Khatti were in Nukhasse, they went into Martu, and ravaged Tunip. So it must be close to Tunip and between Nukhasse and Gubla; the same region that we reach by the limitations of Amurri. This region (marked on map) contains a series of place-names in *Mart*; Marata (two), Martaban, Mardib, and Mardina.

MISHTU is in the Tiberias group, and is doubtless *Mushtah*, 14 W. of Tiberias.

NARIBA is mentioned with the Khatti, and is probably *Nerab*, 2 m. E. of Aleppo. As a king of Nariba is named, while the important site of Aleppo does not appear in all the war, it seems likely that Nerab may be the earlier site.

NI is fairly fixed by Egyptian inscriptions to about the S.W. corner of the Euphrates, opposite to Aleppo. Nina is probably the same name.

NUKHASSI was an important kingdom; the king was appointed by Tahutmes III.; it was early in touch with Aziru of Amurri; liable to invasion from the Khatti; lay between the Khatti and Tunip and Martu; is named before Ni and Zinzar; and the people joined Aziru in taking Zumur. This shows that it lay E. and N. of Tunip and Martu, and extended to the Amurri. It cannot, therefore, be Anaugas named by Egyptians near Tyre.

QATNA was in the north, raided by the Khatti. It may therefore be *Katma*, 23 W.N.W. of Aleppo.

GEOGRAPHICAL POSITIONS

QIDESHU is named by Abisharri of Tyre as fighting against Namyapiza, who fled from Bashan to Damascus. Qedesh (Heb.), *Qades*, near Lake Merom, 22 S.E. of Tyre, agrees closely to these condition.

QIDSA, another of the many holy cities, was a refuge from the Amurri, and is referred to from Zidon when writing about Gubla. The name has been preserved in the *Nahr Qadisha*, which points to Tripoli having been a Qedesh before its Greek name was imposed.

RUBUTE, from its linking with Gazri, Gimti, and Qelte, is the *Rabbah*, 6 N.E. of *Beit Gibrin*.

SAMKHUNA was allied with Akku; and the name is exactly preserved in Semekhonitis or Samokhonitis, a Greek name for Lake Merom. Evidently a city Samokhon was on that water, and the name lingers in the *Wady Samakh*, which flows into the east of the lake.

SERDANI appear as a people in the Egyptian interest; probably, therefore, the Shardana mercenaries from the Mediterranean, who later formed the bodyguard of Ramessu II.

SERI was on the hills east of Guti; this is probably *Surah*, on the ridge, 6 S.E. of Gath; or possibly *Surah*, Heb. Zorah, on the hills, 10 N.E. of Gath, which, however, appears here otherwise as Zarkha.

SHANKU, near Irqata, is perhaps *Shakku*, 10 S.W. of Tripolis.

SIGATA, close to Gubla, is *Tell Saukat*, 2 S. of *Gibleh*.

SUNAMA was close to Joppa, and is probably *Selmeh*, 3 E. of Joppa; just as Shunem has become *Sulem*.

TAMBULIYA (or TUBULIYA elsewhere) was near Zumur, and was attacked by Aziru. It agrees closely to *Zambul*, 22 E. of Tripolis.

TUMUR was near Mankhate, Gazri, and Rubute; probably *Tumrah*, 7 N.E. of Gaza.

TUNIP agrees in all respects to the modern *Tennib*, 18 N. of Aleppo.

YARIMUTA was certainly on the coast, and therefore not Yarmuth (Heb.). The site is unidentified.

ZARKHA linked with Ayaluna is doubtless Zorah (Heb.), *Surah*, 11 W. of Jerusalem.

ZARQISABTAT is a compound name; as it belongs to the Tiberias group, it is probably *Kefr Sabt*, Gr. Kaphar Sabti, 7 W. of Tiberias.

ZILU is probably Zelah (Heb.), an unknown site N. of Jerusalem.

ZINZAR, between Ni and Kinanat, agrees in position and name to *Shinshar*, 10 S. of Homs.

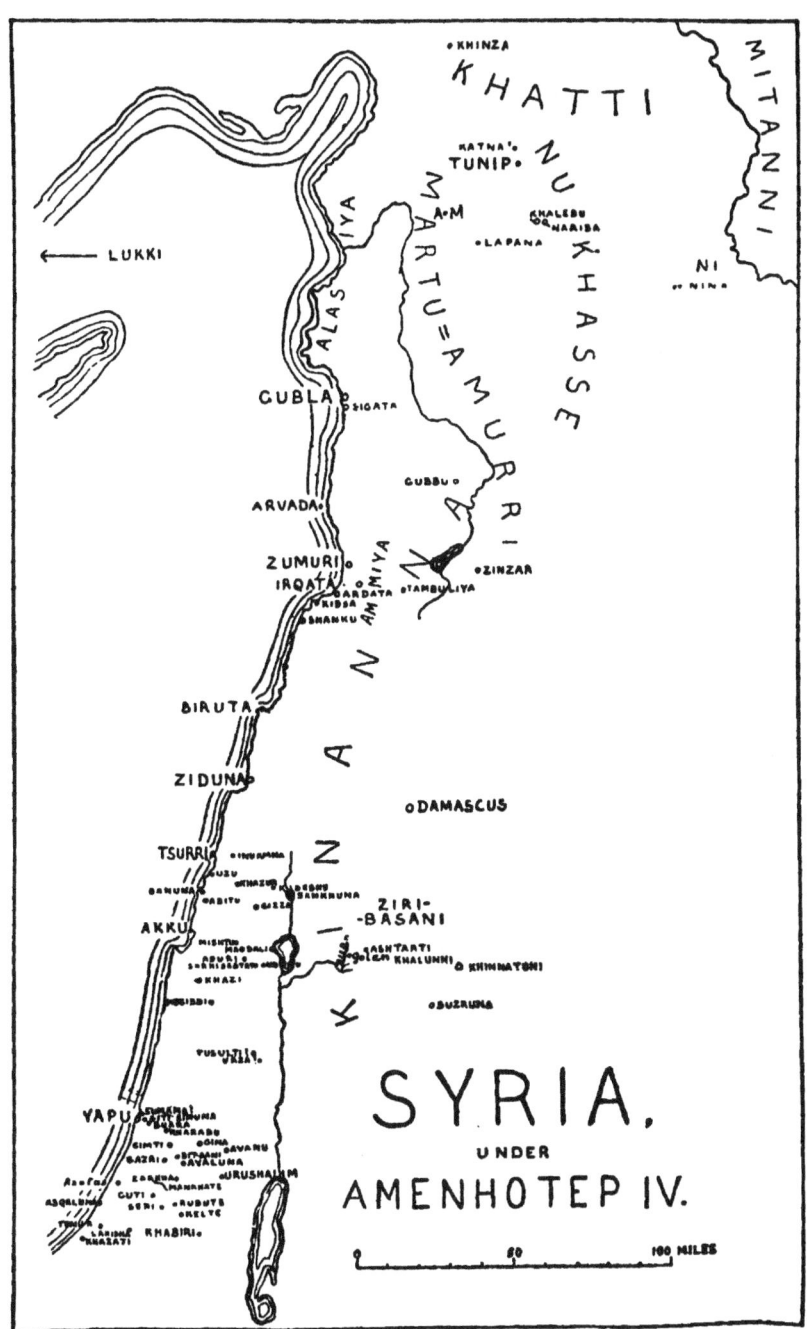

Fig. 162.—Syria under Amenhotep IV.

THE GEOGRAPHY OF THE SYRIAN CAMPAIGNS.

THE long list of the names of conquered places given by the monuments of Tahutmes III., Ramessu III., and Sheshenq, beside various lesser records, have been studied by several authorities. The first impulse under Mariette and Brugsch was to care little for geographical relation, and to adopt forcible changes and inversions in the spelling, if a resemblance to well-known and important names could be thus produced. Their main principle was the presumed importance of the sites named. Maspero gave much more weight to the geographical order, and refused arbitrary alterations in the names. Conder proposed many new and probable identifications. Tomkins endeavoured to make more complete identifications of sites throughout, placing more reliance on similarity of name than on position. Max Muller was far more critical on the exact phonetic equivalence, but did not much use the geographical positions. As these writers came to very different results in some parts, it is desirable to re-examine the matter afresh with their various conclusions before us.

The first consideration is, from what materials these lists have been compiled, and what lies behind the monumental series of names. That the Egyptians had regular maps from which an artist would read off the places in order, is very unlikely, when we see the rudeness of the portions of maps which have been preserved to us. It would rather be from the papyrus records or cuneiform correspondence of the campaigns that the lists would have been compiled. These records would recite the main course of the army, and the various lesser expeditions for plunder or punishment in the remoter parts of the country. Hence we should not expect to find an unbroken series of names, threaded in the neatest order ; but rather a series of short lists, two or three of which might often radiate from one centre, and which might double back or cross one another. In treating the whole long list, then, we ought to find groups of several connected names ; but we should be prepared for sudden breaks from one region to another, where one list ends and another begins.

The equivalence of the Egyptian names with those found in Hebrew or in modern Arabic is a very difficult question, from its vagueness and the many uncertainties of it. No doubt, in carefully transcribed and carefully preserved names, a thorough system of equivalence between hieroglyphs and the Semitic alphabet can be rigidly traced. But the fact of such a precise system existing must not lead us to ignore the many other sources of variation and change that affect the question. It is as well to specify these causes of difference, as they have not all been noticed.

(1) Original mutability of the name often exists. In the present day there is the hard and the soft *gim* side by side ; the g or the hiatus for '*ain*, also together ; the perversion of *gim* into *shin* (as in *wug*), and of k into soft ch (*chef* or *chelb*), inversions of syllables (as in *betà* and *tebà*, and even in place-names), and other variations, which are often enough to make two equally correct ways of writing a name appear very different.

(2) The errors of scribes in hearing and transcribing must certainly have affected the names. When we see the mistakes of Englishmen in writing foreign names of a new country, or, still more, the wild mistakes of the Norman scribes of Domesday Book in writing Saxon names, although they were living in the place for their business, and used almost the same alphabet, how much more in hasty military reports, drawn up in a totally different system of writing, may we credit the

scribes with making strange errors. The variability of spelling of some often-recurring words—as in the Sheshenq list—shows how little precision was sought.

(3) Our other versions of the names may often be altered from what they were in Egyptian days. The aboriginal forms have probably undergone some alteration in passing from Amorite into Hebrew or Arabic, How many different races were in the land at the Egyptian invasions we do not know, but their language, if Semitic, was certainly neither the Hebrew nor Arabic, through which we have the names preserved.

(4) Corruption of names by sheer wear—as Wokingham to Oakingham, or Brighthelmstone to Brighton, or Alexandria to Skandria—is a frequent change; and corruption by making sense of a name whose origin is forgotten is even commoner, as in Kentish Town, Leatherhead, Pepperharrow, Leghorn, the Campidoglio, or Hierosolyma.

Considering, then, the chances of alteration in names, we should give the more weight to the clue that we have in the sequence in the lists, and trust to that if any passable form of the name can be found in the correct order of place. The principle of tracing a Hebrew root-meaning for the Egyptian form by strict equivalence, and then requiring that Semitic root in the modern name, is excellent in theory; but as, in practice, two or three entirely different roots are often proposed for one Egyptian form, this shows how little real certainty there is in such a process, and how readily fictitious results may be gained. This system, moreover, ignores the sources of error (2), (3), and (4), which we have just noticed.

In determining the line of route of the lists, but little weight can be given to the presence or absence of common topographical terms, such as *Ain*, a spring; *Mejdel*, a tower; *Shuweikeh*, thorny place; *Neqb*, a valley; *Gennein* or *Ganat*, gardens; *Abel* or *Aubela*, a meadow; *Hagarim*, apparently stone-walled fields, etc. Such names may easily vanish from their ancient places, or be introduced, according as specific names or descriptive generalities are more in use.

We will now proceed to consider the list of Tahutmes III. of 119 places in the Upper Ruten country, or Palestine. Three versions of this exist on his monuments, and have been published (M.K. 17–21). In these transliterations G is used for the basket *k*, and F for the square *p*, as such is the constant usage in the forms of the Semitic names in this list. Where our present conclusion differs from that of previous writers, it is marked *. Egyptian names are in capitals, and modern Arabic in italics. Positions are indicated by the distance and bearing from well-known places or the last-named site.

1. QEDSHU, named first, as being the most important conquest, *Kadas*, near Lake Homs on the Orontes.

2. MAGETY, Megiddo, *el Lejjun*, 19 miles S.E. of *Haifa*.
3. KHAZAY, *Tell el Kussis*,* 9 N.W. of *Lejjun*.
4. KITSUNA, Kuddasuna in cuneiform, *Tell Keisan*,* 13 N. of *Kussis*.
5. 'AN SHIU, now plural *Ayun Shâin*,* 16 S.E. of Keisan, 3 E. of Nazareth.
6. DEBKHU, Tubikhu cun., *Tabghah*? 16 N.E. of *Ayun Shâin*, on N.W. of Sea of Galilee. Or *Jebel Tubakat*, 17 N.N.E. of *Ayun Shâin*.
7. BEM'AY, possibly *Bâneh*, 10 W. of *Tubakat*.
8. KAMATA, perhaps *Kama*, 8 E. of Nazareth.
9. TUTYNA, *Umm Tuteh*? 17 N.E. of *Akka*.
10. LEBBANA, *Lebbuna*, 13 N.N.E. of *Akka*.
11. QERET·NEZENA, *Kureiyeh*? 8 E. of *Umm Tuteh*.
12. MARMA, Lake Merom, or *Marun*, 4 E.S.E. of *Kureiyeh*.

This circuit of places northwards through Galilee is evidently connected, and is perhaps continued southward in 20–27, the Damascus road (13–19) having been inserted at the most northern part.

13. TAMESQU, *Dimeshq*, Damascus.
14. ATARU, *Daraya*,* 5 S.W. of Damascus.
15. AUBIL, Abila,* *Neby Abel*, 14 N.W. of Damascus.

SYRIAN GEOGRAPHY UNDER TAHUTMES III 325

16. HEMTU, not found on this road, but perhaps brought in by confusion of the other E. Jordan road of Hamath to Abila.
17. AQIDU, *'Ain Yakut,** pass on the Lebanon, 20 S.S.E. of *Beirut.*
18. SHEM'ANAU, *Beshamun,** 7 S. of *Beirut.*
19. BAARUTU, *Beirut.**

This line is the best road from Damascus to Beirut for slow transit or a large body, as it is better watered than the modern road on a ridge. These places are on the direct line of this old road.

20. MAZNA, *Madin,* Madon, 5 W. of Tiberias.
21. SARUNA, *Sarona,* 6 S.W. of Tiberias.
22. TUBY, *Tubâun* * and well, 12 S.W. of Sarona.
23. BAZNA, *Bessum?* 1 N. of Sarona.
24. A'ASHNA, *Esh Shuni,** 10 S.E. of Sarona.
25. MASAKH, *Mes-hah,* 3 S.W. of Sarona.
26. QAANAU, waters of Qana by Megiddo in campaign.
27. A'ARUNA, Aáruna in campaign, *Ararah?* 7 S.W. of Lejjun.

This group brings us from group 2–12 back to Megiddo, from which we started. There seems to have been a garrison at Sarona making sorties in various directions, which form the group 20–25. The site of Megiddo at *el Lejjun* or *Tell el Mutasellim*, and not at *el Mujedda*, is proved by the campaign, and the relation there to Taanakh.

28. ASTARTU, *Tell Ashterah,* Ashteroth Karnaim, 21 E. of Sea of Galilee.
29. ANAU·REFAA, *Rafah,* Raphon, 9 N.E. of *Ashterah.*
30. MAQATA, *Migdad,** 4 N. of Rafah.
31. LIUSA, Laish, Dan, *Tell el Kady,* 11 N. of Merom.
32. HUZAR, Khazura cun., *Hadireh,* 6 W. of Merom.

33. FAHEL, Pella, *Fahil,* 18 S. of Sea of Galilee,

34. GENNARTU, Khinneroth, about Tiberias.
35. SHEMANA, *Sebana,** 3 W. of Magdala.
36. ATMEM, *Admah,* 5 S. of Sea of Galilee.
37. QASUNA, Qishion * of Issachar, about the head of river Kishon.
38. SHENAMA, Shunem, *Solam,* 7 S. of Nazareth.

39. MASHAL, *Meselieh*, 15 S. of Shunem.
40. AKSEF, *'Asâfeh*,* 9 S.S.W. of *Jeba*.
41. GEB'A·SU'AN, Geba, *Jeba*, 6 S.W. of *Meselieh*.
42. TAANAK, *Tànnuk*, 4 S.E. of Megiddo.

---

43. YEBLAMU, Ibleam, *Yebla*,* 17 E. of Megiddo.
44. GENTU·ASNA, En Gannim, *Jenin*, 11 S.E. of Megiddo.
    "The Gardens of Asnah" (a man's name; Ezra ii. 50).
45. RETA·'AREKA, *'Arrakeh*, 6 W. of *Jenin*.
46. A'AYNA, *Anin*, 3 N.W. of *Arrakeh*.

---

47. A'AAG, *'Ajjeh*, 7 S. of *Arrakeh*.
48. RUSH·QEDESH, "The holy hill" = any hill sanctuary; possibly *Kudeis* on hill of Shechem.
49. GELIYMNA, *Jelameh*, 9 E.S.E. of Megiddo.
50. BAR, *Bireh*,* 13 E.N.E. of *Jelameh*.
51. SHEMASH·ATUMA, *Shemsin*, 6 N. of *Bireh*.
52. ANUKHERTU, Anaharath, *en Naurah*, 9 S.W. of *Shemsin*.
53. 'AFEL, *el Fuleh*, 5 W. of *en Naurah*.
54. 'AFEL, *el 'Afuleh*, 1 W. of *el Fuleh*, 7 E. of Megiddo.

---

55. KHASHBU, Khasabu cun., *el Kusab*, 5 W. of Megiddo.

---

56. TASURET, Tusulti cun., *Taâsur*, now *Teiasir*, 11 N.E. of Shechem.
57. NEGEBU, "a pass" in the hills, *Wady Beidan*,* ? N. of Shechem.
58. ASHU·SHEKHEN, "Plain of Shekhem."* *Ashedah*, the plain below hills, or place of streaming out, would be a root familiar to Egyptians as *Ash*, effusion, and therefore shortened to *Ashu*.
59. LENAMA, *en Nahm*, 13 N. of Shechem.
60. YERZA, *Yerzeh*, 11 N.E. of Shechem.

This group, 28–61, begins by crossing the Jordan into Bashan, 28–30; thence striking N.W. round the head of the Jordan, 31; from 32 a branch expedition goes down the east of Jordan to Pella, while the main line goes south through Samaria to 40, and returns to Megiddo (41–42). Another expedition from Megiddo goes out east to 43, and back by a south circuit, 44, 45, 46. Then another expedition goes south to 47, and perhaps even to Shechem, 48; then up north to 49 and on to 50, returning by 52, 53, 54 to Megiddo. Khashbu (55) seems to be an isolated foray. Then another expedition strikes out to Shechem and the eastern region, 56-60. The manner in which the line of these names recurs to the Megiddo region shows that though that city is not named (having appeared before), it was the garrison centre of these several raids, the records of which are strung together to form the list. Leaving Megiddo, the next itinerary is southward.

61. MAAKHASA, *el Maghasun*, 14 N.E. of Joppa.
62. YEFU, *Yafa*, Joppa.
63. GENTU, "gardens" of Joppa.
64. RUTHEN, LUTHEN, has been proposed at Ludd, 11 S.E. of Joppa.
65. AUANAU, Aunu, Heb. *Ana*, 7 E.S.E. of Joppa.
66. AFUQEN, Peqiáin, between Yabneh and Ludd, Talmud.
67. SAUQA, "thorny place," a common name.
68. YEHEMA. There were mentioned probably two, and there now are three places of this name; as it is a very important key position, it must be cleared up. It occurs here between Joppa and Migdol; but in the Tahutmes III. campaign (p. 104) it is certainly near Megiddo, and just at the required place on the road is the name *Yemma*, 17 S.S.W. of Megiddo, before entering the hills. Therefore we can equate . ·. YEHEMA = *Yemma*, 17 S.S.W. of Megiddo, and *Yemma*, 6 S.S.W. of Tiberias = Jabneel; . ·. Jabneel, Jamnia, or *Yebnah*,* 13 S. of Joppa = YEHEMA.

These equivalents prove that Yehema has changed into Yemma, Yebma, Yebna, Yamnia, and Yabniel. And the position of Jamnia is exactly in the right place to agree with the list.

69. KHABAZANA, a compound name by its length, *Butani*,* 8 S. of Jamnia.
70. GENTHU, "gardens," by Migdal.
71. MAGTAL, *Migdal, Mejdel*, 13 N.N.E. of Gaza.

72. AFTHEN, *Fatuneh*, 15 N.E. of Migdal.
73. SHEBTUNA, *Shebtin*, 9 E. of Ludd.
74. TAY, *Atya**? 19 E.N.E. of Shebtin.
75. NAUN, *Naaneh*, 7 E. of Jamnia.
76. HUDITA, *Haditheh*, 3 E. of Ludd.
77. HAR, "a hill."
78. YESHEFAR, *es Suafir*, 7 E.N.E. of Migdal, Shaphir.

79. LEGAZA, "unto Gaza."* The position next to Gerar shows the name to be about this region, and Gaza is properly written in this manner. The particle *le*, "unto," has been accidentally retained in transcribing from the bulletin, or from a road list, like the Antonine itinerary prefix of *Ad*.
80. GERURU, Gerar, *Jerrar*, 6 S. of Gaza.
81. HARAR, *Abu Hareireh*,* 7 S. of Gerar, up large valley.

In these groups, 61-81, we have the circuits about Migdal, like the previous expeditions around Megiddo. First is the line down from Megiddo to Migdal, 61-71. Then an expedition north-east into Dan, or perhaps Ephraim, returning by nearly the same line, 72-78. It must be remembered that often an isolated site of small importance may occur (such as Atya, 74) far ahead of an expedition, when a body of the enemy were chased and at last caught in some small village, the action and the capture of which gave it a place in the annals. The record of Chalgrove and Quatre Bras has no relation to their size. Objection has been made to 78 being es Suafir, on the ground that it would be more closely rendered Yusef-El, a place of the god Yusef. If so, it has been proposed that it be *Yasuf*, 23 N. of Jerusalem, and in that case the itinerary ends out in Ephraim without a return line to Migdal. The next itinerary, 79-81, is, however, from Migdal, through Gaza to Gerar, and on up the important Wady esh Sheriah to Hareireh, 81.

82. REBBAU, Rabbah, *Rubba*, 23 E. of Migdal.
83. NUMANA, *Deir Naman*, 9 N.W. of *Rubba*, 12 E. of Ashdod.
84. NAMANA, *Arak Naman*, 1 N. of *Deir Naman*.
85. MALEMAM, *Umm el Hemam*, 1 S. of *Deir Naman*.
86. 'ANI, *'Ana*, 3 N. of *Arak Naman*.
87. REHEBU, *er Rohban*,* 5 E.N.E. of *Ana*.
88. AQAR, *Aqir*, Ekron, 4 E. of Jamnia.

89. HAYGERYM, *'Ain el Hejeri*, 4 S.W. of Hebron.
90. AUBAL, "a meadow."
91. AUTAR·A'A, Autar the Great, Adoraim, Adora, *Dura*, 5 W.S.W. of Hebron.
92. AUBAL, "a meadow."

93. GENTHAU, "gardens."
94. MAQEREFUT, Maqor (Heb.), *Majur*, "reservoir," of *Rafāt*,* 10 S.S.W. of Hebron. (*Majur* appears in this district 5 W.S.W. of Hebron.)
95. A'AYNA, "a spring."
96. QAREMAN, Carmel, *Kurmul*,* 7 S. of Hebron.
97. BATYA, supposed to be Beth Yah. Hebron* is in the right position in the series, and an altar of Yahveh was there in early times: so Batya may be Hebron.
98. TAFUN, Taphon, *Tuffuh*, 5 W.N.W. of Hebron.
99. AUBIL, "a meadow."
100. YERUTA, *Jeradat*,* 4 E.N.E. of Hebron (for Y changing to J, see Yotapata = Jefat).
101. HALKAL, *Halhul*,* 2 N. of Hebron.

These two itineraries may well belong to the expedition which we last saw coming round from Migdal up the Wady esh Sheriah eastward; a party on such a line might well divide, and while one half pushed through by Rabbah to Ekron, 82–88, the rest might scour the hill country ridge in the sites 89–101.

102. Y'AQEBAAL, *Ikbāla*? 6 W. of Jerusalem.
103. QAFUTA, *Kefrata**? 3 E.N.E. of Gezer.
104. QAZIRU, Gezer, *Jesar*, 16 S.E. of Joppa.
105. REBBATU, "a chief city."
106–7. MAQELTU A'AMQU, *Wady el Miktely*,* 7 E. of Gezer.
108. SARUTA, *Sira*,* E. side of *Wady el Miktely*.
109. BAARUTU, Beeroth, *Bireh*,* 10 E. of *Sira*.

110. BAT·SHAR, Beth-sura, *Beit Sur*,* 4 N. of Hebron.
111. BAT·ANTA, Beth-anoth, *Beit Ainun*, 3 N.N.E. of Hebron.
112. KHALQETU, *Kilkis*,* 2 S.S.W. of Hebron.
113. 'AN·QENA, *'Ain el Qana*, 1 N.W. of Hebron.

114. QEB'AU, *Jibia*, 16 N.N.W. of Jerusalem (or *Jebā*,* 7 N.N.W. of Shechem).
115. ZERER, *Jerir*,* 13 N.N.E. of Jerusalem (or *Jerrar*,* 8 S.S.W. of Megiddo.
116. ZAFTA, *Suffah*,* 1 N.W. of *Jibia* (or *Zebdah*,* 4 S. of *Jerrar*).
117. BERQENA, *Berukin*,* 6 N.W. of *Jibia* (or *Burkin*, 9 S.S.E. of Megiddo).
118. HUMA, *Hamid**? 4 N.E. of Gimzo.
119. AGTAMES .. or AGMES .. Gimzo, *Jimzu**? 15 S.E. of Joppa.

Fig. 164.—Map of Northern Syria.

These three lists may perhaps be only two, the section 110–113 having been inserted in the middle; for Jibia, 114, is only 7 miles N.N.W. of Bireh, 109. Hence there may be one line from near Jerusalem going west to Gezer, then turning back and going north to Bireh, 109; Jibia, 114; and on to Berukin, 117, whence it turns back to Jimzu, 119, on the return to the centre at Migdal. If this be so, the Zafta, 116, cannot be the Zefta of the annals, which was near Megiddo; or, if the latter be adopted, some of the other names, 114–117, may be reasonably grouped in the same region, as entered above in parentheses. The group of four names, 110–113, is well established by the close relation of these places. This section has probably been transposed with 102–109; as, if reversed, the Hebron group continues naturally from 101, Halhul, to 110, Beit Sur close by; while 109 joins to 114, as we have noticed.

The general scheme of the original documents which were drawn upon to form this long list, appears to have been as follows:—

2 to 12. From Megiddo northward about Galilee.
13 to 19. Damascus-Beyrut road inserted at the most northern part.
20 to 27. Return route from 12 south to Megiddo.
28 to 42. Across Jordan and back round the north to Megiddo.
43 to 46. From Megiddo to east and south, and back to Megiddo.
47 to 54. From Megiddo to south and east, and back to Megiddo.
56 to 60. From Megiddo round Shechem region.
61 to 71. From Megiddo to Migdal.
72 to 78. From Migdal to north-east, and back to Migdal.
79 to 81. From Migdal to south and east into hills.
82 to 88. Part of army from hills across to Ekron.
89 to 101, 110–113. Rest of army around the Hebron ridge.
102 to 109, 114–119. Up to Jerusalem region, working west, then north and east, and back to coast region, return to Migdal (?).

Such seems to be the structure of these lists when examined in the obvious light of their being edited from a series of military reports. Their relative order may not necessarily be the order in the history ; but it would be very reasonable to take it as such, knowing that Megiddo was the first centre of operations, and seeing that Migdal, on the road to Egypt, might well be the centre of later operations in the south country.

The lists of places in Northern Syria are far less certain, as our knowledge of the country is so poor. Some connections may be traced with more or less probability, and they are indicated by the map, though they scarcely need to be here discussed.

RELATIONSHIPS OF THE SEVENTEENTH DYNASTY.

For the obscure period of the rise of the Egyptian power against the Hyksos oppression, we have but little material to guide us. Few names remain, and the order and relationship of those is very uncertain. Two tombs at Thebes of officials (*sedem ash em ast maāt*) attached to the service of the royal tombs, provide the best information we have; though, as the rows of figures of kings and princes whom they adored is not professedly in chronological order, and as they lived four or five centuries after those kings, the material is not satisfactory. We may first notice the structure of these tomb lists. Both tombs have an upper and a lower row of seated figures, each one with a cartouche, adored by the official. Anhur·khau (L.D. iii. 2 d), in the upper line, records Amenhotep I.; behind that king is his father and father's mother (Aahmes and Aah·hotep); and then his brothers and sisters (Meryt·amen, Sat·amen, Sa·amen, Kames, Hent·ta·meh, all known as such), Turs and Aahmes, probably also sisters, and Sa·pa·iri, his brother. In the lower line are the founders of dynasties, Nefertari of the XVIIIth, Ramessu I. of the XIXth, Mentuhotep III. of the legitimate part of the XIth dynasty; then Amenhotep I., Seqenenra, Uazmes, Ramessu IV. (the reigning king) (blank), and Tahutmes II. Thus the order has no obvious meaning in the latter part. In the other tomb, Kha·bekht (L. D. iii. 2 a) records in the upper line Amenhotep I., next his mother (Nefertari), and then, presumably, her father and mother (Seqenenra and Aah·hotep), after whom come a row of Amenhotep's brothers and sisters. In the lower line come the two founders, Mentuhotep III. and Aahmes; next, Se·khent·neb·ra and Uaz·kheper·ra; and then a line of princes and royal wives, who are probably the brothers and sisters of those who precede them.

Such a general structure of these lists is closely in accord with that of the lists on family tablets; first the parents, then grandparents and ancestors, and then a row of brothers and sisters or children. Not a single known fact of relationships in this dynasty disagrees with this presumed system here; and therefore, in some cases where we know nothing about the relation of the persons named, we may accept this scheme as a probable clue. The results indicated to us by this view of the lists are (*feminine):—

Parents of Nefertari.	Brothers and sisters of Aahmes	Children of Aahmes.
Se·qenen·ra	Kings { Uaz·kheper·ra	Amenhotep I.
*Aah·hotep.	S·khent·neb·ra	*Meryt·amen
	Aah·mes	*Sat·amen
	Bin·pu	Sa·amen
	Uaz·mes	*Ka·mes
	Ra·mes	(or Sat·ka·mes)
	Ken·nu·aru	*Hent·ta·meh
	Aah·mes	*Turs
	*Ka·mes	*Aahmes
	*Sat·iri·bau	Sa·pa·iri
	*Ta·khredqa	*Ta·iri
		(mother, Kasmut)

(*Note.*—The children of Aahmes often compound "Aahmes" in their names.)

In only one point do these conclusions vary from these already stated by Professor Maspero, in his elaborate study of the mummies of Deir el Bahri. On the strength of the name of Sat·kames, the daughter of Aahmes and Nefertari, he supposes that Kames was probably her grandfather, and therefore father of Nefertari; whereas here, on the strength of the position of Seqenenra and Aah·hotep next after Nefertari, it would seem likely that they were her father and mother.

From the stele of Iufi (Rec. ix. 92) it is certain that Aah·hotep was mother of Aahmes I., and hence Aahmes and Nefertari were of the same mother. But yet we cannot suppose them to have had both parents alike; Aahmes is always (except once) shown of the same colour as other Egyptians, while Nefertari is almost always coloured black. And any symbolic reason invented to account for such colouring applies equally to her brother, who is nevertheless not black. As Nefertari was specially venerated as the ancestress of the dynasty, we must suppose that she was in the unbroken female line of descent, in which the royal succession appears to have been reckoned, and hence her black colour is the more likely to have come through her father. The only conclusion, if these points should be established, is that the queen Aah·hotep had two husbands: the one black (the father of Nefertari), namely, the celebrated Seqenenra, who was of Berber type (Ms. M. 528); the other an Egyptian, the father of Aahmes and his elder brothers, Kames and Skhentnebra, which explains why those three kings are separated from the other children of Aah·hotep by her husband Seqenenra, and placed in a different line in the tomb of Khabekht.

Now Aahmes was rather over fifty when he died (Ms. M. 535), and he reigned 25 years; hence he was about 25 to 30 years old when he came to the throne. As there is but little memorial of the reigns of his presumed brothers (see above), Uaz·kheper·ra and S·khent·neb·ra, they are not likely to have reigned for 30 years between the death of Seqenenra and accession of Aahmes. Hence it is probable that her Egyptian husband, the father of Aahmes, preceded her black husband, Seqenenra, the father of Nefertari. Two other reasons appear for Nefertari being the daughter of Seqenenra, and not of his son Kames: (1) as Seqenenra died at about 40, and Kames probably reigned but a short time, his daughter would be rather too young to be the great queen of his brother, Aahmes I.; (2) as Nefertari's daughter was named Aah·hotep, it is more likely that her mother was Aahhotep and not her grandmother, as names were repeated usually in alternate generations in Egypt.

It is needful to enter thus fully on this family history if we are to obtain any results; but for the less important members of the family we merely notice the occurrence of their names, and refer to the discussion by Maspero (Ms. M. 615–639) as the best statement known about them. When in the preceding details we have ventured to vary slightly from that memoir, it is not with any dogmatic assurance, but only to show the possibility of an alternative view which may be preferable in a doubtful detail.

THE MUMMIES OF DEIR EL BAHRI.

As we have frequently referred to this deposit of mummies, we here give an outline of its history.

The tombs of kings as well as private persons were continually liable to be plundered by unscrupulous thieves; what we now find are but the last leavings of a hundred generations of incessant pillage. Such robbery began even during the life of the workmen who had been employed upon the construction; and though royal tombs were cared for by priests and officials, yet they were not secure from attack. In the 16th year of Ramessu X., a special commission investigated the state of the tombs, owing to various reports being spread as to their violation. They found, however, only one tomb opened, out of ten between the XIth and XVIIIth dynasties; but two others had been attacked, though unsuccessfully. The disorders of the close of the Ramesside period made the question more pressing; the officials, despairing of the safety of so many scattered and out-of-the-way tombs, gave orders to bring some of the royal mummies into the great tomb of Sety I. for safety (Ms. M. 551, 557, 560). This must have been done by the tunnel at the back of the tomb, now choked up, as the proper entrance was intact when opened by Belzoni. Hence this tunnel must lead through the cliff to the Deir el Bahri. The successive renewals and removals took place as follows, according to the endorsement of the scribes upon the mummies and the coffins :—

Pasebkhanu I.—
   6th year, Paophi 7.   Herhor renewed wrapping of Sety I.
   6th ,,   Phamenoth 15. Herhor renewed wrapping of Ramessu II.

THE MUMMIES OF

Pasebkhanu I. (or Sa'amen)—
13th year, Pauni 27.   Painezem I. restored mummy of Ramessu III.

Pasebkhanu I.—
17th year, Phamenoth 6.   Painezem I. removed Ramessu II. and renewed his wrapping *in the tomb of Sety I.*

Sa'amen—
6th year, Phamenoth 7.   Painezem I. restored mummy of Tahutmes II.
6th ,, Pharmuthi 7.   Painezem I. renewed wrapping of Amenhotep I.
7th ,, Khoiak 8.   Painezem I. moved mummy of Sat·kames.
8th ,, Phamenoth 29.   Painezem I. moved mummy of prince Sa'amen.
8th ,, Phamenoth 29.   Painezem I. moved mummy of Aahmes I.
16th ,, Pharmuthi 11.   Masahart renewed wrapping of Amenhotep I.
16th ,, Pharmuthi 13.   Sety I. taken *from his tomb to the tomb* of Anhapu.
16th ,, Pharmuthi 17.   Ramessu II. taken *from tomb of Sety I.* to tomb of Anhapu.
16th ,, Khoiak 13.   Ramessu I. taken *from tomb of Sety I.* to tomb of Anhapu.

Amenemapt—
7th year, Mekhir 9.   Menkheperra re-wrapped Sety I.
10th ,, Pharmuthi 20.   Sety I. moved *into tomb of Amenhotep I.*
10th ,, Pharmuthi 20.   Ramessu II. moved *into tomb of Amenhotep I.*

Sa'amen is here treated as not being the same as Herhor; the names of the officials sufficiently prove this; and we see it also in Ramessu II. being in Sety's tomb under Painezem I., while he was removed from that place under Sa'amen.

For the discussion of the XXIst dynasty, and the assignment of the dates in the above reigns, see S.B.A. xviii. 56–64.

We see here how the bodies were shifted into Sety's tomb; then again to the tomb of Anhapu; yet again to the tomb of Amenhotep I.; and lastly, though unrecorded, they were all carried into the burial-place of the priest-kings of the XXIst dynasty. There they remained until, about twenty years or more ago, the Arab dealers found the tomb, and gradually drew out one object after another for sale. By the arrest of the sellers in 1881 their secret was by threats—and they say force as well—wrung from one of them, and the confused mass of a dozen kings and queens of the XVIIIth–XIXth dynasties, many royal children, and a large part of the family of the XXIst dynasty, together with such portions of the funeral furniture of the various persons as had survived the many removals of the bodies, was all brought to the museum at Cairo. The list of personages is as follows, with the pages where the remains are described in Maspero's " Momies Royales de Deir el Bahari" (M.A.F. i. 4).

			P.	Pl.
XVII. 7?	Seqenen·ra III., Ta·aa·qen	mummy and coffin	526	iii.
	Râa, nurse of queen Nefertari	coffin	530	
	Anhapu, queen	mummy	530	
XVIII. 1.	Aahmes I.	mummy and coffin	533	iv. a
	Nefertari	mummy and coffin	535	v. a
XVIII. 2.	Amenhotep I.	mummy and coffin	536	iv. b
	Sa·amen, infant	mummy and coffin	538	
	Sat·amen, infant	false mummy and coffin	538	
	Seniu, keeper of palace	coffin, re-used	539	
	Merytamen	mummy and re-used coffin	539	
	(Priestess of Amen, XX. dyn.	coffin, re-used	540	
	Sat·kames	mummy	541	
	Hent·temehu, dau. of Tenthapi	mummy and coffin	543	
	Mes·hent·temehu, infant	false mummy and coffin	544	
	Aah·hotep II.	coffin	545	v. b
XVIII. 3.	Tahutmes I.	{ coffin { mummy	545 581	vii. viii. b
XVIII. 4.	Tahutmes II.	mummy and coffin	545	vii. viii. a
XVIII. 6.	Tahutmes III.	mummy and coffin	547	vi. a
	Poisoned prince	mummy and coffin	548	ix.

XIX. 1.	Ramessu I.	mummy and lid	551	
XIX. 2.	Sety I.	mummy and coffin	553	xi. a, xiii.
XIX. 3.	Ramessu II.	mummy and coffin	556	xi. b, xiv.–xvi.
XX. 1.	Ramessu III.	mummy and coffin	563	xvii., xviii. a
XX. 10.	Ramessu XII. (?) Khaemuas	mummy	568	
XXI. 1.	Nezemt, queen	mummy and 2 coffins	569	xix. a
XXI. 2.	Painezem I.	mummy	570	
XXI. 3.	Masahart	mummy and coffin	571	vi. b
XXI. 4.	Painezem II.	mummy and coffin	571	
	Zed·ptah·auf·ankh	mummy and 2 coffins	572	
	Nebseny	mummy and coffin	574	xviii. b
	Hent·taui	mummy and 2 coffins	576	xx. a
	Makara and Mut·em·hat	2 mummies and 1 coffin	577	xix. b
	Ast·em·kheb	mummy and 2 coffins	577	vi. c
	Hatet, altered for next	2 coffins	578	
	Tayuhert	mummy and 2 coffins	578	
	Nesikhonsu	mummy and 2 coffins	566, 578	
	Nesi·ta·neb·ashru	mummy and 2 coffins	579	xx. b

ADDITIONAL NOTES

I owe the following notes about the tombs at Thebes, etc., to Mr. Percy Newberry, who has seen the proof-sheets of this volume.

Page 39, line 3. *Huy* tomb at Drah abul Negga.
,, 41, ,, 28. *Bak* was a son of a keeper of cattle of Nefertari. Tomb, Qurneh.
,, 44, base. Cone of *Tahuti*, priest of Aahmes (M.A.F. viii. 15).
,, 68, officials. *Bak*, chief steward, cone (M.A.F. viii. 15).
       priests. *Mut*, priestess, in tomb of Ka·em·her·ab·sen, Qurneh.
              Neferhotep(Ram. II.). Tomb of Khonsu, Qurneh.
              Nay, ,, ,, ,, ,,
              Auy, ,, ,, ,, ,,
,, 69, line 10. And in a tomb at Hieraconpolis (B.E. 243).
,, 78, ,, 13. *Sen·men* was an official of princess Neferu·ra, named in Senmut's tomb (M.A.F. viii. 16).
,, 90, ,, 19. Base of black granite statue of *Senmut* found at Deir el Bahri (N.D.B. i. 19).
,, 90, ,, 23. A third glass bead was bought at Luxor (Newberry).
,, 95, ,, 15. At Qurneh are tombs of *Hapusenb*, 3rd *kherheb* of Amen, of *Anna*, and of *x*, an overseer of works of great obelisks.
,, 164, ,, 21. *Amenken's* wife was royal nurse.
       Tombs at Qurneh of *Neb·en·kemt*, palace keeper; *Tahuti·nefer*, treasurer; *Amenemapt*, vizier; *Mery*, high priest of Amen.

ADDITIONAL NOTES

Page 164, line 30. *Mentuhotep*, *kherheb* under Ram. II. Tomb of Khonsu, Qurneh.

,, 172, ,, 12. *Ry*, chief of engravers. Tomb, Qurneh.
Sebekhotep, chief of Fayum. Tomb, Qurneh.
Ta, keeper of cattle, Ram. II. Tomb, Khonsu, Qurneh.

,, 173, base. *Meryt*, nurse of royal children. Tomb of Sebekhotep, Qurneh.

,, 198. *Amenemapt*, keeper of palace. Tomb. Qurneh.

,, 200. *Nebamen*. Tomb, Qurneh.

,, 229. *x*, overseer of workmen, Tomb, Assassif.

INDEX

Names of persons and places in Syria which only occur on the cuneiform correspondence, will be found separately indexed on pp. 308–311.

The references here in thick type show the beginning of the principal account of each royal person.

AA, 39.
Aah·hotep I., 1, 2, 3, 5, 6, 7, 9.
Aah·hotep II., 1, 3, 34, 42, 43, 46, **52**, **54**, 333, 334, 339.
Aahmes, K., 1, 2, 3, 7, 9, 13, 20, 25–29, **34**, 333, 334.
Aahmes, monuments, 34.
,, mummy, 37, 338, 339.
,, worshipped, 38.
,, family, 41.
Aahmes, Q., 1, 46, 54, 59, **69**, 85, 333.
Aahmes, Q., portraits of, 70.
Aahmes, princess, 5, 6, 333, 334.
Aahmes, general, 21, 30, 34, 35, 45, 46, 61.
Aahmes, official, A, 198.
,, ,, B, 225.
Aa·kheper·ka, 68.
Aa·kheper·ka·senb, 68.
Aamathu, 140.
Aanen, 198.
Aaruna, 105, 106.
Aata, Hyksos, 23, 35.

Abeha, 180.
Abhat, 181.
Akenkhres, 25–29.
Akhenaten (see Amenhotep IV.), 25–29, **205**.
,, portraits, 208, 209, 213, 217, 224, 230.
,, change of type, 211.
,, conversion, 211.
,, hymn to Aten, 215.
,, length of reign, 219.
,, monuments, 220.
,, tomb, 220.
,, ushabti, 222.
,, in early style, 224.
,, family, 229.
,, in cuneiform, 308.
Akhenuthek, 181.
Akherres, 25–29.
Akina, 181.
Alisphragmouthosis, 20, 25–29.
Amen proscribed, 212.
,, reinstated, 236.
Amen·em ant, 127, 141.

INDEX

Amen·em·apt, A, princess, 165.
," B, 39.
," C, 341.
," D, 198.
," E, 225, 308.
Amen·em·hat, officials, 45, 68, 101, 141, 163, 198.
Amen·em·heb, 45, 123, 141, 163.
Amen·em·ka, 141.
Amen·em·meruf, 141.
Amenhotep I., 1, 3, 10, 25-30, 34, 38, 42, 43, 54, 55, 333, 334.
," festivals, 32.
," monuments, 45, 50.
," head of, 47.
," history of, 46.
," mummy, 50, 338-339.
Amenhotep II., 25-29, 32, 54, 55, 56, 78, 100.
," monuments, 152, 157.
," youth of, 153.
," and nurse, 154.
," portrait of, 156.
," statue of, 160.
," scarabs of, 162.
Amenhotep III., 25-29, 56, 57.
," monuments, 174, 187.
," portraits of, 177, 184, 186, 188, 202.
," and his *ka*, as children, 178.
," dated events of, 178.
," lion hunting, 180.
," marriages, 181-3.
," length of reign, 186, 208.
," associates his son, 186.
," tomb, 187.
," funeral temple of, 192.
," adored, 202.
," family, 202.
," in cuneiform, 308.
Amenhotep IV. (see Akhenaten), 25-29, 177, 205.
," marriage of, 181, 186, 207.
," associated, 186, 187, 208, 210.
," dates of, 207, 210.
," portraits of, 208, 209, 213, 217, 224, 230.
," upholds the Aten, 210.
," in cuneiform, 308.
Amenhotep, officials, 44, 46, 68, 69, 171, 173, 188, 197, 198, 223, 308.
Amenhotep, son of Hepu, 192, 196.
Amen·ken, 163, 341.
Amen·mery, 308.
Amen·mes, prince, 46, 52, 53.
Amen·mes, officials, 46, 141, 223.
Amen·nekht, 198.
Amen·nekhtu, 46.
Amenofis, 25-29.
Amenofthis, 25-29.
Amen·user, 141.
Amersis, 25-29.
Amesses, 25-29.
Amorites, 229.
Amos, 25-29.
Amu, invasion by, 19.
," captured, 123, 124.
Amukehak, 47, 48.
Amunzeh, 141, 199.
An, nurse of Hatshepsut, 95.
Anaugasa, 102, 110, 117, 120.
Anay, 38.
Ancestors, chamber of, 130.
Anebni, 78, 95.
Anhapi, 35, 43, 338-9.
Anhur, 164.
Anhurkhaui, 39, 42, 46, 333.
Anhur·mes, 199.
Aniy, 225.
Ankhefenamen, 46.
Ankhsenamen, } 207, 232,
Ankhs·en·pa·aten, } 235.

INDEX

Anna, 78, 341.
Anrathu, 114.
Antef, 141.
Antoninus, 131.
Anui, 226.
Anukhenti, 35, 47, 62, 73, 157.
Apepa II., 17.
  ,,   tale of, 17.
Apis tombs, 189, 245, 252.
Apiy, 226.
Apthentha, 181.
Apuy, 226.
Arat, 170, 174.
Arem, 118.
Arerpaq, 181.
Armais, 26–29, 250.
Armour, suit of, 122.
Aroana, 119.
Arqantu, 122.
Arseth, 155.
Art of Akhenaten, 219.
  ,, changed by Syria, 150.
Artist from Syria, 109.
  ,,   sculpturing, 171.
  ,,   painting, 204.
Arurekh, 120.
Arvad, 101, 102, 113, 114, 310.
Asi (Cyprus), 102, 118, 120, 121.
Assassif, 131.
Assuru tribute, 112, 181.
Ast, 39.
  ,, queen, 72.
  ,, princess, 177, 203.
Aten worship, 184, 211–218, 251.
  ,, upheld by Amenhotep IV., 210.
  ,, cartouches, 212.
  ,, hymn, 215.
  ,, duration, 236.
Aten·neferu boat, 184, 211.
Aten·nefer·neferu, 210, 230.
Ater·maiu, 181.
Aty, queen of Punt, 83.
Aururek, 181.
Auta, 204, 226.
Auy, 341.
Avaris, 21, 22, 35.
Axe of Aah·hotep, 11.
  ,, of Kames, 14.
Ay, 25–29, 226, **238**, 240.

Ayhatab, 181.
Azenunian, 181.

BAHESHEKU, 141.
Bak, 226, 341, 341.
Bakenkhonsu, 199.
Bakta, 142.
Baktaten, 177, 203, 227.
Battle of Megiddo, 107.
Beba·ankh, dagger of, 16.
Berber type of Seqenenra, 4, 335.
Betehamen, 39.
Binpu, 7, 13, 334.
Birth-ring of Tahutmes III., 100.
Birth-scarab of Amenhotep II., 162.
Birth-scarab of Amenhotep III., 195.
Boat, golden, of Kames, 12.
Bows from Syria, 119.
Bull's head vase, 121.

CAMPAIGNS, records of, 320, 331.
Canal of Aswan, 67, 135.
Canon of proportion, 138.
Captives (see Syrians), 22, 23.
Carmel, 101, 104.
Carnelian, artificially whitened, 51.
Chair from Syria, 111.
  ,, of Hatshepsut, 92.
Chariot from Syria, 110.
  ,, of Kha·em·hat, 179.
Chester, Mr. Greville, 92.
Chief of Tunep and artist, 109.
Chiefs "smelling the ground," 109.
Chronology, 3, 25–33, 52–56, 60, 61, 186, 208, 219, 246.
Coffin of Seqenenra III., 8.
  ,, Aah·hotep I., 12.
  ,, Aahmes, 37.
  ,, Nefertari, 40.
  ,, Amenhotep I., 49.
  ,, Tahutmes I., 64.
  ,, Tahutmes II., 76.
Colonnade of Tahutmes III., 129.
  ,, Amenhotep III., 191.

Colossi of Thebes, 192.
Constantinople obelisk, 132.
Corn imported into Egypt, 112, 115, 117–123, 149.
Coronation edict, 60.
Cows, sacred, 90, 91.
Cuneiform correspondence, 259–319.
Cups from Syria, 114.

Dagger of Aahhotep, 11.
,, Kames, 14.
Death mask of Akhenaten, 230.
Decline of Egypt in Syria, 259–319.
Deer's head of gold, 120.
Deir el Bahri, mummy pit, 7, 337.
temple sculptures, 82, 84, 85.
Dishes from Syria, 111, 112.
Draughtmen of Hatshepsut, 93.
Duaheh, 95.
Dudua, 39.
Dushratta, 181, 187, 309.
Duy, 168.

ECONOMIC state of Egypt, 149.
Education of Syrians in Egypt, 114, 185.
Egyptian taste changed, 150.
Egyptian type of face, 148.
Egypto-Syrian type of face, 149.
Elephant from Syria, 124.
Eshmunen, origin of XVIIIth dyn., 15.
Ethics of Akhenaten, 218.
Ethiopian origin of XVIIth dyn., 4, 17.
,, monuments, 68.
,, expedition of Tahutmes III., 103.

FALCHION, 122.
Fenkhu (Phoenicians), 36, 37, 73, 101.
Foliage on column, 219.

Foundation deposits of Hatshepsut, 94.
Foundation deposits from Am, 126.
Foundation deposits of Amenhotep II., 161.

GAZA, 101, 104, 185, 311.
Genbetu, 115.
Gilukhipa, 177, 178, 181, 182, 203.
Glass of Tahutmes III., 139.
Gureses, 181.

HA·ANKH·EF, 170.
Hanebu, 72, 253.
Hanefer, 46.
Hapi, 308.
Hapusenb, 341.
Harakhti, 210, 223.
Har·nekaru (Ras Nakura), 110.
Harosheth, 155.
Hatet, 340.
Hatshepset Merytra, 78, 99, 143.
Hatshepsut, 25–29, 32, 52, 61, 71, 72.
,, co-regency of, 66, 69.
,, monuments of, 79.
,, portrait, 80.
,, temple at Deir el Bahri, 81.
,, statues, etc., 91, 92.
,, chair of, 92.
,, position in kingdom, 95, 96.
,, inscription hidden, 130, 170.
Hatuart (Avaris), 22, 35.
Haworth, Mr., 92.
Hayt, 46.
Heby·khetf, 199.
Hek·er·neheh, 165, 172.
Hent·mer·heb, 177, 203.
Hent·ta·meh, 35, 42, 43, 333–4, 339.
Hent·ta·mehu, 35, 42, 43, 339.
Hent·ta·neb, 177, 203.
Hent·taui, 340.

INDEX

Henut·anu, 100, 145.
Herhor, 39, 337.
Herkhuf, 48.
Hermopolitan origin of XVIIIth dyn., 15.
Hersekheper, 227.
Hery, 45.
Hin, contents of vases, 51.
Hor, 38, 199.
Horames, 142, 173.
Horemheb, K., 26-29, 131, 222, 223, 232.
,, monuments, 242, 246.
,, general and king, 244.
,, length of reign, 245, 251.
,, portraits, 245, 253.
Horemheb, official, A, 56; B., 142, 165, 171, 199.
Hor·em·heb·pa·hor·ur, 256.
Horos, 25-29, 236, 250.
Hotep, 199, 308.
Hotepbua, 39.
Hotepra, 308.
Hui, 235.
Humai, 141.
Huy, A, 39; B, 218, 221, 227.
Huya, 203, 227.
Hyksos, expulsion of, 16-24, 35.
Hymn to Aten, 215.

IAIRNUF, 39.
Imadua, 142.
Isiemkheb, 140, 340.
Iuf, 38.
Iufi, stele of, 10, 69, 335.

JAR of wine, 112.
Jewellery of Aah·hotep, 10-13.
Joppa, 185, 311.
Jug of silver from Syria, 123.

KA as a child, 178.
Kaha, 46.
Kahu, 199.
Kallimmasin, 181, 309.
Kames, K., 1, 2, 3, 7, 9, 12, 13, 20, 333, 334.

Kames, princess, 7, 13, 334.
,, private, 10, 15.
Karaindash, 181.
Karduniyas, 311.
,, alliance with, 181.
Kargui, 141.
Karikamasha, 124, 181.
Kars, 46.
Kary, 158, 168, 181.
Kasa, 38.
Kasmut, 35, 43, 334.
Kedesh, 102, 103, 105, 114, 122, 124, 125, 181, 311.
Kedet, 227.
Kedina, 181.
Kefa, 181.
Kefti, 118, 123, 157.
Kenamen, 142.
Kenaru, 7, 13, 334.
Kepni, 118.
Khabekht, tomb, 9, 13, 39, 42, 46, 333.
Khaemhat, head of, 199.
,, head of servant of, 150.
,, chariot of, 179.
Khaemuas, 142, 159, 164, 227, 308.
Khafra on Sphinx stele, 167.
Khalubu, 124, 311.
Kharu land, 105, 111, 119, 227.
,, official, 141.
Khay, 200.
Khebres, 25-29.
Khebron, 25-29.
Khebtneferu, 54.
,, figure of, 71, 85.
Khent·hen·nefer, 22, 62, 73.
Kherfu, 188, 200.
Khita, 102, 116, 122, 168, 181, 185, 253, 311.
Khonsu, 142.
Khonsuhotep, 256.
Khutany, 257.
King's son, title, 68.
Kirgipa, 177, 178, 181, 182, 203.
Kom el Hettan, 192.
Kurigalzu, 181.
Kush, 47, 62, 73, 118, 119, 121-3, 236.

INDEX

LIBYANS, 48, 229.
Lion's head of gold, 120.
Lotus flower group, 169.

MAA, 144.
Maat, 212.
Mahler, 31.
Mahu, A, 44; B, 227.
Maitariaa, 181.
Maiu, 181.
Makara, Q., 340.
Makautuash, 181.
Maktaten, 207, 231.
Manuareb, 181.
Map of approach to Megiddo, 104.
„ Syria under Amenhotep IV., 320.
„ North Syrian towns, 330.
Marriages of Egyptians and Syrians, 147, 181.
Marseille altar, 16.
„ forgeries at, 139.
Masahart, 338, 340.
Matnun, 181.
Matur, 181.
Mau·en·hequ, 141.
May, people, 181.
May, official, 227.
Meframouthosis, 25–29.
Mefres, 25–29.
Megiddo, 101, 105, 107.
Mehpeni, 181.
Men, 200, 202.
Menaunu, 181.
Menkh, 69.
Men·kheper, 142.
Men·kheper·ra, 200, 201.
Men·kheper·ra·senb, 133, 141.
Mennus, 157.
Menofres, era of, 29, 33.
Mentiu of Setet (Bedawin of hill country), 22, 35, 73, 157.
Mentuhotep II., 33.
Mentuhotep III., 333, 334.
Mentuhotep, official, 342.
Merenptah, 26–29, 32.
Meriptah, 197.
Mermes, 200.

Mernebptah, 257.
Mertaten, 207, 221, 229, 231, 233.
Mery, 200, 341.
Mery·neit, 227.
Meryt, 342.
Meryt·amen, 34, 38, 39, 42–44, 333, 334, 339.
Meryt·ptah, 100, 144.
Meryt·ra, 54, 72, 78, 99, 143.
Mesamen, 39.
Mifris, 25–29.
Military oppression, 251.
Min, official, 157.
Min·nekht, 239, 241.
Misafris, 25–29.
Misfragmonthosis, 25–29.
Mitanni, 181, 185, 311.
Mummies, royal, 337–340.
Music school, 222.
Mut, 341.
Mut·em·hat, 340.
Mut·em·ua, 173, 174, 192.
Mut·nefert, Q., 46, 59, 71, 198.
„ bust of, 71.

NAHARAINA, 62, 102, 105, 116, 119, 122, 123, 124, 157, 158, 167, 181.
Names of places often perverted, 321.
Nanay, 227.
Napata, 156.
„ ram from, 194.
Narkihab, 181.
Nayu, 341.
Nebamen, 142, 342.
Nebankh, 170.
Neb·en·kemt, 341.
Nebmes, 39.
Nebnefer, 39.
Nebra, 39.
Nebseny, 340.
Nebsu, 38.
Nebta, 46, 57.
Nebt·ka·bani, 200, 203.
Nebtu, Q., 99, 144.
Nebua, 164.
Neby, 142.
Nefer·amen, 100, 145.

INDEX

Nefer·ay, 257.
Nefer·em·hotep, 173.
Nefer·hat, 172.
Nefer·hebt·f, 164.
Nefer·hotep, officials, 39, 68, 250, 256, 341.
Nefer·neferu·aten, 207, 232.
Nefer·neferu·ra, 207, 232.
Nefer·pert, 36.
Nefer·renpit, 144.
Nefer·sekheru, 200.
Nefertari, 1, 3, 9, 34, 38, 40.
,, black, 335.
Nefertiti, 207, 229.
,, origin of, 183, 209, 229.
,, portrait of, 182, 213, 217, 230.
Neferu·er·hatf, 144.
Neferu·khebt, 54.
,, figure of, 71.
Neferu·ra, 72, 78.
,, bust of, 77.
Negeba, 123.
Negroes, 254.
,, and Asiatics, 249.
Nehi, 136, 142.
Nekht, 39, 46.
Nekht·pa·aten, 227.
Nekhtu, 46.
Neserna, 114.
Nesikhonsu, 340.
Nesi·ta·neb·asheru, 340.
Neta, 69.
Nezem·mut, 209, 232, 244, 250, 256.
Nezemt, 340.
Niy, 63, 116, 123, 124, 126, 155.
Nubian gods, 136, 159, 170.
Nubians capture animals, 159.

OASIS of Farafra, inscription, 77.
Obelisks of Hatshepsut, 85-87.
,, of Tahutmes I., 67.
,, of Tahutmes III., 127, 131.
,, makers of, 134.
Oros, 25-29, 236.
Oxen drawing sledge, 37.

PA·AA·AQA, 38, 172.
Pa·amen, 46.
Pa·ari, 227, 308.
Pa·aten·em·heb, 227.
Pafuenamen, 51.
Paheri, tutor of Uazmes, 52.
Painezem I., 64, 131, 338, 340.
Painezem II., 340.
Pakha, 225.
Pakhen, 77.
Palette of Seqenenra, 6.
Pa·nefu·emdu·amen, 39.
Panehsi, A, 39; B, 200; C, 227.
Pa·nehy·amen, 159.
Panekht, 38.
Pa·nekhu, 201.
Pa·neter·hon, 200.
Pa·rohu, king of Punt, 83.
Pasar, A, 163; B, 200; C, 241.
Pasebkhanu I., 337, 338.
Pashed, 46.
Paynamen, 50.
Penaati, A, 50, 68, 77; B, 142.
Penamen, 46.
Penbua, 39.
Penbui, 39, 256.
Pendant of Tutankhamen, 237.
Pennekheb, 30, 34, 35, 45, 47, 62, 69, 73, 77.
Pen·ta·en·abtu, 39.
Pentaurt, 46.
Penthu, 228.
Pepy I., 33.
Perversions of names, 321.
Petahuha, 100, 144.
Petau, 157.
Petenra, 68.
Petpui, 100, 144.
Phoenicia, 101, 113.
Phoenicians, 36, 37, 101, 157.
Physiognomy changed in Egypt, 148.
Piankhy, 140.
Piay, 172.
Pillars, granite, of Tahutmes III., 130.
Plunder of Syria, 110.
Police, 227.
Priestess, head of, 151.

Ptahmer, 200.
Ptahmery, 228.
Ptahmes, A, 142; B, 200; C, 200; D, 201.
Ptolemy X., 131.
Pu, 68.
Puamra, 133, 142.
Punt, 73, 82, 181, 253.
,, houses of, 84.
,, tribute of, 102, 117, 121.

QEDESH (see Kedesh).
Qen, 38, 39.
Qina, 107.
Queens transmitted royal right, 183, 209.
Quiver from Syria, 120.

RA, A, 37; B, 142, 162, 163.
Raa, 339.
Raentuy, 257.
Rahotep, 4, 308.
Ram of Amenhotep III., 194.
Ramery, A, 173; B, 228.
Rames, son Seqenenra, 7, 13, 334.
Rames, officials, A, 201; B, 201, 228; C, 210, 224, 228.
Ramessu I., 26–29, 33, 333, 340.
Ramessu II., 26–29, 32, 38, 337–340.
Ramessu III., 338–340.
Ramessu IV., 333.
Ramessu XII., 131, 340.
Ran, 142.
Rany, 173.
Rapeam, 257.
Rathos, 25–29.
Ratothis, 25–29.
Rauserkheper, 257.
Rekhmara, 133, 142.
Relationships of XVIIth dyn., 1, 3, 333.
Remenen (Lebanon), 116, 120.
Restoration after Hyksos war, 36.
Restorations of Medinet Habu, 131.
Rhind, labels from tomb, 139, 143.

Rhind, toilet box, 161.
Ring of Aah·hotep, 9.
,, Tahutmes III., 100.
,, Tahutmes IV., 171.
,, Amenhotep III., 195.
,, Smenkh·ka·ra, 234.
,, Mertaten, 234.
,, Tutankhamen, 236, 238.
,, Ankhsenaten, 237.
,, Nezem·mut, 250.
,, Silver from Syria, 117.
Rock tablets of Tell el Amarna, 222.
Roy, A, 126; B, 342; C, 256.
Rudua, 228.
Ruten, 62, 101, 102, 112, 114, 115, 118, 122, 133, 156, 157, 235.

SA·AMEN, 35, 42–44, 333, 334, 338, 339.
Sa·ast, A, 34; B, 201.
Sakedenu, 142.
Samanurika, 181.
Samut, 201.
Sangar, 102, 116, 123, 124, 181, 195.
Sa·pa·ir, 3, 34, 43, **44**, 333, 334.
Sat·amen, dau. Amenhotep I., 3, 34, 38, 42, 43, 333, 334.
,, dau. Amenhotep III., 159, 177, 203.
Satharna, 181, 203.
Sat·hora, 100, 145.
Sat·ir·bau, 7, 13, 334.
Satiu, 155, 311.
Sat·kames, 34, 42, 43, 334, 338, 339.
Sat·ra, 95.
Scarabs, figured of Aahmes, 36.
,, ,, Aahotep II., 52.
,, ,, Amenmes, 53.
.. ,, Nebta, 57.
,, ,, Tahutmes I., 69.
,, ,, Neferu·ra, 78.

INDEX

Scarabs, figured, of Hatshepsut, 94.
,, Tahutmes III., 114, 140, 145.
,, Amenhotep, II., 162.
,, Tahutmes IV., 171.
,, Amenhotep, III., 195.
,, Amenhotep IV., 210, 225.
,, Ay, 242.
,, ,, Horemheb, 251.
Scarabs with double cartouches, 94.
School of music and dancing, 222.
Scribes, group of, 228.
Sebekhotep, officials, A, 68 ; B, 342.
Sebekmes, 201.
Sebeknekht, A, 69; B, 201.
Sed festivals, 31–33.
Sekhentnebra, 1, 2, 3, 7, 9, 16, 334.
Sekhet'am, 157, 181.
Sektu, 118.
Semnefer, 69.
Semneh, 35, 67, 136.
Seniu, 339.
Senekhtenra, 16.
Senemaah, 46.
Senmen, 38, 341.
Senmut, 78, 88.
,, statues, 89, 341.
Sen'nefer, 142, 163.
Sensenb, 1, 46, 57.
,, figure of, 58.
Seqenenra I., 4, 5.
Seqenenra II., 4, 7.
Seqenenra III., 1, 2, 3, 4, 7, 333, 334, 339.
,, Berber type, 4, 335.
Serenyk, 181.
Sesu, 258.

Set, official, 142.
Setet, 181.
Sety I., 26–29, 38, 50, 131, 223, 340.
,, tomb of, 337.
Shabaka, 169.
Sharhana (Sharuhen), 22, 35, 104.
Shasu, 73, 121, 181.
Shemeshatuma, 155.
Sheshenq I., 190.
Shields from Syria, 120.
Shooting at a target, 166.
Si, 144.
Siege of Megiddo, 108.
Simyra, 102, 114, 311.
Sirius festivals, 31–33.
Sitatama, 181.
Sledges for drawing stone, 37.
Smenkh·ka·ra, 25–29, 219, 221, 229, 231.
,, monuments, 233.
Smensheps, 172.
Soldiers, figured, 85.
,, oppression by, 251.
Sons of chiefs taken to Egypt, 114.
Sotep'en'ra, 207, 232.
Spear head of Kames, 14.
Speos Artemidos, inscription, 19, 81.
Sphinx tablet of Tahutmes IV., 166.
Staff with human head, 111.
Stand for sacred bark, 138.
Sunuga, 181.
Suta, 228, 308.
Sutekh, worship of, 17.
Suten du hotep formula, 38, 40, 95, 202, 218, 257.
,, offering made by king, 172.
Sutharna, 181, 203.
Suti, 228, 308.
Syria, Egyptian remains in, 145, 157, 188.
,, high civilisation of, 146.
,, loss of, 259–319.

Syrian influence on Egypt, 145–152, 181.
,,   marriages, 181.
Syrians brought to Egypt, 22, 23, 62, 109–125, 147, 185, 229.

TA, 342.
Ta·aa, 164.
Taanaka, 105.
Tables, inlaid, 111.
Tables of families, 1, 3, 54.
,,   dynasties, 4, 25–29.
Tadukhipa, 181, 183, 187, 207, 310.
Taharqa, 131.
Tahennu, 48, 101, 157, 181.
Tahured, 68.
Tahuti, officials, A, 342; B, 68; C, 95; D, 142; E, 142.
Tahuti·nefer, 341.
Tahuti·sena, 68.
Tahutmes I., 1, 25–30, 46, 54, 55, 85.
,,   festival, 32.
,,   monuments, 59, 65.
,,   coronation, 60.
,,   history, 61.
,,   head of, 63.
,,   mummy, 64, 339.
,,   officials of, 68.
,,   family, 69.
Tahutmes II., 25–29, 54, 55, 61, 333.
      monuments, 72.
      mummy, 74, 338, 339.
      portrait, 75.
,,   head of coffin, 75.
Tahutmes III., 25–33, 50, 54, 55, 56, 61, 72.
      festival, 32.
      descent of, 78.
      monuments, 97, 126.
      family, 99, 143.
      dated events, 100.
      annals, 103.

Tahutmes III., portraits of, 102, 137, 138.
      obelisks of, 132, 134.
      a great builder, 136.
      in cuneiform, 308.
      list of towns, 320.
,,   mummy, 339.
Tahutmes IV., 25–29, 54, 56.
,,   monuments, 165.
      portrait of, 168.
      scarabs of, 171.
      offering to Osiris, 172.
      marriage, 181.
,,   in cuneiform, 308.
Tahutmes, son of Tahutmes IV., 171.
Tahutmes, son of Amenhotep III., 203.
Tahutmes, officials, A, 45; B, 142, 201; C, 201.
Tair, 35, 43, 334.
Takheta, 100, 144.
Takhetaui, 100, 144.
Takhisi, 124, 156.
Takhredqa, 7, 13, 334.
Tanai, 123.
Ta·nezemt, 46.
Tank of Amenhotep III., 184.
Tares, 181.
Target, shooting at, 166.
Tarobenika, 181.
Tarosina, 181.
Tartar, 181.
Taui, 100, 144.
Tayuhert, 340.
Tell el Amarna, 205, 210, etc., 221, 251.
,,   cuneiform tablets, 259–319.
Temahu, 48.
Tent·hapi, 35, 43, 339.
Teta·an, Hyksos, 23, 36.
Tetamerenptah, 257.
Tethmosis, 25–29.

INDEX

Thenau, 173.
Thent·nub, 39.
Thenuna, 164, 171.
Thmosis, 25-29.
Throw-stick of Thuau, 6.
Thuau, son of Seqenenra I., 5, 6.
Thuna, 172.
Thuthu, 239, 242.
Tita, 181.
Tombs, inspection of, 5, 7, 15, 48, 337.
Touthmosis, 25-29.
Tugay, 144.
Tunep, 101, 103, 109, 113, 122, 181, 311.
Turo, 67.
Turrah quarry, 36, 37, 188.
Turs, 35, 42, 333, 334.
Tursu, 181.
Tutankhamen, 25-29, 32, 222, 223, 232.
,, monuments, 235.
,, portrait, 236.
,, inscription, 237.
Tutu, 229, 308.
Ty, 226, 242.
,, portrait, 239, 240.
Tyi, 176, 187, 192, 202, 209.
,, portrait of, 182.
,, origin of, 182.
,, influence of, 183.
,, reigned alone, 203, 207.
,, family, 204.
,, in cuneiform, 308.
Tyuti, 39.

UAAY, 100, 145.
Uazit·renpitu, 90.
Uazmes, pr., 7, 13, 46, 333, 334.
,, nursed by Paheri, 52.
,, temple of, 57, 65.
,, official, 39.
Uaz·shemsu, 69.
Unfinished state of monuments, 158.

Unnef, 38.
Unnefer, 39.
User, 142.
Useramen, 100, 140.
Userhat, A, 68; B, 142; C, 201.
Usertesen I., head of, 149.

VASES, with contents marked, 57, 139.
,, from Syria, brought by captives, 111.
,, of copper, 113.
,, with goat's head, 116, 118.
,, of glass and stone, 139, 163.

WAN, 124.
Wand, of ivory, 70.
,, human-headed, 111.
Wawat, 102, 115, 117, 118, 121-3, 168.
Women, group of, 219.
,, brought into Egypt (see Syrians).
Workmanship, rapid, 87.

YANKHAMA, 185.
Yatibiri, 185, 310.
Yehem, 104.
Yenuamu (Inuamma), 110, 311.
,, man of, 182.
Yeruza, 104, 311.

ZAHI (Phoenicia), 35, 101, 102, 113, 117, 118, 119, 120.
Zalu, 101, 103, 184, 252.
Zamara (see Simyra).
Zamerkau, 39.
Zanuni, 142, 171.
Zay, head of, 149.
Zed·ptah·auf·ankh, 340.
Zefta, 105.

www.ingramcontent.com/pod-product-compliance
Lightning Source LLC
Chambersburg PA
CBHW061250230426
43664CB00024B/2908